Kenneth Cox. His popular books *Garden Plants for Scotland* (2008) and award-winning *Scotland for Gardeners* (2009) have made him Scotland's best-selling garden writer. Ken is a plant hunter, nurseryman, gardener and garden centre owner at Glendoick, near Perth, Scotland, world famous for rhododendrons. He has written 11 books on plants, gardens and plant-hunting.

Caroline Beaton. From a family of enthusiastic amateur gardeners, former librarian Caroline has worked in a therapeutic garden in Perth and now lives in Orkney where she works part-time for Trellis, Scotland's therapeutic gardening network, as a fundraiser. She is a fish-eating 'vegetarian', interested in food and where it comes from. Her new veg plot in Orkney is a challenging work in progress.

FRUIT AND VEGETABLES FOR SCOTLAND

Kenneth Cox and Caroline Beaton

BIRLINN

To Katy and Ingrid with love, CB

To Jane, KC

First published in 2012 by
Birlinn Limited
West Newington House
10 Newington Road
Edinburgh
EH9 1QS

www.birlinn.co.uk

Reprinted 2015

ISBN: 978 1 78027 046 3

British Library Cataloguing-in-Publication Data
A catalogue record for this book is available
from the British Library

Designed and typeset by Mark Blackadder

Printed and bound by Livonia, Latvia

Contents

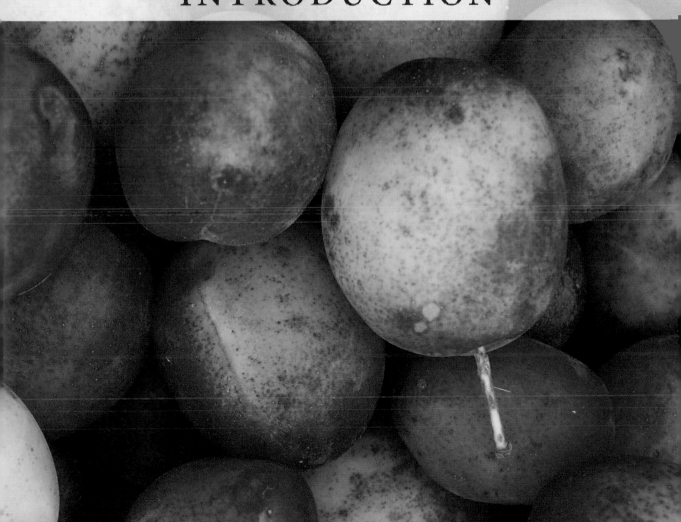

INTRODUCTION

Ken Cox with his giant 'Sárpo Mira' potatoes.

Caroline Beaton and Peter Milne lifting kohlrabi.

CHAPTER 1

Why Grow Fruit and Vegetables?

Vegetables beckon and intrigue in a way that no fish or piece of meat ever could.

Nigel Slater

Vegetables are the food of the earth; fruit seems more the food of the heavens.

Sepal Felicivant

Sex is good, but not as good as fresh sweet-corn.

Garrison Keillor

You are what you eat. For example, if you eat garlic you're apt to be a hermit.

Franklin P. Jones

And for a little balance:

I don't dislike vegetables, I hate them. Not all of them but certainly the common types such as cabbage, turnips, onions, Brussels sprouts and lettuce.

John Cushnie (BBC *Gardeners' World*)

For Ken

I'm a nurseryman by trade, growing mostly orna-mental plants, so I love growing things. I'm fasci-nated by plant breeding and the history of fruit and vegetables – where they come from and how they evolved throughout history. I've really enjoyed listening to and recording Scotland's fruit and vegetable gurus waxing lyrical – Willie Duncan on apples and Alan Romans on potatoes, for example. And then, of course, there's eating the stuff – fresh asparagus spears straight from the garden to the steamer and dipped in pools of lightly salted melted butter; dark-red, sweet 'Tulameen' raspberries plucked from the canes and popped straight into the mouth; removing a few earwigs from home-grown artichokes; young broad beans shelled from their downy pods and fried in bacon, tomatoes and garlic in a recipe from Catalonia . . . These are a few of my favourite things.

For Caroline

My passion for growing vegetables is the direct result of my passion for food. But that's only part of the story. It is the joy of connection with the soil, the relaxation engendered in an hour or two in the sun (and even in the rain) encouraging beautiful plants to do their best for you, the challenge of beating the slugs and bugs without actually poisoning the earth in the process and the tremendous satisfaction of the harvest and the resultant sharing (174 cucumbers and counting). And gardening is a great cure for grumpiness, too.

Why a Book on Fruit and Vegetables *in Scotland*?

With the plethora of fruit and vegetable books available, you might wonder why we need a Scottish one. Quite simply, existing fruit and vegetable books tend to been written by southerners who fail to mention that the Scottish climate demands a different approach to gardening, whether in timing of sowing crops or selection of appropriate varieties. You would not know by reading Alan Titchmarsh or Carol Klein that you might struggle to ripen sweetcorn or peaches or quinces in Scotland.

What's more, this country has a fascinating but largely untold history of fruit and vegetable growing, and of the breeding of some of the world's most important fruit and vegetable crops – onions, raspberries, blackcurrants and potatoes.

We wanted to share and celebrate the knowledge of Scotland's fruit and vegetable experts, few of whom have put pen to paper, and, by pulling all this together, give as much practical advice as possible to Scotland's gardeners, whether they garden in mild or severe climates, from Stornoway and Lerwick to Galloway and Jedburgh.

Why Would/Should You Grow Your Own Fruit and Vegetables?

As you can buy a huge range of fruit and vegetables from your local supermarket, there are many people who don't see the point of growing your own. But deep inside almost every human, there seems to be an urge to grow things to eat. Humans have been sowing seeds and eating the results from the moment nomadic hunter-gatherers first settled in villages and communities. Many of our twenty-first-century fruit and vegetables find their origins in the Tigris and Euphrates valleys in what is present-day Iraq and Iran, an area known as 'the cradle of civilisation', where humans first began growing things to eat rather than simply gathering from the wild. Scotland's crofters and farmers have grown both to eat and to sell over hundreds of years, while our parents, grandparents or great-grandparents lived through government-inspired vegetable production when the Second World War's 'Dig for Victory' campaign encouraged them to grow food crops in every available space to guard against starvation in the face of U-boat blockades.

'Grow your own' is something that has inspired generations of gardeners, passing down from parent to child. Interest in fruit and vegetable growing has intensified in recent years as concerns have increased over imported food, pesticide residues and food miles. We are now encouraged to grow things to eat, no matter how small a space we have in which to garden. A generation back, in the 1970s, it was the growbag that inspired many first-time gardeners to have a go. I remember television footage of London East End tower blocks transformed using Fisons growbags, filled with cascading flowers and fruit, changing concrete balconies into modern Hanging Gardens of Babylon. These days, television chefs and gardeners such as Nigel Slater, Bob Flowerdew and Alan Titchmarsh as well as Scotland's own Jim McColl and the *Beechgrove Garden* team encourage us all to grow things to eat. This new level of interest means that the demand for allotments has never been higher.

Two other questions that this book has forced us to examine are: what might be done about the notoriously poor Scottish diet? and why, despite having an excellent climate and ample rainfall, does the UK import 65 per cent of the vegetables and over 90 per cent of the fruit we eat?

CHAPTER 2

A Short History of Fruit and Vegetable Growing in Scotland

Early History

What were Scotland's early inhabitants eating and did they practise 'grow your own'?

The Pictish and Celtic inhabitants of Scotland were hunter-gatherers or nomadic herders who existed on a diet of meat and wild fruit and vegetables. The Iron and Bronze Ages saw the founding of the first Scottish settlements. Archaeologists have found remains of up to 160 different edible plant species including raspberries, blaeberries, brambles, sloes, bird cherry, cloudberry, wild vegetables, herbs, grains and hazelnuts at Oakbank and other crannogs (loch dwellings on stilts) on Loch Tay.

However, most fruit and vegetables grown in Scotland are not native and find their origins far from our shores. The Persian Empire of Darius in 510–450 BC was well known for its extensive collections of peaches, apricots and other cultivated fruit which spread to Greece via Alexander the Great and later to the Roman empire. Despite Roman historian Tacitus's description of Britain's climate as 'wretched', the Romans are known to have introduced large numbers of fruit and vegetable crops into Britain, many of which had come along trade routes into Europe – cucumbers from India, eating apples from Central Asia and onions from Egypt – which were dispersed throughout the empire. As the

Falkland Palace Orchard, Fife. Some of Scotland's earliest orchards were planted at monasteries and palaces.

Roman incursions into Scotland were short-lived and the long-term frontier was established at Hadrian's Wall, it is unlikely that they introduced anything of note directly into Scotland, but plants which began to appear in English gardens would have moved north via merchants and farmers. Roman fruit-growing was sophisticated and included complex training and pruning, grafting of best varieties onto rootstocks and winter storage of apples and pears. Roman literature contains several detailed manuals on fruit and vegetable husbandry.

Much Roman knowledge of gardening was lost in Britain during the Dark Ages and was not rediscovered until the establishment of Christian monasteries and abbeys. Records suggest there were gardens and orchards associated with Cistercian and other religious orders throughout much of Scotland during the Middle Ages, from St Andrews, Dunfermline, Lindores and Balmerino in Fife to Borders towns such as Jedburgh and north to Pluscarden near Elgin. Plants were grown for both their nutritional and healing properties – parsnips were thought to cure digestive problems, leeks to help heal bone breakages, celery was used as a contraceptive, lettuce for cleansing the blood. Turnips and tomatoes were considered aphrodisiacs. Strangely, the radish was condemned by Culpeper in his famous herbal of 1652, as 'they breed but scurvy humours in the stomach and corrupt the blood'.

The Scots are considered to have been rather slow starters in the world of gardening compared to much of Europe, reaching horticultural pre-eminence only in the last 250 years. My grandfather, Euan Cox, paints a very gloomy picture of the state of Scottish horticulture before the seventeenth century in his 1935 book, *A History of Gardening in Scotland*: 'In Truth, we were a barbarous nation . . . Scotland lay in a backwater . . . out of touch.' Scotland's political instability, he argues, prevented advances in agriculture, horticulture and garden fashions from spreading from the Continent and from England. More recent research published in Forbes Robertson's *Early Scottish Gardeners and their*

John Reid's *The Scots Gard'ner*, 1683, was probably Scotland's first gardening manual.

Plants concludes that Euan Cox's account is over harsh, citing seventeenth-century travellers' reports of what were clearly well-established non-monastic gardens and orchards in Dunfermline, Glasgow, Paisley and Linlithgow and the King's Knot Garden below the walls of Stirling Castle. Robertson has found contemporary accounts of cultivation of onions, leeks, turnips, carrots, parsnips, beetroot, radish, cabbage, kales, peas, beans and lettuce in the gardens of rich estates from the seventeenth century onwards. In 1692, the Earl of Crawford recorded in his diary the fruit he sampled on a tour of Scottish estates. He lists 22 varieties of apples, 40 of pears and 36 of plums, as well as apricots and gooseberries.

Walled Gardens

From the Middle Ages onwards, at the back of town houses, long, narrow, often walled plots of land,

Culross Palace in Fife, with its re-created seventeenth-century Scottish merchant's garden.

known as 'rigs', were used as smallholdings to raise livestock and chickens and to grow vegetables. You can still see the layout of rigs in towns such as Linlithgow, St Andrews and Newburgh in Fife. At Culross Palace, Fife, a seventeenth-century merchant's house has a garden re-created in the style of the period. Here you'll find Scotch Dumpy hens rooting around the medicinal and culinary herbs, vegetables, Scottish apples, quince and medlar, all of which were planted in Scots gardens of this period.

The late sixteenth and early seventeenth centuries saw the beginning of Scotland's love affair with the walled garden. The first were extensions to the walls of the L-shaped baronial castle but, as the need for fortification passed, the gardens became larger and more elaborate. 'The kitchen garden is the best of all gardens,' John Reid writes in the first-ever Scottish gardening manual, *The Scots Gard'ner* (1685). He gives specific instructions on how to make one – 'Make the bordures 6 foot broad' – and

explains where it should be sited – 'The kitchen garden may be placed nearest the stables, for the convenience of wheeling in manure, and out of sight of the house; because of the impropriety of the view.'

One of the reasons for the popularity of walled gardens in Scotland was that the microclimates and shelter afforded by the walls allowed a wide range of otherwise tender fruit and vegetables to be successfully grown, and over a much longer season. The warmth of south and west walls was perfect for protecting blossom and ripening fruit, and their height protected tender plants from the full force of Scotland's ferocious winds. The series of eighteenth-century walled gardens along the coasts of Caithness and Sutherland – Dunbeath, Langwell, Castle of Mey and Sandside – are carefully sited to afford the maximum amount of shelter. Horticultural consultant Colin Stirling gives the example of a walled garden in Orkney where the wind shelter allows potatoes to be harvested three weeks earlier than

Inverewe, Wester Ross, showing the curved walled garden which follows the line of the beach.

those planted outside the walls.

By the mid eighteenth century, the fashion was to build walled gardens away from the house and often on a considerable scale. Some of the largest in Scotland include Hopetoun (over 20 acres), Brechin Castle (13 acres), Blair Castle's Hercules Garden (9 acres), Amisfield (7 acres) and Wemyss Castle (6 acres). Some walled gardens were divided into two or more compartments – for orchard, cut flowers and vegetables, for example. By the end of the eighteenth century, a country estate was not considered complete without a productive walled garden. A permanent monument to the art of eighteenth-century fruit growing is Scotland's most extraordinary garden building, the Dunmore Pineapple near Falkirk, constructed *c.*1775 to celebrate the first production of pineapples in heated frames.

Not all walled gardens are fully walled and not all are of conventional shapes. Many have three walls, leaving the lower end fenced to allow frost to drain. There are several oval walled gardens in Scotland but Netherbyres, near Berwick, is the only elliptical walled garden in the world. Others follow the contours of the land or, in the case of Inverewe, the curved beach. One important eighteenth-century Scots fruit and vegetable expert was author James Justice, whose *The Scots Gardiner's Director* (1765) was a primer for anyone running a walled garden. Another was William Forsyth, who ran the Royal Kitchen Gardens for George III at Kensington Palace in London. He was famous for treating fruit-tree canker with a mixture of cow dung, lime and wood ashes.

Crofters and Peasant Farmers

While the rich landowners and merchants were extending their palette via their well-staffed walled kitchen gardens, the ordinary peasant or crofter living off the land in the seventeenth century had a restricted and monotonous diet based on oats – made into porridge, gruel and oatcakes – barley, for making alcohol, and a limited number of vegetables, such as kale and pea flour used to make bannocks. Most crofters would have had hens and possibly a

A planticru on North Ronaldsay, Orkney, formerly used to grow kale (photo Linda I. Weston).

cow or some goats for milk and cheese. Meat and herring were available from time to time. All but the rich faced the common threat of starvation. Historian T. C. Smout describes the 1690s as the worst recorded period of famine, with huge numbers of fatalities, which he attributes mainly to price rises following several poor oat harvests. Before the invention of canning and refrigeration, fruit and vegetable storage was all-important. Crops were dried, clamped, bottled, kept in ice houses or salted to keep them edible for as long as possible. The 'hungry gap' in late spring and early summer was the period of lowest food resources, when fresh, new-season food was not yet available and stored food had run out or spoiled.

On the west coast and islands, many practised the lazy bed cropping system – raised beds in strips, often on rocky, boggy or peaty soil, with paths dug out to provide drainage and the planting area in between filled with composted seaweed waste, dung and any other available organic matter. Many west-coast gardeners still use adaptations of this system. In the Northern Isles, young kale was planted out in

small circular drystone walled enclosures called kail-yards, known as plantie-crubs on Shetland and planticrus on Orkney, where they were still used until relatively recently.

The eighteenth century saw a revolution in Scottish agriculture. A raft of innovations, technology and knowledge improved the Scots diet immeasurably. New practices were popularised by crusading improvers such as farmer, geologist and evolution pioneer James Hutton, judge and writer Lord Kames and farming innovator John Hamilton, Lord Belhaven. They sought to make Scottish agriculture and horticulture more productive, adopting practices from England and the Continent. Improved ploughs and harvesting equipment allowed greater productivity, as did increasing understanding of soil fertility and the benefits of crop rotation. Viscount 'Turnip' Townshend from Norfolk promoted the use of turnips as a large-scale agricultural crop while, in Scotland, it was the hardier swede which became more widely planted from the 1770s onwards. These provided winter feed for animals as well as humans, allowing dairy produc-

The Pineapple, Dunmore, near Falkirk, is Scotland's most unusual garden building.

tion year round and more reliable supplies of meat.

Lowlanders were early adopters of new agricultural practices, while the Highlanders and Islanders were more resistant to change. The eighteenth century saw the addition of New World plants to the Scottish diet – many via Scottish plant hunters – including tomatoes, peppers, marrows, pumpkins and Jerusalem artichokes. Most were initially met with suspicion. Though introduced to Europe from South America in the late sixteenth century, the potato did not find favour in Scotland until the eighteenth century, when it transformed the calorific intake of crofters and farmers. It was arguably a potato-fuelled increase in life expectancy for both adults and infants which prompted the movement of labour to the newly expanding cities of the early Industrial Revolution.

Victorian Innovation

The nineteenth century saw another golden age of horticultural innovation born of new technologies. Gardeners were expected to keep their employers' tables filled with fresh food year-round. Melons, cucumbers, pumpkins, squash and other tender vegetables were produced with the aid of artificial heat. From the 1750s onwards, hot beds of manure, heating up as they composted, provided a source of warmth for protecting and forcing crops in winter and early spring. The National Trust's garden at Acorn Bank in Cumbria has been experimenting with raised beds heated through the winter under low plastic tunnels by the composting of a mixture of manure and sawdust. I was amazed at the results of this 'free' heat, allowing perfect crops of lettuces ready to harvest from March onwards. As fuel prices rise ever upward, I suspect that some of these old and forgotten methods of raising food will come back into vogue. The late eighteenth and nineteenth centuries also saw innovation in fruit growing, with heated walls, stove houses and glasshouses allowing crops such as pineapples, apricots and vines to be grown in Scotland's walled gardens.

The nineteenth century witnessed the first celebrity garden writers in horticultural magazines and books. Despite being crippled with arthritis, Scots polymath J. C. Louden (1783–1843) sustained a career as a botanist, garden designer and town planner, prolific writer and garden magazine editor. He had an opinion on almost everything and is said to have published a mind-boggling 66 million words in a lifetime's writing. His *An Encyclopaedia of Gardening* (1822) (available to download free from Google Books) is surely the most ambitious Scottish horticultural book of all time. The 1,052 pages cover every aspect of gardening: the origins of garden plants, botany, soils, fertiliser and the cultivation of fruit and vegetables in Britain and other countries. Much of his advice on crop rotation, prevention of disease, manures, propagation and pruning is as sound today as it was then, and the range of wisdom and common sense puts many more recent authors to shame. However, his views on crop protection would raise a few eyebrows these days. In the chapter 'Means of Defence', Louden recommends 'the man trap . . . a barbarous contrivance though rendered absolutely necessary in the exposed gardens around great towns'; the humane man trap, 'which simply breaks the leg'; and the spring gun, 'a variety of blunderbuss . . . found extremely useful in the neighbourhood of London'.

By the mid nineteenth century, hot beds and heated walls had gradually fallen from favour. The rapid evolution of glasshouse technology led to the construction of large-scale practical and ornamental greenhouses, vineries and palm houses. Scot Charles McIntosh published the influential *The Greenhouse, Hothouse and Stove* (1838), a manual of new techniques for forcing exotic crops. Greenhouses were used both to supply tender and out-of-season fruit and vegetables and to house the now-fashionable exotic plants sent back from all over the world by intrepid plant hunters such as the Lobbs, employed by Veitch Nurseries of Exeter. Many Scottish landowners had access to abundant coal, which they used to heat glasshouses to produce tropical delicacies. Edinburgh-based greenhouse company MacKenzie and Moncur designed and built many of Scotland's finest greenhouse complexes, such as those still extant at Geilston, Kailzie and Dunskey.

In parallel with the fruit and vegetable adven-

MacKenzie & Moncur, Scotland's greenhouse dynasty, supplying much of Britain in the nineteenth and early twentieth centuries.

tures of Britain's upper classes, an entirely different strand of gardening evolved through the eighteenth and nineteenth centuries – that of competitive fruit and vegetable shows, held amongst the workers in the newly industrialising cities. Lancashire weavers became fanatically competitive gooseberry growers, producing fruit the size of apples, and this craze spread north to Scotland. The 1827 catalogue of Edinburgh nurserymen Dicksons and Co. lists an astonishing 194 varieties of gooseberry. Competitive showing of vegetables continues to this day with the Scottish branch of the National Vegetable Society.

Plant breeding is something we now take for granted, but deliberate hybridising for desired characterics, such as larger yield or disease resistance, is a relatively recent science. Nobody knew, 250 years ago, that you could breed and hybridise plants. Pioneer Thomas Knight from Herefordshire began deliberately crossing strawberries and peas in the 1780s and 1790s. Before this, seed was simply collected from crops and stored for the following year with no deliberate human intervention. Local crop landraces such as Shetland kale had evolved over time to suit local conditions but, once Gregor Mendel's experiments in the 1850s revealed the laws of inheritance, breeders could begin to deliberately manipulate crops, resulting in more productive strains and increases in yields and disease resistance. Scottish potato breeders William Paterson and Archibald Findlay were amongst the first to take advantage of this new-found knowledge.

Second World War vegetable propaganda, including the 'Dig for Victory' campaign. Scottish-raised potatoes saved Britain from starvation.

The Twentieth Century

The Edwardian mansion and walled garden at Manderton near Duns is often referred to as the swansong of the great British country house. The grounds and gardens were once looked after by up to 100 gardeners but, within a few years, everything changed. Many gardeners were among those conscripted and slaughtered in the trenches of the First World War, and Europe-wide food shortages saw the government, through the Defence of the Realm Act, requisition land and triple the number of allotments for growing food to 1.5 million. Most walled gardens were given over to feeding the population. Even Buckingham Palace had its flower borders replaced with a cabbage patch, and parts of Kew Gardens became fields of potatoes. Wounded soldiers were encouraged to turn to gardening as physical and mental therapy in order to overcome the horrific injuries and experiences they had suffered. Only 20 years later, the Second World War saw a return to large-scale vegetable growing, this time under the banner 'Dig for Victory', the brain-child of Aberdonian professor John Raeburn.

Schools were required to grow food too; and great Scottish gardens, such as Drummond Castle in Perthshire, were turned over to market gardens. Scottish-raised potatoes were a key to the avoidance of starvation for Britain's population during the U-boat blockades. This countrywide, cross-class experience of growing things may have been responsible for the post-war gardening boom which has seen the British become some of the world's keenest and most talented gardeners.

The expansion of the railways and the ability to move fresh produce around the country saw Scotland's commercial fruit production expand, reaching a peak in the early twentieth century with apples, soft fruit and heated greenhouses full of tomatoes. Sadly, it was not to last, as Scottish growers found it increasingly hard to compete with growers in more favourable climates further south. Scotland's tree fruit industry went into decline, although our commercial fruit and vegetable sector is still a significant part of the country's GDP. Potatoes, soft fruit, turnips/swedes and peas are the most widely grown crops.

CHAPTER 3

Why Eat Fruit and Vegetables?
The Scottish Diet

Fresh fruit, vegetables and grains should be the mainstay of the Western diet, for both health and environmental reasons. With one of the worst diets in Western Europe, we Scots eat too much meat, sugar, carbohydrates, fried and processed food and not enough fruit, vegetables or fibre. The Scottish government has been wrestling with the issue of how to improve Scotland's dangerously unhealthy diet for almost two decades. The *Scottish Diet Action Plan* (1996, revised 2005) states:

> A well-balanced diet is vital to good health. Conversely, a badly balanced diet is harmful and predisposes people to a variety of serious illnesses including diabetes, coronary heart disease and some cancers. Our diet in Scotland is notoriously unhealthy and worse than that of almost any other country in the Western world. Indeed, next to smoking, it is the most significant reason for our poor health record. Children's diets are particularly poor, with many failing to eat green vegetables and fruit.
>
> Fruit and vegetables provide a wide range of nutrients . . . increasingly recognised as protective of health. These foods are rich sources of several vitamins, including folic acid, which, in addition to preventing deficiency diseases such as anaemia, are important before and during early preg-

nancy for the developing foetus and will help prevent arterial damage, coronary heart disease and strokes later in life.

The Scottish Executive laid down its targets for fruit and vegetable consumption in 1996 for 'average intake to double to more than 400 grams per day', which is equivalent to 'five portions'. So what progress has been made? From 2001–08 average intake increased from 3.1 portions to 3.4 per day per head, so there is still some way to go. In comparison, England and Wales claim an increase from 3.7 to 4.3 portions. One way of achieving the 5-a-day target is for more people to grow their own. If children can be inspired to grow and eat fruit and vegetables, they'll understand where they come from and hopefully learn to enjoy eating them for the rest of their lives. The challenge for policy makers is to break the cycle where the parents and grandparents don't and won't eat vegetables or fruit so don't encourage their children and grandchildren to do so. Food tastes are set very early in life, and studies suggest that children follow their parents' example. Telling children to eat fruit and vegetables without leading by example tends to have the opposite effect, putting children off. Some studies suggest that the mother's diet during pregnancy and breastfeeding may affect food tastes in children. Social class is a factor here, with A, B, C1 adults and children tending to eat a better diet, contributing to significantly greater longevity

Above. Bridgend Allotments, Edinburgh, comprises organic allotments, the Caley Allotment Demonstration Garden and a local therapeutic horticultural project all on one site.

Left. The Fife-Diet is a successful local food initiative founded by Mike Small, with assistance from the Climate Challenge Fund.

and reduced incidence of obesity and obesity-related disease. The Scottish government has pledged that all schoolchildren will have food education as part of the curriculum. Not before time.

Of Scotland's adults, 27 per cent are obese (2009), a figure which is increasing all the time. This has been described as Scotland's major public health time bomb. The reasons given for the obesity increase include poverty, poor education, lack of exercise, restricted access to fresh food, limited cooking skills and the time-poor adult preference for foods that are high in fat, and salt- and sugar-processed food (especially processing that uses high fructose corn syrup). Politicians, policymakers and campaigners have acknowledged all these issues but have yet to come up with joined-up and radical governance which actually delivers their targets.

Scotland's primary schools have seen a dramatic decline in organised sports outwith the statutory PE lesson, although attempts are being made to reverse this through the Scottish government-funded 'Active Schools' programme. The Westminster coalition government's laissez-faire attitude to school meals, probably prompted by the food industry's campaign contributions, may have disastrous consequences. Thankfully, Scotland's government continues to take such matters more seriously and has been examining Finland's successful intervention into its population's diet, which has reduced heart disease and obesity. We need successful, proven schemes which can be rolled out nationally. Scotland has good role models such as the Shotts Healthy Living Centre: its café, fruit and vegetables sales and education have had a major impact on the local diet for many families. The 'Big Eat In' (2010) saw several Glasgow schools opt for compulsory school meals for 11–12-year-olds for a period of a year. Supported by parents, teachers and pupils, the scheme may be rolled out to other schools. The *Daily Mail* loves to decry such intervention as part of the 'nanny state' but, in other countries, this would be viewed as a common-sense approach to saving lives by improving health and well-being. Tesco's lobbying scuppered the UK government's attempts to have 'traffic light' food labelling to allow people to see at a glance what might be good for them. What an opportunity for Scotland to take a lead on this – just as it did with the smoking ban. Successive UK and Scottish government reports on diet and health come to similar conclusions but vested interests, such as the food industry and the supermarkets, always manage to prevent action being taken. If our politicians don't have the courage to stand up to them, then we'll be looking at US levels of obesity and diabetes in the next 20 years. We have no choice but to act.

In 2005, the World Health Organization highlighted the correlation between the consumption of fruit and vegetables and reduced risk of heart disease, diabetes, cancer and other illnesses. Ironically, the adoption of a Western diet, with its increase of processed foods and calorific intake, and the decrease in exercise are having a catastrophic effect on health and obesity levels in many parts of the developing world. The evidence that fruit and vegetables are very good for you is unambiguous, but scientists are still trying to work out exactly *how* this happens. These beneficial effects appear to be the combination of fibre, vitamins and antioxidants, minerals, proteins, amino acids and polyphenols which fruit and vegetables contain. Most importantly, these effects are strongest with *fresh, naturally ripened* fruit and vegetables. Long transportation and storage, juicing and most processing also reduce efficacy. The claims on the packets of fruit-based pills and tablets on sale in health food stores are likely to be largely wishful thinking, as the production process will have removed most of the good-

Leaflets from some of the many organisations encouraging 'Grow Your Own', at Glasgow's Nourish Conference, 2011.

ness.

The James Hutton Institute (formerly Scottish Crop Research Institute) in Invergowrie is a key player in this research, examining the absorption of antioxidants through the gut into the colon and the bloodstream. Significant health-promoting fruit and vegetables which have come to light in recent years include blackcurrants, raspberries, *Aronia* (chokeberry), which inhibits colorectal cancers, rhubarb, which has significant cancer treatment properties, and spinach, which appears to help prevent cataracts in the eye. Even if we don't understand exactly what the causes are, there is universal agreement that a diet high in fruit and vegetables is good for us. All we have to do is persuade people to act on this information. It should be a win–win situation.

Where Do the Fruit and Vegetables We Eat Come From? World Food Production and Distribution

Scotland's climate is suited to growing a wide range of fruit and vegetables. Scotland was self-sufficient in apples, tomatoes and many other crops 100 years ago. Now we import most of them. A quick look at the labels of the fruit and vegetables in any supermarket shows how much is flown in from afar – blueberries from Chile, beans from Kenya, apples from New Zealand and so on. An Oxfam publication, *Fair Miles* (2009), reported some key statistics. The UK is the world's largest destination for food transported by air, and the amount of fresh food shipped in has been growing at a rate of about 6 per cent a year for much of the last two decades. Before this, Britain, like other countries, enjoyed mainly seasonal, locally produced food – rhubarb in March–May, asparagus in May–June, strawberries in June, raspberries in July, brambles in September and so on. The concept of fruit and vegetable seasonality has largely disappeared in northern Europe and now you can buy strawberries at any time of year, picked green in some far-flung corner of the world, ripened in a CO_2-filled shed and often tasting like turnips. Chefs, garden writers and campaigners such as Hugh Fearnley-Whittingstall and Jamie Oliver have been promoting local produce and seasonality for many years, with only limited success as far as the supermarket offerings are concerned.

Though it is certainly desirable for us to eat crops grown locally and in season and to reduce 'food miles', it would be naive to believe we can produce all our fruit and vegetables in Scotland. Don't assume that it is better for the environment to eat a locally grown tomato if it needs to be produced in a heated greenhouse. Producing the same crop outdoors or in unheated tunnels in a warmer country and flying it in will use significantly less fossil fuel energy and release less carbon dioxide. The Oxfam report also pointed out that fruit and vegetable production in Africa sent to the UK (a value of £1 million per day) directly sustains the livelihood of over a million Africans. The report concludes that simply adding up food miles does not always lead to helpful conclusions on sustainability.

Most fruit and vegetables – organic and non-organic alike – are now produced commercially in vast, water- and fertiliser-intensive monocultures, often under plastic tunnels. Crops are transported at significant expense in refrigerated planes and trucks, from continent to continent. Intensive agriculture in hot and often desert climates causes the draining of aquifers and the diverting of rivers so they no longer reach the sea. The result is irreversible salination of river deltas and permanent loss of marsh habitat such as is happening in Almeria, Spain, and in the Nile delta, Egypt. Except when consumer pressure can be brought to bear, supermarkets aim to maximise shareholder value by buying the cheapest available fruit and vegetables, largely without considerations of fair trade, environmental impact or sustainability. The long-term results of the degradation of soil and water quality are largely ignored by governments in the face of economic necessity, in the case of producers, and political pressure from the vested interests of powerful multinational food conglomerates in Western countries. The consequences will be irreversible and, for some afflicted by water shortages, life threatening.

THE TROUBLE WITH SUPERMARKETS

Almost all of us use supermarkets to buy most of our food. Due to competitiveness in retailing, Britain has relatively cheap fresh fruit and vegetables compared with some other Western countries. The downside is that the supermarkets have more or less destroyed the local food economy in Britain. Aggressively cheap supermarket pricing, sometimes selling at a loss, also means that small-scale local fruit and vegetable growing and retailing is almost always

Good for Ewe community allotments, Wester Ross, which unusually include some indoor allotment sites.

uncompetitive – which is why your local green-grocer probably closed down years ago. The consequences of pressure to produce cheaper and cheaper food often forces farmers to compromise on the long-term sustainability of their production activities just to remain viable. One major Scottish supermarket vegetable supplier told me, off the record, that the supermarkets regularly break contracts with and impose unfair terms on most of their suppliers. Though they are invited to testify at government inquiries into supermarket practices, producers can't afford to speak out, as their supermarket customers will immediately cease trading with them.

Fair trade principles need to be applied to smaller UK producers who simply cannot remain in business in the face of sustained supermarket pressures to cut costs. The UK Groceries Code Adjudicator, charged with ensuring fair play, has no power to fine or force supermarkets to act fairly. The Scottish government claims to want a viable local food economy in Scotland, but there is no real hope of this happening without the help of legislation, through intervention in the supply chain, taxation

and changes to local government business rates. The 2002 Small Breweries Tax Relief scheme, brought in under Gordon Brown's chancellorship, allows a 50 per cent excise duty reduction for small breweries so they are able to compete with the economies of scale of the big four multinational breweries. The result is a boom in microbreweries all over the UK. Scotland's local food economy could be encouraged by just such an initiative, with reduced rates and taxation for small independent businesses and increased rates for larger corporations.

Food waste expert Tristram Stuart (www.tristramstuart.co.uk) reports that, in the UK, 20–40 per cent of fruit and vegetables grown for supermarkets is rejected because it is the 'wrong' size, shape or colour. Perfectly edible, the produce is dumped. Globally, the figures are shocking. In the USA, households, retailers and food services throw away 40 million tonnes of food each year, enough to feed all of the one billion malnourished people on the planet. Despite claims of supply chain efficiency by the supermarkets, Stuart estimates that up to half of the entire Western food supply is wasted between

The Food Link Van, Skye, is an excellent local food economy initiative, allowing distribution of local produce to hotels and shops (photo Carole Inglis).

the farm and the fork.

Don't be fooled by the 'we support local producers' banners in your local supermarket. These are Scottish producers who supply the whole of the UK with strawberries, potatoes and turnips. Supermarkets rarely deal with suppliers who cannot supply countrywide. As the *Food Justice* report (2010) concluded, we need to focus on the *real* cost of food, taking into consideration the full environmental impact of its production and distribution, including transport and wastage. Only then do locally produced food crops on smaller-scale mixed farms of livestock, grains, fruit and vegetables become an obvious solution both economically and environmentally. Several organisations are campaigning for such change in Scotland, including Transition Scotland and Nourish Scotland. Is this a pipedream or the only sustainable way forward? We live in interesting times.

Increasing Fruit and Vegetable Growing and Consumption in Scotland

The SNP Scottish government, elected in 2007 and re-elected in 2011, believes in the importance of locally grown food and has invested considerable time and funding into commissioning reports and

research in this sector. *Recipe for Success: Scotland's National Food and Drink Policy* (2009) supports the increased provision of new allotment sites and aims to help public bodies, communities and individuals to set them up. The 2009 Grow Your Own Working Group brought together policy makers, allotment representatives and others to develop a strategy which allows everyone in Scotland to have access to land to grow their own food and to encourage more people to do so. A further report, *Community Growing in Scotland* (2011), spelled out the wider strategy:

There is also a need to explore alternative, more flexible and adaptable approaches to both individual and community urban food growing. A broader approach to community growing has the potential to increase the amount of land available and provide growing opportunities for a wider range of people . . . Whilst allotments are the most prevalent form of community growing, a range of other models are in use. These include community gardens, community orchards, landshare, community supported agriculture and workplace growing . . .

This report provides the basis for concerted and coordinated cross-sector action to secure a step-change in the scale and impact of community growing in Scotland . . . Allotments are only part of the picture.

Campaigning organisation Nourish Scotland encapsulates the goals: 'For Scotland to grow more of what we eat and to eat more of what we grow.' Which sums it up perfectly.

The information and strategies that these reports contain and recommend are all well and good, but it will take joined-up national and local government to make widespread change happen, particularly in the current economic climate. One key problem area is the difficulty of accessing mean-

Knowetop Community Farm, Dunbartonshire, is sadly closing through lack of funding.

ingful funding, especially for existing projects. Trellis, the umbrella organisation for Scotland's therapeutic horticulture, works side by side with the Federation of City Farms and Community Gardens from an office in Perth. Involved in over 250 Scottish projects between them, Fiona Thackeray, Development Manager at Trellis, eloquently describes the struggle for funding that many projects experience:

> Photo opportunity funding is obsessed with innovation . . . because funders are all into this idea that you must have brand exposure/publicity . . . and the way to do that is [by] getting news headlines and photo opportunities. Hence 'more of the same' proposals are not so fundable because they are not new – even if good/proven. I am not sure how to challenge that except by convincing funders to dare to say, 'We will fund tried-and-tested, good projects, inno-

vative or not, because we care about the results more than our own profile.' This could be radical, refreshing and very popular.

Politicians and funders seem unable to concede that community grow-your-own initiatives need funding and good management over a significant period of time to have any chance of long-term success. Bringing fruit and vegetable crops to market is a complex business and requires a range of skills. Poorly planned and short-term funding for such projects is often money wasted. Those who run these projects tend to need a modest amount of core funding over several years but, in place of this, all they are offered is short-term or one-off funding for new initiatives for infrastructure only. As Fiona Thackeray has pointed out, funders fall over themselves to fund novelty at the expense of tried-and-tested schemes, often for political expediency – it makes them look good. Common sense says they should do exactly the opposite – fund schemes which work and replicate them elsewhere.

A great initiative which can't find funding, and which illustrates the lack of joined-up government thinking, is the Food Link Van in Skye and Lochalsh. Set up in March 2000 with a grant of £1,000, this excellent scheme now annually distributes £100,000 worth of Skye and Lochalsh-produced cheese, fruit, herbs and vegetables to local retailers and restaurants, who proudly advertise their locally sourced food. Skye is now a favourite destination for food lovers. The current Food Link van is now nearing retirement age and a new refrigerated van is required, which will enable it to carry fresh meat and fish as well as fruit and vegetables. Try as they might, the Food Link members can't find any funding which they can use to help replace the van and, as a result, the scheme may not survive. Why are we willing to subsidise farmers via EC grants to produce food which is not required, but not to subsidise local food producers whose food already has a market? Why will governments subsidise rural bus transport year after year, but not food distribution? As scheme member Dede MacGillivray says, 'The economic and social benefits the van brings to Skye and Lochalsh, particularly through the tourism sector, are enormous – many local restaurants and hotels have built their reputation upon using high-quality local ingredients.' Here is a model scheme which fulfils so many criteria deemed important by the Scottish government but which cannot find funding. Not only should this scheme be supported but the government could and should help roll out similar schemes in other parts of Scotland.

Another worthwhile project, set to close due to lack of funding, is Knowetop Community Farm, Dumbarton, established for over 30 years and with up to 25,000 annual visits. Despite its key role in the deprived local area, encouraging the growing and eating of fresh fruit and vegetables through a community allotment, further funding for their core activities is not available.

Many older funding schemes, such as the Sustainable Action Fund and the Greener Initiative, have been replaced as a major source of finance for grow-your-own initiatives by the Climate Challenge Fund (CCF). The Scottish government has pledged to cut Scotland's carbon emissions by 42 per cent by 2020, apparently one of the most ambitious targets in the world. Reducing food miles is seen as part of this strategy. The Climate Challenge Fund has given grant funding of almost £30 million to community groups throughout Scotland in the last five years. The aim is 'to help communities take local action to tackle the global threat of climate change'. Projects have included alternative transport, waste disposal, forestry, and fruit and vegetable growing.

The Barra and Vatersay Northbay Garden Project received £60,000 from the CCF to reduce food miles by establishing island production of fresh food for homes, hotels and restaurants. Produce was hitherto shipped on the five-hour journey from Oban. The project has a parallel role as a therapeutic garden and includes a heated greenhouse powered by renewable energy. Caroline visited an equally inspiring CCF-funded grow-your-own project on Unst, the most northern of the Shetland Isles. Fife Diet is an award-winning Scottish initiative, part financed by the CCF, which encourages the sourcing of as much food as possible from the local area and the preparing of meals from scratch using raw ingredients. Founder Mike Small's target is for individuals living in Fife to live on food which is 80 per cent locally produced, perhaps very wishful thinking, as the current figure is thought to be 0.6 per cent. Clearly a revolution needs to take place.

Some CCF-funded projects have undoubtedly been successful, but others have already floundered. A major flaw was the funding timescale, demanding that applications be placed within a few months of the announcement and that all funds be spent within 6–12 months of the awards being made. The rushed timescale was not a recipe for well-planned and well-embedded, sustainable schemes. Communities rushed headlong to grab the available cash, filling in the forms with fanciful carbon-saving data.

Worse, some funds for grow-your-own projects did not reach their applicants until late summer, entirely missing the growing cycle because the scheme demanded that all funds be spent by the following March. Neither the Green MSP I interviewed, whose party supported this project, nor the Scottish government's then environment minister was willing or able to concede there was a problem or to agree to do anything about it, blaming 'treasury rules'. The *Review of the Climate Challenge Fund* (June 2011) does address the need for longer term funding and future applications, and we have been assured that the new funding rounds will have longer lead times. It is a pity that significant funds have already been wasted.

If the Climate Challenge Fund is not always the solution, then what sort of funding *would* make a lasting difference to this sector? Voluntary community-based growers can't become experts on horticulture, management, fund-raising or food distribution and storage overnight. New initiatives need careful planning and ongoing mentoring, evaluation and advice from those who already run successful schemes. Replication of success rather than looking for novelty is the best driver for grant applications. Throwing short-term funding at Scottish fruit and vegetable growing will have no lasting impact unless the big issues are considered. We can't afford simply to tinker at the margins. For example, if the Scottish government insisted on a quota of locally produced food for all public sector food procurement in prisons, hospitals and schools, it would create a sustainable large-scale, cost-effective and resilient local food economy and producers would reduce their dependency on the supermarkets. As the Greenspace Scotland report proposes, *all* government departments – health, education, environment, agriculture – as well as retailers will need to work together for this to happen.

Scotland already boasts dozens of excellent businesses and initiatives to serve as models. The Food for Life initiative in East Ayrshire, where the council uses locally raised produce to feed its school-

La Boqueria market in Barcelona, one of Europe's outstanding produce markets (photo Jane Cox).

children healthy meals, is a beacon of best practice which could be rolled out nationally. Binn Skips near Glenfarg is planning an ambitious integrated food and energy scheme. If it works, this looks like a model to emulate elsewhere. Earthy Foods in Edinburgh and Portobello demonstrates a viable growing and distribution model for local organic fresh vegetables. Further south, Riverford in Devon runs a franchise network of participating organic farms, delivering over 47,000 meat, fruit and vegetable boxes each week from Yorkshire to Cornwall. Riverford's philosophy is to deliver locally produced food where possible, and anything that has to be imported must come by road/ship. Nothing can be flown in. The Findhorn Community in Moray pioneered the Community Supported Agriculture (CSA) model in Scotland in its EarthShare scheme, where the food consumer buys a share of the food production and/or exchanges labour for food.

Members had an organic vegetable box delivered each week. Sadly it was forced to close in 2010, after 16 years, largely due to issues of tenancy on its rented land, but the CSA model they pioneered has been copied successfully elsewhere. Other CSA schemes in Scotland include the organic vegetable box scheme H.O.P.E., in Arbroath; Whitmuir the Organic Place, in West Linton; and Good for Ewe, near Poolewe in Wester Ross. To grow a sustainable Scottish local food economy, the CSA model has considerable further growth potential – as does the setting-up of mutual/cooperative schemes. Pete Ritchie, chair of Nourish Scotland, suggests the establishment of thousands more crofts and smallholdings for small-scale produce growing.

If Scotland wants a national sea change in how we produce and buy food, we need to think big but recognise that small is often beautiful.

Produce Markets

Like many others, I love visiting and shopping at food markets, and every time I visit one in France or Spain – or London, for that matter – I wonder why we can't do it here in Scotland. As long as the big four supermarkets have a stranglehold on the distribution of fruit and vegetables, there will be little or no change to the availability of locally produced fresh food. Supermarkets demand suppliers who can supply nationally. They won't look at small local suppliers. Re-establishing retail produce markets in Scotland's towns and cities for fruit and vegetables, baking, meat and fish is one way to really make a difference. Great though they are, we are not talking about once-a-month farmers' markets. Food markets need to be open much more often – for several days a week – so that they change people's buying habits for the weekly shop. This requires large-scale markets where producers and stallholders can sell directly to the public, creating a proper local food economy and an attractive alternative to the supermarket. Almost every town in southern France

has them. Closer to home, Borough Market in London, St Nicholas Market in Bristol, Kirkgate Market in Leeds and the Bull Ring Market in Birmingham are all thriving. Markets are traditionally the hub of the town and a way for local producers and fishermen to sell the volumes of food that they need to so that they are not slaves to the whims of the supermarkets and their restrictive terms. For produce markets to happen on a significant scale, there has to be government and local council support, and politicians need to have the courage to resist the inevitable heavy-handed lobbying of the supermarkets. Indeed, it should be possible to make approval for a supermarket development site to be conditional on the building of an independent produce market for the community which might even share a car park with the supermarket.

A successful produce market can revitalise a town centre and bring associated benefits to other retailers and services. Produce markets need decent, cheap car parking because what people buy in markets is heavy – potatoes, pumpkins, apples, haunches of meat. Whether we like it or not, people go shopping in their cars and many markets have failed because councils restrict or over-price parking. Campaigning organisation Common Ground has been pushing for more food markets for several years. I'd certainly support Climate Challenge Fund money being spent on re-opening markets around Scotland, which would make a long-term difference to our producers, the supply chain and shopping habits alike, and thus reduce carbon emissions. Wholesale food markets like the one in Glasgow, for instance, could provide a hub for Scotland's markets, receiving and distributing a core of essential goods. Buying from markets makes sense for the consumer too. The price of fresh fruit and vegetables could be cheaper than the supermarket offering, as it tends to be in London, for example. Why can't Glasgow and Edinburgh, Stirling, Dundee and Aberdeen have retail produce markets?

In 2007, Perth Council trumpeted its joining of the Slow Food/Cittaslow movement. The Cittaslow

Northbay Garden Project, Barra, was supported by the Climate Challenge Fund.

charter states, 'Consumers are encouraged to support and buy from local artisan producers through markets, fairs and other activities that keep consumers in direct contact with makers and producers.' Perth is the perfect location for a new produce market, a core Cittaslow activity, which could and should be the model for the rest of Scotland. Perthshire can provide the produce. The old city hall in the city centre, threatened with demolition, would be the ideal site. It just requires some courage and vision.

Making a Difference: A Strategy for Change in Scotland's Fruit and Vegetable Growing, Distribution and Consumption

- A poor diet is almost as damaging to health as smoking. UK governments at last stood up to the tobacco industry and banned smoking in public buildings. Eating fruit and vegetables saves lives and governments have a moral duty to stand up

to vested interests in the food industry and make policy decisions on health grounds as they did with the smoking ban. Traffic light indicators on food packaging and warnings of high levels of fat, sugar and salt would be a first step.

- Children's tastes in food are set early in life. Developing a fruit-and-vegetable-eating habit needs to begin from weaning onwards. The challenge is that children copy their parents' eating habits. The Royal Horticultural Society campaign for School Gardening aims to have 80 per cent of UK primary schools growing food, but this will need cooperation from government and councils. Any produce grown should then be cooked, served and eaten in school. RHS training courses are being run in Scottish primary schools.

- Public food procurement (for schools, hospitals, etc.) should have a minimum statutory requirement for locally raised/grown produce.

- Fair-trade principles need to be applied to supermarket–farmer relationships in the UK. Much commercial fruit and vegetable production in

Redhall Walled Garden, Edinburgh, is an excellent example of therapeutic horticulture.

Scotland is in a precarious state due to the power and conduct of supermarkets and their payment terms.

- Policy makers can level the financial/economic playing field by using the tax system to reduce business rates to locally owned food-related small businesses, and increasing them for supermarkets and major food chains. This was partly addressed by the Scottish government in 2011.

- As part of the development of a sustainable local food economy, daily or weekly produce markets in Scotland's major cities should be established so that suppliers can deal directly with the public.

- As the Greenspace Scotland report states, there is a need to free up the bureaucracy involved in acquiring land for growing things, particularly in the short term, and for short- and medium-term leases. There is more than enough suitable land out there to meet demand, if red tape and legal fees can be reduced/eliminated. The Community Land Advisory Service has been established to fulfil this role. It needs to be properly funded and

given teeth to succeed.

- If we and our government want sustainable, economically viable local food production, then we will need to rethink the way schemes are subsidised and funded. One-off grants from the Climate Challenge Fund are not a sustainable answer. New business models such as social enterprises, mutuals and community-supported agriculture will be required for growing, distribution and retailing. And microcredit interest-free loans will need to be offered to allow projects to get off the ground and bed in. Core funding should be provided for proven and effective projects and rarely for novelty.

- Town planning for new building estates should include mandatory provision for grow-your-own space/allotments.

- Enough glossy reports have been published and enough talking has been done. Now is the time for the implementation of a top-down sustained strategy for the growing, distribution and eating of locally grown produce, encompassing the

Scottish government, Departments of Health, Education and Environment, local councils, farmers, gardeners and consumers. Will the SNP National Food Policy deliver this? Time will tell.

Fruit and Vegetables in Community Gardens and Therapeutic Horticulture

Scotland boasts a huge range of community gardens from Skye to Shetland, from the Central Belt to South Uist. Many have been assisted by BBC Scotland's *Beechgrove Garden* and, more recently, the Climate Challenge Fund. Projects focus on education for schools and colleges, the promotion of organic gardening and minimising community carbon footprints as well as sharing unused land for the benefit of all and building community cohesion. A good example is Assloss Walled Garden. This old walled garden in Kilmarnock is being opened up for schools, families and community groups to grow their own food. Two Glasgow-based projects, the Children's Orchard and the Hidden Gardens at Tramway, are both examples of creative ways of engaging local people in education, food production and healthy eating.

A newer project – so far, funded and working well – is the restoration of the old market garden at Royal Edinburgh Hospital in Morningside, now called Royal Edinburgh Community Gardens. The key to this project is the 11 partner organisations involved, which include the Cyrenians, Shandon Local, Transition and Veterans First Point. Produce is mainly grown in raised beds, while new fruit trees have been planted alongside the old orchard of 70 mature apple trees. Chairman of NHS Lothian, Dr Charles Winstanley, stresses the many benefits of the project – exercise, improved diet, community involvement and mental well-being.

Trellis, the umbrella organisation for Scotland's therapeutic gardens, currently supports over 190 different projects, ranging from dementia groups to adults with learning difficulties at sites including prisons, hospitals and community gardens. Trellis actively promotes, supports and develops the 'use of gardening to improve the health, well-being and life opportunities of all'. A large proportion of these projects grow fruit and vegetables. The Walled Garden, based in the grounds of the Murray Royal Hospital in Perth, supports 40 adults recovering from mental health problems, while Gardening Leave, at Auchincruive in Ayrshire, founded by Anna Baker Cresswell, is an excellent therapeutic project for servicemen suffering from combat trauma and psychological damage. Bridgend Allotments, Edinburgh, provides space for fruit and vegetable growing but, perhaps more importantly, also offers a covered social space where the food grown is prepared, cooked and eaten by the participants. The focus of this scheme combines community inclusion and horticultural therapy and is a perfect example of how the Scottish government's drive to encourage healthy eating could be fulfilled. And yet its future looks precarious because of cutbacks. Another inspiring but underfunded project is Redhall Walled Garden, also in Edinburgh. This eighteenth-century walled garden offers training in horticulture, conservation, maintenance skills, IT and life skills for up to 50 people recovering from mental health problems. The demand for places is large enough to fill it four times over. I can't do better than quote Fiona Thackeray, Development Manager of Trellis, in summing up the challenges faced by this sector:

> Politicians and public alike don't see what gardening can do – from neurological rehabilitation after a stroke to teaching numeracy and literacy skills to people who have missed out on this at school, to building self-esteem, to recovery from mental illness. People tend to think it is 'just nice' or it keeps folk busy/off the streets. Hence garden therapists are underpaid and undervalued, resources are scant and projects are overlooked.

CHAPTER 4

The Ground Rules for Growing Fruit and Vegetables in Scotland

Scotland's Climate: What Grows Well, Where, How and Why?

Scotland's northerly latitude and Gulf Stream-influenced climate provide cool summers, low sunlight intensity, plenty of rainfall and lots of wind. The climate is ideal for many fruit and vegetables – raspberries, strawberries and potatoes, to name but three. However, the climate also dictates that many crops which grow fine outdoors in the south of England struggle in Scotland. Cucumbers, most tomatoes, figs and peaches are barely worth growing outdoors here – although you won't find this information in most fruit and vegetable books. Many other crops are excellent as long as they have a little protection in early spring or are started off indoors. This is particularly important for exposed sites, inland and more northern and island gardens.

Scotland boasts a considerable range of climates, from milder parts of the west coast and islands with little frost, to near Arctic conditions in the Cairngorms and the wind-battered Shetlands with little summer heat. As Jedburgh is further away from Shetland than it is from the south coast of England, you'll understand why there is no one-size-fits-all advice for Scottish gardeners. Even within a single region there can be big differences. Borders growers explained to me that distance from the North Sea is a key factor in what they can grow. Towards the east it is milder but windier, while west

of Galashiels it is much colder, with late frosts, but more sheltered from the wind. So, what grows well in Coldstream, for example, may not grow in Peebles. Scotlandwide, fruit crops do better in the drier east of the country than in the wetter west. However, every corner of Scotland can grow a huge range of edible crops as long as you select the most suitable varieties and adapt your husbandry a little. The key is both to manipulate conditions through shelter and soil preparation and to work with nature, choosing plants suited to local conditions and ensuring that you get the timing right. If you sow too early, for example, your newly germinated seedlings will be stunted by cold or wind and you'll never get a bumper crop.

Whatever we say in this book about what can and can't be grown in different parts of Scotland, there is always someone who can prove us wrong. Much of the fun in gardening comes from successfully growing the most unlikely things – especially if you have been told it is not worth trying. Seek out local wisdom, as most gardeners love to share their knowledge. Treat this book as a general guide to what *should* do well in your area, but remember there are no absolute rules. Growing most fruit and vegetables demands a certain level of planning, commitment and nurturing. You can't expect to have a perfect patch of fruit and vegetables without a bit of research and at least some hard work. There are undoubtedly easier-to-grow choices like potatoes and strawberries to start with. We would not recommend jumping straight in with growing Florence fennel, asparagus and peaches unless you are really up for a challenge. We give an indication of how easy it is to succeed with each fruit or vegetable through the text of the book, using easiness ratings of E1 (easy) to E3 (challenging).

Sun, Light and Heat

In Scotland, most fruit and vegetables benefit from as much sunlight as possible. South- and west-facing sunny walls are ideal for fruit and climbing vegetables such as beans. If you have a very shady garden, there is a limited list of crops which are likely to do well. These tend to be the ones where you eat the leaves rather than the roots or the fruit. The sun in Scotland weakens fast from September onwards, slowing growth outdoors, but protected cropping under cloches and tunnels will prolong the growing season.

Top. Experimenting with artificial lights on salads, David Newman, Benbecula.

Above. Hotbeds at Acorn Bank, Cumbria, where heat from composting manure and sawdust is used to force early vegetables.

Food Crops for Shady Gardens
Alpine strawberries
wineberries
blackcurrants
salads such as lettuce, endive and cress
beets
radishes
Swiss chard and spinach
mint, lovage, parsley

Several Scottish growers are experimenting with artificial lighting to produce early and late crops, particularly in the Northern and Western Isles, which have a short growing season. High-pressure sodium lights, with an orange-red glow, encourage budding and flowering while the blue spectrum of metal halide lights encourages bushy, leafy growth. At Glendoick we tried expensive grow lights for seedlings in winter but found that good old-fashioned fluorescent lights were just as good. Alan Crowe on mainland Shetland starts his brassicas under metal halide lights in early spring and he uses sodium lights to obtain early crops of tomatoes. On Benbecula, David Newman has been experimenting with salad crops under wind-powered red and blue LEDs and noticed a difference in growth rate after only two weeks.

Left. Seaside gardening at Plockton, Wester Ross (photo Elspeth Bruce).

Top right. Extreme greenhouse wind protection at the Big Garden, South Uist.

Above right. Wind shelter for brassicas at Laura Donkers' garden, North Uist.

Frost and Frost Pockets

Frost damage takes place when moisture in soft plant tissue freezes and ruptures cells in the leaves, stems and flowers. This can kill tender plants such as potatoes and beans. The key is not to plant out tender vegetables until frost danger has passed, unless you have the wherewithal to cover them or you have some spare plants indoors as an insurance policy. Keep an eye on the weather forecasts so you can cover with fleece or cloches. Many gardeners improvise using plastic bottles and other waste materials to make individual protective cloches for tender crops. It is also useful to have some idea when the last frosts in your area tend to be – typically April for mildest coastal areas, May for most of coastal southern Scotland and as late as June in inland valleys and other frost pockets. When the temperature drops below zero, frozen water crystals, heavier than air, sink to ground level and then flow downhill. Frost will settle in hollows, along rivers, at valley bottoms and, in a garden, it can sink to the lowest point against walls and fences. Some of Scotland's coldest, most frost-prone areas include inland river valleys such as those of the Tweed, Clyde, Dee, Don and Spey. The temperature in the valley bottom can be several degrees colder at dawn (the coldest time) than on the surrounding hillsides. Those who garden on the slopes above the river may escape damage as the frost drains downhill. Higher altitudes may, of course, bring other problems, such as strong winds and more persistent snow.

Certain tough fruits, vegetables and herbs are good choices for frost pockets. These include currants, gooseberries, rhubarb, beetroot, Brussels sprouts, chard, kale, leeks, parsnips, radishes, chives, horseradish, lemon balm and mint.

Microclimates

Microclimates are local variations in climate created by shelter, frost drainage, slope or aspect, as well as by man-made intervention such as the walls of heated buildings. Cities and towns have a 'heat island' effect – the cumulative heat escaping from buildings artificially raises the temperature compared to the rural equivalent. Microclimates can also occur within gardens, even very small ones, and they can also be created and manipulated by changing a garden's structure and planting. It will be warmer and more sheltered beside a house than near the property's boundary. South- and west-facing walls are warmer than north- and east-facing walls because they soak up the sun's warmth for the longest daytime period and then slowly reflect this heat back. Old stone and brick absorb and radiate more heat than other materials, acting like storage heaters. Pale-coloured paints and renders reflect heat and light too, helping plants to ripen in time for cold weather. Scotland's plethora of walled kitchen gardens are an example of a human-manipulated microclimate, using walls for growing plants which benefit from the shelter and warmth provided.

Expanses of water – the sea and nearby rivers or lochs – can have a moderating effect on climate, and relatively mild climates (although often very windy ones) can be found by the estuaries of the rivers Forth and Tay and beside the Moray Firth, as well as by many west-coast sea lochs.

Wind

Wind damage is one of the major causes of plant failure in Scotland. The prevailing winds come from the south-west and west, and the coldest winds from the east, particularly in spring. Infrequent strong gusts do most of the damage to buildings and trees but, for plants, it is as much the constant buffeting in exposed sites which can lead to failure. The leaves of newly planted fruit and vegetables are vulnerable at any time of year to desiccation from wind as the roots cannot yet take up moisture easily from surrounding soil. Each time the wind rocks a plant, it tears the tiny, delicate new roots, requiring the plant to start root production all over again and, as a consequence, young growth is severely stunted and the plant may die. The most frequent wind damage is to newly planted-out vegetables in May, started off under cover, where the tender, soft new growth is fried by cold easterly winds or westerly gales. Tall and vigorous plants such as peas and beans are particularly vulnerable, as are any plants on the tender side, such as basil and tomatoes, which are best grown indoors. Keep them protected until June or July. Salad plants tend to bolt if they are dried out by wind, so you get few edible leaves. Coastal garden winds are often laden with salt, which burns young foliage. Wind also hampers pollination of flowers by flying insects so some fruit trees, such as pears, and some types of bean tend to set poorly in windy sites. Crops that stand over winter, such as Brussels sprouts and kale, are vulnerable to wind rock, so need to be firmly stamped in at planting time, and you may need to stake them.

Internal windbreaks, also useful for attaching fleece and mesh, at the Big Garden, South Uist.

The frequency of strong winds and gales is significantly higher in Scotland than in other parts of the United Kingdom. The windiest areas are the western seaboard, particularly Wester Ross and Sutherland, the Atlantic side of west-coast islands and Orkney. Windiest of all is Shetland, averaging as many as 30 days of gales per year. During her trip through the Outer Hebrides, Wester Ross, Orkney and Shetland in summer 2010, Caroline discovered just what a challenge growing any fruit and vegetables can be in areas with extreme wind. Many gardeners there divide their plots into small sections that are walled with stone or wood or fenced with woven plastic, to shelter everything from wind and salt. Polytunnels and greenhouses are invaluable there, but they are always at risk of blowing down or away. At the Big Garden on South Uist, Denise Bridge has to batten her greenhouses with a slatted wooden casing to prevent windborne objects from crashing into them. Keder houses are polytunnels that have been aerodynamically designed to withstand severe winds, and these are being used with success by the Good for Ewe community garden in Wester Ross and allotments and gardens in the Western Isles. Another technique used at Good for Ewe is to make sunken beds sheltered by low walls constructed from turf – a good solution, provided drainage is sharp, on a raised beach, for example. In

the windiest sites, horticultural advisor Colin Stirling advises 'bunding' – constructing soil banks around the tunnels on the windward side – which helps them survive severe storms. Trials of vegetable growing on Benbecula on alkaline machair soil by the Sustainable Uist group demonstrate the value of wind shelter. Project manager David Newman reports that, even in summer, severe storms of over 60 mph have killed most peas, beans, salads and brassicas in unprotected beds, with only kales surviving. Next door, plots sheltered with woven polypropylene or covered with fleece produced good crops of courgettes, salads, brassicas, beets and leeks.

Filtering the wind's strength creates a microclimate, giving immediate improvement in growing conditions. The traditional solution has been to build walls or a walled garden. Most gardens along the Caithness and Sutherland coast and in towns and townships in Orkney and Shetland can be found inside walls. These protect plants from the almost constant winds and salt-laden air. But walls are expensive to build and maintain, and there are cheaper and easier solutions. Fencing panels and wire netting with woven polypropylene attached are often used. Waste materials such as recycled wood from pallets can often be picked up for nothing; look at allotment sites for ideas. Walls are not always the best solution, as solid barriers tend to divert wind, which can strike with even more force beyond the barrier at a distance of roughly three times its height. Damaging eddies and undercurrents can be created too, as the wind swirls around when it strikes the ground again. A permeable barrier, such as a hedgerow or a shelterbelt of trees and shrubs, filters the wind rather than redirecting it. The famous Scottish west-coast woodland gardens tend to use shelterbelts of wind-tolerant trees and shrubs such as *Escallonia*, *Griselinia* and *Olearia* to protect the garden from salt-laden winds. On Iona, and commonly in Orkney and Shetland too, vegetable gardens are protected with low walls and hedges of *Fuchsia magellanica*. When choosing shelter planting, consider the impact of the roots on your crops

Wind protection at Northbay Garden Project, Barra.

Above. Machair soils (such as here on Benbecula) present particular challenges for growers.

Right. Ken liming the vegetable patch in winter.

as well as the shade cast. Conifers and other trees will spread their roots sideways and take nutrients from the soil quite some distance from the hedge, so reducing the area available for cropping unless you create raised beds. Sycamore is the only broadleaf tree which will grow in some of the windiest sites on Orkney and Shetland, for example, so while most of us curse it for seeding everywhere, this tree can be invaluable in extreme conditions. In conclusion, wind is the most significant predictor of success or failure in such climates and so investment in strong and durable wind protection is essential.

Climate Change

Central Scotland lies at a latitude of 55° north, on the same latitude as Labrador in Canada and parts of southern Alaska, both of which have much colder climates. That Scotland's climate is relatively mild for somewhere this far north is mainly down to the Gulf Stream, an 'oceanic conveyor belt' bringing warm air and rainfall from the Gulf of Mexico to north-west Europe. Some scientists believe that climate change may weaken the current, which would make Scotland colder, not warmer as elsewhere. The significance of Scotland's northerly latitude is that cool summers and relatively weak sunlight mean that many plants whose origins are from nearer the equator may struggle to ripen. Examples include walnuts, sweetcorn and apricots. Journalists may lead you to believe that we'll be starting vineyards in Scotland soon, but I would not hold my breath. Even if the planet is warming up, the relative weakness of the sun's strength is a key predictor of which fruit and vegetables will grow well.

Many of us gardeners had become complacent with a run of mild winters for 20 years, but we were brought back down to earth with the extreme cold of 2009–10 and 2010–11. Torrential downpours in summer and salt-laden summer gales which batter the west coast can also do terrible damage to food crops. Climate change is undoubtedly taking place:

as reported by Scotland & Northern Ireland Forum for Environmental Research (SNIFFER – www.sniffer.org.uk), the length of the growing season, from last to first frosts, in northern Britain has increased by an average of more than four weeks over the last 30 years, and the number of nights with air frosts has decreased by almost 25 per cent. Heavy rainstorms are deluging us with up to 20 per cent more precipitation in one go (bigger rainstorms, less often), with more rain in winter and less in summer. The longer growing season should help to ripen borderline crops such as sweetcorn and allow late crops to remain in the ground longer. The downside is that climate change tends to bring new pests and diseases.

Soils

Investing in your soil is one of the most important aspects of growing your own fruit and vegetables. As well as the soil particles which make up the soil structure, one teaspoon of soil contains millions of micro-organisms, each constituting a small part of a bigger underground ecosystem. If your growing space has never been cultivated before, it will need to be weeded and well dug over and you'll need to mix in some goodness in the form of organic matter. Once your soil has a good 'tilth' – when it has been well dug over and mixed – you may be able to move towards a no-dig approach, but this is only possible once the soil is well worked. Digging is best done in summer or autumn in dry weather – don't leave it till winter when the soil tends to be heavy and wet. As well as the extra effort digging wet soil, tramping on soggy ground can damage soil structure. All soils benefit from a significant amount of added compost and/or manure, although it may take a number of years of adding such material to crop fruit and vegetables at an optimal level. Fruit and vegetables do tend to use up much of the available soil nutrients over time so annual replenishment of compost, manure and fertilisers is advisable.

SOIL TYPES

Experts categorise soils into several types. Two of these, silt (found in river valleys) and chalk soils, are rare in Scotland. The main Scottish soil types are:

Clay

Most gardeners can recognise a clay soil – it feels lumpy and sticky when wet, is heavy to turn with a spade, dries rock hard and drains poorly due to the tiny particles which stick together, leaving few airspaces. It does hold lots of nutrients, however, and a good number of fruit and vegetables will grow well in clay soils – potatoes, cabbage, kale and sprouts, for example. Heavy clay soils often stay cold, wet and airless for long periods, and some vegetables and herbs cannot tolerate such conditions. You can smell badly drained clay soils when you dig them up! Adding well-rotted organic matter, such as dung, leaf mould, peat and compost, will improve the structure. Many wide river valleys such as the Carse of Gowrie between Perth and Dundee have predominantly clay soils. Most vegetable gardeners who garden on clay soil end up making raised beds so they can garden *on* and not *in* the clay (*see* p. 34).

Sandy

Sandy soils have everything that clay soils don't. The larger, gritty particles form a light soil which is easy to work and drains very well – too well in many cases, as it can dry out very rapidly and hold few nutrients. Vegetables and fruit grown on sandy soil can easily run out of puff early in the season. Many coastal gardens, such as those in Fife, East Lothian and Angus, have sandy soil which needs plenty of feeding and organic matter added for best results.

Loam

Loam is the halfway house between clay and sand. It is often considered the perfect soil – easy to work, with good structure and drainage qualities but retaining moisture and nutrients well. You can grow the widest range of plants in loam.

Peat

Much of Scotland has peaty, acidic soil, which is dark in colour and often fibrous in texture. Heather and other acid lovers (known as ericaceous plants), such as rhododendrons, grow well in it. Peaty soil is too acidic (*see* soil pH below) for most vegetables and its water absorption qualities can create boggy conditions, unless drainage is improved. In a peaty garden, consider creating raised beds, adding compost and composted seaweed, to grow in.

SOIL PH (ACIDITY)

The pH scale gives a measure of a soil's acidity or alkalinity and runs from 0 (very acid) to 14 (very alkaline). A pH of 7 is neutral. Scotland, for the most part, has soil and water on the acidic side, from 4.5–6.5. There are some naturally alkaline spots such as the limestone seam, which starts on the west-coast island of Lismore and works its way north across the Great Glen towards Orkney. Most fruit and vegetables prefer a near-neutral pH of around 6.5, though author and recognised vegetable expert Joy Larkcom reckons that pH 5.5–6 will do for most of them. The exceptions are blueberries and their heath family relatives, which prefer a very acid soil (pH4.5–5.5). For the most part, assume that your soil acidity is OK unless you garden on peat. If you want to test your soil, basic soil testing kits (available in most garden centres and DIY stores) should give a pH reading and an indicator of key nutrient levels, but they are not always very accurate. The James Hutton Institute (formerly the Macaulay Institute) in Aberdeen can conduct soil tests and analyses. If rhododendrons and other acid lovers grow well in your garden, then liming the vegetable patch is probably worthwhile to raise the pH a little. You can buy lime at most garden centres either in powdery form (hydrated) or granular form. The powdery form is cheaper and more concentrated. Wear thick gloves when putting lime on, as it can burn or irritate skin. For those with an organic bent, using dolomitic lime

Raised beds in wet, heavy soil at the Walled Garden in Applecross, Wester Ross.

or calcified seaweed is the thing. These are slower acting but longer lasting than the hydrated version. It is advisable to apply lime in small doses and over several seasons to change the soil pH gradually. Too much lime can be as damaging to plants as too little. As a guideline, it is best not to apply more than 500g per square metre per dose. And be warned that lime dissolves in water in the soil, so a rhododendron bed downhill from a limed vegetable patch is not a good idea. Liming is best done when the bed is empty, during the winter and before digging it over and preparing for the season but, if you forget, just do it four weeks before sowing or planting. If you manure your beds, then wait at least four weeks before applying the lime and vice versa. Lime washes out gradually over three to five years, depending on drainage and rainfall. Botanist and author of the 'Expert' series of gardening books Dr Hessayon recommends that, as part of crop rotation, you only lime the brassica plot so that each plot is limed every three to four years. And he recommends 250g per square metre for this rotation. For a new garden, you can use double this. For a very peaty soil, you can add up to 2kg per square metre in several smaller doses over a year or more.

Drainage and Raised Beds

Most fruit and vegetable crops like a well-drained soil. Only a few, such as blueberries and cranberries, like it to be really moist. To test the drainage of different parts of a garden, dig down a spade's depth, fill the hole with water and watch how long it takes to drain away. If the water drains very slowly, then you have a problem which needs to be resolved before you plant fruit and vegetables. Deep digging can break up any pan (solid compacted layer) that has formed, but often there is an underlying problem with the soil structure. Many new-build properties have gardens with poor drainage because the topsoil has been removed or compacted and the structure ruined through the traffic of heavy construction machinery.

Drainage is, of course, mainly a question of gravity – there is no point in installing drainage pipes if there is nowhere for the water to go. You may be able to link drains to the ones which take your roof water away or to dig a soakaway, filling it with coarse gravel. Heavy clay soil is the greatest challenge and it is often a more realistic alternative to raise the planting area instead of fighting the drainage. Vegetables do particularly well in raised beds and many great vegetable gardens use them. Beds around 1.2m wide are sensible so that all parts can be reached without the need to stand on them. Bed edges can be constructed using wood, log-roll, stone, concrete, metal lawn-edge, mature (but not freshly treated) railway sleepers, strong wire netting or anything else that comes to mind. Garden centres stock easily assembled kits. Fill beds with topsoil and/or a mix of garden centre composts. If you can, add a significant percentage of home-made compost and/or well-rotted manure.

Less work than raised beds is the practice of planting rows of fruit or vegetables on raised ridges. The ridges or individual mounds can be as little as 15cm higher than the surrounding soil to make the difference between success and failure. Plums, pears, cooking apples, blackcurrants and brambles are more forgiving of poor drainage than most fruit, while raspberries, strawberries and cherries usually cannot tolerate it.

Feeding Your Crops

The soil is the engine room of the garden and, if you don't feed it, then it will gradually grow nutrient poor and less able to support a wide range of plants. Fertilisers can be organic – animal manure, green manure or animal by-products such as bone meal and dried blood – or inorganic – manufactured from rock or chemicals. There is no real difference in the nutrients supplied, but organic fertilisers are claimed by some to work more in harmony with the soil's micro-organisms and some high-nitrogen inorganic fertilisers are inclined to leach away in heavy rain and may contaminate watercourses.

Most fruit and vegetable crops benefit from fertiliser. Garden centres contain a bewildering range of feeding options, but all fertilisers contain one or more of the three key nutrient elements – nitrogen (N) for plant growth, phosphorus (P) for root growth and potash/potassium (K) for flowers and fruit. Some fertilisers, known as straights, contain only one of these – ammonium sulphate (nitrogen), superphosphate (phosphorus) and sulphate of potash (potassium). Most general fertilisers such as Miracle-Gro and Growmore contain some of each of the three key ingredients, differing only in the ratio of one to the other. The relative quantities are given in the NPK ratio, which is clearly noted on the fertiliser packs. So, for example, 8:4:4 contains a higher ratio of nitrogen, while in a ratio of 4:4:4 the amounts are even. Most fruit and vegetables enjoy a fairly high ratio of nitrogen. In addition to the three key elements, many fertilisers also contain trace elements, such as iron, zinc, copper, manganese and molybdenum, which plants require in tiny quantities. They are essential for different aspects of plant health. Despite the array on offer in garden centres, you don't need to

Fertilisers mostly contain the same key ingredients – nitrogen, phosphates and potash.

buy lots of different feeds for different plants – indeed, if you are gardening organically, you may choose to rely on manure and your own compost for nutrients. Most fertilisers can be used for a wide range of subjects. It is more important to feed at the correct time of year, and don't be tempted to over-dose as it can make plants weak and floppy, burn foliage and even kill. Inorganic fertilisers such as Growmore are useful because they are formulated to supply a good general nutrient mixture that will benefit a broad range of plants. Slow-release fertilisers, which release feed gradually throughout the growing season, are particularly useful for containers, where there is a high demand for nutrients. Liquid feeds are useful for containers, whilst granular ones are easier to apply in the garden. Many fruit and vegetables benefit from high potash feeds, often sold as tomato food, but equally good for strawberries, rhubarb, potatoes and salad crops. Some growers recommend Perlka, particularly for brassicas, which is high in nitrogen, dicyandiamide, which holds the nitrogen in the soil, lime and magnesium, which help raise the pH. You'll probably need to buy this online.

Rockdust, first promoted by Cameron and Moira Thomson from the Seer Centre in the Perthshire hills between Pitlochry and Blairgowrie, is ground rock from the Collace Quarry near Perth. The claims made for this substance 'remineralising

the earth' are dismissed by many scientists. Rockdust is not a fertiliser but instead contains most of the minerals and trace elements required for growing plants. It probably has a useful role, particularly in improving marginal land such as machair or moorland, which contain few nutrients. It may have limited value on well-established and productive fruit or vegetable plots, which probably contain most of the elements already. Many Scottish fruit and vegetable growers swear by Rockdust's results, and it is sold by a limited number of garden centres. The *Beechgrove Garden* trialled it in 2009–10 and found no significant benefits. John Ferguson, part of the new marketing team for Rockdust at Binn Soil Nutrients, explained that the benefits are not always apparent in the first season and he is working on long-term trials to demonstrate what it can do over time.

Many organic gardeners recommend home-made comfrey 'tea' – as long as you can stand the awful smell. Comfrey is a good source of potassium, as well as calcium, iron and manganese. Simply fill a lidded bucket with comfrey leaves, weigh them down with a stone, add a little water and leave for three to four weeks out of direct sun. Once you have a rich brown liquid, strain the bucket contents through muslin or, as Jekka McVicar (2002) suggests, a pair of old tights. Keep the 'tea' in a screw-top bottle, clearly labelled, out of the sunlight. Dilute 12ml per litre of water as a foliar feed or 25ml for a root feed. Either grow your own little comfrey patch (don't let it get out of control) or pick comfrey in the wild but away from busy roadsides. Nettles can be used in a similar way.

ORGANIC MATTER, COMPOST AND MANURE

Well-rotted organic matter made from composted green and household waste is a 'magic' ingredient which acts as a soil conditioner and a feed, both improving the structure and helping to maintain

A display of compost bins by Borders Organic Gardeners (BOG) at Woodside Walled Garden, Monteviot.

Composting bays using recycled pallets, Caroline and Peter's garden.

healthy nutrient levels. Worms and soil micro-organisms will break down these materials, converting them into a form that plant roots can use known as humus. If you can, add organic matter to the soil whenever you plant. It is important that this material is well-rotted rather than fresh because micro-organisms require a huge amount of energy to break down raw matter. If substances such as fresh sawdust or bark are added directly to the soil, the composting process will rob the soil of the nitrogen your fruit and vegetables need, so they tend to turn yellow and grow stunted, with poor yields. The solution is to leave fresh matter to compost for six months to a year before using it – farmyard manures, leaf mould, kitchen waste, bark and grass cuttings all provide invaluable organic matter once they have been composted. Some councils offer compost free if you go and pick it up.

Leaf mould from well-rotted leaves is a wonderful soil improver. You can make your own by raking up autumn leaves, putting them in net-sided bins or black bin bags with holes pierced in them and letting them compost for a year or more. If you have any space at all in your garden, a compost heap for garden and kitchen vegetable waste (but not meat or cooked food) is really worth having. Some

wire netting or four old pallets for the walls are all you need to get started, or you can buy all sorts of composters from your local garden centre. The Internet and local councils can be good sources of guidance on composting. The secret of good compost is a decent container, a good mix of non-woody ingredients and moisture. If your mix is good enough and you have some grass cuttings to provide plenty of heat as they break down, you may not need to turn it. You can also purchase enclosed hot composting systems which can compost all food waste, including cooked food and meat. Those in search of composting perfection may wish to try managing their own wormery. Ronald Gilchrist of Greenway Consulting is a key vermiculture advocate in Scotland. His book, *Grow Food Nature's Way*, details the best way to make a wormery, as does the website www.vermico.com.

If you live near the coast, you may wish, like many of our forebears, to feed or mulch with seaweed, which rots down into good compost quite quickly and is rich in potassium (potash). Try to take the stuff the sea has thrown to the shore, give it a rinse when you get it home, then heave it onto your empty vegetable beds in winter or mulch with it in summer. Do not layer it too thickly, as it may end up going slimy, smelling badly and breeding vile clouds of flies. You can add it to your compost heap instead, if you like. Les Bates, gardener at the Torridon Hotel, Wester Ross, gardens on a raised beach. He makes his special compost using seaweed along with cattle manure, shredded paper, annual weeds and autumn leaves. He turns/mixes it at least once. He also uses 'neat' seaweed to mulch his fruit bushes. Laura Donkers of North Uist pointed out how the gelatinous seaweed helps to bind the sandy soils of the machair, preventing it from blowing away. Almost everyone we visited in Orkney, Shetland and the Western Isles used seaweed to grow fruit and vegetables, and swore by its good qualities. Their forefathers will have used it in the lazy bed system (*see* p. 9). If you are not yet sold on the idea of using seaweed then consider this – its saltiness makes it a natural slug repellent.

If you need to fill containers or raised beds and head off to the garden centre in search of bags of growing media, what should you buy? A mixture of several things is probably the best advice. Manure, topsoil, fine composted bark and peat-based or peat-free multipurpose compost will all do. You may have access to spent mushroom compost, sometimes offered in bulk from farms. This is a mixture of well-rotted straw or horse manure, peat and chalk and is a good soil conditioner mixed with garden soil, usually with a good pH balance for vegetables.

Well-rotted horse and cow manure is a great material for most fruit and vegetables as it contains feeding for plants and roughage to improve soil

Lazy beds, a form of raised bed used on the west coast, piled with seaweed in winter for nutrition.

Constructing raised beds in Cris Stubbington's garden, Carloway, Lewis (photo Cris Stubbington).

Good in a compost heap	Bad in a compost heap
Raw fruit and vegetable scraps	Anything treated with weed killer
Non-woody plant material	Raw or cooked meat or fish scraps
Crumpled newsprint	Diseased plants
Comfrey and nettle leaves	Woody plant trimmings unless shredded
Seaweed	Perennial weeds
Annual weeds that have not gone to seed	Cat and dog manure
Brassica stems, but chop them first	

structure. It usually comes mixed with straw bedding material. Don't use it fresh, as it is too strong and can burn young growth; rather let it sit for a year. There have been incidents with cattle and horses eating grass which has been sprayed with weed killer, producing manure that still contains enough chemical to damage plants. It can't do any good to the livestock either. Pelleted chicken manure is concentrated nitrogen, so use with care; it is best used well mixed into the soil rather than scattered on top and I would not put it on young seedlings. Conventional wisdom was that you should not manure root crops such as carrots and parsnips, as it encourages bifurcation (split roots in funny shapes). Joy Larkcom says that research now suggests that this common advice may be erroneous. Brassicas won't take kindly to too much manure, as it tends to lead to soil acidification which can, in turn, lead to club root disease.

Another form of soil food you might consider is a green manure, many of which are legumes with nitrogen-fixing properties (but only in summer when in active growth). They are usually sown and allowed to grow for two to three months and then cut down and dug in. They can be used to keep weeds down in an empty plot as well as preventing nutrient leach during winter. A good source of information on green manures can be found in Joy Larkcom's book, *Grow Your Own Vegetables*. Not all are hardy enough for Scotland. For autumn sowing, try field beans (*Vicia faba*), winter tares (*Vicia sativa*) or grazing rye grass (*Secale cereale*). All should be cut down before they flower and dug in or left as a mulch to rot down. Mild coastal gardens may be able to grow other green manures over winter but, for most of Scotland, the more tender green manures are best sown in spring and cut down in summer.

PEAT AND PEAT ALTERNATIVES

It probably won't have escaped your notice that peat is getting a bad rap these days. You don't need peat in the fruit and vegetable garden – it is mainly used in container growing and propagation. Peat-based composts have long been the standard for germinating and potting on young seedlings. UK environmentalists have been trying to convince us to stop all horticultural peat use. The campaign, begun by David Bellamy to preserve lowland peat bogs in England, has been largely successful and these rare habitats have now mostly been protected. I interviewed David Bellamy recently and he was at pains to point out that his campaign was never intended to lead to a ban on peat use. Indeed, he positively encourages peat use, as long as it is extracted from

Green manures, *Phacelia*, rye and clover, planted in empty sections of the garden and then dug in for nutrition.

suitable sites. The reality is that there is no shortage of peat at all. Worldwide, it grows faster than it is currently extracted. Scotland has a layer of peat on around 50 per cent of its landmass so there is no good reason we should not be able to exploit it in a sustainable manner and place a carbon tax on it as we do with fuels to offset carbon released. As long as there is a layer of live sphagnum, peat continues to grow and, in Scandinavia, it is produced as a commercial crop on a 100-year cycle. The UK is out of step with the rest of the world on this issue. For example, the UN has recently reclassified peat as a 'renewable biomass resource' and is actively encouraging its use, provided it is harvested in a sustainable way. Environmentalists try to blame horticulture for the loss of peat bogs but, in fact, more than 90 per cent of English peat bogs have been lost to farming and forestry. The dilemma for the gardener is that most of the trials we looked at suggested that peat-based composts are significantly better than most peat-free composts for sowing seeds and potting on young fruit and vegetable seedlings. *Gardening Which?* 2009 trials found that some peat-free composts had improved in the last 10 years, with New Horizons and Vital Earth coming top. Many of the rest performed poorly. RHS trials published in January 2011 showed poor results for germinating seedlings and potting on young plants in most peat alternatives, including loam, wood fibre and coir, particularly for plants with very small seeds. *Beech-grove Garden* trials in 2010, growing potatoes in containers, reported poor results with peat-free composts compared with composts containing at least 50 per cent peat.

I'm sure that, with more research and better formulae, peat-free composts can be improved but, at the moment, they tend to be inconsistent, harder to water correctly and often require the addition of extra food and trace elements. You might be advised to continue using composts containing at least 50 per cent peat for germinating seedlings and rooting cuttings and using peat alternatives in larger containers, raised beds and for soil amelioration. At

Glendoick, we grew good garlic, radishes, carrots, rocket and reasonable lettuce in our peat-free compost trials in a raised bed but extra nutrients were required. So, if you combine peat-free media with plenty of good home-made compost, you will probably get excellent results. My advice is to reduce peat use to a minimum but not to be put off using it in propagation.

Organic Gardening

Most fruit and vegetable gardeners make a conscious decision as to whether to garden 'organically' or not. The word 'organic' is rather a curious choice to describe a way of agriculture or gardening as, previously, the word was mainly used to describe a type of chemistry which is concerned with compounds containing carbon. Surprising as it might seem, the organic movement grew out of a collection of quasi-fascist organisations such as Kibbo Kift shortly before the Second World War. The Soil Association was founded in 1946 by Oswald Mosley's former farming advisor Rolf Gardiner and Scot Eve Balfour, author of *The Living Soil* (1943). Post-Second World War, a gradual increase in environmental awareness was prompted by the publication of Sir Albert

The organically run vegetable garden at Harmony, Melrose.

Well-rotted manure – invaluable for fruit and vegetable growing

farms/producers the length and breadth of Scotland, many of which sell at farmers' markets and run vegetable box schemes.

Organic growing has several key principals or beliefs centred on sustainable environmental practice:

1. As crop production takes nutrition out of the soil, so this needs to be carefully replenished and managed to maintain soil fertility. Composts and manures are advocated as well as crop rotation using nitrogen-fixing plants, such as legumes.
2. Synthetic fertilisers should be avoided. 'Natural' fertilisers such as seaweed, bone meal and manures are claimed to be better for the soil than artificial and synthetic ones based on ammonia.
3. Non-organic weed killers and pesticides are considered dangerous to humans and other creatures in the food chain. Ideally, techniques such as mulching, intercropping, netting and encouraging natural predators should reduce or eliminate the need for artificial herbicides and pesticides. Organic pesticides are promoted as a safer and more natural way to treat pests.
4. Organic food is claimed to be better for you and to taste better too.

The first of these is widely accepted but the evidence for the other three is less straightforward. One difficulty is that organics is part science and part faith in the way it is practised and it polarises opinion, leaving few agnostics. Writers and broadcasters tend to give only one side of the argument – either for or against, depending on their point of view – and there appears to be pressure on television gardeners to sing from an organic hymn sheet, even if, as I suspect, they are not quite so purist in private!

One of the few sources of balanced information is the book *The Truth about Organic Gardening* (2008) by American horticultural lecturer Jeff Gillman, and we follow much of his logic here in assessing the issue. Like him, we conclude that supporting a broadly organic approach is mostly

Howard's wartime studies of soil fertility, J. I. Rodale's 1948 book, *The Organic Front*, which considered the use of artificial fertilisers and Rachel Carson's bestseller, *Silent Spring* (1962), which warned of the dire consequences of the use of DDT and other pesticides. The 'organic movement' really really took off in the 1960s and has gained ground ever since. While many are devoted to the organic cause, the majority of the scientists and papers we consulted were sceptical of the role of organics in feeding the current world population, let alone in the face of a predicted increase in food demand of 30 per cent by 2050. Our conclusion is that there is room for both organic and non-organic methods of production.

Scotland's Findhorn Community near Elgin was one of Britain's organic pioneers, while John Butterworth in Ayrshire, now retired, ran the first certified organic tree fruit production in Scotland. John has been one of the gurus of fruit tree grafting and orchard restoration throughout the country, generously sharing his practical knowledge, including invaluable advice for this book. There are now dozens of impressive organic vegetable and fruit

A series of raised vegetable beds on a slope at Craigievar, Aberdeenshire.

common sense when we grow things for ourselves to eat, but that not all the claims and assumptions made for organic foods and practice stand up to scrutiny.

While many organic gardeners may shun pesticides, you may be surprised that organic farmers are allowed limited use of quite a number of them – not all of which are particularly safe to use and with some just as toxic as the non-organic ones. The Environmental Impact Quotient (EIQ) is a useful rating of chemical danger and toxicity. We give the ratings on pages 71–76 so you can assess the relative impact of common garden chemicals, including the organic ones. Research findings on this subject may surprise you too. 'Some evidence suggests that when toxicity and volume are considered in an overall pest management strategy, organic practices may have greater environmental hazard than conventional ones' (Kovach et al., 1992). This is often due to the large number of applications that may be required to control something organically when a single non-organic chemical application might take care of it.

In theory, organic farming ought to be better for the environment because of improved mainte-nance of soil conditions, less use of dangerous chemicals, little or no pesticide residues and so on. And, in the garden, organic approaches do make environmental sense. But organic gardening and organic farming are very different practices. The recent evolution of industrial-scale organic produc-tion in North America to supply the supermarket appetite for organic food is often far from sustain-able or good for the environment. The trend is for the establishment of giant monoculture 'organic' farms, in California and elsewhere, growing thou-sands of hectares of lettuce and tomatoes and most other fruit and vegetables, often under polythene, irrigated from aquifers or from water diverted from rivers, which no longer reach the sea. The produce is packed in plastic bags and trucked and flown thousands of miles in refrigerated lorries and planes. The environmental impact of all these food miles is, of course, unsustainable. The old locally based, seasonal organic model is falling by the wayside while Walmart and other giant conglomerates flaunt their new-found environmental credentials. In the USA, Wall Street now controls much of US organics, as they do most other forms of US food production.

A similar consolidation is starting to happen in the UK. Your local supermarket will source organic vegetables from wherever in the world they are cheapest and without considering sustainability or food miles. For example, southern Spain is vastly overusing its limited water supplies to produce fruit and vegetables for the UK market, both organic and conventional.

Consider which is better for the environment – organic sweetcorn flown thousands of miles or a local non-organic sweetcorn which has travelled a few miles from the grower to your plate. We certainly encourage you to garden organically but don't assume that your organic supermarket supplies are always an ethical or sustainable buy and, if they are flown in, it may be better to leave them on the shelf. Buy local produce when it is in season, and not from supermarkets, if you want to make a difference.

Though organic campaigners will claim otherwise, we have struggled to find much hard evidence that the source of nutrients (organic or not) makes much long-term difference to the quality of plants or the soil. They all contain the same basic elements of nitrogen, phosphates and potash. Organic feeds do often release their nutrients more slowly than synthetic feeds, which may protect water courses. A more persuasive argument in favour of organic feeds is that most inorganic fertilisers are based on ammonia extracted from urine or made from combining nitrogen and hydrogen in an energy-intensive, hot, high-pressure Haber-Bosch process, while phosphates are mined. However, many 'organic' fertilisers such as blood, fish and bone and bone meal are made from the ground up remains of animals reared for meat, seldom on organic farms. Organic growers can use 'vegetarian' fertiliser options, with feeds based on seaweed, alfalfa, etc.

Are organic vegetables more nutritious and do they taste better? Most of us might assume that the answer is 'yes' to both questions. The UK Food Standards Agency conducted a survey of 162 studies on nutrition and concluded that 'consumers may choose to buy organic fruit, vegetables and meat because they believe them to be more nutritious than other food. However, the balance of current scientific evidence does not support this view.' *Gardening Which?*'s taste trials in 2009–10 revealed the surprising conclusion that non-organic vegetables (calabrese, tomatoes, potatoes) tasted better than organically grown ones and they had higher levels of antioxidants and vitamins. In double blind tests, there is very little evidence that anyone can taste the difference between organic and non-organic food. This may well be beside the point for many people who garden organically as a matter of principle and belief. It can probably be explained as a 'placebo' effect – it tastes better because you want it to. The produce from my garden probably tastes better because it is fresh and picked ripe rather than because it is organically grown.

Biodynamics

For gardening 'in tune with nature', you may be interested in looking into the growing practice of biodynamics, as promoted by its inventor Rudolf Steiner. Biodynamics shares many of the principles of organic gardening but is more prescriptive as to how soil fertility should be maintained. Various herbal and mineral treatments, including the unlikely cowhorn preparation, are added to garden soil and composts. Planting times are chosen with reference to the astronomical calendar, paying strict attention to the cycle of the moon. You'll either buy into this or think it sounds daft, and we don't have space in this book to cover this subject in any depth. If you wish to investigate further, there is an extensive literature, both in books and on the web. Scotland has several farms and nurseries run on biodynamic principals. At Drimlabarra Herb Farm on Arran you can volunteer or attend courses. The Aberdeen Biodynamic Land Trust aims to purchase land to be biodynamically farmed.

CHAPTER 5

Getting Started: What Do I Need?

As a first-time grower, you'll be faced with endless choices – from selecting what to grow from garden centre seed racks, to the bewildering number of varieties of fruit trees and bushes, not to mention the plethora of 'grow-your-own' accessories. Fruit needs a bit more planning but, to grow vegetables all you need is a container and some seeds. How much to grow depends on how much space you have and how ambitious you want to be. If you have never grown anything before, then start with the simple and quick crops – salads, carrots, radishes, potatoes and the easier fruits such as rhubarb, strawberries and gooseberries. Most of these crops can be grown in a modest space and are suitable for containers and raised beds. Garden centres now have a baffling range of equipment for grow-your-own enthusiasts. Much of it is very useful but some is largely gimmickry. You don't need wicker-edged raised beds or strawberry towers but, by all means, buy them if that's what you want. If your budget is tight, a lot of what you need may be available for nothing – ask fellow gardeners for their spare old pots, canes for making bean and pea wigwams, etc. Gardeners often pride themselves in ingenious ways to grow vegetables without spending money. Shetland allotment holders, for example, found that used tyres were being given away, so they snapped them up for perfect raised beds and containers. Buy seed of the things you'll want lots of and want to sow several times – carrots and salads, for example. Vegetable seeds can remain viable for a year or two as long as they are stored in a cool, dry, dark place. If you freeze seed, it will keep for several years. With the exception of F1 hybrids, you can collect seed from many vegetables and sow them the following year. For vegetables that you only want a few of and if you don't have a greenhouse, tunnel, cold frame or

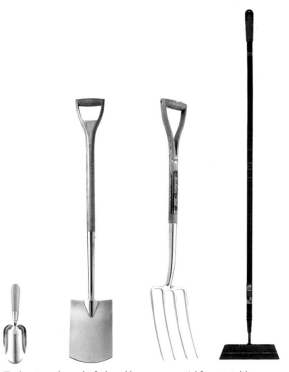

Tools – trowel, spade, fork and hoe are essential for vegetable and fruit growing.

Mesh and fleece tunnels protect from weather and insect pests and are all but essential for many vegetables.

windowsill to raise tender plants in early spring, it is often cheaper to wait until May, when garden centres sell trays of small seedlings – tomatoes, courgettes, beans, Brussels sprouts, cabbage, etc – ready for transplanting. Above all, you should invest in compost and soil preparation. Best results come with well-drained fertile soil enriched with lots of organic matter, manure, household compost, etc. And you must start with a clean, weed-free patch or bed. If you are gardening in containers, the best medium to fill them with is a combination of different things – John Innes compost, topsoil, farmyard manure and composted bark can be combined to make an ideal fruit and vegetable cocktail. Beware of using peat-free compost alone as many brands are not ideal for all crops (*see* p.38).

Some crops – salads and radishes, for example – go from seed sowing to harvesting in a matter of weeks, while most vegetables take less than six months. It takes at least a year to get a decent crop on currants, raspberries, brambles and other soft fruit, two to five years for tree fruit such as apples and pears and, with them, you'll need to do some pruning and training.

You will need some basic tools for any serious vegetable growing. A spade and a fork, a rake and a hoe, some secateurs and a hand trowel are probably the most useful. Don't go for the cheapest option if you can afford to spend a little more – the really cheap tools tend to be heavy, fragile, bend or rust easily and are harder work to use, whereas a good stainless steel spade with a 10-year guarantee may cost four times as much but it will last longer and be easier to use. The cheapest form of frost protection is a roll of frost-grade fleece, which can double up to keep off pests, but it does sag after rain and it can blow around. Also offering some shade and a little frost and wind protection, but better for pests, are rolls or sheets of fine mesh sold as Wondermesh (from a fine Scottish company) or Enviromesh and other cheaper but often less robust brands. With so many uses, protective mesh is probably the most worthwhile investment you can make. Laid over and around crops, this acts as a barrier to many of the worst pests – snails, larger slugs, rabbits and household pets. Although it is relatively expensive, it lasts for several years and will save many crops – brassicas from birds and cabbage whites, carrots from carrot fly and fruit from birds. Don't wait until you see the problem, as you'll risk keeping it in rather than out. Get the mesh on as soon as you have planted/sown.

Whatever you do in the garden, the key is to enjoy it. Don't try to do too much so you resent the time spent. Make your gardening activity fit your lifestyle, your world view, your pocket and, of course, your site and prevailing weather conditions, and then give it a go. Early success is likely to encourage you to greater gardening feats. Early failure hopefully won't stop you. Start with what you have, get to know your piece of land – however tiny – and then grow what you would like to eat.

Your vegetable plot or planting space should, ideally, be south-facing, not shaded and have a very slight slope from north to south. This allows for the maximum sunlight to reach your fruit and vegetables and ensures frost rolls away without damaging them. Although not always possible, certainly go for the best position within your garden. If you are starting from scratch, you will need to prepare your patch, border, beds or vegetable space. This will involve assessing the kind of soil you have (*see* p. 32) and understanding what is most likely to be happy in it. Don't despair if you have very soggy ground, what looks like a pebbly beach or even a brownfield site, or if you live in a perpetual wind-tunnel. There are ways of eventually making all of these produce-friendly. For example, soggy ground can be turned into something productive by building raised beds, and brownfield sites might lend themselves to 'pop-up' style gardens, where builders' yard one-ton bags are used as giant planters, safely keeping the roots of the plants away from the contaminated ground.

For a new or overgrown site, you need to get rid of the weeds. Perennial weeds and grass need to be killed before you start, as you can't do it once the vegetables are in. Glyphosate in the growing season is the best weed killer but, if you shun chemicals, then you may have to cover the whole area with cardboard, plastic or similar for a year to suffocate the weeds (*see* p. 76). Almost every gardener in Scotland needs to contend with strong winds and most

fruit and vegetable gardens require some moderation to provide shelter. You can plant windbreaks or hedges, attach a wind-absorbing material to an existing fence, build a new fence or grow under protection, in a polytunnel, although this needs wind shelter too (*see* p. 57). We observed great ingenuity in wind barriers on our vegetable tour of the Northern and Western Isles and the west coast. In Wester Ross, Barra, the Uists, Benbecula, Lewis, Orkney and Unst in Shetland, tyres, pallets, scrap metal, woven materials and lots more were used as protection.

Planning Your Fruit and Vegetables

Whether you are growing your fruit and vegetables in containers on a patio, in a small town garden or in a giant Scottish walled garden, there is a certain amount of planning required. You can garden formally (in rows) or informally (all mixed up or in irregular patterns). The traditional kitchen garden is an ordered affair, with crops in rows and vegetable types rotated from plot to plot each year to reduce soil pests and diseases. Even in a traditional garden, there are other options – at Castle Fraser in Aberdeenshire, Damon Powell has used a centrepiece of a bean wigwam with circular patterns of marigolds and leeks and other crops to produce edible pattern bedding to great effect. Gardeners who don't have space for a dedicated vegetable plot can grow edibles and ornamentals in a series of raised beds, and why not grow attractive combinations together in the style of the potager (*see* p. 54). Marigolds, nasturtiums and other annuals are useful for distracting and confusing pests as well as providing an attractive contrast to the foliage of the potager produce. What's more, many annuals have edible flowers (*see* p. 284). At some gardens – such as Cambo, in Fife, and Johnstounburn House, south of Edinburgh – large-scale potagers have been created and in many other gardens – such as Malleny, near Edinburgh, Culross Palace and Kellie Castle, both in

Fife, Fyvie, in Aberdeenshire, and Inverewe, in Wester Ross – flower-food combinations are practised each year. Some gardeners don't have access to soil at all and so are forced to garden in raised beds and containers. This too can produce excellent crops of fruit and vegetables (*see* p. 55).

Seeds

Most fruit varieties don't come true from seed so other propagation methods are used, but seeds are the way to propagate most vegetables. Seeds need four things to germinate and grow successfully – moisture, air, appropriate temperature and light. Sowing them too early, when the earth is still cold, or too deeply will not lead to a successful outcome. For a first-time vegetable grower, the range of seeds available at most garden centres may be daunting – 30 different tomatoes and 25 beans is not exceptional. You'll find recommended varieties listed under each fruit and vegetable entry in this book, so that's a good place to start, but you'll find many varieties which we have not listed and which might be perfectly suitable. Seeds vary significantly in price, with new varieties and F1 hybrids (it will say so on the packet) tending to be the most expensive and with the fewest seeds. F1 hybrids are produced by controlled pollinations, which is time-consuming and expensive – hence the higher price. Many of the most vigorous, high-yielding and disease-resistant vegetables are F1 hybrids and we recommend many of them in this book. Practitioners of biodynamic growing (*see* p. 42), and some organic growers, object to F1 hybrids, as seed collected from them doesn't come true so that, in this case, saving your own seed is not worthwhile. In contrast to F1s, many older vegetables are strains, meaning that they do come true from seed as long as they don't cross with other varieties nearby. Sweetcorn, for example, cross readily so you should only grow a single variety if you want to save seeds. Most seed can be stored for a year or two in a dry, cool place or frozen to keep

Caroline sowing seeds in various modules and trays.

for longer. Many allotment groups share seed as packets frequently contain more than you need. Gardeners hate to throw away unwanted seed or seedlings we don't have space for and it is so satisfying to share with others.

You may find tiny seeds easier to sow if you mix them with a little dry sand. You'll find seed tapes and seed pads available too. These are biodegradable paper with seeds set into them at the correct spacing. They are great for salad crops you want to sow every few weeks. You don't have to thin them and they are also useful for children and anyone who finds it difficult or time-consuming to sow seeds thinly and evenly. Seeds, whether sown in long rows or in blocks of shorter rows, are generally sown in drills which can be made with a cane, the corner of a rake or hoe or, in the case of a broad drill for peas, with the flat edge of a draw hoe. The soil should be moist when seeds are sown. If it is not, water the drill before you sow rather than once the seed is sown and covered. Once sown, pull the soil very gently over the drill with the back of your rake. For the tiniest of seeds, you can pinch the drill closed with your fingers then pat it flat. When sowing seeds in trays or modules, water the compost before sowing.

Remember the benefits of succession production of many vegetables – a sowing of small amounts every few weeks rather than a single larger amount in one go. This avoids a short-term glut and extends availability across the longest possible season. Sprouting seeds, rocket, radish, carrots, peas and lettuce are good subjects for repeat sowings. The freezer is the vegetable grower's friend and Caroline gives advice for freezing vegetables throughout the text.

You'll find seed racks from companies such as Suttons, Thompson and Morgan, and Unwins in almost every garden centre. For vegetables, Suttons are perhaps the most innovative, with new developments such as club-resistant brassicas and grafted tomatoes. They were also the most helpful of the bigger seed companies when researching this book. Most of the others were frankly hopeless, with no knowledge of Scottish conditions, no trialling done in Scotland and no appreciation of the different conditions we garden under. Their replies and submissions were laughably ignorant. As far as we can ascertain, only the *Beechgrove Garden* and *Gardening Which?* run vegetable trials in Scotland. The lack of information of this kind is one of the reasons we decided to write this book in the first place. In short, take what you read on a seed packet with a pinch of salt, as whoever wrote it won't be referring to Scotland. If you can't find seeds of what you want locally, there are lots of great mail order specialist seed companies, some of whom sell unusual new or heritage varieties (*see* p. 286 for contact details). Two of the cheapest are Dobies of Devon (not to be confused with Dobbies) and Rebekah's Veg. You'll enjoy the wonderfully written catalogue of Thomas Etty and sound advice from Medwyn Williams, of Chelsea fame, who runs his vegetable seed business from Anglesey, Wales. Closer to home, Alan Romans sells seeds and potatoes from Fife. For organic seeds, try Garden Organic and The Real Seed Catalogue, who have good advice on seed saving on their website. Another amazing resource is the French Association Kokopelli which, in a previous incarnation, was sued and bankrupted by the EU for distributing heritage fruit and vegetable seeds not on some bureaucrat's list. Their catalogue/book of over 2,000 varieties is now available in English and is a work of art. You join for a fee and they give you the seed, to circumvent the idiotic legislation.

The Scottish Seed Savers Exchange Network project aims to develop and select hardy cultivars of vegetables suited to Scottish conditions and to re-establish Scottish landraces of the best vegetable strains for Scotland which come true from seed. Matthew Love told me that 'we even have bush tomatoes that grow well outdoors, even here in East Kilbride at 600ft'. I have not managed to test this unlikely claim but, if it is true, then we should all be growing them. The Network distributed over 14,000 free packets of vegetable seeds in 2010 running Scotland's biggest annual seed-sharing event in East Kilbride. Chris Scatchard is running a similar scheme, Highland People's Food Seedbank Project, in northern Scotland.

Hardening Off

You'll find many a mention of 'hardening off' throughout the text. Plants which are started off indoors and/or with artificial heat are not able to withstand the sudden drop in temperature if they are planted straight outside. The cells of the plant need to build up a resistance to cold so that the plant's growth is not stunted and, in addition, many

Hardening off in spring using home-made cloches and plastic bottles.

Strawberries with spun polypropylene mulch.

vegetables are tender and certainly not frost resistant. Scotland's spring weather is fickle, with cold and freezing nights as well as biting east winds possible in late May and into June in the coldest gardens. It is therefore advisable to gradually harden off tender and soft crops by moving them from a heated to a cold greenhouse or frame before moving them outdoors or, if started indoors, by putting them outside during the day and bringing them back in at night. Using cloches or fleece will give a little night-time and wind protection once they are finally transplanted.

Mulching

'Mulching' means adding a layer of organic matter such as compost, dung, green manure, seaweed, straw, composted bracken (watch out for ticks when cutting it) or gravel on top of the soil. This brings a number of benefits – reducing the need to weed, helping to retain moisture and moderating soil temperature, keeping it warmer in winter and cooler in hot summers. Mulching also encourages worm and micro-organism activity. A straw mulch can protect courgettes and strawberries from rotting due to contact with the soil. It also prevents mud splashing on foliage and soil capping after heavy rains, where an impervious layer is created which stops moisture getting down to the roots. You can use thin layers of grass cuttings to mulch some vegetables such as peas and beans, but only if the grass has not been treated with weed killer. Mulches can have drawbacks, as they may harbour insect eggs, slugs and the spores of rusts and other fungal plant diseases. Dave Allan at ASK Organic suggests removing or digging in mulches on perennial vegetables and soft fruit in winter. Any old mulch can be dug into the vegetable patch or added to the compost heap. Strawberries and other fruit are often planted through black polythene or a permeable membrane which acts as a mulch, keeping weeds down and moisture in. In the Western Isles, we saw onion sets planted in this way.

Crop Rotation

Farmers and vegetable growers practise crop rotation of annual and short-term crops, both to avoid the build-up of pests and also to replenish nitrogen and other essential elements. Long-term crops, such as asparagus, raspberries and rhubarb, can be left to grow for many years but, once replaced, are best replanted in another area of the garden.

You can practise crop rotation with three to five crop categories. The most common is a four-group crop rotation. If you are short of space, you can combine groups one and three. It is recommended to follow the succession given in the table below, with brassicas following legumes and root vegetables following onions or brassicas.

Crop rotation is not always easy to manage, and the desired results are not perfect – some pests and diseases remain in the soil for ten years or more so crop rotation is not going to prevent club root or onion rot, for example, but it should reduce them. If you have enough space to rotate your vegetable plot into an entirely new area of the garden after eight to ten years, this is a good idea. In a small garden, the lack of available space means that, even with strict rotation, soil pests can easily spread sideways. However, it is still worth carrying out the simplest rotation and following the rule of not putting the same crop in the same soil two years running. In containers, new compost can be provided or a different crop can be grown in the old compost with the addition of manure or fertiliser. Overwintering vegetables can make rotation a bit tricky but most plots will be cleared by March or April in time for new and rotated sowing and planting.

Rotation group	Vegetable examples	Benefits to soil	Ground preparation
1. Legumes and fruiting vegetables	Peas, beans (outdoors), tomatoes, aubergines (indoors)	Fixes nitrogen, which fertilises the soil.	Manure ground at digging time. Add lime if soil is acidic at least one month after manure and one month before planting.
2. Brassicas, turnips	Cabbages, sprouts, broccoli, kale, radishes, swedes and turnips	Prevents build-up of club root.	Only dig in compost or manure if soil is poor. Lime soil one month after manure and one month before planting.
3. Onion family and salads	Onions, garlic, chives, marrows, lettuce, sweetcorn	Prevents build-up of fungal disease such as onion white rot.	Manure ground at digging time. Add lime if soil is acidic.
4. Root vegetables	Carrots, parsnips, celery, celeriac, beetroot, potatoes	Avoids build-up of potato eel worm.	Do not add manure, do not lime.

CHAPTER 6

Where to Grow Fruit and Vegetables

The Traditional Vegetable Plot

Larger gardens can give space to a dedicated vegetable plot. In designing it, it is desirable to be able to reach all your plants from the paths, so a sensible bed width is no more than 1.2m (4ft). The typical design is a pair of 1.2m-wide beds with a wide path down the middle, hard enough for walking on in wet weather and wide enough for wheelbarrow use, and a narrow path, which may just be flattened soil, down the outside. For a tidy edge, use wood, bricks or plant a border with perennial or shrubby plants which can be clipped formally – a box hedge, for example. Be aware that live edging plants will vie to some extent with your crops for nutrients and water. The whole garden can be planted as a parterre, with patterns of low hedging in-filled with edible plants. Be adventurous with the plant choices to line or define the border of a vegetable plot. Trish Kennedy, at Newhall in Midlothian, uses a hedge of

Caroline and Peter's garden, a traditional vegetable plot with leanings towards a potager, Glendoick, Perth.

Jerusalem artichoke while, at Hatton Castle, Aberdeenshire, the paths are lined with *Astilbe*. One edible solution is to use trained step-over apples (*see* p. 89) as practised at Fyvie Castle, Aberdeenshire and Dunrobin Castle in Sutherland. For Scotland, unless you garden on the east coast, I'd advise against lavender or other herbs as a permanent edging as they tend to die off in parts after a year or two, making a messy and uneven border.

If you don't have a rectangular shape to work with, don't worry. There are lots of layout variations which work, whatever shape your plot is, including triangular or tapering beds. In poorly drained or heavy soils, the best advice is to plant the whole fruit and vegetable plot in raised beds, as is the case in many Scottish gardens – Craigievar and Fyvie in Aberdeenshire and the walled garden at Applecross House are good examples (*see* p. 34 for more details on raised beds). If it fits with your rotation, it makes sense to plant crops which need netting, such as strawberries, blueberries, currants and brassicas, close together. The same applies to tender crops – peas, beans, corn and so on – which might need fleecing or cloching in late spring to protect from cold winds and late frosts.

There are several advantages to growing in rows. You should be able to differentiate the young seedlings from the weeds, and the row gaps can be used to step on when thinning, weeding, hoeing and harvesting. Overcrowding tends to encourage disease so having gaps between rows increases air circulation and maximises sunlight to speed ripening. Mulches of composted green waste or black horticultural fabric between rows will help suppress weeds and retain moisture.

Allotments

Allotments are small parcels of land rented to local people, usually for the purpose of growing fruit and vegetables. The traditional allotment size is 200–250m² which allows around 45–50 plots per hectare.

Planting in rows, allowing hoeing to take place between them, at Phantassie Farm, East Lothian.

The National Society of Allotment and Leisure Gardens (NSALG) reports that the average allotment holder tends their allotment for 200 hours a year, or the equivalent of eight whole days or 25–28 working days.

With the huge increase of interest in grow-your-own, the demand for allotments in Scotland has never been higher, and is becoming a significant political issue. On 17 December 2009, the Scottish Parliament held a debate on the issue, opened by Liberal Democrat MSP Jim Tolson, who stated:

> According to recent figures produced by the Scottish Allotments and Gardens Society, Scotland has 1 plot per 700 people. England has 1 plot per 170 people. That contrasts starkly with the situation in 1945, when Scotland had 90,000 plots, or one plot per 60 people. At the moment, 55 per cent of sites are outwith Glasgow, Edinburgh, Dundee and Aberdeen – in other words, outwith the main centres of population.
>
> Encouraging the provision of more

City Road Allotments in Dundee.

allotments and community gardens through-out the country will contribute to the Scottish Government's agenda . . . By increasing the amount of food that we grow in this country, we will contribute by reducing food miles, and emissions from food production. We could eat more seasonal food, which has travelled fewer miles.

In 1998, the waiting list for an allotment in Edinburgh had around 400 names on it. By 2009, the number on the waiting list had reached 2,000. Edinburgh City Council owns just 1,233 plots and the waiting lists show no sign of falling. The waiting list for Inverleith Allotments is currently likely to take 180 years to clear! The demand is almost exclusively in the areas of densest population – the very areas where there are the fewest potential sites. Imaginative schemes are being proposed to find more space for allotments, with more than 70 groups throughout Scotland seeking land for new sites. Some have even proposed that urban golf courses should be appropriated. The Scottish Allotments and Gardens Society (SAGS) represents allotment sites and plot holders throughout Scotland and promotes the value of allotments for healthy activity and good food. You can download their leaflet, 'Allotments – A Scottish Plotholder's Guide', from the SAGS website, www.sags.org.uk. SAGS, led by the irrepressible Jenny Mollison, has a target by 2018 of more than doubling the availability of allotment plots to a ratio of one per 300 inhabitants and, by 2028, to one per 100, with a higher provision in heavily populated areas. The SNP administration has broadly agreed to try to attain these targets. Councils have a statutory duty to respond to demand for the provision of allotments. It only needs six or more residents on the electoral roll to make representation in writing. The Scottish government is considering legislating for a 'community right to grow', which may force councils to act on grow-your-own provision. In May 2011, Westminster Tory minister Eric Pickles called for the removal of any requirement for councils to provide allotments, calling the 100-year-old legislation 'burdensome'. Thankfully, Scotland's government is taking a more enlightened view.

The Climate Challenge Fund (*see* p. 20) has

Kirkwall Allotments in Orkney.

An example of private allotment provision at Scotlandwell, Kinross.

given out £2 million to 34 allotment and community garden sites throughout Scotland. Glasgow & Clyde Valley's Green Network Partnership's report 'Sow and Grow Everywhere (SAGE)' has led to a number of abandoned and unused sites being colonised for community food-growing/allotments. Glasgow's ambitious project at Shettleston, in the East End, plans to create 40 raised beds, seven tunnels and greenhouses, an orchard and a café on an old builder's yard, with a part-time project officer. Edinburgh City Council's impressive document 'Cultivating Communities: A Growing Challenge – An allotments strategy for the City of Edinburgh (2010–2015)' empowers partners such as the NHS and local and neighbourhood groups to form associations to clear suitable land for allotments and to develop them.

Though there are abandoned, vandalised green spaces and brownfield sites in many of Scotland's urban areas which may be suitable for allotments (once checked for possible contamination), the legal and bureaucratic hurdles discourage many groups. The 2011 'Grow-Your-Own Working Group Report' found that:

Land supply does not appear to be the problem ... The missing link appears to be a trusted intermediary to broker acceptable tenure terms and conditions between landowners and community gardening groups.

This issue will need to be addressed by both government and local authorities to make a significant increase in sites. Many landowners are willing to offer land to communities for sale or rent but, in urban areas, the costs can be considerable. The Bridgend Allotment site in Edinburgh spent £230,000 to purchase and equip 58 plots. That works out at almost £4,000 per plot. Contrast this with the ongoing issue of the traditionally low rents paid for allotments, which do not sustain the cost of maintaining infrastructure. For example, Edinburgh City Council currently charges £54 per year per allotment. Because of this, councils often see allotments as a drain on resources and of benefit to a relatively small number of people. If councils were able to charge more money for allotments, it might encourage them to look more enthusiastically at trying to create more. Perhaps some degree of means-tested charging might be the fairest way, so that those receiving benefits would pay less rent. The private sector can almost certainly provide more allotments. Scotlandwell Allotments near Kinross are probably Scotland's poshest and show one possible way forward. The brainchild of Bob McCormick, the 17.5-acre site has room for 200 allotments and for £300 per year you get a 'stone-free plot', access to water, toilets, a clubhouse and a huge library of cooking and gardening books. Rouken Glen Garden Centre near Linlithgow has recently opened an allotment site next to their garden centre. The first 70 plots were quickly snapped up.

Not all allotment sites are urban. The new allotments at Mossbank in Shetland enjoy a stunning hilltop view, perhaps a challenging choice for Britain's windiest place. Good for Ewe at Inverasdale, near Poolewe in Wester Ross, is a community allotment project on land rented from a local crofter. Wester Ross's ferocious winds make vegetable growing a serious challenge and the solution has been to have indoor allotment plots in Keder greenhouse tunnels.

In many allotment sites, 10–20 per cent of plots are 'dirty' – that is, not being actively used. With the waiting lists which exist, this should be addressed. Abandoned sites quickly fill up with brambles, nettles, willowherb and thistles and the seeds are blown onto neighbouring plots. I would strongly urge all allotment sites to take steps to change their constitutions to allow the immediate takeover of any abandoned sites by people on the waiting list, even for short-term leases of a year or two.

Not everyone loves allotments – that much is clear. I would have to concede that the 'do-it-yourself' ethos which allows an eccentric range of buildings, crop scarers and polythene crop protective measures can be a bit of an eyesore. Many allotments have rules as to which constructions are acceptable. Some extraordinary narrow-mindedness has been expressed in the objections to new allotment sites in recent years. For example, residents at St Monans, Fife, suggested that 'it would be off-putting to tourists to have visible allotments'. Another feature of allotments is the tension which can arise between allotment holders. I heard horror stories from one waterside Edinburgh allotment site of inter-plot vandalism, sabotage, shed arson and other less-than-charming behaviour. I'm surprised we don't yet have a TV soap opera set on an allotment site. The potential is considerable.

The Potager

You don't need to have a dedicated vegetable plot to grow edibles in the garden. One alternative is the potager. Taking advantage of the striking flowers, foliage and produce of fruit and vegetables to make gardens and borders which are both ornamental and edible is an age-old tradition that is very much back in vogue. The restoration of the potager at the Château de Villandry in France in the early 1900s, with its planting of 30,000 vegetables annually to recreate a 1600s design, seems to have inspired many British gardeners, and Scotland now boasts some impressive potagers. Herbs such as lavender, rosemary and chives have obvious ornamental appeal and can be used anywhere in the garden. Rhubarb, artichokes, coloured-stemmed chard, blue-leaved cabbage, purple sprouting broccoli, coloured salads, beans and peas on wigwams and many other edibles make fine ornamentals and they can be mixed with shrubs, fruit, perennials and annuals. The French style usually involves a degree of formality, including a parterre design with low hedged sections and trained fruit infilled with annual flowers, fruit and vegetables, such as is practised at Johnstounburn House near Edinburgh. Some potagers, such as the one at Cambo in Fife, although containing edible plants as well as flowers, are grown exclusively as an ornamental display. And this points to the difficulty with potagers – when you harvest crops, you start to break up the design. We succession-sowed salads, radishes and other quick crops in our rather informal potager each time we had a patch of bare earth and this worked well into early August and later for some salad crops.

Ken's potager in August 2010 is a melange of edibles and ornamentals.

The potager at Malleny in Balerno, near Edinburgh, incorporating annuals, herbs, potatoes, leeks, rhubarb and more.

The largely ornamental potager at Cambo in Fife is changed each year and features spectacular planting combinations dreamed up by head gardener Elliot Forsyth.

Fruit and Vegetables in Containers

Not having access to soil in the ground is not a barrier to growing fruit, vegetables and herbs. Even a window box can provide enough space for a range of herbs such as chives and parsley, and salads such as rocket. When space is limited, it makes sense to plant crops which produce maximum yield in the smallest area – cut-and-come-again salads, potatoes and climbing beans, for example. Seed companies have now developed a range of patio and container vegetables. Tree fruit has limited scope in small spaces but there are patio and columnar dwarf apples suitable for containers (*see* p. 96). Raised beds

An example of imaginative potager planting at Cambo – lettuce 'Lollo Rosso' and *Stipa tenuissima*.

A hanging vegetable garden at Tufnell Park, London. You can't do much better than this! Scotland's wind would make this sort of thing a little tricky, but it can be done.

Wicker-edged raised beds, Hampton Court Palace Flower Show.

The 'Burgon & Ball 5-A-Day Garden', an RHS Gold Medal winner at the Hampton Court Palace Flower Show 2011.

A Scottish invention – Geocell pots can be placed on any surface (Gardening Scotland).

made of wood or plastic can sit on any hard surface such as paving or balconies, as can growbags for tomatoes, herbs, strawberries and salads. You do need at least part-day sun to grow most food crops, so north walls and dark basements are not usually suitable.

We have tried growing fruit and vegetables in an assortment of pots, baskets and raised beds, and most have grown reasonably well. As a general rule, a few larger containers or raised beds are often easier to look after than a whole series of small ones, but large individual pots are also worth trying for raising potatoes, carrots, strawberries and other crops. Bear in mind that, in pots and containers, plants tend to be buffeted by wind, their roots are more vulnerable to freezing, compost can become waterlogged and

Ken's herb and vegetable barrow. It proved excellent for stumpy carrots, rocket, garlic and herbs but too dry for salads.

plants need more feeding than they would in the ground but, above all, plants in containers need watering. In midsummer, that means every day for many crops, unless it rains. Make sure that pots and containers have adequate drainage holes, covered with crocks (broken bits of terracotta) or rough stones to keep the holes clear. Perlite and/or coarse grit can be mixed into the compost to improve drainage. For container-grown crops, it is worth moving the pots up against the walls of the house in winter to keep them warmer and drier. Try to shelter plants from strong winds, particularly in their soft young growth phase in spring. Most fruit and vegetables appreciate regular feeding or slow-release fertiliser mixed into the compost, which lasts for several months. If you can't find anyone to water your containers when you are away on holiday, then move them to a shady spot where they won't dry out too fast or think about investing in an automatic irrigation system, as most annual vegetables will not tolerate drying out for long.

Fruit and Vegetables for Containers

- **Chillies** – keep indoors (one plant can provide plenty of fire for a whole season).
- **Compact bush tomatoes** ('Tom Thumb', 'Tumbler', etc.) – best kept indoors until they have flowered.
- **Cut-and-come-again or baby salads** ('Little Gem' lettuce, rocket, etc.) – harvest in six to eight weeks, grow two to three crops per year and, with protection, you can get early and late crops.
- **Herbs** – rosemary, parsley, mint (a container stops it taking over), coriander, dill, tarragon and chives.
- **Courgettes** – use a large container, expect the plants to spill over, huge yields are possible.
- **Potatoes** – 'Anya', 'Charlotte', 'Duke of York', etc.
- **Radishes**
- **Carrots**
- **Dwarf beans**
- **Strawberries**
- **Blueberries** – in ericaceous compost.
- **Cape Gooseberry 'Little Lantern'.** Can go outdoors in midsummer.
- **Apples on dwarf rootstocks** – ensure good wind shelter.

Gardening shows such as Gardening Scotland and Hampton Court usually have innovative displays of fruit and vegetables in containers. Two Scottish companies have caught our eye. Gilchrist's Geo Cells (gilchristlandscapes@live.co.uk – no website) offers a series of deep containers made of recyclable fabric which form a honeycomb of planters that can be used on any hard surface to grow significant crops. On a smaller scale, Whirligro offers vertical gardens, spirals of tubes or pots, designed for very small spaces and ideal for salads and herbs (www.whirli-gro.co.uk).

Greenhouses, Tunnels and Frames

Most Scottish vegetable growers find some form of protected cropping invaluable. This allows for early and late sowings and protection of tender crops from the crueller aspects of the Scottish weather, as well as extra warmth for growing tomatoes, peppers, chillies, grapes and many other less hardy crops. While you can use cloches for a degree of protection, most opt for a walk-in covered growing space – a greenhouse or tunnel. You can spend a considerable

Scotlandwell Allotments. Allotment holders often show great DIY ingenuity to create cheap protective cropping. Whatever you use, ensure it is robust enough and well anchored so it does not blow away.

Some of Scotland's finest greenhouses are the restored vine houses at Culzean, Ayrshire.

fortune on a bespoke traditional greenhouse, but there are plenty of cheaper options both in greenhouses and plastic tunnels. The most important factor to consider is wind. Unless the site is very sheltered, both greenhouses and tunnels need to be strongly constructed and properly anchored. The storms of May 2011 carried off many of the soft fruit tunnels in Perthshire and Angus, and wind is a threat to all crop-protection structures. Crop consultant Colin Stirling stresses the importance of getting tunnel skins really tight. To do this, you need to choose a warm, still day to allow the polythene to be stretched and anchored. Once it is attached and dug in, the skin should make a distinct 'ping' if you tap it. If it flaps in the wind or makes a dull thud when you tap it, it probably is not tight enough. And don't forget to screw the tunnel corner hoops to the bases so the tunnel can't take off in gales.

Greenhouses are usually more attractive and easier to shade and ventilate than tunnels but they cost two to five times as much as tunnels of the same size. Greenhouses should last longer but are more complex to erect. By using an existing back wall, a south- or west-facing lean-to greenhouse needs less glass and is usually cheaper to heat – also the back wall is ideal for fan-training peaches, apricots, figs and other fruit. Tunnel-house plastic skins last for two to five or even up to seven years, depending on quality as well as the amount of wind the tunnel is subjected to. A 3m × 2m tunnel-house frame and skin typically costs under £300, a 10m × 3m around £700. A tunnel house should have 1m of polythene to dig into the ground all round to anchor it securely. If you can, invest in both the structure and the anchoring/foundations to give yourself the best chance of longevity. Tunnel-house ventilation can be a challenge, especially in a large one, as they can easily get too hot. Tunnels with sides which can be opened up in summer are ideal, but they are more expensive. Tunnels can be installed on slightly sloping sites too, although the more level the site, the better. You may spot tempting £99 plastic-framed greenhouses and tunnels at your local garden centre. In our experience, these tend to buckle and blow away into the North Sea after the first storm, as they just are not designed for average Scottish weather. Use them for summer protection or as a propagating house within a larger greenhouse or tunnel only, and fold or roll them away for at least six months of the year. You'd probably be better off with a cold frame than one of these.

Scotland's winters of 2009–11, with their heavy

snowfalls, saw many a collapsed tunnel or greenhouse – only some designs shed snow easily. Tunnels with steep sides, without flat tops and with heavy-gauge frameworks are the most robust. Likewise, single-span greenhouses with well-pitched roofs are best, while multi-spans with valley gutters are prone to snow overloading. Wherever possible, don't let heavy, wet snow lie – knock it off with a broom or a heavy rope dragged from side to side. This is much more easily done when snow is soft and powdery. If you can't get out to knock snow off, then consider extra bracing or props which can be removed in summer.

A cheaper alternative to greenhouses and tunnels is the traditional cold frame, which is ideal for starting off vegetables in the spring. The old-style wooden and glass frames are quite expensive. Aluminium and polycarbonate are lighter and cheaper. Plants soon get too tall for cold frames so you need to bear this in mind with timing of sowings. Frames can be opened and closed to suit weather conditions and, if you visit almost any allotment, you'll see a great range of DIY frames, cloches and other forms of protection. These can be made from discarded building materials, which are often available for nothing if you keep your eyes open. I've seen excellent frames made of breeze blocks and second-hand windows.

There are several irrigation systems with capillary action, seep hoses and micro-drips available to water plants in tunnels and greenhouses, some of which can be put on timers for several weeks. These are invaluable if you are away from home for some time and don't have anyone to keep an eye on the watering.

Cloches, Fleece and Protected Cropping

Scotland's fickle spring weather, with sudden frosts and cold east winds in April and May, means that newly planted out or freshly germinated vegetables are vulnerable to damage, which can be fatal. A fine mesh covering will provide a little frost protection. Better are the two versions of 'floating mulch' – moisture-permeable perforated plastic film and spun polypropylene 'fleece', which tends to prevent water getting through. Both are available in rolls of various widths and are the cheapest form of weather protection. Anchoring the material and holding it off the crops below to stop it from flapping wildly is crucial, as this can do as much damage as the cold itself. A light framework gives something to attach the material to and keeps it tight. Caroline uses hoops of 23mm polypropylene water pipe cut to size to create a low tunnel. Remove the fleece before it

Snow damage to tunnel houses. Avoid multi-spans and flat-topped tunnels and knock the lying snow off as soon as possible.

An insulated Keder house at Northbay Garden Project, Barra.

Classic old-style glass cold frames at Mertoun in the Borders.

The Rolls-Royce of cloches at Inverewe, Wester Ross.

rains, as the weight of water-soaked fabric can damage soft young crops. Fleece can also be used for shading and for protection from birds and insects. Cloches and low tunnels are portable methods of protection which can be moved from crop to crop as needed and stored when not in use. You can choose glass or polycarbonate versions, often decoratively made, or go for cheaper, more functional hoops covered with fleece or polythene. Cloches are invaluable but don't always stay put in high winds; try a series of canes pushed in at either side at an angle and so crossed over the top of the cloche to

help secure it. If your local garden centre does not stock a good range, there are lots of online sellers. Harrod Horticultural and Garden Organic websites both have extensive listings.

Hydroponics

In place of soil, hydroponics uses mineral nutrient solutions dissolved in water to produce crops which are usually grown indoors in tunnels and greenhouses. It is claimed that this method of production requires only 5 per cent of the water used by traditional farming to produce the same weight of food. This may be relevant in areas with water shortages and dwindling rainfall – so probably not Scotland. The original Scottish Hydroponicum in coastal Sutherland has been closed and the business relocated to Achiltibuie Garden close by. The hydroponic fruit and vegetables are grown in a double-span Keder house, with energy supplied from a wind generator and water collected from the roof. Tomatoes, strawberries, salads and lots of other crops can be seen growing in their special nutrient solution. You'll find further information about their activities as well as mail order for all things hydroponic at www.thehydroponicum.com. The Polycroft on Lewis runs a hydroponic system using containers filled with Siar Glass (recycled glass 'gravel') to grow a wide range of crops, while at Glendrynoch on Skye, the Peppes produce watercress and strawberries hydroponically to supply local restaurants.

Companion Planting, Polyculture, Permaculture and Forest Gardening

Organic gardening emphasises the benefits of planting certain fruit and vegetables next to one another to offer protection from pests or disease. Planting carrots next to onions, leeks or French marigolds gives some protection against carrot fly, for example. The organically run vegetable garden at Kellie Castle

Hydroponically grown watercress, Skye (photo D. Peppe).

Companion planting – *Calendula* planted with carrots to deter carrot fly, Scotlandwell Allotments, Kinross.

in Fife manages a complex range of plant associations, with rows of complementary plants side by side. Head gardener Mark Armour believes these are simple and effective and he showed me examples – using borage and pot marigold to act as decoy plants for blackfly on broad beans and having onions and chives planted between rows of strawberries to reduce fungal disease. Mark also notes that certain plants attract the same pests and so are better not planted adjacent to one another. Potatoes, cabbages and beans should not be planted next to onions apparently. In our experience, rotation and companion planting often contradict one another and you may find yourself tearing your hair out!

Former *Gardeners' World* presenter Alys Fowler has been promoting a style of gardening which she calls 'polyculture', where shrubs, fruit trees, flowers and vegetables are grown mixed up together. Spreading plants around rather than in blocks or rows is said to reduce pest damage and disease. As an experiment, I tried this approach for a year at Glendoick, planting a variety of vegetables, fruit and herbs with edible flowers in a bed 8m × 3m. I would

say that it was a qualified success. The promised benefits of companion/association planting to confuse pests did work to some extent. I was determined not to use mesh or netting against birds or insects, as I wanted as 'natural' an effect as possible. Sadly pigeons came by each night and stripped the newly planted brassicas and, by the end of June, I had to throw out the shredded remains. Another problem was weeding. Without clearly defined rows which can be hoed, it is hard to ascertain which small seedlings are the vegetables you have sown and which are weeds. I found that hand weeding required stepping on the bed, which made a mess and compacted the soil. If I did this again, I'd incorporate stepping stones for easy access. On balance, I'd conclude that, if you need to maximise your yield, it is best to grow things in traditional rows but, if you are not so worried about quantity and care more about the visual impact, then go for a polyculture approach. The effect is one of lush disorder – edible flowers, beans on wigwams, salads, herbs, strawberries, currants and root vegetables all growing into a vigorous mass, some being lost under their

1. Canopy (large fruit and nut trees)
2. Low tree layer (dwarf fruit trees)
3. Shrub layer (currants and berries)
4. Herbaceous (perennial plants, herbs)
5. Soil (root vegetables)
6. Soil surface (ground cover, e.g. strawberry)
7. Vertical layers (beans, peas etc.)

A schematic diagram of forest gardening, showing the various layers from an over-storey of trees to root vegetables in the ground.

more enthusiastic neighbours in chaotic fecundity. I was pleased to see that Alys Fowler's television version looked as messy as mine. Visitors seemed to like it and, to a large extent, this informal melange is the point of it. You may tire of telling onlookers that 'it is meant to look like that'!

Permaculture (from 'permanent agriculture') is said to have been 'invented' in the 1970s in Tasmania, but what was new was more the term itself rather than the practice. Many tribal people in the Americas and Asia instinctively follow permacultural approaches, where crops, and often animals, are grown/farmed together so providing positive interdependence, whether in preventing pests and disease, providing shelter or a support to climb on, or dung for fertiliser. Most importantly, the agriculture practised is sustainable, as it does not degrade the soil and, in theory, the land can remain productive indefinitely.

Permaculture, in turn, inspired gardeners such as forest garden pioneer Robert Hart in Shropshire,

Graham Bell's Coldstream forest garden.

who wrote about his experience of growing over 100 different varieties of fruit and nuts, climbers, perennials, vegetables and herbs together. Hart stresses the importance of various forest layers, designing a self-perpetuating ecosystem where plants provide their own nutrient replenishment (legumes and leaf mould) and are perennial or self-seed. Robert Hart advises using fruit and nut trees to provide the forest layer, planted 6m apart, then fruit bushes such as currants in between and, as an understorey, herbs and perennial vegetables with fungi in the soil beneath.

Hart's ideas have inspired many others, including Martin Crawford in Devon (Agroforestry Research Trust), Ken Fern in Cornwall (Plants for a Future) and Sandy Masson, who founded the Rhuba Phoil forest garden on Skye, situated by the ferry terminal to Mallaig. To learn more, I visited Graham Bell, author of two books on permaculture. Graham and his wife Nancy garden in Coldstream in their quarter-acre, where they have spent over 20 years developing a productive small walled 'forest garden' of fruit trees and bushes, soft and hardwood trees, ground cover and edible plants. At first glance, the garden looks like chaos but, on closer inspection, you can see the method. Fertility is maintained by composting and mulching, soil is protected from heavy rain by carpets of ground cover and a huge range of edible plants occupies almost every nook and cranny. Crops include quince, plums, cherries, apples, pears, apricots, pumpkins, hazelnuts, strawberries, gooseberries, raspberries, red-, white- and blackcurrants, blackberries and a whole host of hybrid berries. Raised beds, tyres and pots jostle for space and are filled with salads and vegetables. In Scotland, most annual vegetables need to be grown in full sun/light, so forest gardening needs substantial clearings to grow sun-loving plants this far north.

Permaculture is a complex and challenging practice – as much a philosophy and an approach to life as a way to garden – with every aspect of the process of living off the land carefully designed. Food, soil, water, fungi, insect and micro-organisms, sustainability, energy inputs, waste management and community well-being are all considered. It can have something of the 'religious' about it, with some zealot-like adherents convinced that theirs is the only true path to gardening heaven. Permaculture gardens often look a bit of a mess, to be perfectly honest, although I'd be afeared of voicing this opinion! Beechgrove's Jim McColl is not a fan either. 'We did it at Beechgrove for four to five years and quite honestly it's a footer,' was the conclusion he voiced in a *Beechgrove Potting Shed* podcast in November 2011. If you want to know more, we'd recommend attending a permaculture lecture or course, or perusing the literature on the subject. The concept of permaculture will certainly make you think more deeply about how you garden.

Gardening on Land That is Not Yours – Guerrilla Gardening

As the demand for allotments demonstrates, not everyone has access to land to grow fruit and vegetables – particularly those who live in densely populated urban areas. Historically, the concentration of landownership in small numbers of large estates and the enclosure of common grazing grounds have denied citizens the right to grow their own crops. Nonconformist dissenter Gerrard Winstanley and his band of 'Diggers' invaded and planted vegetables on common land in Weybridge, Surrey, in 1649 in an act of land squatting. Oliver Cromwell sent in his heavies to evict the protesters, but the Diggers have inspired land reformers worldwide ever since. More recently in Britain, Richard Reynolds' book *On Guerrilla Gardening* and the associated website have inspired a generation of British gardeners to take over land on derelict building sites, roundabouts and anywhere else that comes to mind to plant flowers and vegetables. Scotland's own guerrilla gardeners have been active since 2008 and Glasgow's Darren Wilson is credited with the invention of the favourite

Guerrilla Gardening – a homage to Che Guevara at the headquarters of Garden Organic, Ryton, Warwickshire.

weapon of the guerrilla gardening movement, the 'seed bomb'. Glasgow Guerrilla Gardening have planted vegetables on several sites and their website (www.glasgowguerillagardening.org.uk – please note that 'guerrilla' is misspelt as 'guerilla' in the web address) gives further details on where to meet them.

As has already been mentioned, Scotland has significant tracts of unused urban land which could become temporary or permanent growing spaces – parts of parks, railway sidings, land-banked or derelict industrial sites, unused walled gardens and land owned by many non-profit organisations. Among the proposals put forward in the 2011 report of the Scottish government Grow-Your-Own working group are:

- to create a land bank of potential sites
- to allow 'meanwhile' (short-term) use of sites earmarked for development in the future
- to encourage NGOs and government to lease land at less than market rates for 'grow-your-own' initiatives.

The report also urges community credit loans to purchase infrastructure and stresses the need for joined-up thinking on training, qualifications, dealing with red tape, planning and consistency amongst councils. As long as this report is implemented by subsequent administrations and not left to gather dust, this should make a significant improvement to the availability of land on which to grow produce.

SAGE, based in Glasgow, has developed the 'growing toolkit', a specially designed modular system of grow boxes/bags made from recycled materials which allows growing on brownfield sites and other places normally deemed unsuitable.

Sometimes the best way to find growing space is simply to look around your neighbourhood. There are hundreds of unused private gardens all over Scotland which owners can't or won't look after, perhaps through old age or lack of skills or interest. Owners are often delighted if someone else wants to use the space. And you can always share produce instead of paying rent. Nationally, Landshare (www.landshare.net), founded by Hugh Fearnley-Whittingstall, attempts to match landowners with those who want land to grow on. It is supported by Creative Scotland north of the border.

CHAPTER 7

Pests, Diseases and Weeds

All growers of fruit and vegetables have to contend with weeds, pests and disease. Some are annoying or cosmetic, and others can completely ruin crops. A garden's ecosystem is best served by balancing the needs of our stomach with the needs of the soil we work and the animals and organisms that live in and on it, many of which will be useful natural predators. Prevention is better than cure – keep watch over your patch so that you can, sometimes literally, nip problems in the bud. Choose disease-resistant varieties and those best suited for your climate. Tidying up prunings, diseased and dead plants, and general hygiene will help keep fungal spores to a minimum. The benefits of crop rotation (p. 49) have already been discussed. Pests cannot be eradicated – we just have to find ways of reducing them to acceptable levels so that crops retain vigour and can be harvested. Legislation means that fewer chemicals are available to combat problems, so gardeners are finding new and often ingenious ways to deal with the nasties, using biological controls, companion planting and barriers such as fleece and fine mesh. Worldwide, plant breeders make pest and disease resistance a key goal in their newest hybrids. Most people who grow fruit and vegetables as a hobby, working in their own garden and putting produce into the mouths of their family, are quite logically inclined towards the idea of gardening without using chemicals where possible. We realise that there is a broad range of attitude to dealing with garden pests and disease which we try to accommodate in this book. We summarise several broad approaches here:

1. **No chemicals** – Caroline's preferred approach
2. **Strictly organic** – no man-made chemicals or fertilisers but using feeds and chemicals that are passed as 'organic'
3. **Pragmatic minimum pesticide use** – for example, accepting the use of glyphosate (Roundup) on stubborn weeds, or fungicides to combat apple scab, and only using chemicals when essential
4. **Use all available chemicals** to get the best results. Gardeners in this category are unlikely to change their ways unless forced by legislation and are probably not concerned with 'green' issues. The end justifies the means to obtain the giant blemish-free show vegetables or the perfect lawn. Such gardeners may, for example, be prepared to kill worms in revenge for leaving worm casts on a golf or bowling green, despite the obvious benefits that worms bring to soil ecology and lawn quality.

Some of the most common and intractable fruit and vegetable problems include carrot fly, cabbage white caterpillars, vine weevils in strawberries and scab on apples and pears. And the rainfall in Scotland seems to be the principal reason why slugs and snails are many Scottish gardeners' worst enemy. As the *Beechgrove Garden* factsheet describes:

Some Slimy Facts: One individual grey field slug can produce 90,000 grandchildren; a cubic metre of garden will contain on average up to 200 slugs; it is estimated that slugs consume twice their own body weight every day; a slug weighing 0.10z would, over a 20-week growing season, consume an astonishing and expensive 1.75lbs of plants and vegetables each.

'Beechgrove Factsheet', 2004, no 4

Many an organic-leaning gardener is willing to make a chemical exception to combat slugs (and snails). Slugs are much worse in wet/damp weather and do the most damage with young seedlings – a mature leaf can take a few holes but a young seedling can be a slug mouthful. Jim McColl advises putting an old slate in the vegetable patch to gauge slug activity. Turn it over and see how many are hiding underneath. There are more alternative remedies for slugs than any other pest, but trials indicate that most of them are of limited use. By all means try copper tape, caffeine, garlic and lots more. Biological controls (*see* p. 68) are only partly effective on slugs and not effective on snails.

Caroline is more of a purist than I am but, despite some misgivings on my part, we do both broadly support organic gardening as the way ahead. As author Jeff Gillman concludes in *The Truth about Organic Gardening*, 'organic gardening should be about making safe and smart choices' rather than being obsessive about 'natural' choices which are not necessarily better (*see* p. 39). The organic movement has been responsible for important and lasting change in our attitude to the production of food in a sustainable and less environmentally harmful way. Many toxic chemicals have been removed from the market and there is a huge increase in public awareness of issues such as GM crops, monocultures, pesticide resistance and unsustainable use of water supplies.

Most fruit and vegetable gardeners are concerned about their environment and will do all they can to preserve the quality of their soil and local watercourses by composting waste and reducing chemicals used. Gardeners don't have the stress of supermarket price pressure and the demands of perfect, unblemished crops to worry about, so they can afford to go for reduced yields and share their crop to some extent with local wildlife. We recommend a pragmatic rather than a dogmatic approach. There are many disease- and pest-resistant cultivars of fruit and vegetables which reduce the need for chemical intervention. Overall, our advice would be to practise sound and proven organic techniques such as composting, rotation and companion planting. I reckon that you should not be put off from using occasional useful chemicals such as Roundup, limited use of targeted fungicides and insecticides and inorganic fertilisers when this is the best practical solution to the problem. I use them and Caroline chooses not to. Both positions are valid.

Measuring the Dangers of Using Pesticides – the EIQ Rating

Almost all pesticides, including organic ones, present possible dangers to the user and can contaminate the environment so it is important to know any potential risks or dangers in order to aid decision-making. The best objective measurement is the Environmental Impact Quotient (or EIQ), devised by Dr Joseph Kovach at Cornell University, New York. Chemicals are rated in three areas:

- Danger or risk to the person applying the chemical – from spray, mixing the concentrate, getting the chemical in the eyes or on the skin.
- Danger or risk to anyone else who might come into contact with the chemical – from drift from agricultural spraying or eating a treated apple, for example.
- Danger or risk to the environment – to bees, ground water and things which live in the soil, the time taken to break down in the soil, collateral damage and so on.

The higher the aggregate EIQ score (1–100), the more potentially harmful and dangerous the chemical is. Most chemicals now available for use in gardens have an EIQ of 30 or less and, when used correctly, they are relatively safe and well targeted. Where the data is available, we list the EIQ of pesticides and herbicides, both organic and non-organic, in our table on p. 71 to aid your decision-making. We think that the UK and European chemical industry should publish the EIQ score on all chemicals to allow customers to make informed decisions. The full list can be found online.

Due to legislation, the range of chemicals available to amateur growers has halved in recent years and many useful pesticides for ornamental plants and flowers are not licensed for use on fruit and vegetables, making the range of available products even more restricted. Chemical companies are sometimes forced to re-formulate their brands to comply with legislation, but they tend not to tell you on the packaging when chemicals change. Often the new version is less effective than the old and can be more expensive. Some chemicals have rightly been banned because they are toxic or dangerous, but others are taken off the market for purely economic reasons. Because EC licensing of chemicals is very expensive and the licence needs to be renewed every ten years, less profitable chemical licences are allowed to lapse. In some cases, the chemicals are still available but no longer listed for use in the garden. Armillatox, for example, was formerly advertised as a treatment for vine weevil and honey fungus. These uses are no longer listed on the label and it is now sold purely as a disinfectant. Of course, it still does what it always did, but now you can't find any instructions and you are apparently breaking the law if you use it as a pesticide. There are some chemicals which would be useful for gardeners if the UK would only get round to approving them. A good example is neem oil (azadirachtin), which is relatively safe to use (EIQ 12). It is used in organic farming in some countries and is effective against both insects and disease. For reasons I can't quite fathom, in the UK you can buy it for treating

Biological control or trade name	Pests treated and use
Bacillus thuringiensis	Caterpillars. Rather slow to act and you need to cover every leaf. Also used in breeding GM crops. Very safe.
Phytoseiulus	Red spider under glass, minimum temperature 16–20°C.
Slug nematodes *Phasmarhabditis*	Kills immature slugs, may not control adults and not effective against snails. Not good in heavy clay soil.
Steinermena krausii	Vine weevil, new formula works in soil above 5°C. Controls larvae, not adults, so most useful in late summer when larvae hatch.
Mixed nematodes	Carrot, cabbage and onion root fly, cutworms, caterpillars, sawfly, thrips, codling moth.
Pheromone moth traps for codling and totrix moths	A chemical (pheromone) attracts male moths which end up glued to the trap surface. It captures males to reduce the females' mating success. Commercial growers use them to monitor crops and identify when to use insecticides.

humans and pets but not for putting on your garden. Pesticide legislation is often a saga of confused, inconsistent regulation, changed at very short notice, which is unhelpful to manufacturers, gardeners and nurserymen alike.

Most, but not all, organic pesticides are relatively benign. One or two naturally occurring pesticides, permitted for organic gardeners, can be relatively dangerous to use, and this is reflected in their high EIQ rating. Bordeaux mixture (copper sulphate and lime), used for spraying against potato blight and apple scab, is permitted under organic cultivation and yet it has an EIQ of over 50, as the copper can leach out and poison watercourses. Likewise the insecticide rapeseed oil has an EIQ of 27. Some 'organic' chemicals need to be applied sparingly, with as much care and as much protective equipment as non-organic chemicals. In some cases,

the non-organic choice may be less dangerous, better targeted and less harmful to the environment. Some organic pesticides need to be applied every few weeks, and the combined effect of so many doses can accumulate in the soil or water as well as posing more of a threat to the user.

Biological Controls

One important recent breakthrough is the development of biological controls such as ladybirds, nematodes, parasites and predator insects which prey on pests such as aphids, weevils or slugs. Some have disconcerting names like *Heterorhabditis megidis*. Biological controls are particularly effective on crops indoors, where the temperatures are more consistent. Safe to apply and more or less harmless to the

Aphids on apples.

Cabbage white butterfly (note the black spots on the wings).

Botrytis (mould) can affect fruit such as strawberries, raspberries and tomatoes and vegetables such as courgettes. It is also common on young seedlings, particularly if over-watered.

Cabbage white caterpillars on brassicas.

environment, they need to be applied regularly, usually mixed with water and drenched or sprayed on. Detailed information on these is available on the Royal Horticultural Society website. The main drawback is the cost – even in a small garden, you can easily spend a small fortune if you apply them as often as instructed. As they contain live ingredients, most have a short shelf life, need refrigeration and so are mostly sold by mail order rather than in garden centres. The table below shows some of the most useful for vegetable and fruit growing but there are lots more.

'Integrated Pest Management' is becoming the norm for much commercial UK food production. This can be defined as a mixture of methods used to control pests, using predators, organic methods and traditional chemicals to control problems with the lowest overall environmental impact. This seems to be a sensible way forward for gardeners, too.

Controlling Rabbits, Deer and Other Mammals

With very good reason, many Scottish gardeners bemoan the attentions of rabbits and deer – two out-of-control pests. You can be as sentimental as you like about fluffy bunnies but they can destroy your vegetable patch. Co-existence is not an option. Fluffy bunny websites tell you that you can keep rabbits off with chilli powder and other home-made remedies. Don't believe a word of it. One useful rabbit-repelling product is a calcium solution marketed as Grazers, which you can paint on foliage. The vegetables taste horrible for rabbits, pigeons and deer but apparently humans don't notice, so you can spray right up to harvesting.

For long-term peace of mind, bite the bullet and agree that rabbits need to be fenced out or killed. Fences need to be partly buried in the ground down to 20–30cm and, even then, rabbits may dig underneath. For rabbits, the fence needs to have a mesh of 2.5cm diameter and a height of 1–1.2m.

Rabbit Resistant Fruit and Vegetables

Hungry rabbits will eat anything, but the following are some of their least favourites:

blackberries/brambles	leeks
currants	onions
gooseberries	garlic
rhubarb	tomatoes
asparagus	squash
potatoes	herbs – most
broad beans	courgettes
wild rocket	

Deer are most likely to damage plants in winter, when they are most hungry. Barking of fruit trees can be fatal, so individual tree guards are a good precaution. Roe deer can leap a 2m-high fence, so it is an expensive business keeping them out. Grey squirrels, particularly in urban gardens, rats, mice and voles can also be a serious problem when they discover and eat your growing or stored crops before you do. Mice are particularly fond of eating newly planted seeds such as peas and beans. At the RHS Wisley garden, they use electric fences to discourage squirrels and badgers from digging their way into the fruit and vegetable cages. Patrick Kelsey from Sutherland told me that his dog dug up and ate his carrots and broccoli! Mine just dug a large hole in the vegetable garden.

Diseases and Pests – Dealing with the Most Common Problems

The diseases and pests listed below affect many different crops. More detail on problems with specific crops can be found under individual entries.

Netting brassicas and other vegetables for protection against pigeons, Hatton Castle, Aberdeenshire.

Sawfly larvae can strip the foliage of gooseberry, usually around fruiting time.

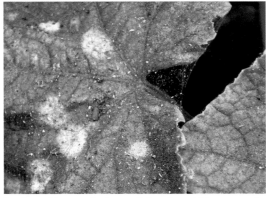

Powdery mildew can attack many fruit and vegetables – courgette (left) and goji berry (right).

Rust (on blackcurrants).

Slug damage (cabbage). Slugs can also devastate small seedlings.

Problem and plants affected	Non-chemical and cultural controls	Chemical control
Diseases		
Blossom end rot – tomatoes, peppers, aubergines	Grow plants in as large containers as possible. Caused by erratic watering, so water regularly. Remove and destroy affected fruit.	No chemical treatment
Black leg – potatoes	Remove and destroy affected plants. Ensure drainage is good for future crops. 'Charlotte' and a few other varieties show some resistance.	No chemical treatment
Blight – tomatoes and potatoes	Crop rotation helps. Grow resistant varieties. Grow only earlies. Keep potatoes well earthed up. As soon as you see the signs of blight, remove all the potato shaws and destroy – crop could be all right. Do not store any affected potatoes. Destroy affected tomato plants. Do not grow tomatoes and potatoes near each other.	Bordeaux mixture (or) – EIQ 62 Copper oxychloride – EIQ 30–50
Botrytis (mould) – seedlings, plants indoors, strawberries and other fruit	Maintain good hygiene. Handle plants carefully to avoid damage. Keep greenhouses well ventilated. Don't over-water. Remove and destroy all affected parts.	Bordeaux mixture (or) – EIQ 62 Sulphur (or) – EIQ 32
Canker – tree fruit	Select resistant varieties. Don't plant apple trees in poorly drained soil. Prune out affected branches and destroy.	Bordeaux mixture (or) – EIQ 62 Copper oxychloride – EIQ 30–50
Club root – brassicas (cabbage, cauliflower, etc.)	Plant good strong specimens started in modules. Soil should have good drainage. Lime the soil (*see* p. 31). Plant resistant varieties. Practise strict crop rotation. Keep weeds at bay. Remove any brassica debris after harvest.	No chemical controls permitted for amateurs.

(or = organic. For details about EIQ rating, see p. 66 – the higher the number, the more potentially harmful or dangerous is the substance.)

Problem and plants affected	Non-chemical and cultural controls	Chemical control
Cucumber mosaic virus – cucumbers but also affects tomatoes, celery, spinach, marrows, beans and peas	Control aphids. Maintain good hygiene and wash hands after handling an affected plant. Keep weeds at bay. Select resistant varieties. Destroy affected plants.	No chemical treatment
Damping off – young seedlings	Keep growing space well ventilated. Use clean pots and compost. Sow seeds sparsely and thin, holding the seedling by the leaves, as soon as you can. Avoid water on foliage in dull weather and late evening. If you can, water from below. Avoid overcrowding and remove affected parts.	Bordeaux mixture (or) – EIQ 62 Copper oxychloride – EIQ 30–50
Downy mildew (fuzzy, pale grey patches) – brassicas, lettuce, grapes, spinach, onions	Keep the garden tidy – spores overwinter in plant debris. Plant out good strong specimens. Ensure good air movement round plants. Do not wet leaves when watering. Destroy any affected parts.	No chemical controls permitted for amateurs.
Gooseberry mildew – gooseberries but affects blackcurrants too	Don't crowd plants. Prune well to aid air circulation. Feed with a balanced fertiliser. Remove and destroy affected parts. Plant resistant varieties.	Myclobutanil – EIQ 24 Sesame and fish oils (or) Sulphur (or) – EIQ 32 (NB some varieties will be damaged by sulphur.)
Onion white rot (fungus that eats bulbs and roots) – onions, garlic, leeks	Maintain crop rotation. Destroy affected plants. (This is a problem in cool wet climates so plants in Scotland are badly affected by it.)	No chemical treatment
Powdery mildew (white powder coating leaves) – apples, blackcurrants, gooseberries, grapes, courgettes, cucumbers, peas	Keep plants well watered but water from below. Don't overcrowd them. Destroy any affected parts. Plant resistant varieties.	Difenoconazole – EIQ 41 Myclobutanil – EIQ 24 Potassium bicarbonate – EIQ 8 Sulphur dust (or) – EIQ 32

(or = organic. For details about EIQ rating, see p. 66 – the higher the number, the more potentially harmful or dangerous is the substance.)

Problem and plants affected	Non-chemical and cultural controls	Chemical control
Rust (orange pustules) – leeks, currants	Select resistant varieties. Remove and destroy affected parts. Keep beds weed free. Rotate crops.	Bordeaux mixture (or) – EIQ 62 Difenoconazole – EIQ 41 Sulphur (or) – EIQ 33
Scab (worst in wet springs) – apples and pears	Do not grow fruit trees on badly drained soil. If feeding, select a balanced fertiliser. Select resistant cultivars. Remove and destroy all affected parts. Remove fallen leaves.	Bordeaux mixture (or) – EIQ 62 Difenoconazole – EIQ 41 Myclobutanil – EIQ 24 (Spray at bud burst to formation of first fruit.)
Silver leaf (silvery leaves and death of branches with affected branches stained inside) – plums, apples, apricots, cherries	Keep pruning tools clean. Destroy all affected branches. Do not leave wood debris lying around.	Paint pruning cuts with sealant.

Pests

Aphids (small green, grey or black insects that suck leaves on fruit and vegetables – leaves have crinkled appearance)	A fleece barrier will help. Start vegetables early and maybe in modules. Larger plants can stand any aphid attack better. Autumn plantings less prone to attack. Spray them off with a fine jet of water. Pinch out the tops of broad beans (*see* p. 156). Tidy up all brassica remains from the garden. Grow chives and *Limnanthes douglasii* (poached egg plant) to attract ladybirds and hoverflies. Companion plant French marigolds or nasturtiums. Grow *Plectranthus tomentosa* in the greenhouse (very soft so overwinter indoors). Biological controls (*see* p. 67). Use yellow sticky traps in the greenhouse but remove them if you introduce parasitic wasps.	Acetamiprid – EIQ 29 Deltamethrin – EIQ 28 Lambda cyhalothrin – EIQ 47 Plant oils (or) – EIQ 0–10 Pyrethrum (or) – EIQ 18 Soft/insecticidal soap (or) – EIQ 19 Thiacloprid – EIQ 31

(or = organic. For details about EIQ rating, see p. 66 – the higher the number, the more potentially harmful or dangerous is the substance.)

Problem and plants affected	Non-chemical and cultural controls	Chemical control
Cabbage root fly larvae (white maggots eat roots of brassicas and burrow into turnips, swedes, radishes)	Grow in large modules so plants have strong root system on planting out. Cover plants with fleece or mesh from at least mid spring to midsummer. Put collars of underlay or cardboard tightly around the stems. Crop rotation essential.	No chemical treatment
Carrot root fly – carrots but also affects parsnips, parsley and celery	Full details found under carrots on p. 244.	Lambda cyhalothrin – EIQ 47
Cabbage white caterpillar – brassicas	Cover your crops when you plant them out in late spring with fleece or mesh. Winter brassicas are usually not affected. Biological controls (*see* p. 67).	Acetamiprid – EIQ 29 Lambda cyhalothrin – EIQ 47 Pyrethrum (or) – EIQ 18 Thiacloprid – EIQ 31
Codling moth – apples and pears	Site bird boxes and hang bird food in winter to encourage natural predation. Biological controls (*see* p. 67).	Deltamethrin – EIQ 28 Lambda cyhalothrin – EIQ 47 Pheromone traps
Cutworm (roots severed below soil surface by creamy-brown caterpillars) – carrots, potatoes, cauliflowers, lettuces, leeks	Fine netting will prevent moths from attacking the plants, as will individual plastic bottle greenhouses. Water root crops heavily in summer to kill. Dig in winter to expose them to predators. Biological controls (*see* p. 67).	No chemical treatment
Flea beetle (mass of small holes in leaves) – brassicas, rocket, swedes, turnips	A fleece barrier or very fine mesh will prevent an attack. Frequent watering helps keep them at bay. Plant in to early summer to avoid them. Remove weeds to minimise overwintering opportunities.	Deltamethrin – EIQ 28 Lambda cyhalothrin – EIQ 47 Pyrethrum (or) – EIQ 18 Thiacloprid – EIQ 31 – on seedlings only
Onion fly (small maggots in bulbs) – onions, leeks, garlic	Destroy any affected plants. Cover bed with fleece. Use sets rather than seeds.	No chemical treatment

(or = organic. For details about EIQ rating, see p. 66 – the higher the number, the more potentially harmful or dangerous is the substance.)

Problem and plants affected	Non-chemical and cultural controls	Chemical control
Potato cyst eelworm	Use resistant varieties. Practise crop rotation. Discouraged by interplanting with French or African marigolds.	No chemical treatment
Raspberry beetle (larvae eat the ends of berries) – raspberries, brambles and hybrid berries	Try sticky traps.	Deltamethrin – EIQ 28 Pyrethrum (or) – EIQ 18 – sprayed as flowers go over. Once you see it, it is too late.
Red spider mite (tiny red insects on leaf undersides, indoors) – citrus, tomatoes, peaches	Keep your greenhouse clean, well ventilated and moist in hot weather. Put badly affected plants outside for the summer. Biological controls (*see* p. 67).	Acetamiprid – EIQ 29 Deltamethrin – EIQ 28) Fatty acids (or) – EIQ 5–10 Insecticidal soap (or) – EIQ 19 Lambda cyhalothrin – EIQ 47 Plant oils (or) – EIQ 0–10
Sawfly (strip leaves) – gooseberries, currants	Pick them off! Hang bird feeder nearby or sprinkle seeds and nuts below the bushes to attract natural predators – birds. Chickens below the trees will eat the larvae. Nematode – Nemasys Grow Your Own Pest Control	Lambda cyhalothrin – EIQ 47 Pyrethrum (or) – EIQ 18
Scale insect (small grey-white shells on leaf undersides) – indoor citrus, etc.	Biological controls (*see* p. 67).	Deltamethrin – EIQ 28 Fatty acids (or) – EIQ 5–10 Plant oils (or) – EIQ 0–10
Slugs and snails – young seedlings, mature leaves, anything really	Try a barrier, such as wood ash, crushed eggshell or sawdust, or traps, such as a dish of beer. Start vegetables early. Minimise hiding places by keeping garden tidy. Deterrent plants are said to be mint, chives, geraniums and fennel. Oat bran for them to eat apparently makes them bloat and die. Parasitic slug-destroying nematodes (*see* p. 67).	Aluminium sulphate (or) – EIQ 5 Ferric phosphate (or) – EIQ 5 Metaldehyde – EIQ 11

(or = organic. For details about EIQ rating, see p. 66 – the higher the number, the more potentially harmful or dangerous is the substance.)

Problem and plants affected	Non-chemical and cultural controls	Chemical control
Vine weevil (white grubs that eat roots) – strawberries, etc.	Beware of presents of strawberry runners from friends as they may have weevils in the soil. Commercial plants will be treated with insecticide. Kill adults at night by searching with a torch. Insect glue traps, biological controls (*see* p. 67).	Acetamiprid – EIQ 29 Thiacloprid – EIQ 31
Whitefly (sap-sucking white insect, mainly a problem indoors) – cucumbers, tomatoes, peppers	Biological controls, sticky traps (*see* p. 67).	Acetamiprid – EIQ 29 Deltamethrin – EIQ 28 Fatty acids (or) – EIQ 5–10 Insecticidal soap (or) – EIQ 19 Lambda cyhalothrin – EIQ 47 Plant oils (or) – EIQ 0–10
Wireworm – potatoes	Keep your ground well weeded. Dig soil in winter to expose them to predators. Crop early to limit damage.	Acetamiprid – EIQ 29 Deltamethrin – EIQ 28 Fatty acids (or) – EIQ 5–10 Insecticidal soap (or) – EIQ 19 Lambda cyhalothrin – EIQ 47 Plant oils (or) – EIQ 0–10

(or = organic. For details about EIQ rating, see p. 66 – the higher the number, the more potentially harmful or dangerous is the substance.)

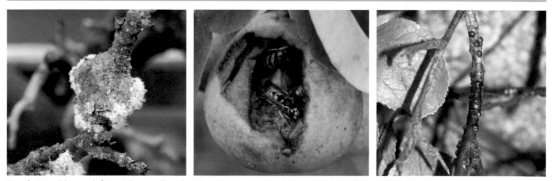

Tree fruit problems – left to right: woolly aphid (in winter), wasps and scale insect (hard to eradicate).

WEEDS

Vegetables are mostly shallow rooting, and they don't compete well with weeds, so take steps to keep the latter to a minimum. Prevention is better than cure, as a square metre of ground can contain up to 100,000 weed seeds. Perennial weeds such as ground elder, bindweed and brambles are a nightmare to remove in a plot full of plants, so it is far better to get rid of them before you start. The key is to kill or dig out the roots. If you don't, they'll simply re-sprout. Organic gardeners use old carpets and black polythene to cover weedy beds for long periods to starve perennial weeds of light and water. Sadly the worst perennial weeds can survive such treatment. Most chemical weed killers are no longer available to amateur gardeners, leaving Roundup, or glyphosate, as the main weapon against perennial weeds. It only works when plants are in active growth, so apply from March/April to October. It is neutralised in the soil soon after it is applied so you can safely sow as soon as the weeds have died back and you have removed them. You can use it amongst existing plants but make sure you keep the spray off any green parts of plants you want to keep. Cover them to be on the safe side. You may need to spray two or three times to get rid of the deepest-rooted and most persistent weeds such as ground elder, creeping buttercup and creeping thistle, which can spread underground. Painting glyphosate gel (Roundup) onto foliage is excellent for brambles and other weeds amongst plants you wish to keep. Mare's tail (*Equisetum arvense*) can survive almost anything and is perhaps the hardest weed of all to get rid of. It needs to be smashed and painted several times with neat glyophosate and even then it may bounce back. It can break concrete. A recent Greenpeace report (*see* bibliography) questions the safety of glyphosate so be aware that there may be dangers.

Annual weeds are easy to hoe or pull out but they can come up in their thousands, so you have to catch them before they bloom. I am amazed to see allotment holders tolerating abandoned weed-filled plots, with weed seeds blowing all over the place. Some of our worst weeds include thistles, bittercress, groundsel and chickweed, all of which flower and seed fast. Don't let this happen! Once you have a clean bed and are sowing and planting, a hoe is invaluable. It's best used in dry weather. Using it well takes a fair bit of practice – don't drag too much soil off and don't slice up your delicate young produce.

Mulching and growing green manures (*see* pp. 38 and 48) are other useful ways of reducing patches of bare earth and therefore keeping weeds to a minimum. Alternatively, cover temporarily uncultivated areas with three layers of old newspaper topped with grass clippings or cover with two layers of cardboard or black horticultural fabric.

HARDINESS AND HARDINESS RATINGS

Hardiness ratings are invaluable in choosing what to grow for local climate conditions and these are included for fruit and vegetable entries. Winter hardiness ratings are useful for trees, shrubs and perennial fruit and vegetables while, for annual vegetables, ratings can be used as a guide to when young plants can safely be planted outside. These ratings are adapted from those produced by the Royal Horticultural Society. I was a member of the RHS committee which revised these ratings in 2011 to make them more suitable for the whole of the UK, including Scotland. See p. 78.

EASE OF GROWING RATING E1–3

We have added an 'easiness rating' of E1–3 to give you a rough idea of how much effort each fruit and vegetable will take a beginner to grow. We have considered many aspects together to get our frankly fairly subjective rating – so ease of germination, cultural requirements, pest and disease problems, climatic sensitivity and productivity. The rating runs from 1 (very easy) to 2 (requires some care) through to 3 (quite challenging).

CHOOSING WHICH VARIETIES TO GROW

Under each vegetable entry we recommend some of the most popular and reliable varieties for Scotland. Many of these we have grown ourselves and we have received recommendations from gardeners all round Scotland. You'll find particular recommendations for cold, inland gardens, the Western Isles and Orkney and Shetland as these are some of the most

PLANT HARDINESS RATINGS		
H rating, H5 hardiest	**Fruit and perennial vegetables**	**Annual vegetables**
H5	Hardy throughout Scotland, the toughest-rated plants for the book. Extreme weather and wind can still damage plants. Minimum temperature -20°C.	Can be overwintered in the open, even in severest climates – kale, Brussels sprouts, parsnips, etc.
H4	Reliably hardy in most eastern gardens fairly near the coast or on hillsides – Perth, S Edinburgh, Tayside, Fife, Aberdeen, Inverness. Hardy in colder inland gardens except in severest winters; inland, frosted flowers may result in poor or no crops for fruit trees. Minimum temperature -15°C.	Young plants with some hardiness, so can be sown early. Harvesting possible throughout the winter in most areas, with crops such as winter brassicas and leeks.
H3	Hardy on west and south coast, in a sheltered site in most of coastal eastern and northern Scotland, N Edinburgh, mildest parts of Forth and Tay. Hardy plants may suffer winter wet or damage to unripened wood and damage may occur from early or late frosts or east winds. Minimum temperature -12°C.	Spring-sown vegetables need some protection from wind and cold in May. Suitable for harvesting into autumn except in cold snaps. Coastal gardens may be able to keep going well into winter. A little cloche/tunnel protection will be a benefit.
H2	Hardy over winter in mildest parts of west coast and west coast islands. May well grow in colder areas with protection. Minimum temperature -8°C.	Spring-sown vegetables for outside growing in the summer will need protection from frosts and cold winds. Peas, beans, etc. For annual crops, may tolerate near freezing temperatures if hardened off, but best with protection.
H1C (cool greenhouse)	Tender fruit and vegetables such as citrus need to be grown indoors in heated greenhouses. They can go outside in summer. Minimum temperature 0°C.	Basil, tomatoes, peppers, chillies. Greenhouse cultivation or artificial protection except in mildest parts of the country. Many H1C-rated plants can be grown outside in midsummer but they will probably yield better under glass or polythene.

challenging climates to garden in. There are so many vegetable varieties available that we could only list the most popular and the most successful ones; many others will probably grow perfectly well. Keep your options open and find out what friends and neighbours are having success with. The Award of Garden Merit ♀ symbol is the Royal Horticultural Society's award for the best performing plant varieties. Bear in mind that this is generally evaluated for growing in England and not Scotland, although it remains a valuable guide.

You'll find lots of Scottish growers and experts quoted in the text. We list them in the bibliography and acknowledgements.

FRUIT

Fife fruit expert Willie Duncan with his apple display, Glendoick Apple Weekend.

Our prehistoric ancestors gathered blueberries and nuts from the moors and forests. Later on, they learned to make alcohol from wild fruits and to dry them for eating in winter. A hundred and fifty years ago, before sugar became generally affordable, fruit was one of the few sources of sweetness for the majority of Scotland's population. The nineteenth and early twentieth centuries saw the peak of Scotland's commercial fruit production while, more recently, Scotland has become a world centre of soft fruit breeding, particularly for raspberries and blackcurrants. A recent resurgence of interest in heritage fruit varieties has led to the setting-up of several collections of Scottish-bred fruit trees and the formation of local apple/orchard groups which hold fruit festivals, juicing days, grafting and pruning workshops and identification displays. Organisations such as Common Ground, the Commonwealth/Child-

ren's Orchard, based in Glasgow, and Abundance, in Edinburgh, have encouraged school and community orchards to be planted the length and breadth of Scotland with, for example, at least 20 in Fife alone. However, while gardeners in larger numbers than ever grow fruit, the commercial fruit sector is in a precarious state, having become over-dependent on strawberries and raspberries and been battered by severe weather and unreasonable supermarket terms. Growers need to innovate with more profitable crops and to add value by processing them locally. Why does the UK import 80 per cent of its blueberries when they can be grown very well in Scotland, for example? Devon-based Martin Crawford's Agroforestry Research Trust, run on a shoestring budget, has produced exemplary and exhaustive publications on both well-known and obscure fruit and nut crops, many of which may have potential in Scotland.

Fruit grows better on the eastern side of Scotland, where the rainfall is lower, than on the west. Where rainfall is above 1000mm per year, fruit diseases, such as canker, scab and mould, make commercial and amateur fruit growing more of a challenge. Much of western Scotland receives up to double this rainfall. The further north you go or the higher the altitude of your site, the more shelter is required. North of Aberdeen, away from the favourable Moray Firth, tree fruit is best grown on walls. Boggy, acidic peaty soil is not suitable for most fruit either and wind presents another challenge. Good drainage and careful selection of varieties are the key. Tunnel-house growing provides the best conditions for many fruit on the west coast.

All fruit is good for you but there are some which have significant health benefits, not yet fully understood by scientists. These so-called fruit 'superfoods' contain the largest concentrations of antioxidants, measured by the oxygen radical absorption capacity (ORAC) value. Top of the charts are chokeberries (*Aronia*), prunes, raisins, blueberries, brambles (blackberries), strawberries and raspberries. Dark (but not milk) chocolate scores very highly too, which you might be pleased to hear. It is

Fruit cage, Culzean walled garden Ayrshire.

worth stressing that picking early and ripening artificially, processing, cooking and pasteurising all reduce beneficial properties, so fruit is best eaten fresh and therefore grown locally. Home-grown fruit can be picked at the optimum time, eaten straight off the tree or bush and usually has little or no pesticide residue. Some of the fruit which grows best in Scotland – rhubarb, gooseberries, currants and Scottish-bred apples – are seldom offered by supermarkets. What's more, fruit trees and bushes are often ornamental, both at blossom time in spring and when laden with fruit in summer and autumn. As well as the fruit trees discussed in this section, Scotland boasts rowans, hawthorns, sloes, roses and other native trees and shrubs which produce fruit and hips that not only feed birds in the autumn but can also be made into jellies and drinks.

When planning your fruit garden or plot, bear in mind that some crops will need to be protected against birds, so it is useful to plant soft fruit in a block where it can be caged and to plant plums and cherries on a wall or fence where they can be easily netted. Lowest growing fruit (strawberries, gooseberries, etc.) should be planted on the south side of a plot, with the taller (raspberries, brambles and fruit trees) at the north side so that all receive maximum direct sunshine. For wall cultivation, south- and west-facing walls are best for fruit. East-facing walls are not ideal but are suitable for tougher and later-flowering fruit such as apples. Few fruit do really well on north-facing walls due to cold and lack of sunshine. If you only have a north wall, try cooking apples, gooseberries and currants. And, of course, trained trees and bushes add structure and shape to the garden on walls, over pergolas and along fences.

CHAPTER 1

Tree or Stone Fruit

Apple blossom bee pollination.

Willie Duncan festooning apples. Bend and tie down a long whippy shoot back to the main stem to encourage bud breaking and new growth along the branch.

Apples, pears, plums and cherries, known as tree or stone fruit, can all be excellent in Scotland as long as you follow a few basic rules and choose the best varieties for your local conditions. Many fruit varieties won't fruit well in Scotland, while others seem to do better in one part of the country than another. Tree fruit growing is possible in all areas with careful selection of scab-resistant varieties. Peaches and apricots will only fruit reliably in the warmest and most sheltered south-facing sites.

TREE FRUIT POLLINATION

Plums and many cherries are self-fertile but most apples and pears require a different variety as a pollination partner to ensure good fruit set. Pollinating insects fly from tree to tree carrying pollen from the stamens (male) of one tree to the stigma (female) of another. How far away the pollinating tree can be depends on temperature and wind. Warm temperatures encourage pollinating insects to fly further. In a mild spring, pollen may be carried up to two miles, while in cold weather, insects are less inclined to fly. Garden tree fruit is pollinated by flies and wild bees as well as honeybees. Some fruit varieties need more pollination than others and there is no doubt that the more varieties you have, the better the pollination will be. There are a few 'triploid' pears and apples such as 'Bramley' whose pollen won't pollinate other apples and so require two other compatible varieties to ensure all three are pollinated. Frost pockets and very exposed sites tend to suffer from poor fruit set due to poor pollination. Former Royal Horticultural Society (RHS) fruit expert Harry Baker reports that most fruit blossom is destroyed at temperatures lower than -2°C.

ROOTSTOCKS, PRUNING AND PLANTING

Almost all tree fruit is grafted onto selected rootstocks that will determine the size and vigour of the tree. You should find the rootstock used listed on the fruit tree label. Many rootstocks were developed at the East Malling Research Station in Kent and so are prefixed by the letter M – for example, M26. Dwarfing and semi-dwarfing rootstocks are ideal for containers and small gardens. You'll find these discussed in more detail under the fruit entries below. Another space-saving idea, apple and pear 'family trees', have two or more varieties grafted onto a single stem. You need to be vigilant in pruning these to prevent the most vigorous variety/ies from overwhelming the others. You can take the family tree idea a lot further – the BBC's *Gardeners' World* showed Paul Barnett's single-trunk apple with 250 varieties grafted onto its branches. Fife fruit expert Willie Duncan likes to graft new varieties onto the lower branches of his older trees.

All fruit trees should be staked when young, until the trunk is strong enough to withstand wind and the weight of heavy fruiting. Trees on dwarfing rootstocks need permanent staking or support on wires as they don't develop a robust trunk or root system. On windy sites, use a stout stake with the base 30–50cm into the ground. The stake should be placed on the side of the tree from where the prevailing wind blows (usually south-westerly). When trees are young, they are best staked at around 75–100cm high, tied below the lowest set of side branches. On windy sites, tie higher up or use more than one tie. Use rubber ties which can be loosened as trees

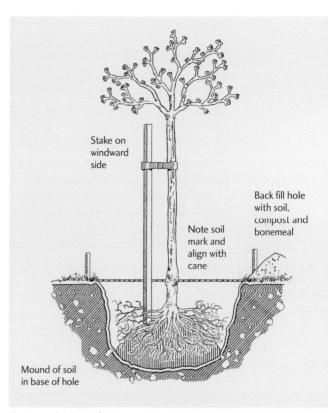

Planting and staking a fruit tree.

Staking fruit and nut trees, essential for all but the most sheltered sites.

83

mature and which are unlikely to cause bark rubbing. It is important to keep the union where the graft was made above soil level. Consider additional shelter while the tree is establishing and bear in mind that, in the longer term, fruit trees require a certain amount of wind shelter for pollination and to hold fruit on the tree. Most trees, these days, are planted from containers in early spring or autumn. Autumn is best of all as it allows plenty of time for roots to start establishing before young growth starts. Summer planting is fine, as long as you can keep the newly planted tree watered in dry periods. Avoid pot-bound trees, as they will be slow to establish. If you want to plant a substantial orchard, it is cheaper to buy bare-rooted trees in the winter from a specialist grower, usually available from late November to early spring. Unless the area is deer and rabbit proof, you would be advised to put tree guards on young fruit trees to prevent barking, particularly in cold winters. To keep weeds down and retain moisture, you can use weed mats or a good layer of mulch around each tree. Once the trees mature you can spray with herbicide around the base but try to avoid any weed-killer drift on to the trunk or foliage. Traditionally, livestock would graze

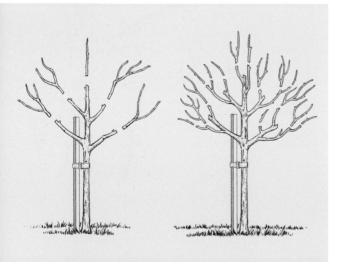

Pruning a young bush fruit tree for the first few years after planting to maintain a tidy open shape.

under fruit to keep the grass down and the trees manured.

PRUNING TREE FRUIT

Fruit trees are structural plants which provide features in the garden, whether free-standing or trained on a wall or wires. It is therefore desirable to prune them in a way which is both pleasing to the eye and productive, as well as to keep the tree within the space that is allocated to it. As long as you follow some basic principles, you should not go far wrong. For complex pruning, it is worth investing in a specialist fruit book. A mature fruit tree will probably produce more fruit than you can eat, so you don't have to prune perfectly – there is considerable margin for error. For a standard bush apple or pear, when trees are young, pruning is done to create a balanced goblet-shaped head on the tree. Subsequent pruning is used to keep the tree in bounds, to thin out congested, damaged or diseased shoots and to rejuvenate it if yields are reducing. Apples and pears can be pruned at any time, but it is usually done in midsummer or winter. Winter was the traditional pruning time, when the tree was dormant and gardeners had time spare. Advantages of summer pruning are that wounds heal quickly, growth can be restricted and you can thin and/or remove diseased fruit at the same time.

Tree nurseryman John Butterworth of Ayrshire advocates winter pruning for young trees, while Nick Dunn, of top English fruit growers Frank Mathews, is happy to prune in summer or winter. Nick gave us a simple and effective masterclass on pruning young apple and pear trees, which is detailed here. His advice assumes that you are starting with a two- to three-year-old, spur-bearing apple or pear tree, known as a maiden whip – the size of tree typically sold in garden centres. Stone fruit trees (cherries, plums, etc.) should only be lightly pruned in late spring or summer – avoid autumn or winter pruning, which can let in disease.

PRUNING BASICS

1. Cut tidily and don't leave snags.
2. Horizontal branches fruit better than vertical ones.
3. Remove a dominant leader (strongest shoot) so that five to six side branches form the structure of the tree.
4. In summer, pinch out or prune back the growing tips of any long growth extensions to half or one-third their length to encourage shoots from side buds which will bear fruit the following year. This is particularly important with really vigorous apple varieties such as 'Bramley', to avoid a gaunt-looking, leggy mature tree. Willie Duncan suggests 'festooning' (see picture, p. 82) as an alternative – that is, bending leggy shoots down and back towards the main trunk and tying them to it. This encourages several fruiting spurs along the branches and later you can prune the leggy tip off.
5. Remove any damaged or diseased branches back to wood which is green rather than brown inside.
6. Keep an open, uncongested tree with plenty of room for fruit, so remove one of any pair of branches that are too close together and remove any crossing branches that might rub. Leave branches which will grow into space and remove those which are growing into other branches.
7. Don't leave too many fruiting spurs on each branch – every 10cm is close enough. Remove every second one if they are overcrowded.
8. To keep a clean trunk, take off any lower branches that are tending to bend down towards the ground.
9. Thin clusters of fruit to one or two so that branches are not broken by the weight. For the first year or two, it is better to remove most fruit to encourage growth. If you leave too much fruit on the tree, it may not bear fruit the following year.
10. Tip bearers – a few apples and pears are tip bearers. The only variety recommended in this book is the pear 'Jargonelle'. In this case, you need to remove long shoots on only part of the tree each year so that the following year's fruit can form on the ends of the branches.
11. Apples or pears on dwarfing rootstocks such as M27 should be only lightly trimmed unless they start to become misshapen.

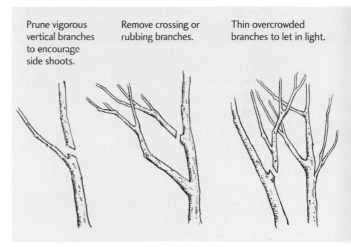

Prune vigorous vertical branches to encourage side shoots.

Remove crossing or rubbing branches.

Thin overcrowded branches to let in light.

Tree fruit pruning: select the outward pointing branch of a pair to keep; also remove crossing or over-crowded branches.

As overcrowded fruiting spurs can weaken the tree, remove some of them, particularly those which are weak or misshapen.

OLD OR NEGLECTED TREES

Pears can live for hundreds of years and apples for over one hundred, so you often inherit old trees when you buy a house and garden. First ascertain if a tree is diseased or healthy. Diseased parts are often warty and produce little or no young growth. Remove the dead wood and see what you are left with. What remains may not be worth saving but old trees can be remarkably productive despite the ravages of time, even if, at first, they seem beyond redemption. Give them a chance before cutting them down. The branches of old trees tend to be congested, so thin them out over one to three years, leaving 60cm or so between main branches. 'Festooning' or tying down long whippy shoots should encourage lots of vigorous new growth, as will feeding your trees. You can use old stumps or trunks of reasonably healthy trees to graft new varieties, so don't be too quick to dig them out. You may need to remove some trees if they are overcrowded but try to taste the fruit first to see which ones to keep, and beware of cutting down your pollinators.

TRAINING TREE FRUIT

Gardeners have trained, clipped and preened their fruit trees for years, with styles and shapes changing from era to era according to fashions. Much of Scotland's most successful fruit is trained on walls, which provide reflected warmth, support and protection from cold, wind and frost. You'll find examples in many of Scotland's walled gardens – espaliers at Castle Fraser in Aberdeenshire and step-overs trained horizontally, low to the ground, at nearby Fyvie Castle, for example. Alec West and Pat Watson's walled garden at Anton's Hill near Coldstream is a masterful demonstration of cordons trained against wire fences. Alec has propagated and trained his own trees over 15 years, resulting in a collection of 240 apple varieties, as well as a good range of pears. Trained fruit does require quite

Cordon apples, Anton's Hill, a walled garden in Berwickshire.

precise annual summer and/or winter pruning to maintain the neat shapes and to produce ample young wood which will bear fruit. You can buy a partially trained tree, usually at some expense or, if up for a challenge, you can start training fruit trees by either grafting your own onto rootstocks or buying maiden whips (young trees).

Cordons are an excellent way of training apples and pears to fit several varieties into a small space. A single stem is trained to have short fruiting spurs along its length. Cordons can be grown vertically but they are more commonly grown at around a 45° angle from vertical, against a wall or supported by a series of horizontal wires. To create and maintain cordons, summer prune all lateral shoots from the main stem/trunk to 7–10cm or three buds in length. From these, further shoots will grow, which should be cut back to 3cm to the first 'true' bud. Once the cordon reaches the desired height, the leader should be pruned back to 1–2m long in late spring or early summer. It is possible to grow two (or more) cordons off a single trunk, grown like the shape of a letter 'Y'.

Fans are as they sound – trained in a flat fan

shape and usually grown against a wall or fence. Most wall-grown cherries, peaches and apricots are trained in this manner. To fan-train a young tree, remove the leader and all but two side branches, which are trained left and right. From these will come the subsequent network of branches. A network of canes is normally used to train the branches.

Espaliers have two to four or more sets of horizontal branches trained along wires on a wall or fence. Though this takes some work to achieve, the results are stylish and yields are good, as the restrictive pruning allows plenty of light into all the forming fruit. Each tier is usually trained to 40–60cm apart, so a 1.2m wall or fence can support two tiers and a 2–3m wall or fence four to five tiers. Start creating the lowest tier by training horizontal branches. It can take three to four years to create three tiers. Damon Powell prunes Castle Fraser's excellent espaliers in both winter and summer. The horizontal branches of espaliers produce numerous vertical shoots in summer which should be pruned in August–September back to 3cm or so. The leaders at the ends of each horizontal branch need to be tied into the training wires. Once they have reached the desired length, they can be pruned back each year in late spring. Gordon Castle near Fochabers has 249 espalliered fruit trees in its 8-acre walled garden.

Step-overs are dwarf espaliers with a single set of low horizontal branches. These can be used to edge parterres or borders. There are good examples of step-over apples at Fyvie Castle in Aberdeenshire and at Dunrobin Castle on the coast of Sutherland, where they line some of the parterres. John and Sara Hulbert have a dense low hedge of step-over apples along the front of their house in Longforgan near Dundee.

There are lots of other complex pruning shapes you can try to attain. The more elaborate forms are suitable for apples and pears only. Complex training and pruning is not advisable for stone fruit (plums, peaches, etc.) as any cuts made provide potential entry points for potentially fatal bacterial or fungal disease. For shaping and controlling stone fruit, such as cherries and peaches, Willie Duncan advises tying

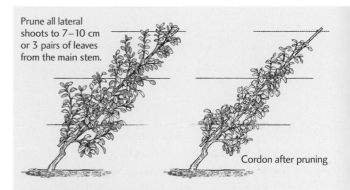

Prune all lateral shoots to 7–10 cm or 3 pairs of leaves from the main stem.

Cordon after pruning

Summer pruning of a Cordon Apple.

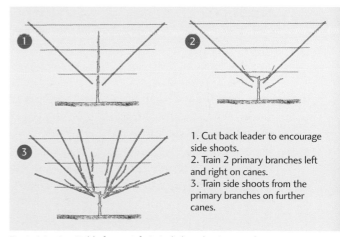

Some of Scotland's finest espaliered apples at Castle Fraser, Aberdeenshire. They are pruned twice a year to keep the neat shape.

1. Cut back leader to encourage side shoots.
2. Train 2 primary branches left and right on canes.
3. Train side shoots from the primary branches on further canes.

Fan-training is suitable for most fruit, including cherries, peaches and apricots.

Young espaliered apples, Frank Matthews Nursery in Worcestershire.

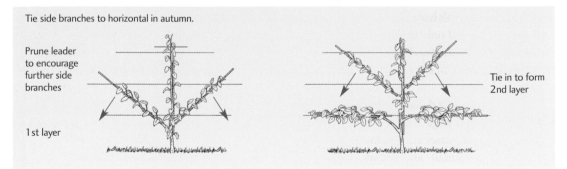

Tie side branches to horizontal in autumn.

Prune leader to encourage further side branches

1st layer

Tie in to form 2nd layer

Training an Espalier. Tie in selected branches to horizontal wires over several years, starting at the bottom.

in branches rather than pruning. He showed me his tunnel house of cherries trained in this way. Many of the Victorian fruit manuals have wonderful drawings of the most elaborate training regimes, some of which look scarcely credible. Such pruning is still being done – Floors Castle's French goblet-style trained apples, for example. The RHS garden at Wisley in Surrey has excellent demonstrations of pruning shapes, including an apple and pear pergola/arched walkway.

COMMON PROBLEMS

The fungal disease **scab** is the scourge of apple and pear growing in Scotland. It causes unsightly greyish-black blisters/pustules on the leaves and branches and spots on the fruit itself. It is worst in wet areas (the west coast) and during wet springs and early summers. If you want clean fruit, stick to the most disease-resistant varieties or spray preventatively against scab from when new growth appears

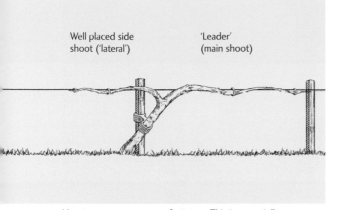

How to create a step-over fruit tree. This is essentially a one-layer espalier but using the leader and one lateral shoot to form a single tier.

Step-over apple, a single-tiered low espalier at Willowhill, Fife. This method of pruning is ideal for small gardens and for edging borders.

until May–June. Once you see the scab, you are probably too late to do much about it, so prevention is the key. Organic gardeners can use copper and sulphur sprays, but they'd be better off selecting scab-resistant varieties. Many of the most effective chemical scab controls have been removed from the amateur market and only myclobutanil is left. In a wet spring, it is worth spraying as flowers finish and fruit begins to form. In dry springs, this may not be needed.

The sometimes fatal disease of **bacterial canker** affects plums and **fungal canker** can affect apples and pears. These diseases are also most prevalent in areas of high rainfall and/or sites with poor drainage. In the west, it is advisable to select disease-resistant varieties. **Fireblight**, another fatal disease, is now affecting apples and pears in parts of the UK. It is not yet a significant problem in Scotland but climate change suggests that it will become more of an issue. **Brown rot** is when the whole fruit turns into a mouldy brown shrunken mess and is worst on apples. There are no preventative sprays for this, so it is best to destroy all infected fruit to try to break the infection cycle.

Codling moth can be a problem on apples in some areas of Scotland. The larvae burrow into the fruit and eat them as they grow. **Woolly aphids** feed on apple trees around young shoots and pruning scars, leaving woolly patches which can turn into hard galls. Dr Hessayon suggests using methylated spirits on an old toothbrush to remove them, while gardener and broadcaster Stefan Buczacki suggests pruning off all the galls where the aphids overwinter, to break the cycle. **Aphid** damage can be an entry point for canker. Tar oil, long used as a winter wash to kill insect eggs, is no longer legally available and the winter wash containing plant oils is less effective, as it only works on contact with the eggs. Jeyes Fluid and Armillatox were commonly used for this purpose and are still sold for other uses but, if you use them as garden pesticides, you now break the law. Grease bands on young trees and sticky fruit tree grease on older trees are used to prevent crawling insect pests from climbing the trees in autumn, winter and spring where they may lay their eggs. Apply round the trunk above the height of surrounding weeds and grass in November and renew in February, if required.

You will find a range of apples, pears, plums and cherries at most garden centres. The selection of varieties offered by some of the chains is often not suitable for Scotland – for example, if you see 'Cox's

Above. Apple scab is an unsightly and serious problem in wet weather and on the western side of Scotland. Select scab-resistant varieties.

Left. With bacterial canker on plums – sudden summer dieback like this is typical. Cut out all dead branches back to green wood and hope for the best, but it is usually fatal.

Orange Pippin' offered for sale, then walk away and go somewhere else with a better informed plant buyer. There are also some excellent mail order nurseries which list heritage and hard-to-find varieties. Try Blackmoor, Keepers Nursery, Plants and Apples in Perthshire and Brogdale (*see* p. 286).

Apple (*Malus domestica*) H4–5 E1

APPLE HISTORY

> I have never met anyone who does not like an apple.
>
> Nigel Slater

> There is no fruit . . . so universally esteemed . . . or any so closely identified with the social habits of the human species as the apple.
>
> Dr Robert Hogg, *The Apple*, 1851

Apples got Adam and Eve kicked out of Eden, one caused the Trojan wars, one was split by William Tell's crossbow while another caused Isaac Newton's 'gravity moment'. Can any other fruit compete in myth and history? The apple has long-proven versatility for humans, fresh or cooked, with long storage qualities when fresh or dried, turned into juice and with numerous products of fermentation (cider) and distillation (calvados). Exploited by many cultures over centuries, there are now more than 7,000 named varieties. And, of course, they are very good for you, with research suggesting that apples can reduce the risk of heart disease, diabetes, Alzheimer's, colon cancer and asthma. Apples are an ideal complement to so many foods and flavours – pork, blackberries, cheese, nuts, cinnamon, nutmeg, custard . . .

Though crab apples are native to the UK, eating apples are thought to be descended from *Malus sieversii*, which is found in the Tian Shan Mountains in Central Asia. As traders between East and West passed though this region, apples were carried into Europe and they gradually spread around the Persian, Greek and Roman Empires. Roman historian Pliny describes over 20 apple types in his *Natural History* of the first century AD and mentions the storage properties of different varieties. The Romans are thought to have established the first British orchards in Kent, and the fruit spread around their settlements in Britain. British apple growing declined after the Romans left and it was the Normans who rekindled an appetite for them. John Parkinson describes 60 varieties in *Theatrum Botanicum* (1640) and, by the late eighteenth century, there were hundreds of apple varieties with confused and duplicate naming. Something needed to be done to sort out the mess. A trial garden was founded in Chiswick, London, in the 1820s while, simultaneously, the Royal Caledonian Horticultural Society (the Caley) began an experimental orchard at the Royal Botanic Garden Edinburgh in 1824, importing the latest commercial varieties from Europe and North America to assess their suitability for Scotland. In 1885, the Caley held its first apple 'congress' of experts to help expand Scottish production. Perhaps the greatest Victorian apple authority was Robert Hogg, who was born in Duns, Berwickshire. His classic work *The Fruit Manual*, first published in 1860 and revised in 1884, is still quoted by present-day apple gurus.

It is impossible to say when the first eating apples were grown in Scotland, but it is a fair guess that it would have happened in the grounds of one of the great Cistercian abbeys and monasteries with French connections. Until the nineteenth century, most apples grown in Britain would have been seed-raised, hard knobbly fruit fit for animal feed, cooking or making into cider. Occasional fine seedlings would be given names, usually after the place they were found – 'Arbroath Pippin', 'Port Allen Russet', 'Galloway Pippin'. Skilled propagators would graft them onto apple seedling rootstocks.

Apples are well suited to Scotland and, 100 years ago, they were an important commercial crop in the Carse of Gowrie in the east and the Clyde Valley in the west. Commercial apples saw gradual decline throughout the twentieth century and most of the significant Scottish orchards have now gone. Common Ground's orchard survey calculated that

Apple 'Discovery' is perhaps the number one eating apple for Scotland. Early ripening, it does not store well but it is prolific, sweet and very ornamental.

64 per cent of UK orchard acreage was lost between 1970 and 1997. The old orchards that are left are a significant biodiversity resource, providing habitats for insects, birds, bats and other wildlife. Sadly, few Scottish apples are put to commercial use these days apart from at farmers' markets. Ron and Judith Gillies at Cairn o' Mohr in the Carse of Gowrie produce apple juice and cider from local apples, while Thistly Cross Cidershed near Dunbar, East Lothian, produces cider from Lothian and Borders apples. UK-wide, more than 70 per cent of apples on sale – a market worth £320 million annually – are now grown abroad and imported. Many American- and Australian-raised varieties, such as 'Golden Delicious' and 'Granny Smith', are unsuited to growing in the Scottish climate. Clearly there is potential for UK growers to gain some of this market, but only if the supermarkets pursue a more broadminded and locally based apple purchasing policy. Why aren't Scottish-grown 'Discovery' apples on sale country-wide in September?

SITE, SOIL AND PLANTING

To be successful in Scotland, an apple needs to be able to set fruit and ripen at relatively low light levels and cool summer temperatures. Many varieties fit the bill but equally many don't. John Butterworth reports considerable regional variations in where apples grow best – 'Galloway Pippin' seems to grow best in the south-west, for example. This variation is not surprising if you consider that the difference in summer temperatures between the north coast of Scotland and the Borders can be as much as that between the Borders and London. Apples need a reasonably sheltered site in fertile, well-drained soil. Feed them for the first few years and mulch with rotted manure if you have access to it. Don't over-feed, as they'll just produce leaves and few fruit. For the first few years, don't let thick grass grow around the trunk. Once the tree is well established, grass won't do any harm.

Named apple varieties cannot be grown from apple pips and must be propagated by vegetative techniques, usually grafted or budded onto a root-stock. Space does not permit the detailed information required on grafting apples – we recommend attending one of the courses run by fruit groups or consult the bibliography.

APPLE ROOTSTOCKS

Apples are grafted onto a variety of rootstocks which affect vigour and ultimate size. You should find the rootstock number on the plant label. The most common are:

- MM106 Medium–large tree, 3–5m in 10–20 years. Needs staking as a young plant but then self-supporting. If you want a significant crop and have the space, this is the one to go for.
- M26 Semi-dwarf, grows to 2–3m. A good choice for a smallish garden as you can get impressive yields on a small tree. It needs to be well staked or grown against a wall.
- M27 This is widely marketed as a very dwarfing rootstock, designed for a small sheltered garden or pot. I have reservations about this rootstock,

as does John Butterworth. M27 trees are essentially deliberate 'runts': weak, fastidious as to soil conditions, easily broken by wind and inclined to produce smaller underwhelming fruit, and they cannot tolerate drying out either, which is not ideal for container growing. Fyvie Castle has some good examples of bush apples and trained step-over apples on M27 in a sheltered walled garden, so they can be grown well in Scotland in good conditions. Nick Dunn recommends M27 to keep the rampant 'Bramley' to a more managable size. Coronet Apples on M27 rootstocks, pruned like bonsais in production, to create a permanently small tree which is suitable for growing in containers.

CULTIVATION, HARVESTING AND STORAGE

To increase fruit size, decrease disease and encourage annual fruit bearing, it is advisable to thin fruit, particularly when trees are young – indeed, most authorities advise removing all fruit for the first year or two. Overcrowded or misshapen fruit can be removed three to six weeks after flowering; aim to leave two fruits per cluster. The earlier this is done, the larger the remaining fruit will become. Cooking apples can be thinned to 15–22cm apart on the branch. Alternatively, thin fruit after the June (or July in the far north) drop, when some fruit naturally falls off the tree. This is nature's own method of conserving energy and not exhausting the tree in overproduction. At Glendoick, we never get round to thinning our old apple trees and this results in small fruit although little reduction in flavour.

Some apples store better than others. Early ripeners like 'Discovery' don't keep, while mid-season to late varieties generally keep longer – 'Fiesta' and 'Egremont Russet' are said to be amongst the best. In ideal conditions, some apples will store until April. Choose apples that are unblemished to store. They should be kept in a cool, dark, frost-free place, not touching one another, so as to maintain good

An apple store with traditional wooden slatted trays at Philiphaugh, Hawick, in the Borders.

air circulation and reduce rot. Some people wrap them in paper. Traditionally, storage is done with wooden apple trays which can be stacked, allowing air circulation above and below the fruit. Many Scottish walled gardens boast attractive apple stores. My favourite is the Robert Lorimer design at Earlshall in Fife, with stone monkeys on the roof.

APPLE VARIETIES

At least 2,000 named apple varieties are known to exist in the UK and there is a national resurgence of interest in heritage varieties, encouraged by local fruit groups and organisations such as Common Ground. We are grateful to Scotland's many fruit experts for invaluable advice, particularly retired fruit nurseryman John Butterworth and Fife fruit expert Willie Duncan. George Anderson and apple collector Alec West from Coldstream have also given invaluable advice. I could not resist quoting nurseryman David Storrie's often grumpy 1950s assessments. His nursery was at Glendoick, near Perth. Harry Baker, former Royal Horticultural Society fruit officer, offers much wise advice too.

The renewed interest in old apple varieties is heartening and many enthusiasts are now propagating local and little-known apples which are seldom available commercially. Romantic though it would be to plant a new orchard of old local apples, it is necessary to warn that many of these varieties were mainly used for cider, cooking and animal fodder. Some may taste good on the right day but few are high yielding, disease resistant or store for long. Journalist Ursula Buchan has described 'heritage apple snobbery', where gardeners outdo one another in planting orchards of only ancient local apple varieties. If you have space, then by all means plant these as part of an orchard or collection, but look beyond heritage varieties if you want a reliable crop of disease-resistant and storable fruit. If you only have room for two or three apple trees, then I'd strongly suggest choosing modern heavy-fruiting and scab-resistant cultivars. Identifying apple varieties is a challenge and few are up to the task. Try the apple displays at some local fruit groups' autumn apple days. Rosie Sanders' *The Apple Book* has excellent botanical drawings of most of the most commonly grown varieties and the website www.orangepippin.com is very useful. The National Fruit Collection at Brogdale offers an identification service.

Eaters (also called dessert apples) are sweet to taste when ripe, whereas cookers are sourer, needing sugar when eaten and usually used to make baked apples, pies and crumbles. Early-ripening varieties are usually ready in August/September in Scotland; the remainder ripen in October and some can remain on the tree until November or even December if the weather is not too cold. If you have space, go for a mix of ripening times and a split of cookers and eaters. If the weather turns cold early, later-ripening varieties may not have time to fully develop their best flavour. Varieties marked **R** are the most resistant to scab disease. For organic gardening and for the western half of Scotland where rainfall is higher, we'd recommend these. Varieties marked ⋈ were bred in Scotland. The number in the square brackets is the pollination group, with [1] the earliest, towards the end of April, and [6] the latest, into June. Actual flowering times vary according to

Some of the most popular apple varieties (left to right, top to bottom): 'Ashmead's Kernal', 'Bramley', 'Ellison's Orange', 'Fiesta', 'James Grieve', 'Katy', 'King of the Pippins', 'Limelight', 'Lord Derby', 'Scrumptious', 'Sunset', 'Worcester Permain'.

Scottish apples: 'Arbroath Osslin', 'Bloody Ploughman', 'Cambusnethan Pippin', 'Galloway Pippin', 'Hawthornden', 'Hood's Supreme', 'Lass of Gowrie', 'Lord Rosebery', 'Port Allan Russet', Scotch Dumpling, 'Stobo Castle', 'Thorle Pippin'.

weather/season and location. Cold springs and higher altitudes mean later flowering and mild springs may bring flowering forward to mid April onwards. Varieties with adjacent numbers will normally pollinate one another – [3] with [4], for example. Crab apples can also be used as pollinators. For hardiness, assume apples are H4–5. Exceptions are marked H5 (hardiest) and H4 (less hardy, needing a warm, sheltered site).

APPLE VARIETIES

'Ashmead's Kernel' ♀ R (eater) *H4* English, dating back to 1700, a growers' favourite with russeted green-yellow fruit and a really good, sharp 'pear drops' flavour. John Butterworth says that it needs a sheltered, sunny site to produce good mature fruit in Scotland and it fruits erratically at best. Alec West at Anton's Hill reckons it is one of the best eating apples for the Borders and George Anderson is a fan for the Lothians. 'Munch with a wedge of cheddar' (Nigel Slater). Pick in October; it stores a long time. [4]

'Blenheim Orange' ♀ (eater) A triploid, so needs two pollinator partners. Large orange and green Cox-like fruit high in vitamin C and very good for tarte tatin. Sets fruit somewhat erratically. [3]

'Bloody Ploughman' ✉ (eater) Raised at Megginch in the Carse of Gowrie in the 1880s, is a striking and handsome dark-red variety which makes a fine ornamental when in fruit. Sadly, when you bite into it, it does not taste of much. It is best in east Scotland, as it is prone to scab in the west (John Butterworth). It was apparently named after a ploughman who was caught stealing the apples and was shot by a gamekeeper. I have seen good yields on this at Culross Palace and Anton's Hill and it does well at Fyvie in Aberdeenshire and in the Walled Garden at Murray Royal Hospital in Perth, but we have found it slow to start producing fruit. It should

apparently have red flesh but there is another form around with green flesh. [3]

'Bramley's Seedling' ♀ (cooker) Large green-yellow apples; this is a great 'tank' of an apple, very vigorous and leggy. The classic baked apple variety, it takes a while to produce its enormous heavy fruit and, though pollinated by others, it does not pollinate in its turn, so you need to grow two other varieties to ensure that all are pollinated. Nick Dunn recommends growing this on dwarfing rootstock such as M26 or M27, even in a larger garden. Jeremy Gilchrist does not recommend 'Bramley' in the Clyde Valley due to scab susceptibility. 'Grenadier' and 'Lord Derby' are better choices for western Scotland. [3] **'Bramley Clone 20'** A little less vigorous and higher yielding; Jim McColl and Nick Dunn recommend it.

'Cambusnethan Pippin' ✉ R (eater) According to David Storrie, 'an excellent scab-free dessert apple', popular in both the east and the west, raised in Clyde Valley or Stirling and a popular Clyde Valley orchard choice. Tender and juicy with mild acidity. [4–5]

'Catshead' (cooker) An old box-shaped green cooking apple, found in many collections, which ripens in October and stores for several months. [3]

'Charles Ross' ♀ R (eater/cooker) Charles Ross was the head gardener at Dalmeny near Edinburgh before he moved south. A versatile orange-red apple, it is good in Scotland, stores well and is good for cooking as well as eating. John Hancox recommends it for juicing. A good choice for the Borders, where it is widely planted. It is also good for coastal gardens, though George Anderson thinks it a bit temperamental. [3]

'Chivers Delight' (eater) Sweet honey flavour; Willie Duncan's choice for flavour and good storage. Good for juicing too. [4]

Columnar Apples These apples originated at East Malling in Kent and have been marketed under several names, including 'Ballerina'. They have a columnar habit to 2–3m, with little or no side branching, and are a possible choice for the smaller garden in eastern Scotland. Fruit experts are often dismissive of their taste and disease resistance, but they look great and are robust trees. 'Bolero' (eater) greenish-yellow, early [1], 'Polka' (eater) green and red, September–October [2], 'Waltz' (eater) red, October [3], 'Charlotte' (eater/cooker) red and green, mid season, does not store well [3]. There are several newer varieties coming on stream, some with improved flavour. Two promising new eaters are 'Moonlight', yellowish-green with orange flushing, scab resistant, late, good storage and 'Sunlight', rich reddish-orange, October harvesting.

'Coul Blush' ✉ (eater) *H5* John Butterworth says, 'Britain's most northerly apple variety raised at Coul, Ross-shire in 1827. Gold with faint flush. Sweet, soft cream flesh. Also makes good sauce.' Not surprisingly it is a good performer up north but Alec West says that in the Borders it drops its fruit very early. The colour is striking and it tastes good if you get it at its peak. [3]

'Court Pendu Plat' R (cooker/eater) An ancient French (possibly Roman) apple with scab resistance and long storage. Apparently, if you keep it all winter, it eventually becomes sweet enough to eat rather than cook. It flowers so late it sometimes fails to be pollinated. [6]

'Cox's Orange Pippin' Not worth growing in Scotland, prone to canker, scab and mildew. If you want a 'Cox'-type apple in Scotland, go for 'Ellison's Orange', 'Fiesta', 'Ribston Pippin' or 'Sunset'. [3]

'Discovery' ♀ R (eater) *H5* Bright red, early ripening, sweet strawberry-like flavour and some pink staining in the flesh. The number-one apple for Scotland and does best in the north of the UK. John Butterworth, Willie Duncan, Alec West and Jim McColl all recommend this; it does not store well, so eat off the tree. An excellent pollinator for other apples too and a good

parent for modern varieties. Of all the early apples, this is my favourite for taste, yield and healthy foliage and fruit. Every garden should have one. [3] 'Rosette' is a new sport of 'Discovery' with pink-patterned flesh. Otherwise identical, so should be excellent in Scotland.

'East Lothian Pippin' ✉ (cooker/eater) Ripening in late August and poor storing, a medium-sized green apple. [2]

'Egremont Russet' ♀ (eater) *H5* Early flowering, cream, tinged yellow, good flavour, keeps well, scab prone in the west but good in the east. Dave Allan rates it for the Borders. Flowers have some frost tolerance. Good for training. [2]

'Ellison's Orange' ♀ R (eater) Yellow overlaid with orange with a distinctive aniseed flavour which is not to everyone's taste. A redder form is also available. September ripening and does not store well. Can be prone to canker but resistant to scab. Its thin branches are inclined to hang downwards. A good alternative to 'Cox's'. [4]

'Falstaff' ♀ (eater) Heavy cropping, not the hardiest and prone to scab but some frost resistance in the flowers. Crisp and juicy but not the best tasting. There is also a redder version, 'Red Falstaff'. [2]

'Fiesta' (syn. 'Red Pippin') ♀ (eater) Sweet, reddish orange, 'Cox'-like in appearance and flavour, heavy yielding, keeps well, but subject to canker in some areas; one of Jim McColl's favourites for Aberdeenshire and good reports from the Clyde Valley. John Butterworth and Willie Duncan report scab issues and Alec West is not a fan either. [3]

'Galloway Pippin' ✉ R (cooker) Large yellow-green fruit with a russet freckle finish. Late ripening but best eaten before Christmas. Raised in Galloway, where it is still popular. Good on a wall at Culross and Kellie Castle, Fife, but less successful for Willie Duncan in Fife as a free-standing tree. [2–3]

'George Cave' (eater) Raised in 1923 in Essex. John Butterworth recommends it for Ayrshire: 'A small, crisp, sweet-sharp fruit, one of our best dessert varieties here.' He reckons it a rival for 'Discovery'. [3]

'**Golden Delicious**' (eater) A supermarket apple, useless in Scotland.

'**Golden Pippin**' **R** (eater) Described by John Reid in 1683 as 'the best apple for Scotland' and used as a parent by Scottish apple breeder Thomas Andrew Knight in 1800. John Butterworth describes it as 'a healthy variety with small, russeted fruit possessing an intriguing "acid drop" flavour'. Willie Duncan comments on its thick skin. [2]

'**Granny Smith**' (eater) A popular supermarket apple, not worth growing in Scotland.

'**Gravenstein**' (eater) A four-hundred-year-old apple said to have the highest vitamin C content of any. It looks a bit like a cooker in colour, yellow-green, but tastes deliciously sweet. It flowers very early, which means it may not be well pollinated and is at risk of frost. Ripe fruit drops rather readily. Triploid so does not pollinate other apples. [1]

'**Greensleeves**' ♀ (eater) *H5* Pale greenish-yellow, crisp and tangy flavour. Partially self-fertile and a good pollinator for other apples. Frost resistant flowers make this a good choice for northerly and cold gardens – it does well on a wall at Leith Hall, Aberdeenshire (600ft). In Fife, Willie Duncan finds it produces small scab-covered apples. [3]

'**Grenadier**' ♀ **R** (cooker) Early with good scab and canker resistance but poor storage. Once popular in the Clyde Valley and good for the western half of Scotland for its disease resistance. More compact than 'Bramley' so a good choice for the smaller garden. George Anderson recommends it, but Alec West comments that it suffers from bitter pip once it drops, so pick it early. [3]

'**Hawthornden**' ✉ (eater) Raised near Edinburgh, this is a George Anderson and Willie Duncan choice as a heritage Scottish variety. Handsome, pale yellow with red flushing, it is prone to scab

in some areas but not for Alec West near Coldstream.

'**Herefordshire Russet**' **R** (eater) A gourmet's apple, this one often wins taste tests and has a 'Cox'-like flavour. Attractive russet-coloured fruit and stores well. [3]

'**Hood's Supreme**' ✉ (eater) Raised in 1924 by Miss B. Y. Hood from Edzell, Angus. John Butterworth writes, 'Large and handsome. Sweet, white flesh but not much taste. Will not keep.' [2]

'**Howgate Wonder**' (cooker/eater) Tough late ripener, red over yellow, sometimes scab-susceptible; Jim McColl, George Anderson and John Butterworth recommend it. Often used to produce giant apples for shows. Grows well at Leith Hall, Aberdeenshire, at 600ft. [4]

'**James Grieve**' ♀ ✉ (eater) The most famous Scottish-bred apple and the easiest to find in garden centres. Raised in Edinburgh and George Anderson reckons it is still hard to beat in the Lothians. Red and green, crisp and juicy, a good pollinator with frost-resistant flowers. Better in the east than the west, as John Butterworth reports that it is prone to canker in wetter climates. A poor doer in the Clyde Valley, but it is still sold in garden centres there. David Storrie rated it poorly back in 1949. You might be better choosing 'James Grieve' hybrid apples such as 'Katy' or 'Falstaff'. [3]

'(**White**) **Joaneting**' ('**June-eating**') (eater) Dating from 1600, it is the first apple to ripen each year, edible in July but drops quickly. It marked the opening of the commercial apple season in Clyde Valley until the 1920s. Small greenish-yellow fruit. [1]

'**Katy**' ('**Katja**') (eater) From Sweden, striking fruit with prolific, early, sweet, juicy red apples, skin rather thick, good in the west. Keeps better than 'Discovery' and recommended by John Butterworth and other Scottish apple experts. [3]

'**Keswick Codlin**' **R** (cooker) *H5* A very tough apple, good in high elevation gardens and valuable for its scab resistance. Sometimes tends to crop biennially, yellow-green fruit, ripening in August. Partly self-fertile. [2]

'King of the Pippins' ♀ (eater/cooker) An old apple, quite common in Scottish collections, with greenish-yellow, red-striped fruit ripening in October. Late flowering. [5]

'Lady of Wemyss' ✉ (cooker) Late-ripening, orange-red, firm flesh, keeps its shape when cooked and stores well. [4]

'Lane's Price Albert' ♀ R (cooker) Fruit green, striped red. Not very vigorous, seen in several old Scottish apple collections and Alec West rates it very highly. Resistant to scab but somewhat susceptible to mildew. A reasonable performer in the west and holds together better than 'Bramley' when cooked. [3]

'Lass of Gowrie' ✉ (cooker) Sweeter than most cookers and holds its shape when baked but does not keep. First recorded at the 1883 Apple Congress. Willie Duncan says that the fruit falls off the tree as soon as it ripens in August and you need to pick them off the ground. David Storrie writes, 'surely the most beautiful of all apples – and one of the most worthless'. John Butterworth rates it highly. You take your pick! [2]

'Laxton's Fortune' ♀ R (eater) Not all that widely grown but a John Butterworth pick as a good performer in Ayrshire and for its richly flavoured and freely produced fruit. It tastes good but can go soft quickly. David Storrie writes, 'pre-eminent, one of the best dessert apples for Scotland.' [3]

'Laxton's Superb' (eater) A 'Cox'-like apple which tends to crop well every second year and has lax, thin branches. Prone to scab. [3]

'Limelight' R (eater) Yellow-green, crisp, high yielding and compact, good for the smaller garden. Partly self-fertile. [4]

'Lord Derby' R (cooker) Irregular in size, square in shape, green, mid season, good disease resistance. Common in the Borders, recommended for the Lothians, the Clyde Valley and other western areas and shows good cold tolerance. The flesh turns pink when cooked and Nigel Slater recommends it for 'frothiness'. Keeps for 1–2 months. [4]

'Lord Rosebery' ✉ (eater) Bright red, strawberry flavour, rather chewy. Raised at Dalmeny Castle, near Edinburgh. Willie Duncan rates this as a good-tasting sweet apple. It is prone to mildew and scab. It grows well at Fyvie Castle. [3]

'Oslin' ✉ (syn. 'Arbroath Pippin') (eater) Early, distinctively bright yellow when ripe. Apple guru and author Joan Morgan says that it was first recorded in 1815 but is probably much older, possibly French, associated either with Arbroath or Lindores Abbey, Newburgh. Slightly scented, rich, distinctive taste with hint of aniseed. John Butterworth thinks that it tastes OK, Willie Duncan does not think much of it but John Stoa, Dundee-based horticulturalist, reckons it is one of the best local apples with great taste. It ripens in August and needs to be eaten quickly. [2]

'Pitmaston Pineapple' R (eater) More than 200 years old, this is a small, oddly-shaped bright yellow somewhat russeted apple with a good sweet, nutty flavour. [3]

'Port Allen Russet' ✉ (eater/cooker) This is presumed to come from the small harbour on the River Tay, used to ship goods from the Carse of Gowrie before the coming of the railway. Several people still grow it in the Carse. John Butterworth describes it as 'a conical, russeted fruit with an even, orange flush on yellow background'. For Joan Morgan, it has a 'brisk, rich flavour'. Willie Duncan says it is only fit for cooking. [2]

'Red Devil' R (eater) Like 'Discovery', with showy fruit and a sweet strawberry-like taste but ripens later and stores well. Makes pink juice. Self-fertile so useful in a small garden. [3]

'Red Windsor' R (eater) Fine red apple which produces masses of handsome fruit for Willie Duncan in Fife. [2]

'**Ribston Pippin**' ♀ **R** (eater) This is a favourite apple of keen 'apple-heads' for its taste, high vitamin C content and cooking properties. Thought to be a parent of 'Cox's Orange Pippin', this York-shire-bred apple does much better in Scotland than 'Cox's'. John Butterworth's favourite apple, and Willie Duncan and Alec West are fans. Sweet, sharp flavour. Some reports of canker but John Butterworth finds it resistant. Early flower-ing. [2-triploid]

'**Scotch Bridget**' ✉ (cooker/eater) Cream, crisp, a Victorian Scottish apple, usually used for cooking but can be eaten off the tree some years. Recommended by Alan Smith in Strath-don, Aberdeenshire, and Nick Hoskins at Broughton, Kirkcudbright. [3]

'**Scotch Dumpling**' ✉ (cooker) Fine pink flowers, large fruit, ripens early. One of the few post-Second World War Scottish-raised apples. [2]

'**Scrumptious**' ♀ (eater) Shiny, deep red, with excel-lent taste, popular with children. Frost-hardy in flower. An improvement on its parent 'Discov-ery' as fruit stays ripe on tree for several weeks. One of Jim McColl's picks but John Butter-worth reports that it is scab prone in the west. Can be grown successfully on its own roots and partly self-fertile. [3]

'**Spartan**' (eater) A handsome Canadian apple with striking, dark-red sweet and juicy fruit. Prone to scab and canker, particularly in the west, but good in the Borders. Best thinned or you get masses of small fruit. [3]

'**Stirling Castle**' ✉ (cooker) David Storrie writes, 'generally cankers badly, but is a grand old apple and a magnificent cropper'. Raised in 1820 near Stirling. A mid-season, greenish-yellow cooker which makes great apple snow, apparently. [3]

'**Stobo Castle**' ✉ (cooker) Willie Duncan recom-mends this variety, introduced by David Storrie from Glendoick and named after the castle near Peebles. Ripens in August. Reddish flushing. Has the odd barren year. [3]

'**Sunset**' ♀ **R** (eater) Raised in Kent in 1920. Like a hardy version of 'Cox's Orange Pippin' with better disease and frost resistance, yellow-orange fruit, sweet-sharp flavour, stores well. Recommended by the Henry Doubleday Research Association for organic gardeners. A good variety for Dave Allan in the Borders, George Anderson in the Lothians and John Butterworth in Ayrshire, who also comments on its spectacular blossom. [3]

'**Tam Montgomery**' ✉ (syn. 'Early Julyan') (eater) A striking, bright-yellow, smallish fruit. Once widely grown in the Clyde Valley. Early eater with some scab resistance. [3]

'**Thorle Pippin**' ✉ First described 1831. A small, flat, red fruit with a sharp taste. Historically used for animal fodder. [2]

'**Tower of Glamis**' ✉ (syn. 'Carse of Gowrie') (cooker) A large, heavy apple, of four-sided shape, grown in Clyde Valley and Carse of Gowrie in nineteenth century. Willie Duncan is not a fan. [2]

'**White Melrose**' ✉ (eater) A large apple raised at Melrose Abbey possibly as early as 1600, it was an important commercial Borders apple in the nineteenth century. Willie Duncan explained that you get giant fruit on this, probably the largest in Scotland, if you thin your apples in early summer. Grown at Pitmedden and Leith Hall in Aberdeenshire, good at Inverewe in Wester Ross and one of the best performers at Elcho Castle on the Tay. Alec West thinks that there are two forms of this in the Borders. *The Herald*'s Dave Allan says it needs to be used quickly or it loses its flavour but says it is very reliable in the Borders. [3]

'**Winter Gem**' **R** (eater) Reddish, russet, late-ripen-ing with good flavour. John Butterworth reckons that this is one of the best late apples for the west, scab resistant. [4]

'**Winter Pearmain**' (cooker/eater) Alec West recom-mends this as it lasts on the tree right up to Christmas and keeps until March in store. Small fruits which sweeten in storage. [2]

'**Worcester Pearmain**' ♀ (eater) Sweet, juicy orange-red fruit, early ripening, best eaten straight from the tree. This was a mainstay of the Clyde Valley orchards in their heyday. Willie Duncan recommends it highly but Jim McColl has no time for it. Resistant to mildew but can suffer scab, as it did for John Butterworth in Ayrshire. Flowers have some frost resistance so a good choice for a cold inland garden. [3]

Crab Apple (*Malus*) H5 E1

Only a few of the many species and cultivars of crab apples have edible fruits which are suitable for jelly making. However, all offer an alternative pollinator for eating and cooking apples. Five-petalled, usually fragrant, white, pink or near-red flowers open in April, May or June, followed by long-lasting reddish, orange or yellow fruit in autumn. Best planted in at least part day sun, they can tolerate light or heavy but not waterlogged soils. Fruit flavour is best if the fruit is allowed to remain on the tree until after first frosts. Like apples, crab apples are subject to **scab**.

'Harry Baker' is the most scab resistant of the edible crabs. You can obtain dwarfing trees on M27 rootstocks but they are rather fussy and need careful staking.

CRAB APPLE VARIETIES

'**Evereste**' ♀ (4–7m × 3–6m) Flowers pale pink to white in April–May, long lasting, small orange-yellow fruits. Though not edible, it is often used as a pollinator for apples.

'**Harry Baker**' (5–9m) Large dark-pink flowers and ruby-red fruit, very good for making jelly.

'**Jelly King**' (6–8m) This is Nick Dunn's choice of the best for jelly making. Good scab resistance. White blossom and large orange fruit.

'**John Downie**' ♀ (6–8m) White flowers, bright orange and red fruits, the most popular variety for jelly making but susceptible to scab.

'**Laura**' (3–5m) A dwarf with fastigiate habit, two-tone pink and white flowers, purple leaves and maroon fruit, good for making jelly, a little scab susceptible.

Malus 'Harry Baker' is an excellent crab apple for jelly making, with showy flowers in spring and fine fruit. Malus can act as pollinators for eating and cooking apples.

Pear (*Pyrus communis*)
H3–4 E2

Pears are native to Britain, but you won't enjoy the fruit of our wild pears as they are small, hard and sour. To create the fruit we eat today, it has taken hundreds of years of breeding, much of this done in France and Belgium, which accounts for the many French-sounding names. One important early British pear is 'Williams' Bon Chrétien' bred in Berkshire in 1770. Eating pears raw, which we take for granted today, is a relatively recent practice. Most older varieties of pears were selected for perry making or for cooking. A great number of such varieties have died out, while others can be found in heritage fruit collections. Many older Scottish gardens have large numbers of gnarled old pears. At Glendoick, ancient cordons and espaliers line the cruciform layout of the walled garden, providing the main structure. Jedburgh, near the English border, used to be an important pear producing area and some giant old trees remain there. These days, most pears planted in Scotland are from the six or seven most popular eating varieties, such as 'Conference'.

A mature bush-pruned pear can produce 15–20kg of fruit or more per year.

Pears are rarely eaten straight off the tree but, instead, are picked slightly hard and stored indoors to fully ripen. It is not an exaggeration to say that some pears remain at perfect ripeness for only a matter of hours, unless refrigerated. As Scottish fruit nurseryman David Storrie writes of some pears, not entirely in jest, 'ripe at noon, rotten by 1 o'clock'. Harvesting a pear at the perfect moment is a bit of an art. When ready to pick, most pears will come away easily with a slight lift and twist and will ripen fully a few days later. Supermarket pears are picked green and hard for transportation and storage reasons. Quite often they never properly ripen, particularly if they are flown in from the southern hemisphere. Pears store best at colder temperatures than apples but make sure that they don't freeze. Lay them on slats or trays in a cool ventilated place. They last well in the bottom of a fridge. Pears such as 'Jargonelle' and 'Beth' don't store well and need eating as soon as they ripen, while others such as 'Doyene de Comice', 'Conference' and 'Invincible' ('Delwinor') store for several months.

A selection of pear varieties: 'Beurre Hardy', 'Conference', 'Doyenne de Comice', 'Humbug' ('Psyanka'), 'Seckle', 'Williams'.

CULTIVATION

Fifty years ago, pears were considered a marginal crop in Scotland, barely worth growing. However, with climate change and warmer weather, they are now widely and successfully grown. Pears are not as tough as apples, flowering earlier and requiring more wind shelter from cold easterlies or salt spray, but they can be long lived and can fruit for 100 years or more. Trees on modern rootstocks seem to be less long lived. In the northern half of the country and in any inland gardens, it is advisable to grow pears on a west- or south-facing wall to protect the early blossom and to help ripening of fruit, as well as providing some protection from wind damage. In the west, scab is a scourge and John Butterworth recommends 'Jargonelle', 'Williams' and 'Bristol Cross' for high rainfall areas. Pears enjoy well-drained, fertile soil in a sunny site but they are more tolerant than apples of a clay soil. Very acid or peaty soils can cause chlorotic leaves (yellow veining) and such soils are best limed. Pears are less tolerant of grass growing over their roots than apples. Harry Baker recommends a 50cm radius of grass-free soil around the base of a pear to avoid competition with its shallow roots. A thick mulch of manure, compost or straw will help to maintain this. Pears appreciate a good feed in spring. Growmore or similar will do.

Some pears are self-fertile or partly self-fertile (as indicated below) so you only need to grow one of these, but most require a pollinator of a different variety. All those recommended below flower relatively late and their flowering should overlap, so ensuring cross-pollination. Pruning is discussed on p. 84 and training on p. 86. Pears are normally grafted and often double grafted for compatibility, onto quince rootstocks. Quince 'A' produces slightly larger trees up to 3–4m, best planted 3–4m apart. Quince 'C' is a little less vigorous, the best choice for training espaliers and cordons, giving a 2–3m tree which can be planted 1–2m apart for cordons and 3–4m apart for bush and espaliers.

A young fan-trained pear, showing the canes used to form the framework to train the tree, at Frank Matthews Nursery, Worcestershire.

COMMON PROBLEMS

Diseases and pests common to pears and apples are discussed on p. 88. As they flower in early/mid spring, frosted flowers and so little or **no fruit set** are common problems for pears in cold and inland gardens. Plant on south and west walls for best results and fleece the blossom if necessary. 'Beurré Hardy', 'Williams' and 'Jargonelle' have flowers with some frost resistance. **Pear rust** is spreading north through England – infected leaves fall off early, which can weaken the tree and reduce fruiting. **Pear midge** damage the young fruitlets, causing them to blacken and drop off. Brush branches with soapy water, meths or spray with acetamiprid after fruit has been gathered. **Birds**, usually bullfinches, can be a problem pecking the blossom, while blackbirds love the ripening fruit.

PEAR VARIETIES

Although there are a number of old Scottish pears, many old varieties are now lost. The Earl of Crawfurd's pear list of 1692 contains 40 different varieties, most of which would have been fit only for cooking.

Stunning use of trained pears to create a fruit walk at West Dean Gardens, Sussex.

The modern pears listed below are grown to eat raw. Two important Scottish collections are at Threave near Dumfries and in the garden of John and Sara Hulbert in Longforgan, near Dundee. Both collections were propagated from Mylnefield in Invergowrie (now the James Hutton Institute) before most of it was short-sightedly grubbed up in the 1970s. Several of the Scottish pears, such as 'Maggie Duncan', 'Goud Knapp' and 'Seggieden', are not in the national fruit collection at Brogdale. I tasted a number of varieties at the Hulberts' garden. Some were pretty good and it would be worth propagating and distributing them more widely.

Varieties marked **R** are the most resistant to scab disease. Hardiness is *H3–4* except where noted. Pollination groups [1–4]. It is best to have pears from same or adjacent groups. Early pears can be picked in late August to early September, late ones in late October.

Asian or Apple Pears *H3* Produced from several Asian species, these crisp pears flower earlier than the European so you need two or more Asian varieties to cross-pollinate. Seldom grown in Scotland, though fruit has been produced in the Borders. [1]

'**Beth**' ♀ Early, conical, pale yellow, juicy, sweet fruit, eat right away. A compact but upright tree which is heavy cropping from a young age, self-fertile; a Jim McColl choice and the best pear for David Catt in Jedburgh. [4]

'**Beurré Hardy**' ♀ *H3* Round, conical fruit, light-green skin with reddish russeting. Tender, sweet, juicy flavour, vigorous and upright, a poor pollinator, needs a warm site and takes a few years to bear fruit. Pick before fully ripe and finish off indoors. It stores for a few months. Good autumn foliage colour. [3]

'**Bristol Cross**' **R** Mid season, a John Butterworth pick for west Scotland climates for its scab resistance. It is a poor pollinator of other pears. Gritty, sweet flavour and white flesh. Grows well for Willie Duncan in Fife. [4]

'**Concorde**' ♀ Good flavour, compact, heavy cropping, partly self-fertile. Willie Duncan's choice as the most reliable and a Jim McColl pick. Nick Dunn recommends this if you want to grow pears organically but in western Scotland it is subject to scab. [3]

'**Conference**' ♀ The most popular pear in the UK both for gardens and commercial production, and perhaps the best for Scotland. A heavy cropper, setting some fruit even if frosted, with good flavour and fairly compact growth habit. Easily recognised by its narrow, elongated shape. Named for the 1885 RHS Pear Conference at Chiswick. Though self-fertile, a pollinator will improve the yield and shape of the fruit. Scab prone in Ayrshire for John Butterworth. [3]

'**Doyenne du Comice**' ♀ *H3* This deliciously flavoured pear is the connoisseur's choice for taste. The downside is that, in Scotland, it needs a warm, sheltered site on a south-facing wall and a pollinator. It is vigorous but scab prone and it is damaged by sulphur fungicides. Best on a Quince C rootstock to control the vigour. [4]

'**Hessle**' **R** An old cooking pear, not the best tasting raw, of dumpy, almost rounded shaped. Said to be one of the toughest of all and good in the west for its scab resistance. Bred in Yorkshire, it was once widely grown in Scotland. Available from specialist growers only.

'**Humbug**' (syn. 'Pysanka') This pear from the Ukraine has extraordinary yellow stripes on the fruit. It may not be the best tasting but it certainly attracts comment and it stores well. The young shoots are striped too. [3]

'**Invincible**' (syn. 'Delwinor') *H4–5* Not the best flavour but this is probably the best choice for severe and northern-most climates, as it is self-fertile and can flower a second time if frosted. It is very free-fruiting from a young age. Nick Dunn recommends this for Scotland.

'**Jargonelle**' R A famous, tough old brownish-yellow cooking pear with fruit that smells of pear drops or nail varnish remover – take your pick! Scab resistant and grows well in western Scotland but triploid, so needs two pollinator partners. It is a tip bearer so don't prune too hard or you'll not get much fruit. Pick early and use fast, as it goes over in the blink of an eye. [3]

'**Seckle**' A rather weak grower with handsome and tasty dark reddish-purple fruit and characteristic white spotting. It flowers early and is not a good pollinator, though it is partly self-fertile. Quite common in older Scottish gardens. [2]

'**Williams' Bon Chrétien**' ♀ *H4* Said to be the world's most popular pear. Early, yellow skin, juicy flesh, good for bottling, a heavy cropper, with some frost-resistance in the flowers. A broad, spreading habit. Best picked before fully ripe or fruit tend to go mushy in the middle. Prone to scab but John Butterworth recommends it for Ayrshire, as does Alan Smith in Strathdon, Aberdeenshire. '**Sensation**' A sport of this variety, with red skin. [3]

Plum Family

Plum (Prunus domestica) H4 E2

Plums and their relatives, which include damsons, gages and bullaces, have a history which dates back to Roman times. Monastic gardens of the Middle Ages are known to have had plums and damsons and there used to be commercial plum orchards in the Clyde Valley and at Gladsmuir in East Lothian. In Scotland, most plums (but not gages) are heavy cropping from a young age and all listed below are self-fertile, so you need only one. Tasting plums from a collection in Worcestershire, I noticed that the sun in England certainly makes plums sweeter than they tend to be in Scotland. If you have space, it is worth planting several varieties – a mixture of early, mid and late. Willie Duncan recommends 'Czar', 'Victoria', 'Oullins Gage' and 'Marjorie's Seedling' as a set of four which fruit from June to early

Plum 'Victoria' is very popular but sadly prone to canker.

Plum 'Marjorie's Seedling' is a good alternative to 'Victoria'.

Plum 'Haganta' is a new tough, late-fruiting variety.

September in his Fife garden. Scotland's woods and hedgerows quite commonly have wild plums and damsons, which may have seeded themselves or might be old rootstocks that have sprouted. The smaller, rounded cherry plum or myrobalan (sweet) and bullace (sour) are used for eating and cooking respectively and both are very hardy and disease resistant.

SITE, PLANTING, ROUTINE CARE AND HARVESTING

Plums are tolerant of any reasonably well-drained soil and prefer a pH of around 6, although they can grow in more acid soils. They dislike grass growing around their roots, so a mulch of manure both keeps down weeds and provides fertiliser. Plums flower early so, in colder and inland gardens, they are best grown fan-trained on a wall. They are not suitable for training as espaliers and cordons. The wall also makes netting against birds and wasps easier and the support may avoid breakage caused by heavy fruiting and subsequent entry of disease. Heavy crops are best thinned to avoid breakage and exhausting the tree, which can result in a bumper/barren biennial cropping cycle. Plums and gages are best pruned in early summer if required, after fruit set. Do not prune after July or in winter because of the risk of disease. Ideally a young bush should have up to five well-spread branches which can be shortened if they become leggy. Prune to upward pointing buds to encourage upward growing shoots. The commonest rootstocks are 'St Julien A' for a full-sized plum (3–4m) and 'Pixy' for a semi-dwarf tree (to around 2.5–3m). Jeremy Gilchrest does not recommend 'Pixy' for the Clyde Valley due to the climate and clay soils – there is no doubt that it does require better than average soil conditions and more wind shelter.

Harvest plums as they ripen around August and September. They are best stored by freezing, bottling or as jam or chutney.

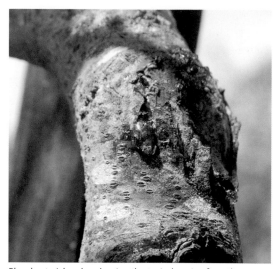

Plum bacterial canker showing the typical oozing from the stem.

COMMON PROBLEMS

Plums suffer from two common and often fatal fungal diseases, **silver leaf** and **bacterial canker** (*see* p. 71). Both enter via wounds and pruning scars so, when pruning plums, disinfect secateurs between trees and only prune in summer and to the minimum. I was dismayed to see the recent devastation of the plum collection at RHS Wisley from bacterial canker and this disease is a serious threat to plums countrywide. Commercial fruit tree production is also badly affected; if your newly planted plum suddenly starts dying back, return it for a replacement. Other problems include **bullfinch** attacks on the flower buds in spring and **wasps** and **birds** going for the ripening fruit. There is normally enough fruit for the humans and the wildlife to share, with 6–10kg possible from a mature tree.

PLUM VARIETIES

'**Czar**' ♀ Sharp flavour, usually used for cooking, early fruiting, tough, spring frost- and shade-resistant, susceptible to silver leaf. Named in honour of the Czar's visit to Queen Victoria in the 1870s.

'**Denniston's Superb**' A green plum, hardier than the gages, self-fertile. Resistant to canker.

'**Early Rivers Blue**' The earliest to ripen, good in the Clyde Valley.

'**Excalibur**' Similar to 'Victoria', with larger fruit and more disease resistance.

'**Gordon Castle**' ✉ One of the few Scottish-raised plums still commercially available. A useful late variety, ripening in September with sweet yellow-green fruit.

'**Haganta**' and '**Haroma**' Two new German late varieties, stunning, damson-like purple skins with a bloom. They tasted great at 'Trees for Life' owner Frank Matthews' trial grounds and we hope that they prove good in Scotland. They are said to be disease resistant.

'**Herman**' Not widely known but Nick Dunn recommends this as an excellent choice, early fruiting and with excellent flavour.

'**Jubilee**' Similar to 'Victoria' but a little earlier.

'**Marjorie's Seedling**' ♀ Sweet but not the best taste, good for cooking, late ripening, long-lasting fruiting, vigorous and upright, heavy cropping. Best in the southern half of Scotland and in a suntrap or against a wall. Resistant to silver leaf and canker.

'**Opal**' ♀ Reddish-purple fruit, tastes like 'Victoria' but less susceptible to bacterial canker.

'**Victoria**' ♀ Victoria plum is the most popular plum, heavy cropping, but very susceptible to canker so often short lived and many garden centre 'Victoria' trees have been badly affected in recent years.

Gage *H3 E3*

These taste wonderful and are worth the extra care; they need more shelter and warmth than plums. They may take years to start fruiting and then may not fruit every year. Apart from perhaps on the

A yellow gage at Kellie Castle, Fife. Gages are best in warm and sheltered gardens on south and west walls.

Moray Firth coast, they are of limited value in the northern half of Scotland, yielding less fruit as you go north. I have seen good fruit yield on gages in Aberdeenshire but owners admitted that this tended to be the exception and not the rule.

'**Cambridge**' Probably the best, green flesh, good raw and cooked, self-fertile.

'**Early Transparent**' Yellow, deliciously sweet and reasonably free-fruiting in Scotland.

'**Oullins**' ♀ Yellow, takes a few years to start fruiting, quite late ripening.

'**Jefferson**' ♀ Yellow, needs a pollinator – a plum will do.

Damson, Bullace (*Prunus insititia*) and Sloe (*Prunus spinosa*) *H4–5 E1*

Damsons and bullaces have smaller fruit but are tougher and more disease resistant than plums. Bullaces are tough and sour, with a large stone and not much flesh. Damsons are purple and most bullaces green but the Langley Bullace, grown at Culross Palace for example, has purple fruit. They

Damson trees are very tough, often with sour fruit, which is generally used for puddings, jams and making damson gin.

Cherries at Charleton Golf Club, Fife. Birds feast on them, leaving piles of stones on the golf course, but there always seems to be plenty of fruit on the trees.

can be used as a windbreak or hedge, thrive in poor soils and can be grown at quite high altitudes. They are often found in hedgerows and formerly used to shelter commercial orchard fruit. Both are cooked or made into jam, wine or gin. Both can sometimes be propagated by removing suckers and potting them up. Sloes are less common in hedgerows in Scotland than further south. As most people know, they are mainly used for making sloe gin (damson gin is almost as good). Freeze sloes to burst the skins and then pop them in a bottle with gin and sugar. (One third of the bottle of fruit and 100g or so granulated sugar.) The longer you wait, the better it tastes.

DAMSON VARIETIES

'Farleigh Damson' Said to the most reliable fruiter for Scotland, self-fertile. 'Merryweather' A good damson for cold and exposed locations and has larger fruit. In the Clyde Valley the 'Shropshire Prune' was widely grown.

Cherry (*Prunus cerasus, P. avium*) H4 E2

A bag of cherries is a bag of happiness.
Nigel Slater

Edible cherries are derived from two species – the native bird cherry or gean, *Prunus avium*, and the sour cherry, *P. cerasus*, which comes from mainland Europe. 'Morello' and other acid or sour cherries are used for making pies and jam. Though the Romans brought some cherries to Britain, Henry VIII seems to be credited with the introduction of commercial cherries, as he sent his royal fruiterer Richard Harris to search Europe for the best varieties and founded the famous Kent orchards. The UK imports over 90 per cent of fresh cherries sold, despite having an excellent climate in which to grow them. Encouragingly, several Scottish growers in Nairn, Montrose and Fife have begun to plant and harvest commercial cherries, mainly under polythene with tunnels on stilts. Many cherries grow well in Scotland and, as long as the spectacular blossom is not frosted, cherries tend to set a good crop of fruit. The challenge is to ripen the fruit without the **birds** getting it before you do. To that end, garden cherries are most commonly trained against a wall, often as formal fan-trained trees, so they can be more easily netted. For smaller gardens, we would recommend buying cherries on 'Gisela 5' rootstocks, as they fruit younger and more heavily on a less vigorous tree/bush only 2–3m high. For a larger tree, select cultivars on the 'colt' rootstock. Whatever the size, cherries need a rich, fertile soil and regular feeding. It is best to do as little pruning as possible, as cuts and scars can lead to infections such as **silver leaf** and **canker**. If you need to prune, do so in summer so the wound can heal. For fan training, rub out the buds of any unwanted outward and inward pointing shoots as they start to swell and tie in the fan branches you want to keep. The National Fruit Collection at Brogdale has over 300 varieties but we'd suggest sticking to those listed below, as they are tried and tested in Scotland and many of the others are not self-fertile. An old avenue of cherries at Charleton Golf Course in Fife is an amazing sight in summer, with the local birds stuffing themselves with the bounty but still leaving plenty on the trees if only you could reach them. Willie Duncan grows a set of cherries in his Fife tunnel house which provides a long season of fruit from 'Early Rivers' in June to 'Napoleon Bigarreau' in August. He grows under cover to reduce **splitting** and keep the birds off.

Cherry 'Morello' with netting against birds at RHS Wisley, Surrey.

CHERRY VARIETIES

'**Lapins**' (syn. 'Cherokee') Sweet, dark-red, good flavour, heavy cropping and seldom splitting; Willie Duncan's choice as the best cherry for east Scotland.

'**Morello**' ♀ A dark-red cooker, very hardy. Late flowering so usually avoids frosts.

'**Regina**' Needs a pollinator, very hardy, late cropping, recommended by Jeremy Gilchrist for Clyde Valley.

Cherry 'Lapins', one of the best self-fertile varieties.

'**Stella**' ♀ Dark-red, sweet, eating cherry, fruit inclined to split. Some bacterial canker resistance.

'**Summer Sun**' ♀ Dark-red, sweet, with good frost tolerance, so good in colder, more exposed locations.

'**Sunburst**' A Canadian selection with sweet, black fruit ripening in July–August.

'**Sweetheart**' Dark-red, late, heavy fruiting and ripens over several weeks.

Quince (*Cydonia oblonga*) H3–4 E3

A fully laden quince with its gnarled branches and furry green or bright yellow fruit is quite a sight to behold. Nigel Slater calls the fruit 'fat cherubs'. Cultivated in Europe for hundreds of years and introduced to Britain in around 1275, quinces grow well and easily through much of Scotland, forming a large, vigorous and sometimes untidy shrub or small tree, up to 3–4m in height and width, producing pink-white flowers in summer. The lack of summer heat tends to mean erratic fruiting, unless you have a warm, sunny site, and fruit tends to be smaller than that produced further south. Quinces need to be cooked to make them palatable and are usually made into ice creams, pies, jams and sauces. The Spanish make a block of thick jelly out of quince, *dulce de membrillo*, and eat it with manchego cheese.

There is a fine old quince at Annet House Museum garden in Linlithgow and one at Culross Palace fruits most years, although fruits are on the small side. The Walled Garden at Murray Royal Hospital in Perth has a cordon quince, while Alan Smith has had small fruit on a 'Vranja' quince in Strathdon, Aberdeenshire. Graham Bell ripens smallish but deep yellow fruit in Coldstream.

Quinces are self-fertile, so you only need one. They need a warm, sunny site, in any reasonable soil. They can be grown as a single-trunked tree or pruned to form a multi-stemmed bush. Cultivars grafted on Quince A rootstocks are slightly more vigorous than those on Quince C. Dr Hessayon advises cutting back any vigorous shoots to half their length for the first few years and, after that, little or no pruning is required. Fruit should be picked in autumn before any serious frosts and can be ripened indoors in a cool dark place until they turn yellow. Cut or snip the fruit off, as they don't come away easily. Fruit forms with a furry covering which disappears as they ripen. Don't store them with apples and pears, as their perfume can taint other fruit. **Quince rust** is becoming quite problematic in England but I have not yet seen it in Scotland. It can defoliate the bush early in the season and it weakens the ability to produce fruit.

RECOMMENDED VARIETIES

Nick Dunn recommends the varieties '**Meech's Prolific**' and '**Serbian Gold**' for Scotland, as they fruit freely. '**Vranja**' ♀ with pink flowers is currently the most planted variety. A quite different plant, the Japanese quince or *Chaenomeles* produces fruit which is inedible raw but can be cooked and made into jams and liqueurs.

Quince 'Meech's Prolific'.

Medlar in flower, in fruit and bletted ready for eating. (Picture © Michael Lean)

Medlar (*Mespilus germanica*) H4–5 E2

Native to southern Europe, *Mespilus germanica* has curious brown, rather sinister-looking fruit and forms a large graceful tree in time, 3–5m × 3–5m, with white flowers in spring and good colour in dry, cold autumns. If you have space, it is worth growing as an ornamental in a warm, sheltered site even if you don't use the fruits. It is self-fertile, so you only need one to set fruit. Long lived, there are quite a number of venerable trees in Scottish gardens and orchards, including the Cruikshank in Aberdeen, Kellie Castle and Culross Palace, Fife, Annet Museum, Linlithgow, and St Mary's Pleasance, Haddington, while a young tree is setting small fruit for Alan Smith in Strathdon. I have to admit that the fruit is more of a curiosity than a delicacy and, if you want to use it for anything other than cooking, you need to 'blet' it (actually let it rot). Some authorities advise dipping the stalks in a water and salt solution and letting them ripen upside down, stalks in the air, in a cool dark place for several weeks. Nigel Slater says they'll do just fine sitting on a plate, while Michael Lean, at Hatton Castle, Newtyle, Angus, told me that the big freeze in late November 2010 bletted his medlar fruit perfectly and they were deliciously edible straight from the tree, 'tasting like Christmas pudding'. I wish I'd been there to try one.

Mulberry (*Morus nigra*) H4 E2

I once tasted Australian mulberries from an overhanging garden tree groaning with fruit that was falling to the pavement and staining the asphalt – certainly one of the best fruits I have ever tasted. Sadly, Scotland's climate can't match this and the few plants I have seen produce only a handful of barely ripened fruit. The black mulberry (*Morus nigra*) was introduced from western Asia by the Romans and was grown in northern Europe by the ninth and tenth centuries. Both leaves and fruit are used in herbal remedies for their antioxidant and other properties. It forms a large, handsome, gnarled tree (up to 10m) which can live for a very long time. Its curious bramble-like, hanging, oblong, purplish-black fruit have a deep, staining juice. The tree is tough and can be grown in a sheltered site through most of Scotland but, if you want fruit, protection and extra heat from a wall are advisable and, even then, you'll never get a big crop. And, in any case, they seldom start fruiting until they reach a

111

Mulberry – you may get little or no fruit in Scotland but it makes a handsome, long-lived tree.

Peach, Nectarine and Apricot (*Prunus persica* and *P. armeniaca*) H2–3 E3

Fruit experts believe that the 'apple' of the Garden of Eden was probably an apricot, which is more likely to grow in the Middle East. In the southern half of Scotland in a warm, sheltered site, it is possible to get reasonable fruiting outdoors on peaches and apricots, after mild springs and good summers. Gardens in the Carse of Gowrie, on the Fife coast, in the Lothians, the south-west and the Borders have regular fruiting trees. Success is usually thanks to walls, particularly those made of brick, as they heat up and radiate warmth back onto the fruit. Luffness in East Lothian has diamond-shaped internal walls within the walled garden for ripening peaches and apricots. Further north, Castle Fraser in Aberdeenshire boasts a fruiting 'Peregrine' peach and a 'Moorpark' apricot, both in sheltered corners.

PLANTING, CARE AND HARVESTING

Peaches, nectarines and apricots are self-fertile, so you only need one. For peaches (*H2–3*), you certainly need a fan-trained tree grown against a wall, whether you want to grow indoors or out, and 'Peregrine' is the best choice of variety. Sadly, those lovely flattish white French peaches from Provence are not suitable for Scotland. You can buy a fan-trained peach tree at some expense or you can try to do it yourself with a cheaper whip or maiden tree by removing the leader and selecting two lateral branches to train left and right, from which the fanning branches will come. It takes several years and some skill to get the framework you need. Peaches (but not apricots) outdoors are very susceptible to **peach leaf curl**, which disfigures the plant and can kill it. You can spray with copper fungicide in April and May or cover the peach to protect from rain in those months. A simple polythene cover will do. At Kellie Castle in Fife an ingenious lean-to frame/greenhouse is used to protect the peach 'Pere-

significant size. With patience, you can espalier one along horizontal wires on a wall.

Mulberries enjoy a slightly acidic soil, pH 5.5–7, and they are self-fertile, so you only need one. Carry out minimum pruning and only in winter, as the sap tends to bleed in summer pruning. Some experts advise 'brutting' or bending almost double but not breaking the ends of shoots to encourage flowering and therefore fruit. Mature mulberries can sometimes disintegrate in gales and many a venerable old tree is propped up with stakes and guy ropes. You'll find an old mulberry at St Mary's Pleasance, Haddington, while Culross has an arched walk covered with mulberry, vines and jasmine. Scotland's cold and wet autumn weather often prevents full ripening to a rich black colour and, in centuries past, gardeners would artificially heat walls to finish the fruit. There are some interesting hybrid forms and selections available from the Agroforestry Research Trust in Devon.

Above. Peach blossom is one of the most attractive of any fruit.

Above right. A vertical peach frame on the outside of the walled garden wall at Kellie Castle, Fife. This protects against frost and peach leaf curl.

Right. An apricot in the corner of the walled garden at Castle Fraser, Aberdeenshire. This would normally be considered too far north for outdoor apricots but this one is quite prolific.

grine' from peach leaf curl and frosts and to help build up enough heat to ripen fruit. Nearby, at Balcaskie, peaches set fruit on the high terrace walls while, along the coast at Culross, a young tree had fine fruit on it in August 2011.

Indoor peaches suffer much less from peach leaf curl and produce larger, sweeter fruit more reliably. Although I saw fruit on an outdoor tree at Culross, nectarines (*H1–2*) are best considered for indoors only and 'Lord Napier' is the usual variety to choose. At Glendoick, we have had good crops of peaches, nectarines and apricots in our greenhouses and our indoor peaches taste better than anything you can buy in the shops. You can tell if they are ripe by the rose-like scent, but don't squeeze them as they bruise easily. Ayrshire's Culzean Castle greenhouse complex has good examples of fruiting peaches indoors and both the Beechgrove Garden and Willie Duncan in Fife grow good peaches in

tunnel houses. Willie advises careful pruning for good crops indoors. He removes all side shoots produced in between set fruit and leaves the side shoot below the ripening peaches to grow, flower and fruit the following year. The nineteenth-century classic on fruit and vegetables *The Book of the Garden* (1853 – available on Google Books to download) devotes almost 20 pages to the pruning and protection of peaches to obtain fruit in northern gardens. Indoor fruit bushes need careful watering and ventilation and can suffer from **red spider**, **scale insect** and **peach leaf curl**. The so-called 'patio' dwarf peaches, nectarines and apricots, usually grown in pots which can be moved in and out as weather dictates, have spectacular blossom but we found them prone to disease.

As they seldom suffer from peach leaf curl, apricots (*H2–3*) tend to perform better than peaches outdoors. However, they flower very early, February–March in mild years, which means that their blossom is particularly vulnerable to **frost damage** without protection. Even if flowers escape the frost, few insects are flying this early so you may need to pollinate the flowers yourself, using a soft paintbrush (traditionally done with a rabbit's tail) to transfer pollen from flower to flower. Indoors, you probably need a wall around 1.5m tall to grow a successful specimen. Apricots like a near neutral (pH 7), well-drained soil. If your soil is acid, lime it at least two months before planting and again every three to five years. They should be planted 15–20cm from the wall. They fruit on the previous year's wood and fruiting is encouraged by pinching out the tips of long shoots in May. Overcrowded fruit will tend to ripen small, so thin when they are the size of a large strawberry, leaving the space of a thumb's width or more between fruits. Apricots like a good feed in early spring, with a high potash fertiliser and a mulch of rotted manure. Keep the tree watered in summer and indoors spray/mist the foliage to discourage **red spider**. You may need to resort to insecticide if you get bad infestations.

The variety 'Early Moorpark' is the only one generally recommended for the north, but it is not the best tasting variety. Jeremy Gilchrist from the Clyde Valley suggests that '**Flavorcot**' and '**Tomcot**' might also be worth trying.

Fig (*Ficus carica*) H3–4 E3

Said to be one of the oldest of all cultivated plants, humans have been growing and harvesting figs for over 10,000 years – longer than they have been growing wheat. Fig plants will grow well on a south- or west-facing wall in Scotland but getting edible fruit is another matter. If you have tasted the super-sweet, oozing, soft, purple fruits on fig trees in Andalucia, for example, then you'll likely be disappointed eating Scottish-grown fruit and, for that matter, supermarket fruit, as they don't travel when they are really ripe. My family and I once made the mistake of eating dozens from a tree we found on a Spanish golf course. The bathroom was busy soon afterwards! Fresh figs go well with cold meats, cheese and tarte tatin, advises Nigel Slater. I love the dried ones too.

A fig outdoors, at Kellie Castle, Fife.

Ripe sweet figs. Sadly we can't produce such fruit outdoors in Scotland but, indoors, sweet figs can be ripened.

FIGS OUTDOORS

Ripening figs outdoors in Scotland is a race against time, as the sun weakens in September and October just when the fruit need a blast of heat to finish off ripening. Figs take over a year to ripen – tiny embryo figs form in the autumn and overwinter before gradually swelling and ripening. A cold snap can kill off the juvenile fruits, though the hard winter of 2009–10 did not seem to have damaged any of the figs I saw later that summer. My investigations indicated more success with figs on the east coast than the west. Culzean Castle in Ayrshire has fine figs on the walls but they seldom ripen. Cambo in Fife, John Hulbert in Longforgan, near Dundee, and John Stoa, in Dundee, manage to get ripe figs on warm, sheltered walls, as does Rora Paglieri at Carestown Steading, in Buckie. Fyvie Castle's walled garden has a series of figs in large pots. Time will tell if they ever bear a good crop of fruit but the advantage is that the containers can be brought indoors in late summer to finish ripening.

FIGS INDOORS

We used to grow figs in a greenhouse at Glendoick but, even indoors, our Scottish figs never tasted like they do in the Mediterranean. We eventually gave up trying to grow them despite being my father's favourite fruit. Mertoun, in the Borders, and Johnstounburn, south of Edinburgh, both ripen figs in September in their greenhouses. I ate some deliciously ripe figs from Willie Duncan's tunnel house in September but the outdoor figs in Fife were a long way from ripening at this time of year.

SITE, SOIL, PLANTING AND CARE

Most fruiting figs in Scotland, both inside and out, are trained onto a wall, which allows maximum light and heat to ripen the fruit. Bend the flexible shoots and tie them onto horizontal wires. Most authorities advise planting in a fig pit which restricts the root-run and therefore encourages fruiting. Fig roots can damage drains and foundations, which is another good reason for restricting them. Fig pits can be made by sinking paving slabs into the ground to make a square cavity around 60cm × 60cm and filling the bottom of the hole with rubble, leaving 30–40cm of depth to fill with soil, compost and roots. You can use a large plastic pot sunk in the ground to similar effect, though the roots will probably break through. In spring, well established figs benefit from periodic hard pruning of long shoots back to 10cm from the main trunk or branches. Figs like to be kept moist in summer while fruit is growing in size. Willie Duncan explained to me that the secret of getting good fig ripening, indoors or out, is pinching/pruning in July. He advocates counting three leaf axils from the last ripening fig and nipping out any further young growth. This ensures three embryo figs for the following year and allows the fig to concentrate on ripening this year's crop. High potash tomato feed will help figs ripen in late summer. In autumn, as figs are ripening, you can cut back on the watering. Any full-sized figs which don't ripen are best removed in winter but leave the tiny embryo ones for next summer's fruit. Figs do best in a well-drained light soil. Rich soils tend to cause lush growth and few fruit.

COMMON PROBLEMS

Apart from the struggle to ripen fruit, **mealy bugs** (white) and **scale** (brown) can suck sap and cause considerable damage, particularly indoors. **Birds** and **wasps** love figs so you may need to net against them.

FIG VARIETIES

'**Brown Turkey**' The most common and probably the best choice for indoors or out.

'Ice Crystal' New and untested in Scotland. Very tough with unusual, attractive, lobed leaves – worth growing for foliage alone. It may not fruit outdoors in Scotland.

'White Lisbon' and 'White Marseilles' Mark Jeffrey, head gardener at Culross Palace, Fife, grows these two on a south wall and they do ripen edible figs. 'You have to get them before the blackbirds,' he advises.

Elderberry (*Sambucus nigra*) ✉ *H4–5 E1*

You may not pay much attention to this Scottish woodland and hedgerow native but Ron and Judith Gillies at Cairn O' Mohr in the Carse of Gowrie have been making elderflower champagne and elderberry wines for many years. Ron has selected the best forms from the surrounding countryside and planted them in trial beds back at the farm, giving them eccentric-sounding names, often to remind him where he found them – 'Stonker', 'Skelper', 'Bell Tree' and 'Car Door' ('We thought we were about to get caught taking that one when we heard car doors slam!'). Ron says that the Carse of Gowrie to the east of Perth is one of the richest wild elder areas and that, as you go west, they thin out considerably. In a larger garden, elder trees can be very ornamental, with frothy white flowers in spring and bunches of

almost black berries on red stems contrasting with the yellow autumn foliage. Easy to grow, you can make delicious cordial with the flowers by adding lemon and sugar, and Nigel Slater makes fritters with them. The autumn-produced berries are high in vitamin C and potassium and scientists in Israel and Norway have found convincing evidence that elderberries can protect against the common cold and influenza, including the deadly H1N1 strain. You can make your own remedy by steeping berries in vodka for a month or more, straining it and taking a teaspoon four times a day. Unripe berries, to which some people are apparently allergic, are toxic, so make sure they are ripe (black and juicy) when picked. Nigel Slater suggests making apple and elderberry pies and tarts.

PLANTING, CARE AND HARVESTING

You won't find fruiting selections at your local garden centre, so collect fruit from the wild (the characteristic smell of leaves helps identification) or propagate your own by hardwood cuttings stuck straight in the ground in winter. Very tough and tolerant of most soils, they grow well in woodland or in the open. Once they get large (up to 3m) you can hard prune them from time to time, but this tends to mean little flower and fruit the following year. Harvest the flowers when they are fully open, probably around June, and the fruit when it is ripe, dark and juicy, probably from August.

Nuts – Hazel, Walnuts, etc. *H4–5 E2*

Scotland does not have much of a commercial nut-growing history, mainly due to a lack of summer heat and a shorter growing season relative to southern England. Don't bother trying to grow almonds or sweet chestnuts for their nuts, for example. But that does not mean that you can't grow nuts in Scotland and our prehistoric ancestors depended on

Ron Gillies with elderberries, at Cairn o'Mohr, Perthshire. Ron has selected prolific fruiting forms for making wine from flowers and fruit.

Corylus maxima (filbert) in the Garden of Scottish Fruits at Fyvie Castle, Aberdeenshire.

A harvest of filberts and hazelnuts, Anton's Hill walled garden, Coldstream.

hazelnuts to a significant extent, judging by archaeological evidence from Peebleshire, Islay and the crannogs site on Loch Tay.

Hazel – Cobnuts and Filberts

Species of hazel, cobnuts (*Corylus avellana*) or filberts (*Corylus maxima*) are UK natives and can be good garden plants in Scotland, with showy catkins. Many garden forms have coloured leaves or contorted stems and these seldom produce good crops of nuts so you are best to choose forms selected for nut production, some of which can start fruiting at a young age. John Cook of Broughty Ferry wrote to us saying, 'First good filbert crop last year, delicious lightly toasted – 5 min at gas mark 6.' And Alec West gets a good crop near Coldstream. You'd be advised to practise some annual pruning in spring to let in plenty of light and remove any suckers growing from the base of the plant. The summer pruning, known as 'brutting', involves snapping long, young growth but leaving it hanging and not cutting it off. This lets in light and encourages fruit (nut) buds to form. Hazels fruit best on poor soils and, if you over-feed them, they'll just grow like mad and not fruit. '**Cosford**' is Nick Dunn's filbert choice.

Walnut

Walnut trees grow well enough in Scotland and we have good crops of nuts at Glendoick in years with hot summers but we find squirrels and birds seem to get at them before they are ready, so they may need to be harvested green and pickled or ripened in a sunny, dry spot on trays. The best nuts are grown on forms of *Juglans regia* from Asia. *Juglans nigra* is a more vigorous and tougher tree but the nuts are not as good. Although they are self-fertile, the male and female walnut flowers sometimes don't flower at the same time so if you want big crops it is best to plant more than one variety. Walnuts need patience and lots of space and they are not suitable for small gardens, as they grow into densely leaved, wide trees and inhibit other plants from growing around their root systems. Nick Dunn recommends '**Broadview**' as the best choice for Scotland. He also recommends a kind of slow strangulation with a cable tie around the main stem from May onwards to encourage fruiting. Remove it or loosen in autumn. Walnuts are probably not worth trying in the coldest or inland gardens as they'll tend to get their early growth frosted, probably meaning they won't fruit very often if at all.

CHAPTER 2

Soft or Bush Fruit

Soft fruit is the generic term for berries and currants. Most soft fruits are hard to transport and so are often picked early to get them to supermarkets, so your garden fruit will generally be picked riper and taste better. Every summer, as a boy, I'd go down to my grandfather's berry fields to pick strawberries. We got tuppence – or was it tuppence ha'penny? – for a 1lb basket and, as a child, it took an age to fill one. I liked strawberries better than rasps and, like most of the children, we went about 'berry-moothed'. Many more ended up in our tummies than in our baskets. We local children were pretty scared of the 'proper' pickers, mostly Glaswegians

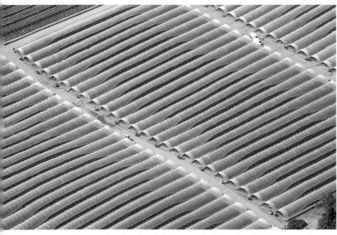

Eastern Scotland soft fruit tunnels from the air. Many people hate the sight of rows of plastic but they are essential for the supermarket demand for perfect fresh fruit (photo James Hutton Institute).

on 'holiday'. Whole families would turn up on barely legal ancient buses (in the 70s, any clapped-out bus was known as a 'berry bus'). The pickers would rough camp at the sides of the fields, while they picked berries for two weeks. What everyone remembers is how little you earned for your hours of work. Perthshire and Angus long boasted the world's largest concentration of strawberry and raspberry production. It even made the *Guinness Book of Records*.

There are still many soft fruit producers in Scotland but now fruit is grown in white plastic tunnels and much of the picking is done by migrant labour from Eastern Europe. Although the tunnels are an eyesore which ruin many of the finest valley views in Scotland, the rationale for them is sound – my grandfather's berries were often spoiled by heavy downpours which rotted the fruit before it could be picked. In those days, much of the fruit went to Baxter's for canning and Keiller's in Dundee for making jam. These days, most of Scotland's berry crop is sold for fresh consumption all over the UK. Tunnels allow for weatherproof production and a long season, which is what the supermarkets demand. Between 80 and 90 per cent of all UK soft fruit is now grown under tunnels, so it looks like the acres of plastic are here to stay. Much of Britain's major soft fruit research is carried out at the James Hutton Institute (formerly the SCRI), in Invergowrie, by Dundee, where many strawberry, raspberry and blackcurrant varieties have been bred.

Apart from blueberries and their relatives, which like very acid, peaty soil, most soft fruit prefers a slightly acid soil, (pH6–6.5), which is easily achieved in Scotland as much land is naturally around this pH level. If your garden is very peaty, or on moorland, then you may well need to lime to bring the pH towards 6. Unlike apples and pears, which can live for a hundred years or more, soft fruit has a shorter lifespan. Currants and gooseberries can produce fruit for up to 20 years, raspberries up to ten years and strawberries three to five years.

Strawberry (*Fragaria spp.*) H4 E1

The commercial strawberry, one of Scotland's major fruit crops, has its origins on both sides of the Atlantic. *Fragaria vesca*, the alpine strawberry, is our native woodlander with tiny but delicious berries. A breakthrough in edible strawberries came from the introduction of *F. chiloensis* to Europe from the Americas in the early eighteenth century. Scotland's climate turned out to be very suitable for strawberry cultivation and the Scottish commercial boom for soft fruit took off in Lanarkshire in around 1870 and soon spread to Perthshire and Angus. It is estimated that, at its peak, around 1910, there were 2,670 acres of strawberries in Scotland. Significant Scottish strawberry breeders include Robert Reid at Auchincruive in Ayrshire in the 1950s who raised 'Talisman' and 'Red Gauntlet', and Ronnie McNicol at the SCRI (now the James Hutton Institute) who raised 'Rhapsody', 'Symphony' and 'Concerto'. More recent work at the James Hutton Institute has included gene manipulation to breed vine weevil resistance.

CULTIVATION

Strawberries from the garden, picked ripe and eaten straight away are a revelation if you are used to the supermarket offerings, which are often picked

The Alpine strawberry is easy to grow and potentially invasive – the fruits are tasty if tiny.

A basket of ripe, freshly picked home-grown strawberries.

Strawberries grown on stilts under polythene for pick-your-own at Belhaven Fruit Farm, East Lothian.

Strawberry ridge planted and mulched with permeable membrane and straw, at the James Hutton Institute, Dundee.

Long one of the most popular varieties, Strawberry 'Cambridge Favourite'.

unripe, flown in from thousands of miles away, ripened in sheds and, to me, can taste like turnips, or 'woolly' according to Nigel Slater, and 'pneumatic' for Alan Titchmarsh. Don't blame the growers for this – the supermarkets are obsessed with shelf life and appearance, both of which override considerations of taste. What strawberries need above all is sun and good drainage. If you don't plant in full sun, you'll tend to produce lush leaves but little or no fruit. In clay or poorly drained soil, mound-plant the strawberries so that the crown of the plant is above any puddles which may occur in wet weather or, better still, build raised beds. In the open ground,

plant them 30–40cm apart in rows or spread them around the garden. If you intend to make jam, you'll need quite a big plot (2m × 2m) but if you just want to put some on your cornflakes, then a few plants will give a good yield. At Kellie Castle in Fife, strawberries are planted with leeks, onions and chives to reduce insect damage and fungal disease. Strawberries are moderate feeders so well-rotted manure or home-made compost is a good addition to the planting site. An annual feed with Growmore or similar fertiliser at 100g per square metre (3oz per square yard) will increase yields, particularly on sandy soils. Some advocate using sulphate of potash in early spring.

The traditional wisdom is to plant or transplant runners in late summer/autumn and container-grown plants in autumn or spring. Though it is tempting to let them fruit straight away, most experts advocate preventing fruiting in the first season by taking off the flowers and removing runners to obtain a really dense plant, which should then fruit heavily the following season (up to 1kg per plant). Scottish gardeners have reported birds, dogs, squirrels, mice, voles and their children appropriating the crop, so most people net them at fruiting time. Rain is the great enemy, rotting the fruit, particularly if left in contact with the soil. Mulches of barley straw are commonly used to prevent this. Not as attractive but equally effective is a mulch of black plastic, dug in or pegged at the sides with crosses cut at 30–40cm intervals for planting the runners into. Straw and other organic mulching materials are best removed after fruiting as they may harbour fungal spores.

If you grow under low cloches (30cm high), you'll often get fruit one to two weeks earlier than outdoors and keeping the fruit dry can avoid loss of crops to mould in wetter areas such as the west of Scotland. This is also a good method of cultivation for windy or cold inland sites. Don't forget to roll up the sides or open the ends to allow good insect pollination. If you have a long cloche run, you may need to put in some drip or trickle irrigation to keep plants watered. Don't slosh water over ripening fruit as it may go mouldy.

For all strawberries, after harvesting, you can cut back the older or yellowing foliage to encourage fresh growth. Some advocate cutting off all the leaves but you can get away with not bothering if you don't need to maximise yield. Don't leave the prunings lying around. Compost or burn them. Strawberry plants have a finite life for good fruiting – after three or four years, yields will decrease and it is best to dig out plants and start again. It is worth planting new runners every second year so you have young plants ready to fruit, otherwise you'll have to wait a year when you throw out an old batch. By all means, sever and pot up runners from young plants in order to increase your stock but I'd advise resisting the temptation to replant runners from old plants as they may already be developing virus. It is best to start again with newly purchased certified virus-free stock from nurseries or garden centres. Strawberries should not be replanted in the same soil/area for three years or more in order to avoid build up of viruses and other diseases, and don't plant them in soil recently used for tomatoes or potatoes. If you don't have ground to plant into, then, of all fruit crops, strawberries are one of the best choices for growbags, containers, raised beds and even hanging baskets. Islay House grows strawberries in growbags on raised platforms outdoors to make picking easier and less backbreaking and many commercial farms do the same in tunnel houses.

COMMON PROBLEMS

Strawberries flower in spring and need to be pollinated by insects. **Frost** turns the eye of the flowers black and they won't set fruit so, in coldest gardens, use cloches or fleece protection. For commercial growers as well as amateurs, **vine weevil** is a serious root-eating pest. The adults are flightless black insects which nibble leaves but their soil-borne larvae are the real enemy as one of their favourite

foods is strawberry root; indeed nurserymen use strawberry plants as an indicator that this pest is present. The crescent-shaped white grubs with a brown head can munch their way though all the roots of your crop. The first you know about it is the wilting foliage which comes away in your hand. Commercially grown plants are treated with insecticide but beware of gifts from friends. Before planting, knock gifted strawberry runners out of their pots and give the roots a good shake before planting, to check for grubs. Chemical vine weevil controls available to amateurs for ornamentals tend not to be licensed for use on fruit, though many people use them anyway. Commercial growers apply large amounts of chemical vine weevil control. Amateurs can use nematodes, a new strain of which is now effective in cooler soils than before. These are probably most useful and affordable for treating young plants and containers. As well as birds and some animals, slugs also love strawberries.

Strawberry virus, which gradually weakens the plants over time, is a serious problem. Infections gradually yellow the foliage and decrease the fruit yield. The only remedy is to dig them up, burn them and start again, preferably on another site. Poor drainage and heavy soil can cause a fatal fungal infection called **red core** (a type of *Phytophthora*), which stunts leaves and turns them red before the plant collapses. *Verticillium* **wilt** is a related disease with similar outcome, which also affects potatoes. The symptoms are the leaves and shoots turning brown and wilting. The only advice for both fungal diseases is to burn plants and try again in a better drained site or a raised bed.

STRAWBERRY VARIETIES

Plant several varieties to extend the season of available fruit. These days many people eat nothing but 'Elsanta', the supermarket favourite, but for the garden you can do much better. You may be tempted by the advertising of varieties known as 'everbearers' or 'perpetuals' which fruit into July and August. These are less hardy, more prone to mildew, produce smaller fruit and only fruit well for two years. They might be worth a try in Scotland under cover but, for most Scottish gardeners, they are probably best left alone. Some Borders growers have tried them and find that they crop in early summer in the normal way and then produce spasmodic further fruits all summer long. Definitely avoid the varieties known as 'day neutrals', which were bred for more southern climates and are not worth growing in Scotland as it is not hot or sunny enough. Those listed below are some of the best of the many varieties on offer. Early varieties tend to ripen in June and later ones in July, but it depends on the site and the weather at the time – sunny weather brings on ripening.

'**Elsanta**' The supermarket favourite, good when ripe but too often picked early and ripened indoors and the resultant fruit taste of little.

'**Cambridge Favourite**' ♀ Still popular, older variety, good flavour, mid season and heavy cropping but prone to disease and virus.

'**Christine**' Very early, disease resistant and good flavour. Early flowers need frost protection in colder/inland areas.

'**Hapil**' Mid season, seems to be tough and a good cropper.

'**Marshmellow**' Slightly later ripening. Seldom offered but recommended by Rosa Steppanova for Shetland.

'**Pegasus**' ♀ Good recent introduction. Large juicy fruit in June and good resistance to wilt. Good reports from Broughton, Kirkcudbright, even in wet weather.

'**Rhapsody**' ♀ ✉ Dundee-raised mid–late season, good flavour, disease resistant.

'**Rosie**' Early, good flavour.

'**Sonata**' Mid season, high yielding and good in *Beechgrove Garden* and *Gardening Which?* trials

'**Symphony**' ♀ ✉ Dundee-raised, a heavy cropper with good flavour, July–August fruiting. Susceptible to powdery mildew but with some resistance to red core, crown rot and *Verticillium* and some tolerance to vine weevil. Recommended for organic growing.

Alpine strawberries (*Fragaria vesca*) H5 Small, fragrant and delicious fruit, they naturalise as groundcover under trees and in borders. You can start them yourself if you collect the fruit, let it dry and separate out the seeds. The white-fruited form 'Alba' is less attractive to birds.

Raspberry (*Rubus idaeus*) H4–5 E1–2

For many, this is the best fruit of all for home-growing, as raspberries don't store well or travel easily and there is nothing to match stuffing them in your mouth straight from the canes. A raspberry is technically a 'drupe' – a cluster of tiny fruits, each

Three Scottish-raised raspberry varieties: 'Tulameen', 'Glen Coe' (photo SCRI), 'Glen Ample'.

Raspberry botrytis (mould), which quickly strikes in wet weather. Commercial growing under polythene reduces mould problems.

Raspberry virus typical on old canes (over ten years old). Plants should be removed and burned and raspberries should not be replanted in the same part of the garden.

with a seed inside. Raspberries take up significant amounts of garden space, it's true, but you can expect to harvest 2–3kg of fruit per metre of raspberries (less for autumn varieties) once the canes are a few years old. Perthshire and Angus are Scotland's raspberry counties and I remember the hillsides covered in neat lines running down the slopes around Dundee and Blairgowrie, planted on a north–south axis to allow the even ripening of fruit. Many are still there but now the fields are covered with plastic and not nearly so visually appealing.

It is believed that cultivated raspberries have their origins in the mountains of Turkey, although wild raspberries, *Rubus idaeus*, occur all over Europe, including Britain. Raspberries contain ellagic acid which has antioxidant properties and apparently reduces susceptibility to heart attacks. Scotland has long been a major player in the commercial production of raspberries and in the development of new varieties. The breeding program at Mylnefield/SCRI (now the James Hutton Institute) began in the 1950s under Derek Jennings, followed by Ronnie McNicol and Rick Harrison. The first of the Scottish 'Glens' series of cultivars, 'Glen Clova', was released in 1970. This was a major breakthrough, with yields 30 per cent higher

than the standard cultivars of the time. 'Glen Moy' (1981) was the first spine-free raspberry cultivar while 'Glen Ample' (1996) is now the UK's most widely grown raspberry. Nikki Jennings (no relation to Derek) is the current senior raspberry breeder and she took a group of us round her tunnels evaluating and tasting the new varieties, mostly still under code numbers. Disease resistance, long shelf life and good flavour are all goals of the programme.

CULTIVATION

Raspberries are best planted when dormant, between October and March–April. They can be obtained bare-rooted from specialist nurseries but are most commonly bought in potted bundles of five to ten canes from garden centres. Raspberries need well-drained but moisture-retentive, fertile, slightly acidic soils and they don't like being planted too deeply. Although they are said to be shade tolerant, in the low light levels of Scotland fruiting is usually significantly reduced. Heavy and waterlogged soils are not suitable, as they usually cause failure due to fungal disease. Try planting in a raised bed or on a 10cm ridge if the soil is heavy or the drainage less than ideal. Plant in a sheltered, sunny position, as early in the year as possible, before the end of May at the latest, and cut the canes back to around 10cm from the ground when you plant them. Compared to east central Scotland, the relative lack of heat in northern Scotland tends to mean that yields are reduced. They don't do very well at Castle of Mey in Caithness, for example, and, in Orkney and Shetland, they are usually grown in polytunnels or in very sheltered sites.

Summer-fruiting raspberries are generally planted in rows about 40cm apart and trained along a post and wire system. The method chosen depends on space and how much effort you want to make. The classic way to grow rasps is along wires which are stretched between 7–10cm diameter posts, placed at 4–5m intervals. Make sure you buy long enough posts to bang them well into the ground so the wires can be tensioned on them. The wires can be single

or double lengths on one or both sides of the posts. The so-called Scandinavian training system uses parallel wires which are more widely spaced, with the canes attached to either one of the wires forming a 'V' shape. Not everyone has room for rows of raspberries, so you can try training two or three canes round a single post or even over an arch or pergola.

Raspberry pruning is not complicated but it does need to be done properly to get good crops year after year. For summer fruiters, cut back fruited canes as soon as picking is done. The strongest young canes, up to eight per plant should be spread out along the wires. They can be tied in or spaced using strings tied back and forth between the two parallel wires. Long straggly canes can be trimmed in winter. One way to make pruning easier is to keep the fruiting canes on one side of the wire or wires (the sunnier side) and the young canes on the other side.

Autumn raspberries produce a smaller crop and are mostly lower growing, so can be grown without supports. Pruning is simpler too. As they fruit on the current year's growth, they should be cut hard back to the ground in spring. If they become congested, you can reduce the number of canes. They can even be grown in a sunny mixed border.

In spring, raspberries appreciate a good feed. You can use organic fertiliser such as fish, blood and bone, for example, and, if you have access to it, plant and mulch with well-rotted organic matter. Sulphate of ammonia, Growmore or dried poultry manure will also give a good boost of nitrogen, leading to vigorous growth.

To try raspberries in a deep container, make up a blend of soil-based compost (John Innes) mixed with a lighter peat-based or peat-free one to obtain a good planting mixture. Use slow-release fertiliser granules or liquid feed through the growing season. Autumn varieties would be best.

COMMON PROBLEMS

Most raspberries succumb to a **virus** which gradually weakens them and, for that reason, after around

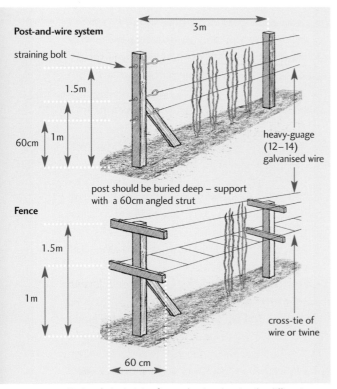

Post and wire training for raspberries showing the different ways of supporting canes.

ten years, it is best to dig up and burn the old stock and replant new canes in another part of the garden. Don't be tempted to replant suckers from the old canes.

Rain when the fruit is ripening is the greatest threat to a good crop. If you can, pick the fruit when it is dry, as mould soon attacks wet picked fruit. Some growers run a tarpaulin rain cover over the posts and wires to protect the fruit. It won't have escaped your notice that, in the last few years, commercial growers now grow most of their raspberries under plastic tunnels, which keep the fruit in much better condition.

In poorly drained and heavy soils, raspberries are susceptible to **root rot** (*Phytophthora fragariae* var. *rubi*), a common problem for commercial growers. Symptoms are the yellowing and wilting of leaves when the ground is clearly moist enough. Plants should be dug out and destroyed. Ridge planting in heavier soils helps to reduce chances of infection and some varieties have some degree of resistance. New James Hutton Institute-raised root rot-resistant raspberries such as 'Glen Ericht' are coming on to the market but these are not the best tasting and there is further breeding to do. **Raspberry beetle** is an annoying pest whose larvae burrow into the fruit and cause grey-brown, dry patches at the stalk end. They normally crawl out when the fruit is picked and you can still eat it. Other insect problems can include **large raspberry aphid**, **raspberry cane midge**, **raspberry moth**, **capsid bugs** and **fruit maggots**. Diseases include **rust**, **mildew**, **spur blight** and **cane blight**. There are few chemicals licensed for amateurs for most of these.

RASPBERRY VARIETIES

Summer fruiting E2

'**Glen Ample**' ♀ ✉ Spine free, mid–late July, large fruit with good flavour. Scotland's top commer-

cial raspberry with good pest and disease resistance.

'**Glen Coe**' ✉ A striking new variety, June–August cropping, wilt-resistant, rich, purple raspberry bred at the James Hutton Institute from 'Glen Clova'. It looks spectacular and don't be put off by the 'bloom' on the fruit, as it is naturally occurring. It will really brighten up the dinner table.

'**Glen Doll**' ✉ A mid-season variety, with late bud break, so useful for cold gardens, and good insect and disease resistance, one of the best for freezing. Rather fussy and needs perfect soil conditions.

'**Glen Ericht**' ✉ A new and important breakthrough with significant root rot resistance. The taste is average but this will be the first of a breeding line, invaluable for those who garden with less than ideal soil conditions.

'**Glen Fyne**' ✉ A new James Hutton Institute selection, mid season, resistant to large raspberry aphid but susceptible to *Phytophthora*. Probably of more interest to the commercial market.

'**Glen Lyon**' ✉ Rather a sharp taste, so better for cooking.

'**Glen Magna**' ♀ ✉ Spiny, longest cropping in *Gardening Which?* trials.

'**Glen Moy**' ✉ Spine-free, good flavour, early starting in June, heavy cropping.

'**Glen Prosen**' ✉ Spine-free, needs rich soil, a good all-rounder. Mid season.

'**Malling Admiral**' Spine-free, disease resistant, needs wind shelter. Late.

'**Octavia**' Late July and into August, one of the latest of the summer varieties.

'**Tulameen**' ♀ Late July, long season, good flavour, very sweet and heavy yield. For many, this is the king of raspberries. I liked this best at the James Hutton Institute tastings and it came top in *Gardening Which?* and RHS trials. The supermarkets don't like it so much, as it has a short shelf life, so I'd pick this as an excellent choice to grow in the garden.

Autumn Fruiting E1

'Allgold' ♀ Yellow with very juicy fruit in August to October.

'Autumn Bliss' ♀ Deliciously sweet, best in a sheltered sunny site. Willie Duncan recommends leaving some of the previous year's growth for a July crop and cutting the rest of the canes back in spring to produce an autumn crop.

'Polka' ♀ A Polish hybrid which David McIntyre at Moyness Nurseries reckons is even better than 'Autumn Bliss', ripening seven to ten days earlier and heavier cropping. RHS trials confirmed this.

Bramble (Blackberry)

Wild brambles (*Rubus fruticosus*) H5 provide free fruit all over Scotland in late summer and early autumn and they are very good for you – a serving of only eight berries counts as one of your 'five a day'. Wild brambles soon engulf your garden if you let them so they are best left in the countryside. Cultivated varieties are generally better behaved and many of the newer ones are as sweet as raspberries, unlike the wild ones which have a certain tartness.

Unless supported, cultivated brambles develop into an untidy tangle, so they are usually grown against a wall or fence or trained along a single or double horizontal wire. You'll need two stout and strong 2.3–3m stakes with three or four wires stretched horizontally between them, starting at 1m above the ground then at 50cm intervals, to which the vigorous shoots can be tied. You can shorten all side shoots to allow easy access, keep your plants off the path and save your clothes from being ripped by thorns. Brambles are not really suited to very small gardens, as they do take up quite a bit of room. Vigorous cultivars can be planted 4–6m apart and the less vigorous, thornless and slow-growing types 2–3m apart. Fruit is produced on wood which is already a year old so, for continued production, you need both one-year-old fruiting canes or 'rods' and young growth which will fruit the following year. Sometimes young and old canes are trained on separate wires in a fan-trained or espalier arrangement. So that you know which ones to prune, as soon as fruiting canes have been harvested they can be cut back to the ground. Tie in the whippy young canes ready for flowering and fruiting the following year.

Cultivated blackberries need reasonable soil which is not too wet, in a fairly sunny site. Many varieties are not as tough as you might expect and their early growth can be frosted or wind damaged in colder and exposed gardens, although the flowers

Bramble or blackberry 'Loch Tay' flowers and fruit – Scottish bred and very sweet.

Bramble 'Loch Maree', with attractive double pink flowers, raised at the James Hutton Institute near Dundee.

are relatively late so are rarely frosted. 'Oregon Thornless' was hammered at Glendoick by harsh winters, taking a year to recover. Alan Smith reported similar problems in Strathdon. Frost damage is usually cosmetic and can be cut back. All brambles are self-fertile, so there is no need to grow more than one.

COMMON PROBLEMS

Brambles suffer less from pests and diseases than raspberries, though they can be attacked by **raspberry beetle** (*see under* 'Raspberry'). You may find lots of seedlings coming up under your plants and these seedlings are seldom as good as the parents so it's best to spray them, hoe them or dig them up. Some of the newer, large-fruited varieties have berries which are prone to going **mouldy** in wet weather.

BRAMBLE/BLACKBERRY VARIETIES *H3–5 E2*

SCRI in Dundee has bred the world's most popular bramble/blackberry variety 'Loch Ness' and the newer 'Loch Tay' and 'Loch Maree'. *Beechgrove Garden's* Carole Baxter recommends thornless varieties 'Loch Tay' and 'Helen' (early), which have done well at the cold Beechgrove site west of Aberdeen. Except where marked, assume a hardiness rating of *H4–5*.

'**Black Satin**' Thornless, pink flowers, early.
'**Fantasia**' ♀ Large fruit, vigorous and with vicious thorns. Admired for its flavour. Hard to find.
'**Helen**' Early ripening, this is John Stoa's choice as the best for outdoors with a large crop of long fruit from mid July onwards. Quite tart but very juicy.
'**Loch Maree**' ✉ A James Hutton Institute variety, thornless with attractive double pink flowers and sweet flavour, ripening in early August.

'**Loch Ness**' ♀ ✉ The most widely grown thornless variety, long fruiting period to the first frosts, large firm fruit. John Stoa reports that fruit can go mouldy and it is prone to downy mildew.
'**Loch Tay**' ✉ A new James Hutton Institute-bred early variety, thornless, fruiting in late July. The sweetest flavour I have ever tasted in a blackberry – you won't believe how sweet it is.
'**Oregon Thornless**' *H3–4* The most ornamental choice, thornless, leaves like parsley, good autumn colour. It can produce thorny suckers which should be removed. This is not all that hardy and it suffered in much of Scotland in the winter of 2009–10. It can be frosted in spring, so for mild and sheltered gardens only.
'**Sylvan**' ♀ Early, tends to have rather soft but impressively large fruit. Very adaptable, tolerant of clay soils, wind and drought. Very thorny.
'**Waldo**' Thornless, huge fruit, with good disease resistance, canes can be brittle. Less vigorous than others, so a good choice for a smaller space.

Raspberry Hybrids – Loganberry and Tayberry

Loganberry H4–5 E2

The story of the Loganberry's creation is a happy accident. Its raiser, Judge Logan of California, was actually trying to create new bramble hybrids in the 1880s, but one of them turned out to be a strange dark red fruit. Giving the fruit to his neighbours to try, they were christened 'Mr Logan's Berries'. The judge recognised that the blackberry had crossed with some raspberries growing in his garden nearby. The original loganberry is thorny and the taste is pretty tart, so it is usually used for cooking. It was grown in large quantities to prevent scurvy in Royal Navy sailors. There is also a 'Thornless Variety' which is as it sounds. The **Boysenberry** is three quarters blackberry and a quarter raspberry and, as

Loganberry (photo copyright the James Hutton Institute).

Tayberry raised at SCRI (now the James Hutton Institute), near Dundee.

you'd expect, is closer to the blackberry in flavour. Grow as for brambles/blackberries above.

Tayberry ♀ H3–4 E2 ✖

Raised by Derek Jennings at the SCRI (now the James Hutton Institute) at Invergowrie, near Dundee, by crossing a raspberry with a blackberry, this was a successful attempt to improve on the Loganberry. Derek used the blackberry 'Aurora' with 56 chromosomes, bred in Oregon, USA, as a parent, crossed with a raspberry with extra chromosomes. The breeding took five years and, in 1980, the best seedling was selected as the 'Tayberry'. Derek writes an excellent account of its launch:

> The Tayberry created much interest and I appeared in cartoons, but wearing a kilt and tam-o'-shanter, which I thought was a bit rich for a Welshman from Cardiff. The Americans were worse. They quoted me speaking in a strong Scottish accent – der yer ken? One even assumed that I lived in a houseboat on the River Tay and sent letters

addressed to: River Tay, Scotland, England (congratulations to the postman).

The Tayberry has reddish-purple fruits, larger and sweeter than those of the Loganberry and you can eat it straight off the bush. I have seen its young growth scorched by easterly winds in the spring, so it is best in a sheltered site. In 1998, the normally prickly Tayberry produced a thornless sport in Buckingham, now known as the 'Buckingham Tayberry'. The **Tummelberry** *H4* ✖ is similar, a little hardier but not as sweet tasting.

Cloudberry (*Rubus chamaemorus*) *H5 E2* ✖

This Scottish native, 10–25cm high, has been gathered for centuries from boggy mountainside sites in the Highlands. Traces of cloudberry have been found at the Loch Tay crannog archaeological site. The yellow and red berries have a singular taste of 'honey and apples' and the fruit ripens in July and August. The berries are rich in vitamin C and have a built-in preservative of benzoic acid, which allows them to last for weeks even without refrigeration. The Holt Research Centre, Tromso, Norway, is trying to breed easy-to-cultivate varieties for the farm and garden, so far with limited success. So, if you want to try them, your best bet is to go walking in the Highlands and pick a few of your own. You can find them on north-facing slopes in the Angus Glens, Perthshire Munros such as Schiehallion, the Cairngorms, Sutherland and other locations. They taste great. If you want to obtain plants, Poyntzfield Herb Nursery on the Black Isle sometimes stocks them. They fruit far more prolifically in Scandinavia than in Scotland, so you'll be lucky to see more than a handful of berries. This plant is vulnerable to climate change in its Scottish habitats.

Japanense Wincberry (*Rubus phoenicolasius*) H4 E2

With delicious fruit, this is worth a try in Scotland. The very sweet orange-red raspberry-like berries are produced in late summer in clusters like those of brambles, on a ground cover plant with handsome foliage which will root into the soil as it spreads. For a more manageable plant, grow against a sheltered wall or fence where it will reach 2m or more. Like raspberries, it fruits on one-year-old stems, so cut out old canes once they have fruited. It does not

Japanese wineberry (*Rubus phoenicolasius*).

produce a huge amount of fruit and certainly needs a sheltered, warm situation to grow well this far north. It can seed around in mild gardens and we have had good reports of it from Catriona Murray and Neil Cameron on Jura.

Blueberry Family (*Vaccinium ssp.*) H4–5 E1–2

Blueberry

Blaeberries and blueberries are related to heather and rhododendrons and, like them, enjoy a very acid soil of pH4–5.5. They are often found growing in almost pure peat in nature. Indeed blueberries are one of the best fruits for the acid soils of the Hebrides and other moorland soils. They have clusters of urn-like small white flowers (like those of *Pieris*) in late spring and bunches of fruit in July and August. Our native blaeberries (*Vaccinium myrtillus*) are the wild, dark blue-black berries found on Scottish moorland, which ripen in summer, usually from July to September. Not a commercial crop, they're great for snacking on when walking. If you can be bothered to pick enough of them, you can use them in jams, muffins and puddings, but I'd just eat them straight off the plant. They were long used as a Highland remedy for improving eyesight and stomach complaints and, more recently, hailed as a so-called 'superfood' for antioxidant properties. John Stoa grows blaeberries from berries gathered in the Angus Glens on his Dundee allotment. They do produce a reasonable crop but are inclined to suffer from fungal dieback. Christine Campbell grows them commercially on Skye with some success but the yields are not high.

From North America, the highbush blueberries (*Vaccinium corymbosum*) are now widely available in garden centres and are popular garden plants. They are being grown as commercial farm crops in Scotland and about time too. The SCRI (now the James Hutton Institute) in Invergowrie first planted

Blueberries are highly ornamental plants – white spring flowers, spectacular fruit and red and orange autumn colour.

Three of the mostly widely planted blueberry varieties – 'Earlieblue', 'Patriot' and 'Darrow'.

blueberries in the 1970s, but fruit breeder Rex Brennan told me that their commercial potential for Scotland took 25 years to be recognised. A new blueberry trial, looking at the best varieties for Scottish farmers, was started by the James Hutton Institute in 2009. Blueberries take some considerable time to get established but they go on fruiting for 30–40 years, so the investment in bushes pays long-term dividends. Birds used to strip the James Hutton fruit but for some reason they now leave them alone so they no longer need to be netted. Have the birds gone off them, I wonder. Blueberry research should reveal the most satisfactory varieties for Scotland, as well as selecting those which can be mechanically

harvested without damaging the berries, bushes or soil. Research suggests that UK consumers would like blueberries to have 'more taste', so James Hutton breeders will be working on this too. The UK currently produces less than 10 per cent of the blueberries eaten in this country, but Scotland has an ideal climate and soil to take advantage of current demand.

A Seattle garden centre I visited on a trip to the USA stocked 30 different blueberry varieties. The majority are 'high bush' growing to 2m or more and used for hedging and screening as well as border plants. Half-high and lowbush varieties derived from *Vaccinium angustifolium* and *V. myrtilloides* grow to 1m and 60cm respectively and are suitable for containers. I have not seen much evidence of lowbush varieties in the UK yet and they may not be as suited to the climate. The Seattle garden centre staff explained that, for them, blueberries were pretty trouble-free and fruited so readily and heavily that it was possible to share the crop with birds. Varieties such as 'Duke' can yield up to 10kg of fruit per bush when mature. Back home, I went to visit Peter and Melanie Thomson, who grow blueberries commercially on their farm in Blairgowrie. Grown in open-sided tunnels, the fruit was plentiful and delicious. They specialise in late fruiters such as 'Chandler' and 'Osark Blue'. At Glendoick Caroline and Peter get very good yields on their bushes.

Cultivation

The key to growing blueberries is to give them moist, but not boggy, acid soil. They take a while to establish and, when newly planted, cannot tolerate drying out, so you may need to irrigate for the first few years. Expert Jennifer Trehane suggests removing much of the fruit for the first few years to encourage lots of strong growth and she also advises pruning long straggly shoots to encourage a strong and bushy plant. Once their roots are well established, blueberries need little or no maintenance. The RHS recommends an annual feeding regime of sulphate of ammonia (35g/m²), sulphate of potash (35g/m²) and bone meal (105g/m²) for best yields. I reckon that you could just as easily use Growmore for similar results. And a top dressing of well-rotted manure doesn't do any harm.

Blueberries fruit on two- to three-year-old wood so little pruning is required except to tidy up straggly shoots. On mature plants, thick woody stems gradually become less productive and these can be cut back to the ground in winter to stimulate new shoots. You can spot the non-productive shoots in winter, as the growth buds are much thinner than the wider, fatter fruiting buds. For container growing, use ericaceous compost with added grit.

COMMON PROBLEMS

Many people have trouble establishing blueberries but, once they get going, they are easy to please as long as they have moist, acidic soil. The fruit may be attractive to birds, so you'll probably need to net them when young.

BLUEBERRY VARIETIES

Most experts advise planting more than one variety to ensure the best pollination. Those listed here have a hardiness rating of H4–5. Some varieties are less hardy.

'**Bluecrop**' Fruits well in Scotland and one of the most commonly offered varieties in garden centres.

'**Chandler**' A heavy cropping late variety which is a good commercial plant and grows well in cold areas.

'**Darrow**' Grown commercially in Scotland with huge berries in August and September.

'**Duke**' ♀ Sturdy, upright, tough, good autumn colour. Late, so good for inland gardens. Heavy cropping, mild flavour, keeps well.

'**Hardyblue**' Large, upright, vigorous and hardy – one of the best for heavier or less than ideal soils. Good autumn colour and attractive red stems in winter. Sweet flavour and a good fruiter.

'**Spartan**' ♀ Upright and hardy, late flowering, good autumn colour. Needs well-drained and rich soil. Good flavour.

Cranberry (*Vaccinium macrocarpon*) H2–3 E2–3

There are Scottish native cranberries, but the commercial fruiting varieties are derived from North American stock. Cranberry juice is a popular and delicious drink, as well as having useful medicinal

Cranberries grown in barrels at Woodside Walled Garden, near Kelso.

Lingonberry (cowberry) – a native of Scottish moorland but low yielding as a garden fruit, so more of a curiosity than a viable crop.

properties. In North America, commercial cranberries are grown in cranberry bogs which are harvested by flooding the bogs so that the fruit floats to the surface and is skimmed off from boats.

Cranberries like damp, peaty soil but not stagnant water. They don't like to dry out. The stems will gradually root themselves, forming a thicket which usually needs to be pruned from time to time to allow sunlight to reach the stems. If you don't have boggy conditions, you can create them artificially by lining a bed with polythene about 1m², to a depth of 30cm and fill it with 50 per cent peat and 50 per cent soil. At Torridon Kitchen Garden, an old cold frame has been lined with polythene to grow them. Fruit ripens in October and you can 'comb' it from the stems by spreading out your fingers. Berries last for ages on the bush or in the fridge. Birds tend to find them too astringent to eat. The *Beechgrove Garden* has had some success with cranberries. After a few years and a slow start, they began to fruit well. The varieties '**Franklyn**' and '**Stevens**' were grown. To fruit, a significant winter chilling period is required, so they may not be suitable for the mildest west coast gardens. Fruit expert Colin Stirling recommends planting six or seven plants per square metre. To obtain more plants, simply detach runners. He also recommends rejuvenating mature clumps by removing older plants to allow room for the young shoots. Christine Campbell at Blueberryhill on Skye is successfully growing cranberries commercially. She grows them in boggy peaty soil with four inches of sand on the top. After a couple of years, they began fruiting well and she now has more fruit than she can sell.

Cowberry/Lingonberry (*Vaccinium vitis-idaea*) H4 E2-3 ✉

A major fruit crop in Sweden but little known as a food crop in the UK, this *Vaccinium* grows wild in parts of Scotland with a spreading habit, white to palest pink bells in spring and dark-red berries in autumn. The berries can be used for jams and liqueurs. Plants grow to 25cm × 1m and the berries taste similar to cranberries. Grow four to seven plants per square metre for a good mat of berries. They require an acid but well drained soil in sun or part shade. You'll probably need to net them from birds when they ripen in September. Christine Campbell grows these on Skye but finds that the fruit are small and fiddly to harvest and yields are low so they do not make a particularly successful commercial proposition.

Chokeberry (*Aronia*) grown commercially by Thomsons of Blairgowrie. It provides tart fruit, high in antioxidants, and spectacular autumn colour.

Chokeberry (*Aronia melanocarpa*) H5 E1

The common name 'chokeberry' – so called for the sharp-tasting fruit – may indicate why this fruit has never caught on in Britain. The white-flowered deciduous shrub has black fruit, like acidic blackcurrants, in midsummer, ideal for jams and sauces, and good autumn colour. Scientists have found that antioxidant levels in *Aronia* are more than twice as high as those of blueberries and they are also very high in vitamins. Commercial fruit growers Thomsons of Blairgowrie have been growing chokeberries commercially for Marks & Spencer and Melanie Thomson explained to me that the astringent taste of the fresh fruit means that they are more palatable mixed with other fruit and fruit juices. Peter Thomson took me to see their spreading shrubby bushes laden with dark fruits in August. 'The second berry tastes better than the first – once you get used to it,' he warned. And he was right. Fresh, I doubt they'll catch on, but I'm sure these have a future in jams, juices and sauces and perhaps in ice cream. The Thomsons also praised the spectacular autumn colour and I can vouch that their fields turn fiery red most years. Chokeberry grows well and fruits prolifically on Jura, so this looks like another good west-coast fruit. Two selected clones for fruit production

are 'Viking' and 'Brilliant'. It is worth growing as an ornamental alone and it is clearly tough and easy to manage. Poland produces chokeberries in large numbers.

Currant (*Ribes ssp.*) H5 E1–2

Currants are cultivated forms and hybrids of *Ribes nigrum*, which can be found over much of the northern hemisphere from northern Europe to Siberia. All currants are good for you but blackcurrants are exceptionally high in vitamins C and E. Currants require a sunny site with shelter from cold winds. They are tough but they flower early and, if their flowers are frosted, they will probably not fruit. All currants are self-fertile, so you only need to grow one. They are usually grown in fruit cages or netted, as birds tend to strip the plants of fruit as they ripen. They are best planted in autumn and winter, 1.2–2m apart. Currants are quite heavy feeders so add a general fertiliser when you plant. Alternate this with a high potash feed, most easily obtained as sulphate of potash. If you can get hold of rotted manure to mulch them, so much the better. Currants don't like to dry out, so water them well, particularly as fruit is forming. However, if they are over-watered as fruit is ripening, it may split.

COMMON PROBLEMS

Birds are the most common nuisance as they are happy to eat the fruit at a stage before we consider it ripe. If you don't have room for a fruit cage, then grow currants against a wall, making netting easier. **Blackcurrant big bud** is caused by tiny mites that live in the dormant buds in winter and cause them to fail to develop properly. There are no chemicals available to amateurs to control this. 'Ben Hope' is the most resistant to the problem. Currants are prone to a **blister aphid** which distorts the leaves with coloured blisters. It usually strikes as fruit is ripening and can be ignored or cut off. **Rust** coats the leaf underside with red pustules, usually after harvesting. It's best to just let nature take its course or prune hard. **Blackcurrant fungal diseases**, such as powdery mildew, can be treated with sulphur but red- and white currants are sensitive to this and it may damage them.

Blackcurrant (*Ribes nigrum*) H5 E1–2

Cultivated in gardens from the eighteenth century onwards but never widely popular due to their tartness raw, the commercial importance of blackcurrants is due to their use in drink production – 95 per cent of all blackcurrants in the UK end up in Ribena™ and similar juices. The taste for blackcurrant juice began during the Second World War when schoolchildren were given free supplies. Blackcurrants are an excellent source of vitamin C and polyphenols, thought to have preventative qualities against cancer, diabetes and Alzheimer's. Blackcurrants are seldom eaten raw but more usually pulped for jams and sauces. Seventeenth-century herbals refer to the medicinal properties of the fruit and leaves for gallstones and chest infections. The leaves are aromatic (although some find them somewhat unpleasant) and can be used themselves as a basis for a drink.

Scotland has had a major role to play in the development of the world's blackcurrants, as most commercial and garden varieties, named after Scottish mountain peaks, were bred at the James Hutton Institute, near Dundee. Beginning in the 1950s under Malcolm Anderson, the breeding programme's aims were to increase cold tolerance, especially of cold spring weather, and to improve even fruit ripening and fungal disease resistance. UK clones were crossed with varieties from Canada and Scandinavia, with the first, 'Ben Lomond', released in 1972. Currently, the most popular is 'Ben Hope'. Breeding work is ongoing, focusing on pest and disease resistance, frost tolerance and fruit quality. Blackcurrants need cold winters to set good crops of fruit, so northern Britain is better suited to them than the south.

CULTIVATION

Blackcurrants can be grown in acid or slightly alkaline soils. Plant with plenty of organic matter to help retain moisture and nutrients. Clay soils are not ideal but are tolerated as long as they are not waterlogged.

Currant blister aphid, which tends to strike later in the season after fruiting. Affected branches are best cut off.

Harvesting blackcurrants at Glendoick. This can be done by cutting off the whole fruiting branch (which would be pruned later anyway) and pulling the fruit off in the kitchen.

Blackcurrants ready for picking.

Planting deeply is advisable to encourage a mass of basal shoots. Plant up to 5cm deeper than the potted soil level. Planting spacing should be 1.5–2m apart. It may seem extreme but it is advisable to forgo any fruit in the first year and to cut back all stems on newly planted blackcurrants down to one bud, near ground level. Once the blackcurrants are established they need regular pruning to obtain good fruit yields. Blackcurrants fruit on second year wood. Blackish-grey, older wood has already fruited and is removed by cutting to the base in winter. Ideally you want seven to ten stems of young wood (paler in colour). If you need to rejuvenate old or neglected blackcurrants, the best thing to do is to cut them hard back, almost to the ground in winter. You won't get any fruit in the first year following, but you should get a good crop of fruiting wood for the year after. A good feed and mulch with manure is also advisable.

Harvest blackcurrants by taking the whole fruit stem (known as a 'strig'). Early fruiting varieties tend to shed fruit as soon as it is ripe, while the later ones give you more leeway, hanging on to ripe fruit for longer. Picking them can be a laborious job and Bob Flowerdew and others recommend a shortcut, which is to cut the whole stem off and sort the fruit out at the kitchen table. The fruiting stem would be cut back later in any case. Chris Bowers & Sons sell a huge range of currants by mail order.

BLACKCURRANT VARIETIES

'**Baldwin**' A still-popular old variety and a heavy cropper.

'**Ben Alder**' ✉ Small, juicy berries, resistant to mildew and late flowering, so good for colder gardens.

'**Ben Arvon**' ✉ Late, heavy cropping, resistant to leaf midge and other diseases.

'**Ben Connan**' ♀ ✉ Large fruit, good flavour, early, mildew resistant.

'**Ben Hope**' ✉ Late season, good flavour, upright habit, resistant to big bud and mildew. A good choice for benign neglect.

'**Ben Lomond**' ♀ ✉ Late-flowering, so good in frosty areas, some mildew, good cropper, mid season.

'**Ben Sarek**' ♀ ✉ This is Willie Duncan's choice as the best variety for the smaller garden. Large berries, less vigorous than the others and can be planted a little closer together. Willie Duncan explained to me that 'Sarek' is, in fact, the name of a Scandinavian peak, which is why Munro baggers might be scratching their heads.

'Ben Tirran' ✕ Late flowering, large fruit, later than the other 'Bens'.

'Titania' A new Swedish variety bred for frost, mildew and rust resistance.

Red, White and Pink Currant (*Ribes rubrum*)

Cultivated since the fifteenth century, the first large-fruiting redcurrant was brought to Britain from Europe by John Tradescant in 1611. Redcurrants and white currants are less popular than their black relatives and have somewhat different cultural requirements. White currants are simply a white variant of the red ones. Both are excellent for cooking, in jams, jellies and summer pudding, and the pectin they contain is used to set jams of other fruit. Pink currants are a colour sport in a very attractive translucent pink colour.

CULTIVATION

Choose a sunny site, in well-drained but moisture-retaining soil. Space at 1.2–1.8m apart. Cut back a newly planted red- or white currant to leave two to

White currant 'White Dutch' fan trained at Fyvie, Aberdeenshire.

three stems which are shortened by around half. The following winter cut back to leave five to seven strong and well-spaced branches and shorten these by half. Then, in subsequent winters, trim any leggy shoots and remove any congested branches. Remove branches which grow horizontally near soil level or any which are pointing downwards.

Red- and white currants (but not blackcurrants) respond well to training as cordons or fans. Fyvie Castle in Aberdeenshire has good examples of vertical and angled cordon redcurrants and fan-trained white currants growing on the garden walls. Prune side shoots to leave one or two buds. The leader can be pruned a little to encourage branching until you reach the desired height. Some birds

Pink, red and white currants are all forms of the same species.

develop a taste for eating the developing buds of currants and, if this happens, you may need to net or cage the fruit in late winter and spring.

REDCURRANT VARIETIES

If you have room for two or three plants, choose different varieties to get a succession of fruit over four to six weeks. The old favourite redcurrant '**Laxton's no. 1**' (bred in 1911) is early fruiting (July), '**Red Lake**' a little later fruiting, '**Redstart**' later yet and '**Rovada**' latest of all, well into August.

WHITE CURRANT VARIETIES

'**White Versailles**', bred in 1843, is the most common white currant. It ripens in July–August and has sweet fruit which is eaten fresh, used in cooking or made into wine. Birds tend not to spot the white berries, so you may get away without netting them.

PINK CURRANT VARIETIES

'**Gloire de Sablon**' is a disease-resistant pink currant.

Jostaberry and Worcesterberry *H4 E1–2*

The jostaberry is a gooseberry–blackcurrant hybrid which looks like and grows like blackcurrants on steroids, with fruit twice the normal size. They grow large (to 2m × 2m or more) and need plenty of space. Dr Hessayon recommends two metres between bushes. They are resistant to mildew, leaf spot and gall mite. Once they are established, they produce a reasonable crop of berries, usually ripening in late July and early August, but they are not as prolific as currants. They taste more like gooseberries when unripe and blackcurrants when ripe, and make great juice and jam. Several commercial fruit

Worcesterberries at David Catt's garden, Coldstream. They remain ripe on the bush for long periods and are sweet enough to eat raw when fully ripe. The Jostaberry is very similar.

farms in Scotland grow them. Willie Duncan's produce a reasonable crop but, on balance, I'd rather have a good gooseberry and a good blackcurrant. Drawbacks are the size of a bush, the fact that they take a few years to fruit well and that they are sometimes frosted in spring, causing poor fruit set. You may need to net them against birds too.

The Worcesterberry (*Ribes divaricatum*) is a spiny North American species with fruit like gooseberries at first and, when very ripe, like large sweet blackcurrants. Worcesterberries are mildew resistant and the fruit can be eaten raw or cooked and made into jam or bottled. Several people in the Borders grow them, including the Schofields at Tweed Valley Organics and David Catt, whose fruit I tried and liked. Catriona Murray and Neil Cameron grow them on Jura and told me that they found them useful, as they fruited over a two-month period.

Goji Berry (*Lycium barbarum var. goji*) *H2–3? E3*

This is yet another widely proclaimed 'superfood' with significant antioxidant properties, high levels of vitamin C and A and a long history of medicinal use in Asia. It is very vigorous with vicious thorns. Our plants showed no sign of fruiting, so I asked around.

Gooseberry 'Invicta'.

Gooseberry 'Invicta' as cordons at Kellie Castle, Fife.

Despite its wide availability in garden centres, try as I might, nobody seems to be able to get a decent crop of fruit. The *Beechgrove Garden* managed two! I also asked the wholesale nurseries who grow the fruit and even they'd never seen any. I suspect that the lack of summer heat and light intensity in Scotland may have something to do with it. Gojis are said to be suitable for any soil and appear to have reasonable hardiness. Small, white and purple flowers in summer are supposed to lead to fruiting on a two- to three-year-old plant and heavy fruiting on a four-year-old. The small fruits are red and shiny and full of seeds. Apparently, after five years, fruiting declines and you have to start again. Ours was killed in the 2010–11 winter – good riddance and, frankly, in Scotland, the goji is probably a waste of time and space. Better to buy a packet of dried fruits. Perhaps someone can prove me wrong!

Gooseberry (*Ribes uva-crispa*) H5 E1

Amongst the hardiest of all fruit, you should be able to grow gooseberries almost anywhere in Scotland, although harvesting them whilst avoiding the vicious thorns is not everyone's idea of pleasure. They are all self-fertile, so you only need one although, if you have room, a group of varieties will give a longer season and a variety of colours and sweetness. Records suggest that the first gooseberries came to Britain in 1275, when they were imported from France and planted at the Tower of London. Britain enjoyed a craze during the eighteenth and nineteenth centuries for competitive gooseberry breeding – the idea was to produce the largest possible fruit. By 1815, over 120 competitive gooseberry shows were held annually and gooseberries as large as small apples were achieved. Gardeners went to incredible lengths to triumph with giant fruit – rather like competitive vegetable growers do these days with their leeks and parsnips. Charles Darwin described his observations on the achievements in gooseberry breeding in *The Variation of Plants and Animals under Domestication* (1868), examining the human impact of selecting new strains and varieties of plants.

A good reason for growing gooseberries is that you can't easily buy them. And they freeze very well, so you can keep them going for months. Make them into ice cream, fools, crumbles and flavour them with ginger.

A gooseberry grown as a standard, Johnstounburn, East Lothian.

Gooseberries stripped by sawfly larvae.

CULTIVATION

Gooseberries like a fertile, well-drained but not dry soil and will fruit in partial shade, even on a north-facing wall. Plant about 1.2m apart, in autumn if possible but, as long as you keep them watered in the first season, you can plant them any time. Allow space for picking them. Varying greatly in sweetness, most green varieties are tart, best for pies and fools with plenty of added sugar, although some sweeten up if you leave them long enough. The sweeter dessert varieties tend to be redder in colour and when ripe can be eaten raw.

Gooseberries like to be fed with a high potassium fertiliser and mulching with manure will encourage plenty of vigour. You may need to net fruit against birds from May to July/August. To keep yields high and reduce mildew, some pruning is advisable. Prune in winter or after fruiting is finished and remember to wear thick gloves. The idea is to keep the bush open rather than crowded or congested. Pruning young bushes involves shortening all long branches by a third. For mature bushes, old woody (grey-brown) stems should be removed to the base. Cut back the previous year's growth (the thinner, greener stems) in the late summer or winter to two growth buds. You can thin out foliage in summer too, if it looks crowded. The alternative is to shorten all shoots (known as spur pruning). The two methods can be alternated. Some advocate thinning fruit in early June (use the gooseberries for cooking) in order to get larger and sweeter fruit later on.

Kellie Castle in Fife has a fine quadrant of 16 gooseberries grown as single-stemmed cordons trained on a metal framework of single vertical posts to 1.5–2m in height. Mark Armour says that this method of cultivation reduces mildew through increased air circulation and makes picking easier. Kellie also has fan-trained gooseberries on the walls. Training gooseberries does require some well-judged pruning several times a year. To keep the narrow upright shape, prune side shoots back to a few leaves in the growing season to encourage fruiting spurs to form and tie in the growth tip of the leading shoot to the desired height. Until the desired height is reached, shorten the previous year's leader shoot in winter by a third or so to encourage new side shoots which should be kept to 30cm or less (two to three buds) by pruning them back in summer.

Gooseberries: 'Pax', 'Careless' and 'Hinnonmaki Red'.

COMMON PROBLEMS

American gooseberry mildew is a major and serious disease of gooseberries. It appears as a white powder on young shoots and, if not halted, can turn the whole bush greyish-white. The fruit turns brown and, although you can still eat it, gooseberries tend to be smaller and with a much-reduced taste. To prevent it, ensure bushes don't become over-congested (*see* pruning above). Over-feeding with high nitrogen fertilizers can also lead to increased disease, so you may be best feeding with sulphate of potash rather than a general fertilizer such as Grow-more. Windy and cold inland gardens probably suffer less from mildew than mild and sheltered ones. Some modern varieties such as 'Invicta' have been bred with some resistance to mildew, but it has to be admitted that many disease-resistant cultivars have sacrificed the best taste to some extent. The best two varieties for mildew resistance, according to Scottish fruit expert David McIntyre of James McIntyre and Sons, are the forms of 'Hinnonmaki'.

Sawfly larvae, green caterpillars up to 10–20mm long, can strip gooseberry leaves – in a few days, your foliage can be shredded, leaving only the midribs. The problem with using insecticides against sawfly larvae is that they tend to strike when fruit is ripening, which is not the time you want to be spraying. You could try picking them off as soon as you spot an attack. Caroline has done this and, with an initial cull of 78 (counting them counteracted the tedium of the job), the bush was pretty much saved. Bifenthrin, long effective against this pest, has now been withdrawn from the market. Alternatives are thiacloprid, lambda cyhalothrin or pyrethrum (organic). Nematodes can also be used (*see* p. 67). I have observed in several gardens that some gooseberries are stripped while others of the same variety are untouched. Clearly research is needed into why this happens.

GOOSEBERRY VARIETIES

'**Captivator**' Spine-free, sweet dessert variety.

'**Careless**' ♀ Pale green fruit, some disease resistance.

'**Hinnonmaki**' Good mildew resistance, green, red and yellow forms, the red being the sweetest. Alan Smith in Strathdon says the yields are excellent.

'**Invicta**' ♀ Compact and free-fruiting, can be container grown, mildew resistant. Very spiny and older branches can break under the weight of fruit. Shelter from east winds.

'**Lancashire Lad**' 1824 Mildew-resistant, green for cooking or leave longer to turn red and sweet.

'**Leveller**' ♀ Mid–late season, can be eaten raw when very ripe, very good taste. Poor in inland Aberdeenshire.

'**Martlet**' A new red dessert gooseberry, sweet flavour, heavy cropping, good disease resistance to both mildew and leaf spot, said to be suitable for organic cultivation.

'**Pax**' Almost thornless, mildew resistant.

'**Whinham's Industry**' ♀ Red fruited, the best variety for a shady site, and good in heavy soil, can suffer from mildew. Good at Broughton, Kirkcudbright.

Grapes (*Vitis sp.*) *H3–4 E3*

VINES OUTDOORS

Before I started researching this book, I assumed that grapes outdoors in Scotland were largely a waste of time, but we have managed to find a significant number of successful Scottish outdoor grape growers. Admittedly, most Scots do grow their grapes indoors to obtain the extra heat to ripen fruit. To have any success with grapes outdoors, you need a warm, sheltered south-facing site, preferably with a warm wall behind to reflect heat. Culross Palace in Fife has several vines on its high terrace walls. Head gardener Mark Jeffery told me that the grapes tended to ripen quite well in years with an Indian summer. A fine foliage plant at Culross is *Vitis vinifera* 'Ciotat', the parsley-leaved vine, while other varieties include 'Müller Thurgau', 'Précoce de Malingre', 'Triomphe d'Alsace' and 'Gewurztraminer'. John Stoa, in Dundee, has good fruit set on a south-facing brick wall. Most years, his 'Brandt' grapes ripen well enough to eat.

Further research revealed that some people believe we can grow grapes for wine in Scotland. At Ardeonaig on the south side of Loch Tay, enterprising South African hotelier/chef Pete Gottgens planted 248 young vines of 'Solaris', a German hybrid of Riesling, Pinot Gris and Muscat grapes. This was the most northerly registered vineyard in the UK and they hoped to be making wine by 2013. The new owners of the hotel are tending the vines; time will tell how they get on. Les Bates at Torridon, Wester Ross, is growing 'Boskoop Glory' outdoors while, in cold, inland Strathdon, Aberdeenshire, Alan Smith has planted a trial of 25 vines outdoors

Grape 'Sweetwater' in the vine house at Castle Fraser, Aberdeenshire.

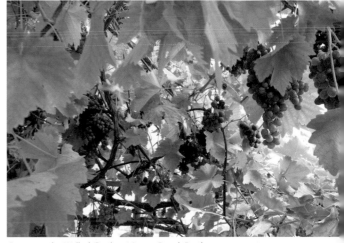

Grapes at the Walled Garden, Murray Royal, Perth.

The vine house at Culzean, Ayrshire.

and 25 varieties under glass. He is hopeful that at least one variety outdoors will be suitable for wine-making. He explained to me that, to make wine, the grapes must produce a minimum sugar content of 15–20 per cent. It is touch-and-go whether, in Scotland, any varieties can achieve this outdoors. By the end of September, the sun appears to be too weak to ripen most grapes further. Alan hopes that Russian and Baltic breeding lines should provide the varieties for Scotland's vineyards. For real success, breeding and selection would probably need to be done here in Scotland to create a grape which will ripen easily at this latitude. I sought advice from the most northerly vineyards in England in Yorkshire. Ian and Becky Sheveling at Holmfirth (www.holmfirthvine-yard.com) opted to plant 7,000 vines, including 'Rondo', 'Regent', 'Acolon' (red) and 'Ortega' and 'Solaris' (white). Ryedale Vineyards near York have planted 'Phoenix', 'Regent', 'Rondo', 'Solaris', 'Seyval Blanc', 'Ortega' and 'Siegerrebe'. They began producing wines in 2008 and owner Stuart Smith supplied the Loch Tay vines. He suggested to me that Scots gardeners could try 'Solaris' for white wine and 'Rondo' for red wine. The latter can be used for rosé wine, if it is not ripe enough for red. Both are disease resistant, as are Stuart's recommended outdoor eaters, 'Polo Muscat' (green) and 'Muscat Bleu'

(black). Nigel Slater recommends 'verjuice', the juice of partially ripened green grapes, as a useful cooking ingredient. I haven't used it, but it sounds worth a try in a poor summer when your grapes won't ripen.

VINES INDOORS

Even with climate change, the intensity of the sun at this latitude is not going to alter, so I don't see much future for commercial grapes this far north. If you want reliable crops, grapes are a greenhouse or tunnel-house crop in Scotland. Scots have a long history of indoor grape growing. Many a Victorian or Edwardian kitchen garden boasted a lean-to greenhouse for vines, back in the days of gardeners, under-gardeners and under-under-gardeners. Grapes were considered an exotic luxury rather than today's year-round supermarket product. Kippen near Stirling once boasted the largest Scottish Victorian vinery, planted in 1891 by Duncan Buchanan – the four-greenhouse complex covered an area of 460m². It became quite a tourist attraction and was producing 2,000 or more bunches of grapes per year. Sadly the vinery closed in 1964 and the greenhouses and vines were crushed to rubble and housing was built on top. The vinery is commemorated in a Kippen street name.

The beautifully restored large-scale working Victorian vinery at Culzean Castle in Ayrshire consists of a series of glasshouses dating from 1880 along the dividing wall of the giant two-section walled garden. The greenhouses were demolished in the 1950s but were recently reconstructed and replanted with 11 of the 12 grape varieties which had been in the original houses. The NTS wisely decided against fertilising the ground with horse carcasses as had been done in the 1880s! The new houses and vines are magnificent, but head gardener Susan Russell showed me the troubles she has controlling mildew on the leaves and fruit. Varieties include 'Black Hamburg' and a selection of Muscat grapes. Further north, I tasted fine grapes at Cambo in Fife and some delicious 'Buckland Sweetwater' in mid August from Castle Fraser's greenhouse vines. The Polycroft on Lewis produces grapes for local farmers' markets, while BBC Scotland's Mark Stephens told me about Jimmy Stout's grapes, which he successfully ripens in his greenhouse on Fair Isle, between Orkney and Shetland. Those may be Britain's most northerly grapes, but the highest must be at Chisholme House near Hawick, where grapes grow in a dilapidated greenhouse at 300m. John Stoa in Dundee has managed to squeeze three vines into his 10ft × 6ft greenhouse, with two single rods and one double. If you are very limited in space, West Dean in Sussex grows trained, half-standard potted vines in their greenhouses. They look attractive but you can't expect more than a handful of bunches on them. They could go outside for a few weeks in midsummer.

Grapes indoors are a rather finicky crop and hard work, but plucking bunches to bring back to the house is surely the peak of fruit romance. Assuming you have a modest greenhouse or tunnel and you don't want huge heating bills, I would look no further than the Sweetwater group of grapes, 'Black Hamburg' (syn. 'Schiava Grossa') with black fruit and 'Buckland Sweetwater' with white-green fruit. These require no artificial heat in winter and ripen early. For more of a challenge, the Muscat grapes ripen later, although are perhaps better flavoured.

Grapes are available on many rootstocks selected for different soil types but, in the UK, where we don't have serious grape soil disease issues, most grapes are grown on their own roots. A south-facing lean-to greenhouse is the classic way to grow grapes. Wires are stretched and firmly attached along the roof and south side at a spacing of around 30cm to support the vines and fruit bunches. Some advocate planting the vine outside and feeding the stem inside through a gap in the bricks or glass. This allows a deep root system and cuts out the need to water except in serious drought periods. Willie Duncan has good success with grapes in his Fife tunnel

house, with wires suspended from the frame, although in 2010 the weight of fruit caused the supporting wires to break. It takes three to four years to get your first decent crop of grapes, but vines are long-lived and you should enjoy a lifetime of fruit production. In Scotland, a greenhouse grape will tend to flower in late May. Shaking the flowering vine in the middle of the day helps to dislodge the pollen and ensure good fruit set. Vines like some, but not too much, nitrogen and lots of potash so Growmore is a good choice for granular feeding and you can supplement with a high potash liquid tomato food.

CARE AND PRUNING OF VINES

The literature on vine pruning can be detailed and complex but most of this refers to grapes outdoors and is for wine grapes. Most grapes indoors are grown as cordons/rod and spur. In this training method, a main stem or trunk is grown to 2–3m or more in height, off which a series of side shoots or laterals are trained along wires. When the vine is young (during its first one to two years), in the growing season, train laterals along the wires and remove flowers/fruit to leave five leaves. In winter, cut the laterals back to 2–3cm from the main stem. After two to three years, you can allow fruit to form – one bunch at first and later two or three bunches. Cut back the lateral beyond the fruit to concentrate energy on ripening the fruit.

It is important to do any winter pruning before Christmas because, once sap begins to rise in spring, any cuts are inclined to 'bleed'. Once you have trained the vine to fill the space, your annual prune will cut back all the shoots from the main woody stems or laterals to one or two buds which will form the fruiting spurs. In Scotland the relative lack of light means that it is a good idea to reduce overcrowding by keeping the spurs 30–40cm apart. If you have to rejuvenate an old, out-of-control vine, don't be frightened to cut or even saw back to a

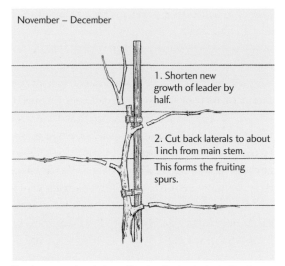

November – December

1. Shorten new growth of leader by half.

2. Cut back laterals to about 1 inch from main stem.

This forms the fruiting spurs.

Pruning grape vines indoors. Shorten the leader by half and cutback laterals to 2–3cm from main stem. Prune before Christmas.

trunk. As long as the roots are in good order, you should soon have it fruiting again. Jim McColl points out that the sap will tend to rise to the topmost buds only. If you want buds to break all the way along the rod, it needs to be more or less horizontal, even if you just lower part of it on a temporary basis until the buds break. In summer, the pruning tactic is to let as much light onto the grapes as possible. Once the laterals have begun to grow, keep a strong shoot and one in reserve (in case of damage) and remove any other shoots from each spur. Most books recommend thinning grapes within the bunches in summer to allow grapes space to develop and reduce mould – as if you'll have time! An easier alternative is to thin out the flower clusters instead and remove bunches that form too close to one another. If you do thin your grape bunches, use scissors or narrow secateurs rather than your hands to avoid bruising the grapes. In summer, don't allow the greenhouse temperature to rise much above 19°C (65°F), so open vents on sunny days. As the light intensity reduces in autumn, it may be necessary to keep the heat up by closing vents. Cut grapes bunch by bunch as you need them, as they keep better if left on the vine. Alan Smith calculates that

Scottish sun is too weak by early October to ripen grapes further, whether inside or out.

COMMON PROBLEMS

Grapes indoors are subject to a range of annoying and sometimes hard-to-eradicate insect pests and diseases. Watch out for **mealy bug**, **red spider** and **scale insect**, all of which suck sap and cause leaves to yellow, and **vine weevil grubs** can munch the roots. Susan Russell at Culzean removes all loose bark on the vine trunks in winter, as this is often where pests hide. **Powdery mildew** on leaves may need spraying with myclobutanil. Most other grape afflictions are caused by poor ventilation, high temperatures or irregular watering – too much or too little water can cause **skanking** (ill-formed fruit) and **leaf yellowing**. Grapes can go **mouldy** if overcrowded or with poor ventilation. **Birds**, **wasps** and your **thieving friends** are more than likely to discover your ripest grapes before you do ... I tucked into lots of grapes on my research travels, I have to admit.

Honeyberry (*Lonicera caerulea var. kamtschatica*) H4–5 E1-2?

This is a shrubby, deciduous honeysuckle with attractive grey-green furry leaves and large, elliptical, edible berries like elongated blueberries and with a similar taste. They ripen in midsummer and fruit can be eaten fresh, made into jam, jelly or ice cream or frozen. Two plants are required for pollination. The Beechgrove Garden near Aberdeen has grown it with some success, although Jim McColl is not too enthusiastic. Catriona Murray and Neil Cameron grow 'Blue Velvet' and 'Blue Forrest' in Jura and get good fruiting, while we obtained three Russian selections, 'Nymph', 'Morena' and 'Latu' from Polish fruit expert Tadeusz Kusibab and are trialling them at Glendoick.

Kiwi fruit outdoors on a south wall at Kellie Castle, Fife – it is a race against time to ripen edible fruit before winter.

Kiwi Fruit (*Actinidia spp.* – *Chinese Gooseberry*) H2–3 E3

We grew these triffid-like, rampant, hairy-leaved vines for many years at Glendoick on a south wall until we wore ourselves out unwrapping the tendrils which enveloped everything they could reach like a family of boa constrictors. Dr Hessayon's sensible advice is that kiwis only produce fruit in areas hot enough to ripen grapes reliably outdoors. The exception which may prove the rule is Kellie Castle in Fife, where male and female plants of *A. chinensis*, on their south-facing walls not far from the sea, give a reasonable fruit set most years. Head gardener Mark Armour explained that the fruit tended to ripen in December and was not large but definitely edible. They need to be harvested before frosts come but picked fruit can ripen indoors. Mark cuts his plants hard back in early spring. Kiwi's rampant growth (up to 10m or more) makes them too vigorous for greenhouse culture and they'd probably bring down the roof, so my advice is to only consider growing them if you have 4–8m spare on a large south-facing wall in coastal south-eastern Scotland. Kiwis like well-drained soil with a pH on the acid side of neutral. An espalier pruning regime would be a good idea to let plenty of light reach the fruit. Alan Titchmarsh suggests that, to save space, you can plant the male and female in the same hole and train the male and female on alternate espalier or cordon branches. As fruit start to form, cut back the tips of the shoots to allow sunlight to ripen the fruit. Fleece to protect ripening fruit from frost. There is a self-fertile variety called 'Jenny' but we don't know anyone who has tried this in Scotland. Hardier than *A. chinensis* is the Mongolian kiwi *A. arguta* with a smoother skin. 'Issai' is the best-known form. Scottish fruit expert Colin Stirling reckons that you'll be lucky to see any fruit on it. The pink- and white-leaved related *A. kolomikta*, commonly found in garden centres, can, in theory, produce edible fruit but tends not to in northern climates.

Rhubarb (*Rheum*) H4–5 E1

Eaten as a fruit but usually more at home in the vegetable patch, rhubarb, like marmite, divides the population into lovers and loathers. I was put off by the endless school meal variations of stewed fruit, crumbles and pies, served with thin, lumpy custard. Rhubarb is an excellent crop for Scotland – almost indestructible – and one you can eat fresh from the garden long before any other fruit is past the flowering stage. I asked a Shetland allotment holder what the best crop for these windswept islands was and he had no hesitation in replying 'rhubarb'. With high levels of oxalic acid, rhubarb was used medicinally as a purgative for hundreds of years and, in Europe, eating it for pleasure is a surprisingly recent idea. It was the availability of cheaper sugar and the persistence of rhubarb grower and breeder Joseph Myatt from Deptford in the early nineteenth century who convinced Londoners to eat it as a dessert. He cannily named his new hybrids after Queen Victoria and Prince Albert, whose royal patronage helped considerably to promote rhubarb's popularity. Forcing rhubarb in warm, dark sheds to crop as early

Left. Rhubarb – one of the toughest and easiest fruits to grow. **Middle**. Rhubarb forcing jar at Kellie Castle, Fife, used to obtain crops a month or so early. **Right**. Rhubarb 'Victoria', one of the oldest selections and still very popular.

as Christmas became popular in the nineteenth century, particularly in the so-called 'rhubarb triangle' around Wakefield, Leeds and Bradford. At one time, 90 per cent of the world's supply of forced rhubarb was produced there. With a nod in the direction of Nigel Slater, Caroline recommends baked rhubarb served with crispy fillets of mackerel. I can't think of anything worse, myself.

More recently, scientists at the James Hutton Institute (formerly SCRI) near Dundee have been investigating polyphenols in rhubarb, which may have a significant role in cancer prevention and as less toxic treatments for the disease.

Only rhubarb stalks are edible. Don't be tempted to eat the leaves, which are poisonous. However, they can be boiled up in water to make an effective insecticide, although apparently bureaucratic European pesticide directives forbid using it. There are recipes for it on the Internet if you fancy risking a criminal record. A plant known as 'monk's rhubarb',

used for hundreds of years in Scotland as a spinach-like vegetable, is in fact a *Rumex* species (dock or sorrel), rather than a *Rheum*.

SITE AND GROUND PREPARATION

Rhubarb forms a handsome foliage plant, as do some of the Asiatic (non-edible) species such as *Rheum palmatum*, and the tall spikes of pink and white flowers are quite attractive. Although growing and yielding best in full sun, we managed to get a reasonable crop of rhubarb at the edge of a conifer wood in some shade. Allow a space at least 1m and up to 1.5m in diameter for each rhubarb clump to expand. One or two plants is more than enough for a family to eat until they won't put up with any more! Rhubarb tolerates most soil except water-logged and heavy clay and, in very peaty soil, you may need to lime regularly. You can grow it as a border plant amongst other shrubs or perennials and it lives for a long time. The young growth is susceptible to late frosts so, in very cold and inland gardens, it is worth having protection ready to cover it.

Plant with manure and, if the soil is well drained, mulch in summer. The dead leaves in autumn are a good mulch in themselves. Rhubarb is easy to force and the paler, more delicate shoots are prized by gourmands. For a really early crop, dig up an early variety such as 'Timperley Early' and pot it or put it in a polythene sack around Christmas time, after some reasonable frosts have occurred. Bring it indoors to a warm dark room and it will start to sprout, providing a crop in February. For a March to early April forced crop, you can leave it in the ground and cover it with straw in early spring and as the leaves develop, put a bell jar or plastic bin over the top to keep it warm and dark. Check that it does not dry out.

HARVESTING

Resist harvesting any stems for the first year after planting or until a decent clump forms. Then harvest as much as you like from April onwards in the open; earlier if forced. To pick, grasp the stem at the base of the plant and pull. Don't cut. After midsummer, the oxalic acid builds up in the thicker stems and it can make them inedible. You may be able to continue picking thinner younger stems. Cut flowering stems off if you want to prolong the crop, as this helps young stem production.

COMMON PROBLEMS

Many authorities claim that, after ten years, rhubarb plants tend to become coarse and less productive. This may be the case for commercial production but we and many others have had rhubarb clumps which go on yielding good crops for much longer

than this. Christopher Lloyd commented on the rhubarb patches he saw growing around long-abandoned, ruined crofts in Orkney – decades old, these clumps still produced edible stems. Mark Armour, head gardener at the large rhubarb collection at Kellie Castle, found that the 20-year-old clumps were producing coarse stems, so he simply dug them up, split them and replanted smaller sections. They were soon back in production again. Rhubarb can become infected with **virus** (shown by yellowing or mottled leaves) and, in this case, the plant should be dug up and burned. It's best to replant fresh stock in another part of the garden. Don't eat stems with frosted leaves as they tend to have high levels of oxalic acid. Wait until new growth comes. Apart from these troubles, rhubarb is pretty tough and trouble free.

RHUBARB VARIETIES

The National Collection of Rhubarb at Harlow Carr in Yorkshire has over 100 varieties. A good Scottish collection is held at Kellie Castle in Fife. You can grow rhubarb from seed quite easily but it is probably not worthwhile, as the seedlings are often rather substandard. It's better to buy potted stock (not expensive) or you can just dig up and detach a section of root with a bud or two from the edge of a friend's clump in winter. There are several Scottish varieties, such as 'Fife Green Jam', but they are not generally commercially available.

'**Early Champagne**' Good flavour, one of the sweetest.
'**Glaskin's Perpetual**' Said to be the fastest maturing, so you can pick it in 1–2 years from seed.
'**Holsteiner Blut**' Early, red stems.
'**Pink Champagne**' Good flavour, pink and green stems.
'**Red Champagne**' Red stems.
'**Timperley Early**' ♀ Good flavour, early variety, good for forcing.

Saskatoons on John Stoa's allotment in Dundee. They taste like blueberries and are as easy to grow.

Saskatoon (*Amelanchier alnifolia*) H5 E1

I'm grateful to *Dundee Courier* garden columnist John Stoa for information about the Saskatoon, *Amelanchier alnifolia*. John saw them being grown in Canada and decided to trial them in Scotland and he is now growing and selling them. *Amelanchier* are tough North American deciduous shrubs widely grown in Scotland as ornamentals with white flowers in spring and often good autumn colour. The saskatoons are selections of *A. alnifolia*, with clusters of dark fruit in summer. They prefer peaty/acidic soils and are best in a sunny site in well-drained but not dry soil. They take several years to start producing but, by the age of four or five, you should get a good crop. Bushes can be pruned from time to time in spring, once they start to mature, either by cutting out older, woody stems or by cutting to the ground. John is growing the forms 'Smoky' and 'Thiessen'. Both have reached around 1.2m after seven to eight years. They are said to reach 2–3m in time. John took me to his allotment in July,

where we picked lots of the delicious and easily harvested fruit. They are like mild blueberries in taste but look like blackcurrants. John nets them against birds when they are ripening. Dried saskatoons were mixed with meat and fats to provide 'pemmican', a winter food in polar regions, which was carried by Captain Scott on his ill-fated race to the South Pole in 1911–12.

Sea Buckthorn (*Hippophae rhamnoides*) H4–5, E1

I first became aware of the spectacular fruit of this plant one winter along the East Lothian beaches at Gullane and Aberlady. Growing to 2–3m and spreading rampantly through the dunes with its thorny branches and narrow, silver leaves, the fruit hangs on into late winter, long after the leaves have dropped, and the bright orange clusters warm the heart on a cold, windy day. Sea buckthorn can spread vigorously, with roots that break paths and possibly even drains and foundations, and you may

Sea Buckthorn (*Hippophae rhamnoides*) in December, the best time to harvest them, on the beach near Gullane, East Lothian.

regret planting it in the garden unless you have lots of room, although a row of them does make an effective screen or barrier. The fruit should be harvested ripe, after the first frosts, so December and January are the months to go for a beach walk. You'll need gloves to protect yourself from the thorns. They start to taste unpleasant if they are overripe and we made some rather rancid ice cream from overripe juice. The fruit is very rich in vitamins, particularly vitamin C, and can be used, as juice, to make jams, alcoholic drinks and sauces. Though little used in the UK, sea buckthorn is widely eaten in other parts of the world and scientists are developing a range of skin care products and cancer-combating drugs from it. Only female plants produce fruit and you'll need a male to pollinate a group of females. There are a number of selected clones, but I have not seen any of them offered for sale in Scotland. Catriona Murray and Neil Cameron imported clones 'Hergo' and 'Leikora' (female) and 'Polmix' (male) from Devon to Jura, where they have done very well. Horticultural advisor Donald McBean has been trialling buckthorn in Forres with a view to commercial production, while a Perth ice-cream parlour, Lickwid, sold delicious sea buckthorn ice cream for several years.

Indoor Fruit

Citrus (oranges, lemons, etc.) *H1C E3*

We now take citrus fruit for granted but, 100 years ago, oranges and lemons were an exotic luxury. The glasshouse boom of the eighteenth and nineteenth centuries saw several orangeries built in Scotland – the best known of which you can visit at Culzean Castle on the Ayrshire coast. Mertoun in the Borders

Citrus – lemon, the easiest of the larger citruses to grow.

has another. Of course you don't need an orangery to grow citrus and, under glass, you can certainly get fruit on your lemons with a bit of patience. Scotland's low light levels tend to cause relatively small fruit which may not ripen to the level of imported fruit. The attractive, scented white flowers open in spring and summer and the resulting fruit takes up to six months to ripen. Citrus are self-fertile, so you only need one.

ROUTINE CARE

Citrus can grow quite happily outdoors in a sheltered site for four to five months of the year, but they need to be brought indoors in winter. Keep them inside until June unless you have a warm and very sheltered garden and beware of any sudden changes in temperature, as they can't tolerate this. Ideally they should be kept above 10°C (50°F) in winter but few of us are willing to provide greenhouse heat to this temperature. They can tolerate periods below this but not near freezing. Lemons are slightly hardier than the others. If citrus are kept in low light levels, they tend to drop their leaves. The problem is that a centrally-heated house is too dark, hot and dry for them. They need to be kept cool and the air humid, but with as much light as possible. Such conditions are hard to find in the home. Citrus are almost always pot grown and they like to be slightly pot-bound, so don't repot them until their roots are really matted and filling their container. There are citrus composts available or you can make your own using John Innes no. 2 or 3 with 20 per cent grit or perlite. Citrus need a particular watering regime where they are soaked and then allowed to dry out. In winter they need very little water and can be killed by overwatering.

COMMON PROBLEMS

I have rarely seen a mature citrus which did not suffer from a degree of **leaf yellowing**. This can be caused by several different things. If only the older leaves are turning yellow, then you need to feed. If the leaves are yellowing but the veins on the leaves are green, then your citrus most likely needs iron. If the outer leaves are yellowing and some of the branches are dying back, then cut back on watering. As well as the usual **aphids**, there are several troublesome insect pests which attack citrus, including **scale insects**, **mealybug** and **red spider** (see pp.73–4). All these are hard to eradicate indoors, but are less likely to occur if you put the citrus outdoors in summer. If you keep them indoors, keep the humidity up, spray the leaves regularly and ensure good

ventilation to keep temperatures down. Citrus like to be fed from April to late summer with a high nitrogen feed. Thin fruits if they start to weigh down the branches. You can grow citrus from pips for a challenge, but you won't get a good fruiting variety. Named varieties tend to be quite expensive to buy, but citrus live for a long time if you look after them. Prune long straggly shoots in winter or spring to encourage branching and remove shoots from low down on the stem but, other than that, no pruning is required.

Oranges are not really suitable for Scotland. **Lemons** will tolerate slightly colder winter temperatures than the others. The hardiest seems to be 'Meyer's Lemon', which is relatively compact. Don't be tempted by the very tender variegated form. Two other citrus produce mainly ornamental rather than edible fruit but are easier to keep – '**Calamondin Orange**' has small, barely edible orange fruit and '**Kumquat**' has small, orange, rather bitter fruit.

Cape Gooseberry (*Physalis*) H1C E2

This South American native was introduced to Britain via South Africa in the nineteenth century, hence the name. It has tiny, pale yellow flowers

The dwarf Cape gooseberry (*Physalis*) 'Little Lantern', grown in Caroline's greenhouse in pots, produced abundant crops of small fruit.

followed by small tomato-like yellow fruits which are encased in a green lantern that turns papery and translucent as the fruit ripens. We have grown 2m-high versions against a wall, planted in the soil of a tall unheated greenhouse at Glendoick. They fruited well in their second year and, as with many hot region fruits, it was a race to ripen them in autumn before the light levels and temperature dropped too far. It takes 70–90 days after flowering for the fruit to ripen. A better choice for most gardeners is the dwarf variety 'Little Lantern', which grows to 50cm. Caroline had great success with this, sown in March indoors, without the recommended bottom heat, and, when large enough, moved up to 7cm pots and kept in the greenhouse. In May, these were planted in five-litre pots in pure garden compost and the plants really took off. By August each one had produced up to 100 berries which started dropping off onto the floor as they ripened. Some were ripe enough to eat straight away and those that were a little green were placed in a basket and left to ripen further. Deliciously sweet, even the dog developed a taste for them and hoovered them off the floor. If you keep the fruit in their lanterns in a cool dry place, they last for weeks if not months. Cape goose-berries can be grown as biennials or even perennials, living for up to four years and being pruned back to the ground each winter. Ours survived 12 months in an unheated greenhouse but were killed in the hard 2009–10 winter. They can barely withstand any frost so are not reliably hardy outdoors anywhere in Scotland. John Stoa in Dundee keeps his potted plants outside in summer, bringing them into the greenhouse in autumn once the tomatoes are out of the way.

VEGETABLES

Caroline Beaton with contributions from Kenneth Cox

Beautiful broad bean flowers – don't hesitate to plant a wigwam of them in your herbaceous border.

Climbing French beans at Geilston, Dunbartonshire.

CHAPTER 1

Bean Family (Legumes)

Beans have been cultivated for thousands of years. Their importance is reflected in the many ways we still use the word – *I haven't got a bean, not worth a bean, to know how many beans make five, hello old bean, having a bean feast, full of beans, spill the beans.* Beans and peas are a ubiquitous and protein-rich part of many cuisines to this day, with the added benefits of fibre, folic acid, potassium, iron and vitamin C.

Legumes, or pulses, are a gardener's friend, as they fix nitrogen in the soil. In your rotation plan, contrive to plant brassicas in the space vacated by the legumes. And as brassicas love a firm soil, you need hardly do a thing but chop down the legume crop, remembering to leave the nitrogen-rich roots *in situ*, then plant up the cabbages and their relatives.

Imagine life without peas. Even people who 'don't eat veg' will often eat peas. Few can resist them eaten raw there and then in the garden – including our spaniel, Bramble. Broad beans are another thing altogether. Earthy and somehow old-fashioned, they are at their best picked small. Try them lightly boiled and then mixed while still warm with olive oil, lemon juice, fresh mint and some crumbled feta. French beans are delicate and flavoursome and very easy to grow. The dwarf varieties can be grown in pots on your greenhouse benching for an early crop. Runner beans, originally grown only for their flowers, are rather undeservedly well known as

'string' beans because of the inedible threads that their pod edges develop as they age. Picked young, they are delicious lightly boiled or steamed and then finished with lots of butter and garlic. Don't sow too many seeds, though, or you may be overwhelmed. They are prolific.

PEA AND BEAN SUPPORTS

With the exception of dwarf varieties, most peas and beans are climbers and need support. Broad beans and peas are typically supported on twiggy pea sticks, on netting or on canes with string running between them. Having said that, my stepfather has never staked a broad bean in his life – not even up the Law in Dundee. More vigorous peas, runner beans and climbing French beans produce a long season of flowers in addition to pods, so there is no reason not to place 2–2.5m cane wigwams in your flower borders and let them scramble up. The peas will need help but the beans can do it for themselves. Rows of beans can be planted on pairs of canes tied at the top and joined by further canes to produce a tunnel. Mertoun in the Borders has fine examples, while Damon Powell at Castle Fraser built a tunnel you could walk through upright. For dramatic effect, you could go for designed wooden or metal structures such as obelisks. But remember, nothing permanent, as you should be rotating your crops.

COMMON PROBLEMS

Blackfly infest the young growth on broad beans. This is usually prevented by nipping out the broad bean tops once the plants are a good size – watch out for the first signs. You can try spraying with soapy water. **Mice** love to eat bean and pea seeds and, once they've discovered them, you may lose the lot. Traps might help, both indoors and out. Organic gardener and author Bob Flowerdew suggests that a dash of seaweed solution in with the pea seeds helps to disguise their smell from mice. **Birds** will go for the seedlings but threads, net, fleece or pea sticks will help to protect them. **Pea moth** can be deterred by using fine mesh (sold as Wondermesh or Enviromesh, for example). This will also help to prevent maggoty peas, the maggots being the moth offspring. If you notice any mould or mildew developing, remove and burn the infected plants. An attack of **pea thrips** will result in a silver mottling of leaves and pods. Remove and destroy damaged parts. Companion planting might lure some of the pests away or deter them. Try annual French marigolds or more permanent and attractive bed-end plantings of chives, lavender, thyme, sage, hyssop or rosemary.

 Mildews (downy and powdery) result in white to grey blotches or coatings on the leaves. They occur in wet (downy) or dry (powdery) weather. Pick your remaining crop and burn the foliage. You can use sulphur to prevent powdery mildew. Other fungal diseases include **anthracnose**, with a mild dose causing spotting and a severe dose collapse, and **foot rot** and **root rot**, where plants collapse and die. If plants collapse, pull them up and burn them. If the plant remains green but with stunted growth and there are brown streaks inside the stem, then it is probably **fusarium wilt**. Again, it's best to pull them up and burn them. **No setting of pods** can be caused by lack of pollination or attack by birds.

Broad Bean (*Vicia faba*) H3–4 E2

BACKGROUND

Eaten for millennia, broad beans are a native of Europe as well as west Asia and Africa. Eaten, I should say, despite there being some bad karma attached to them. Ancient Greeks believed that the souls of the dead migrated into them, while the Latin word for broad bean, *anemos,* means both 'soul' and 'wind'.

 There are two main types of broad bean – the longpod and the shorter-podded Windsor. Field beans are a type of broad bean but are allowed to grow larger and are used as a fodder crop. You'll find fields of broad beans grown on a large scale in the Borders and elsewhere in Scotland. They have striking black and white flowers.

Powdery mildew on peas – a particular problem in sheltered plots or dry seasons.

Broad bean tip with a blackfly infestation. Try to avoid this by pinching out the tips.

Well-filled broad bean pods showing the result of successful pollination.

Broad bean 'Bunyard's Exhibition' at Fyvie, in Aberdeenshire, using netting for support.

Broad bean foliage showing chocolate spot damage. At its worst, this may kill your plants.

When truly tiddly in size, the beans can be eaten uncooked. In 2008, *Gardening Which?* trialled very young broad beans cooked and eaten 'pod and all'. Varieties 'Listra' and 'Optica' were recommended for steaming, blanching or serving in vinaigrette. As the pods get larger and older, the beans become increasingly tough but, if you miss the boat a little, cook the beans and then shuck off their greyish outer skin. The flavour of the deep green bean will be transformed. Broad beans go very well with dill weed and Ken loves *faves a la catalana/habas a la catalana*, which are broad beans fried with garlic, tomatoes and bacon.

SITE, SOIL, SOWING AND PLANTING

If, like me, you find it hard to grow enough of this delicious vegetable, you will want to sow it in both autumn (November for me) and spring (mid April) if your conditions allow. Extreme weather and rodents permitting, you do get a succession of beans with a nice early crop to get you started. Only sow seeds in autumn if your soil is well drained. Broad beans like a well-dug and fertile soil, manured the previous autumn for preference.

Relatively hardy and therefore good in our climate, these beans germinate at a lowish temperature. Simply dib the seeds into the soil to a depth of about 4–5cm and space them at about 25cm apart. We tend to plant a double row of beans in a 'staggered' pattern in each drill. If your season is short, you can start the beans off in modules in the greenhouse in the winter to then plant out in spring. This may also give them a head start if mice are a problem in your garden.

ROUTINE CARE

Keep weeded and water well in dry conditions. You may want to protect young seedlings from birds with a cloche of some sort. As the seedlings stretch, you will need to support them. This can be done in a number of ways, but we put tall canes at the 'corners' of the rows and add two or three additional pairs along the row, depending on its length. Next we run twine tightly from cane to cane to cage the plants in a long, thin oblong. As they grow, so we add another run of twine higher up the canes. Once the plants are in full flower, nip out the tops of each (then wash well, steam and eat as greens). This will concentrate the plants' energy into bean production and will also, importantly, discourage blackfly, which are an absolute pest and an eyesore too.

HARVESTING AND STORING

Harvest your beans as they reach your preferred size – although I urge you to pick them small. Keep harvesting until the crop is done. Sometimes you may harvest apparently chunky pods to find few beans inside. This is likely to have been a problem with pollination, which itself may be linked to poor weather at a critical time. If you have a glut, broad beans are easily blanched and frozen.

COMMON PROBLEMS

(*See also* p. 156 for general pea and bean problems) Broad beans (but not other beans) commonly suffer from **chocolate spot**, a fungal disease causing dark spots on the leaves and dark streaks on the stems. To prevent it, try to grow good strong plants in well-fed soil and don't grow them too close together. A mild infection won't do much harm but a severe one can lead to the plants collapsing. Burn infected plants. As noted above, nip out growing tips to discourage **blackfly**.

BROAD BEAN VARIETIES

Autumn sowing

'**Aquadulce Claudia**' 🏆 Very tough, good yields.
'**Imperial Green Longpod**' 🏆 One of the most popular, really big pods and lots of them.
'**Masterpiece Green Longpod**' 🏆 Said to be good for freezing.
'**The Sutton**' 🏆 The most popular dwarf variety, prolific. Good reports from all over Scotland and does well on Lewis and Shetland, where its diminutive stature helps it resist strong winds.

Spring sowing

'**Dreadnaught**' Heritage longpod, very good flavour.
'**Green Windsor**' Very old variety, so has proved itself.

'**Karmazyn**' Beautiful pink beans, relatively dwarf stock, so good for small gardens. Good yield in trials at the Beechgrove Garden.
'**Listra**' Small-podded, medium height plants and early maturing. *Gardening Which?* recommends it as a variety to eat pod and all when young.
'**Medes**' 🏆 Pale beans and good for freezing.
'**Optica**' 🏆 Very good flavour, lower growing, so good for the neater garden. Smaller-podded and prolific. Recommended by *Gardening Which?* as a variety where the pod can be eaten whole when harvested young.
'**Witkiem**' Pale beans from plump pods, good to freeze.
'**Witkiem-Manita**' 🏆 Good cropper, fast growing, good for early and late sowings.

Autumn or spring sowing

'**Bunyards Exhibition**' Over 100 years old and still going strong, pale beans.
'**Red Epicure**' Recommended by Matt Biggs of *Gardeners' Question Time* and Alys Fowler for its reddish-brown beans and low stature. Happy in Torridon.

French Bean (*Phaseolus vulgaris*) H2 E1

BACKGROUND

The French bean or *haricot vert* is, like the scarlet runner, a native of Central America. The word 'haricot' is a corruption of the Aztec name for the bean, *ayecotl*. French beans fall into two main categories – climbing varieties which grow to 2m or more and dwarf varieties which grow to 30–45cm or so and are suitable for containers and growbags. To get a decent crop on the dwarf varieties, you need quite a large number of plants, so, if space is short, plant a few climbing ones for greater yield. French beans can be very decorative, with white, pink or red

French bean varieties 'Borlotto', 'Cosse Violette' and 'Mont d'Or'.

Prolific and delicious dwarf purple French bean 'Purple Queen'.

flowers, and there are many varieties with yellow or dark-purple pods. Although they taste wonderful, French beans are not the ideal crop for much of Scotland, as they are heat loving and very tender. Warm, sheltered gardens can grow great crops but those in less than ideal conditions can struggle. New growth on plants is easily damaged by easterly winds and cold spring nights and, the further north you live, the better the summer you need to ripen a good crop. *Beechgrove Garden*'s Jim McColl has com-

mented that inland Aberdeenshire is 'on the edge' of where they can be grown reliably outdoors. We saw 'Cherokee Trail of Tears' (sonorous and poetic name) growing well in a tunnel on the west side of Lewis. Ken and I have certainly had good success with the very prolific dwarf purple beans – which sadly lose most of their colour when cooked. An American friend serves French beans with a scatter of pecan nut pieces which have been fried in butter. Try it.

SITE, SOIL, SOWING AND PLANTING

French beans need rich, moisture-retentive, well-drained soil and hate damp clay. To plant outdoors, avoid cold and damp weather, as beans won't germinate until soil reaches 10°C. When the soil is warm enough, probably sometime in May, dib the seeds in 4–5cm deep and 23cm apart. Choose a relatively sheltered site and protect the sensitive young growth from winds or start them off indoors. You could prepare a trench in the autumn in which you put materials which will retain moisture – well-rotted manure or shredded newspaper, for example. French beans are self-fertile, so insects are not required. Support the seedlings as they appear with some twiggy sticks for dwarf varieties and with larger structures for the climbing varieties.

ROUTINE CARE, HARVESTING AND STORING

Keep weed-free and water well in dry conditions and, as with all beans, harvest regularly as they become the size you like. If you let pods mature, it switches off the plants' desire to flower and therefore the cropping stops. If some of your bean pods develop beyond the palatable, pod the beans – fresh flageolet, in effect. To store the later crops of beans as a source of winter protein (and remember to boil them well, as they do contain toxins when raw), leave the pods to dry on the plants then pull up the whole stem and hang in an airy place to dry further. The pods will become brown and crispy. Open and remove the beans, storing them in airtight jars. French beans are good to blanch then freeze.

COMMON PROBLEMS

(*see also* p. 156 for general pea and bean problems)
Slugs will come for your young seedlings so take the usual precautions. Soil-living **bean seed fly** might attack your seeds in the ground and are worse in cold, wet conditions. Starting the plants off in modules will help prevent this.

FRENCH BEAN VARIETIES

Climbing

'**Blue Lake White Seeded**' A long-popular variety, 1.5m, with white beans inside green pods.

'**Borlotto Firetongue**' Striking red and white, mottled beans but don't expect a huge crop in Scotland. Keep harvesting them diligently otherwise they'll stop flowering. Mertoun in the Borders grows good crops of this.

'**Cherokee Trail of Tears**' Very prolific with purplish pods and black beans. Great name!

'**Cobra**' ♀ Stringless, reliable and good taste, said to be good in all weathers. Author and broadcaster, Pippa Greenwood rates the attractive purple flowers.

'**Cosse Violette**' Purple flowers and masses of dark-purple pods which are edible even at large sizes. Ken had great success with this, started off indoor in modules, even in the poor summer of 2010.

'**Mont D'Or**' Yellow waxy bean, full of flavour.

'**Valdor**' Waxy yellow pods over a long period, good virus resistance and good for freezing.

Dwarf

'**Blue Lake**' Long season, *Gardeners' Question Time*'s Bunny Guinness rates this as wet or dry weather proof.

'**Cannellino**' Good cropper and successful as a dried bean too.

'**Duel**' Good flavour and high yield.

'**Masterpiece**' Very popular and a Jim McColl favourite which matures early and carries on all summer with long, straight pods.

'**Minidor**' A beautiful yellow-podded variety that

does keep its colour when cooked.

'**Purple Queen**' Another purple bean with a very fine flavour. Pick small. Loses its colour when cooked.

'**Purple Tepee**' High yielding, dark-purple colour which sadly does not remain once cooked. Good flavour.

'**Safari**' ♀ A very fine bean with a good flavour. We saw this on Lewis.

'**Speedy**' In a *Gardening Which?* comparative trial, this modern variety beat the heritage '**Triomphe de Farcy**' in both quality and flavour.

'**Stanley**' ♀ White flowers and white seeds. Recommended for Perthshire and probably elsewhere.

'**The Prince**' ♀ Heavy yields over many weeks, straight pods.

Pea (*Pisum sativum*) H2 E1

Probably European and Asian in origin, this vegetable has been used as far back as records exist. Peas were valued because they could be dried and therefore offer nutrition in the leaner months of the year. The vegetable was originally called pease in Old English, as in 'pease pudding'. I ate a form of this delicious, comforting yellow mash with my student friends in Newcastle in the '70s – in a stottie with a slab of pork (in my pre-vegetarian days!). In this case, the pea is the dried yellow field pea and not the green garden variety. In the past, Scots used a pease-meal to make their bannocks and brose – this latter a mix of meals of some sort, although often oatmeal, with boiling water, stock or milk added and with salt or butter to finish if available. Golspie Mill in Sutherland still makes peasemeal, which can be used for traditional and more modern purposes – for example, coating fish before frying.

The garden pea as we know it was introduced into Europe in the sixteenth century and has been much cultivated since. Wrinkle-seeded varieties are reputedly sweeter although less hardy than the smooth-seeded. The flat-podded mangetout peas

An approach to preventing mouse damage – a pea cradle. Sow seedlings in a rone pipe with shading to prevent them drying out.

Young pea plants with pea stick supports. Pea sticks can form an attractive part of the design and architecture of your vegetable garden.

Peas 'Hurst Green Shaft' at Kellie Castle in Fife.

and chunkier sugar-snap varieties are grown for their especially tender pods, allowing the whole thing to be eaten, pod and all. These are a good idea if you have limited growing space. Peas are not the easiest vegetable to please but they are one of the most popular. They climb readily with their own tendrils although they often need encouragement to start with. Pea tops can be used in salad but need to be eaten immediately after harvest to retain texture and flavour. Scotland has a significant commercial pea production (about 5,000 hectares), mainly in eastern regions in the Borders, Lothians, Fife, Angus and Perth. Tinned garden peas, marrowfat peas or processed peas were certainly still popular when I was a child. I admit to loving them then but they are utterly different to the fresh or frozen things. Frozen peas are now acceptable as a close approximation of the fresh item and are, especially as petit pois, generally very good. They make a great speedy soup too. Talking of soup, don't throw away or compost the pods of ordinary garden peas. Chopped and cooked with onions and garlic in a good veggie stock with maybe a potato added, they are then liquidised and sieved to leave you with a light and tasty summer soup.

The only downside to peas is that what looks like a tremendous amount of foliage can yield a relatively small crop. But with a selection of varieties and some succession sowing, you can have fresh peas all summer.

As Del Boy said, 'Mangetout, Rodney. Mangetout!'

SITE, SOIL, SOWING AND PLANTING

Peas like a fertile, well-drained soil in sun. Incorporate compost or manure the previous autumn. Start succession sowing them from spring to midsummer. They will take 12–15 weeks until they're ready to harvest. Sow them directly into the ground once the heat is in the soil a little – mid April and onwards in my case. Make a broad drill with your draw hoe, a

little less than 5cm deep, and sow the seeds at the edges in a double row 8–12cm apart (5cm for dwarf varieties) using a 'staggered' spacing. You can try planting outdoors earlier if you can warm your soil with a cloche or fleece that will not disappear in a force ten south-westerly. Mice just love to feast on those delicious dried peas you have carefully sown; they had almost all my crop three times in one year. I have been advised to include dried and chopped gorse when sowing peas but worry about the effect on weeding hands later. To start them under protection, try deep modules. We have started ours in rone pipes settled on a shelf slung from the greenhouse roof in order to prevent mice getting to them. It has worked. I think we should patent this marvellous 'pea cradle'! You could also try fine wire mesh to keep the mice out of the pots or rone pipes. Before the seedlings get too large and tangled, harden them off. This way, the plants gain some strength before facing the great outdoors. Then it is just the pigeons you have to worry about. Once the soil is appropriately warm, push them out of the modules and plant or, if you have used rone pipe, make a channel for your peas in the soil, unblock one end and gently launch the peas into their ready-made bed. Dwarf varieties make good earlies. Be warned that, with peas in general, germination may be patchy.

Vegetable expert and author Joy Larkcom quotes research that shows that the wider apart you plant peas, the longer and heavier they will yield, recommending at least 12cm between plants, each way. And, if you are planting several rows, do so 60cm–1.2m apart, at the wider spacing for the tallest, most vigorous varieties. Rows, as with your entire vegetable plot, should run north–south to maximise the sun to the entire crop.

You do not have to plant peas in rows, of course. You could grow them up a tepee or block of canes and string. We tend to grow two rows with a cathedral of pea sticks over the whole thing – usually brashings from a little evergreen wood near the house. Don't make the same mistake as I did a couple of years ago. The brashings were so twiggy that they stopped a lot of light getting to the pea seedlings and a number of them failed to flourish. Oh dear!

You will have to protect the seedlings from birds as soon as you plant them out. Use a web of threads or a nylon mesh supported by short sticks, a loose sheet of fleece (support your fleece with crescents of polyurethane pipe pushed into the ground over the seedlings at intervals) or individual pop bottle cloches if you don't have too many to cover.

ROUTINE CARE, HARVESTING AND STORING

Weed regularly otherwise peas and weeds will tangle, making it near impossible to weed without pulling up pea plants in the process. A thick mulch can keep weeds down. Water in dry spells, especially once the plants are flowering, but avoid over-watering early on to prevent excessively leafy growth at the expense of peas. Once the tendrils appear, keep the plants well supported. If they flop, they will not crop as well. Even dwarf varieties benefit from a little support – who doesn't?

As with many vegetables, peas are much more succulent when picked and eaten young. Pick carefully so as not to damage the soft stems of the plant. Harvesting peas encourages more to ripen. Leaving them on when ripe has the opposite effect, so pick regularly. For mangetout, pick them when you can just see the peas forming in the pods but while the pods are still flat. If you do forget about them, you can eventually shell them and eat them as ordinary peas. Sugar-snap peas are eaten when the pods are rounder. Harvest youngish when you can easily snap the pods.

Eat as quickly as possible before the natural sugars turn to starch – raw in salads or lightly poached in a little water and olive oil. Joy Larkcom recommends cooking peas in their pods and shelling after to conserve flavour. For use later, freeze quickly after blanching.

Remember to cut the plants at the base once the harvest is over. You will leave the nitrogen-bearing roots in the ground for the benefit of subsequent crops.

To save your own seeds for next year (not from an F1 hybrid), leave some pods on the plant. Wait until they turn dry and brown. Bring indoors and remove peas from pods. Label and store in a cold, dry place.

COMMON PROBLEMS

Peas are rather prone to pests and diseases (*see* p. 156 for details).

PEA VARIETIES

Wrinkled varieties are a little less hardy than the round-seeded varieties and not as good in poor soil, but they are sweeter tasting. Heights vary from 30cm to 2.5m.

Earlies

'**Avola**' An early that's compact enough to grow in a container.
'**Celebration**' A quick-growing early recommended by Dave Allan of *The Herald*.
'**Feltham First**' 50cm tall, round seed, an old favourite, used to produce really early peas, from June onwards if sown under cover in winter/spring. A good choice for less-than-ideal soil conditions and relatively tough.
'**Kelvedon Wonder**' ♀ Wrinkled seed, good for repeat sowing from early spring to June for long cropping well into the autumn. Grown successfully in Lewis.
'**Meteor**' A round-seeded pea with a very neat habit – 45cm tall. Recommended for Shetland.
'**Pilot**' 1m tall, round seed, early, tough and good for forcing, sown under cover, for early crops.

'**Twinkle**' Wrinkled seed, first early, good for succession sowing, vigorous, resistance to pea wilt and downy mildew.

Main Crop

'**Cavalier**' ♀ Produces large pods and two of them to each node. Good in Orkney.

'**Duke of Albany**' A whopper of a pea growing up to 2.5m. This heritage variety is recommended by Dave Allan.

'**Hurst Green Shaft**' ♀ 80–90cm tall, wrinkled seed, long pods of up to ten peas, excellent taste, mildew and wilt resistant. Good in Orkney and Shetland.

'**Lincoln**' Compact plants, heavy yielding and sweet flavoured.

'**Lord Chancellor**' Wrinkled seed, a long-popular main crop.

'**Onward**' ♀ 1m tall, for many years the most popular garden pea. Heavy cropping and disease resistant. Some consider it to have been superseded by modern hybrids.

Mangetout and sugar-snap peas

'**Oregon Sugar Pod**' ♀ 1m tall, popular, eat at around 7cm before they get a bit tough.

'**Shiraz**' A new variety with attractive dark purple pods. The pods turn greenish when steamed or boiled but stay purple if stir-fried. Mildew resistant. Bicoloured flowers.

'**Sugar Ann**' ♀ Very early and a good cropper. Pale green and fine flavour.

'**Sugar Snap**' Dual purpose, eat as a mangetout when young, shelled when older, 1.5m.

Asparagus Pea (*Tetragonolobus purpureus*) is a vetch with attractive red flowers and pea-like winged pods in August and September. Eat the whole pod, picked at 2.5cm, steamed like mangetout. I felt they had no taste at all, so won't be growing them again and the *Beechgrove Garden* presenters don't seem to be fans either. Not frost hardy so don't plant out until June. We have seen them doing well from the Borders north to Aberdeenshire.

Runner Bean (*Phaseolus coccineus*) H2 E1

BACKGROUND

This Mexican and Central American climbing bean was introduced to England during the reign of Charles I and was initially grown for its stunning flowers. Most runner beans are eaten lightly boiled in their pods. As with French beans, runner bean

Asparagus peas showing their attractive red flowers (right).

flavour can be improved with the addition of butter and garlic or try adding them cooked to a mix of finely chopped shallot, garlic and tomato sautéed in olive oil. Runner bean plants tend to be prolific, so it is a good thing that they freeze well. Don't be tempted to plant too many. I find that one eight-cane tepee is enough. I have tried two, so I know!

Runner bean plants started in modules and ready to plant out. A well-manured bed will ensure a bumper harvest.

SITE, SOIL, SOWING AND PLANTING

Runners will need a rich, moisture-retentive soil in a sunny site, ideally manured the previous autumn. They have deep roots, so will need a good layer of topsoil. Scottish gardeners are at the mercy of wind and rain with most runner beans, as they need to be insect-pollinated. Windswept wigwams may not set many beans. A hybrid variety, 'Moonlight', does not require pollination. On the Outer Hebrides and in Shetland, I saw runner beans successfully grown in polytunnels. They did not do at all on the test vegetable plots on the machair of Benbecula. And a number of gardeners on Orkney told me that runners just don't do there either. Too much wind. Chisholme near Hawick has had good results in a sheltered garden at 300m.

Runner bean 'Enorma' showing its decorative flowers.

Books recommend thorough preparation of a trench for runners, incorporating materials like compost or even shredded newspaper to improve moisture retention. I have to admit that, as our soil is routinely well fed with bulky organic materials, I have had success simply dibbing two seeds into the ground at the base of each one of eight canes that I have formed into a broad-based tepee. Sow seeds mid to late spring, depending on when your soil warms. Your local conditions might make a start under cover advisable. Sow the seeds in modules and transplant after hardening off once the soil is warm enough. Sown outdoors, seeds should be about 4–5cm deep and at least 15cm apart. If you are growing them in rows, then space rows about 40cm apart. Remember that you will have to get in between to pick the things. Build your support before you plant

A spectacular walk-through bean tunnel at Castle Fraser, in Aberdeenshire.

and, as the bean plants will become heavy en masse, be sure to build something strong. And don't be too modest with the height either, as some cultivars will stretch to 3m and more.

Once the bean seedlings show through the soil and start to stretch, they will need careful tying in to their support to give them a start. They pretty quickly get a grip and off they go without much more help – unless a strong wind batters them a bit, in which case they may need tying in. Warning: bitterly cold east winds in late spring can fry soft young growth and tendrils, which means that plants have to start all over again with new growing tips.

ROUTINE CARE, HARVESTING AND STORING

Try to keep on top of weeding and water very well in dry spells, as runners will not tolerate a drought. A mulch of compost or similar will help to retain moisture in the soil. When the plants reach the top of their support, nip out the growing tips to encourage the production of more flowers and pods too. If you do not do this, they will flop back on themselves and become a bit of a tangled mess.

Modern cultivars are less prone to stringiness than the older varieties, so you can harvest as they reach the right size for your taste – the younger the better, as far as I am concerned. Do harvest nearly every day in the season, as they grow fast. You can leave some to mature and dry on the plant to use as next year's seed. However, do not leave too many of these monsters, as they will cause the curtailment of further pod production. To store, blanch whole or cut into diagonal pieces and freeze.

COMMON PROBLEMS

They're relatively trouble-free in my experience. **Birds** and **slugs** may go for the young seedlings. Cover with pop bottle cloches pushed well into the soil. If you see **blackfly** in the growing tips, nick them out quickly and burn them. If flowers are produced but few or **no pods are forming**, it could be because the weather has been a bit cold and the insects needed for pollination have not been out and about. Some say that spraying flowers with water helps but there is not universal agreement on this. White or pink flowering varieties are apparently less susceptible to this problem.

RUNNER BEAN VARIETIES

Seed companies are phasing out and replacing some older varieties but you can find them online.

'**Desiree**' Stringless, good for freezing.

'**Enorma**' ♀ Really long pods, used for showing.

'**Hammond's Dwarf Scarlet**' 50cm, red flowers, long cropping, not very high yields but good for containers.

'**Lady Di**' ♀ Long, slender, stringless pods from red flowers. Ripen slowly so can be picked over a long period.

'**Moonlight**' A new French/runner bean hybrid which is self-fertile, so should be good in windy and wet weather. Certainly worked in a polytunnel on Lewis.

'**Painted Lady**' Ornamental with its white and red flowers, self-fertile. Short pods. We saw this growing successfully in Torridon, Wester Ross.

'**Saint George**' White seeds, narrow, stringless pods. Good for freezing. Heaviest cropper in RHS (English) trials.

'**Scarlet Emperor**' Long, straight pods from early, red flowers. Can be left to trail along the ground rather than climbing, though yields are reduced. Good in Inverness, Perth and the Borders, even at 300m up, so a good choice for most of Scotland.

'**White Lady**' ♀ White flowers get a reliably good crop. Recommended by Tracy Norman, a Glasgow allotmenteer, and good in the Borders too.

CHAPTER 2

Cabbage Family (Brassicas)

The word 'brassica' is derived from a Celtic word – *bresic* – suggesting how long this group of vegetables has been important to us. Most of this family are simply forms of the wild cabbage *Brassica oleracea*, a common wildflower found all over Europe including Wales and south-west England but not Scotland. An amazing array of seemingly unrelated vegetables such as Brussels sprouts, kale and cauliflower have been bred from this plant. Charles Darwin's experiments on brassicas found that they would all throw back to their wild ancestors, so giving weight to his theory of evolutionary change. Cabbage and kale have been staples in this country for hundreds of years, both as feed for livestock and for human consumption, as the vitamin C they contain turned out to be vital for staving off scurvy. Kale is one of our toughest vegetables and seems to be able to tolerate almost any soil and weather condition. There are now many new and delicious varieties and many innovative ways of cooking brassicas, but many of us were put off them by the soggy mess from school dinners, the result of hard boiling for half an hour. Although we usually think of brassicas as the 'greens' in the vegetable plot, turnips, swedes and kohlrabi are also included in this group.

Sulphur compounds are especially prevalent in brassicas, which explains the rather rank cooking smells they may emit. Stir-frying shredded cabbage or broccoli avoids this and tastes great too. And on the subject of chemistry, red cabbage will discolour in the face of any alkalinity, which is why we often stew it in acidic vinegar or red wine.

Brassicas at Fyvie in Aberdeenshire showing this hardy crop's potential as a decorative feature.

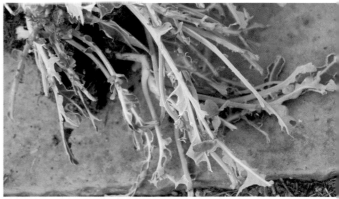

To avoid pigeon shredding of brassicas, netting is the best solution.

Because brassica plants have a significant requirement for nitrogen – lots of green leaves to nurture – they are best to follow the nitrogen-fixing legumes in your rotation plan. Prepare a bed for them in the autumn, adding compost or manure as necessary, so that the soil can consolidate before planting in spring. Getting the pH up to 6.5–7.5 is also important as it reduces the occurrence of the serious disease of club root, so do lime if necessary. As with Greta Garbo, lime likes to be alone so do not add it at the same time as manure. Spread it at least one month before sowing or planting. Planting brassicas requires the use of a strong boot to really firm them in. *Beechgrove Garden*'s George Anderson told Ken that, when he taught students, his traditional test for correct brassica planting out was to tug at the leaves of newly planted seedlings to make sure that they were properly firmed in. The leaf should break before the roots are pulled out of the ground. This requirement for a firm footing makes a no-dig approach ideal for this group. Harden seedlings off for about a week and then plant them very deeply, up to at least one third of their length. Brassica seedlings are then 'puddled in' by watering each one generously at its base. Jim McColl suggests planting young brassicas in drills with ridges between them to give a bit of wind shelter. Don't try this in heavy or clay soils, as the rain will collect at the bottom and rot the plants.

Plantings of brassicas are one of the most attractive features of a great vegetable garden. The rows of coloured kales and cabbages looked so beautiful in the walled garden at Inverewe when I visited while, at Drumlanrig Castle in Dumfriesshire, we saw a square brassica plot planted from corner to corner in mirrored rows – very pleasing to the eye.

COMMON PROBLEMS

With the exception of kale, brassicas share a raft of potential pest and disease problems. Brassica growers used to use a battery of chemicals such as bromophos and bifenthrin to control insects and diseases, but these are no longer available to gardeners who now depend more on crop rotation and barrier methods such as fine-gauge netting. There are nematodes available but they are expensive.

Bird Pests

Pigeons in particular are one of the most prevalent and irritating brassica pests, as they destroy your seedlings by pecking the succulent young growth. Even in Ken's informal potager, with the brassicas scattered around amongst other vegetables and flowers, the pigeons stripped everything in early summer. Most brassicas these days are grown under a framework (canes topped with upturned lager bottles in my case) covered in fine mesh to keep out birds, flea beetle, cabbage white butterflies/caterpillars. You'll see the small, white butterflies circling over your brassicas and any caterpillars laid will shred your leaves. A mixture of half a pint of milk in 1 gallon of water, sprayed onto brassicas in May and every three weeks thereafter is said to help prevent cabbage white butterfly although I haven't tried this myself. It's best to use mesh.

Insect Pests

Underground, **cabbage root flies** munch away and young plants can be killed quickly. Both birds and insects are best prevented by building a cage as noted above and leaving it on for most of the season. Mulching with squares of underfelt or old carpet around the base of the plant also helps prevent cabbage root fly. Greyish, waxy-looking **mealy aphids** and **cabbage whitefly**, the former causing more of a problem than the latter, overwinter on brassica stalks so, as ever, good garden hygiene is important. Remove and burn stalks as the plants finish cropping. **Flea beetles** will eat little holes in the leaves in April and May and their grubs can burrow through stems in late summer. The beetles are deterred by keeping the soil around the brassicas moist. Don't grow brassicas in flea beetle-infected soil for a year or two. **Slugs** can be managed using slug pellets or a range of home-made traps and barriers.

Fungal Diseases

A very serious soil-borne brassica disease spread by tiny spores is **club root**. It is worst in wet summers and in acid soil. The roots of the plants become horribly enlarged and distorted and the leaves will discolour and wilt. Removal and burning of the infected plant is vital – don't put it on the compost heap. The disease will live for years in the soil so strict rotation is only part of the answer. Liming the soil does help and mulching is also reckoned to be useful in this context. Plants raised in modules or pots and planted out with a decent root system may be strong enough to succeed in slightly infected soil. A very significant new development is club root-resistant varieties from Suttons Seeds – Brussels sprout 'Crispus', cabbage 'Kilaxy' and cauliflower

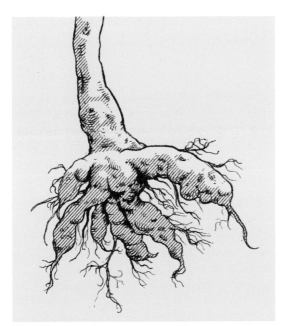

The swollen roots of club root, a serious disease of brassicas, which remains in the soil for many years. Growing club root-resistant varieties is the best prevention.

'Clapton'. *Beechgrove Garden*'s George Anderson conducted an excellent trial of club root-resistant varieties in contaminated soil in 2010. All did well and avoided infection, while the control varieties succumbed to the disease. George recommends liming the soil and growing in pots before planting out to make doubly sure that infection is kept at bay. Clearly this important breeding work is overcoming a serious brassica problem and many of the people who told us they'd given up growing them could consider starting again. Other fungal problems include **leaf spots**, **white blister** (white rust) and **downy mildew**. Avoiding overcrowded planting helps prevent these. Fungicides may help too. Fields of oil seed rape may be responsible for the increase in fungal disease spores blowing into gardens.

Mineral deficiency

A manganese or magnesium deficiency can be the cause of **chlorotic leaves** (yellow veining) although other problems, such as drought or poor drainage, can have a similar effect. The application of trace elements, available in most fertilisers, should clear up the problem.

Once brassicas are finished and heading for the compost, you may wish to chop the thick, woody stems to encourage them to break down. Whole stems take a very long time to decompose. Try using your half-moon lawn-edger in a large plastic flowerpot or bucket for this job – it works well but may not be ideal for the blade of your lawn-edger!

Broccoli and Calabrese (*Brassica oleracea* Italica group) *H4–5 E2*

High in vitamins A and C and iron, and the most popular brassicas for children, it is likely that sprouting broccoli and calabrese are not much more than a type of flowering cabbage. They are first mentioned in print in the eighteenth century and prob-

Succulent broccoli and calabrese harvested at Glendoick. Normally they would not be ready at the same time.

Young broccoli plants in midsummer showing rather close spacing. Thinning would produce larger plants.

Purple sprouting broccoli. There are varieties available which crop at the end of the growing season so there's no waiting until spring.

ably hailed from Italy – in Italian *broccoli* means little arms or little shoots and *calabrese* refers to the south Italian region of Calabria.

Broccoli can take a very long time to mature – nine months is not uncommon – and, with its purple, green or white heads, it is grown in the latter part of the year to overwinter and crop in spring. Calabrese, available as green or purple varieties, is started in spring and harvested in late summer. Having said that, Ken found that calabrese sailed through the terrible winter of 2010 and cropped well the following spring but his broccoli did not make it. Broccoli failure was a UK-wide phenomenon that year. The *Beechgrove Garden* team voted it a waste of space after the 2010 winter although Jim McColl himself said he gave up growing it 30 years before! Lots of Scottish growers are more enthusiastic. Pam Whittle, Chair of the Royal Caledonian Horticultural Society, gets a good overwintering crop in cold Romano Bridge in the Borders.

SITE, SOIL, SOWING AND PLANTING

Broccoli and calabrese require an open, well-fed and well-drained site. Manure in the autumn and lime at least one month before sowing or planting. Ensure a firm footing for the plants. Sow calabrese seed in spring in the ground or, for preference, in modules and then plant out once seedlings are large enough to handle – at least 7cm. Space 30–40cm apart. Start broccoli in modules around May, transplanting to its cropping bed in July. Space 60cm apart each way in a block. To avoid too large a crop appearing all at once use a mix of early and late cultivars. Calabrese can be harvested as so-called 'microgreens' 8–12 weeks from sowing.

ROUTINE CARE

Keep weeded and water during dry spells. You might need to stake the broccoli in winter to help it withstand the weather. Birds may eat the young plants so they are best sheltered under fine mesh or fleece. And again, in the spring, the attraction of the succulent broccoli sprouts may be too much when little else is available – so get the mesh out again!

HARVESTING AND STORING

Calabrese is harvested in late summer of the year it is planted. It will produce a small, cauliflower-like head. Harvest this first and then broccoli-like side shoots should grow to be harvested in their turn. Use a cut-and-come-again approach to encourage new heads, cutting them before they flower. You will be harvesting broccoli from early spring the year after it was planted. Broccoli and calabrese can both be frozen successfully after blanching. For brassica problems see p. 168.

BROCCOLI AND CALABRESE VARIETIES

Broccoli

'**Brokali Apollo**' F1 New, a cross between broccoli and Chinese kale. I tried it and it grew and cropped well. Very tender and sweet.

'**Claret**' F1 ♡ Matures in April, said to be exceptionally high-yielding and tolerant of most soils.

'**Early Purple Sprouting**' Long the most popular variety, ready to harvest in February–March.

'**Late Purple Sprouting**' ♡ Harvest in April. There are 'improved' versions available.

'**Nine Star Perennial**' If you don't let it flower, it should produce spears for two or three years. Harvest the heads in April–June. I have tried this with some success, harvesting succulent white florets. You'll need to give it a semi-permanent home, effectively removing it from your rotation plan. Tall, it may require some support.

'**Red Arrow**' ♡ A new selection which is claimed to

be higher yielding and of better flavour. Good winter hardiness

'**Red Spear**' ♡ Dark coloured, early to mid season, good winter hardiness.

'**White Sprouting**' Early and late versions for harvesting in March–April and April–May respectively.

Calabrese

'**Aquiles**' F1 Alan Titchmarsh recommends this as a long cropper, sown early to late spring and then again in autumn.

'**Arcadia**' F1 ♡ Firm head, quick maturing, robust. Recommended for Shetland.

'**Iron Man**' F1 Recommended by Jane Eastwood on Lewis as it 'just keeps going' and good in *Gardening Which?* trials.

'**Italian Sprouting**' The classic variety with a long cropping season.

'**Shogun**' F1 Tolerant of cold and all soil types. Freezes well.

Brussels Sprout (*Brassica oleracea* Gemmifera Group) *H4–5 E2*

I absolutely love sprouts but, according to the British sprout industry, I am in the minority in the UK – they are most popular in southern England and least popular in Scotland. Undaunted, not only will I eat a pound of them with grated cheese on top for my main meal (and then sleep alone), I have a great soup recipe which confounds sprouts haters with its silky texture and warm flavour. And they provide some colour if you use a red variety. Sprouts probably came relatively late to our tables and were not much known until the late eighteenth century. Now frequently eaten as part of a Christmas meal, this is probably because they last well into winter. Indeed, sprouts are reputed to taste better if picked beyond the first frosts. Convenient for those of us who have, whatever the season, an absolute need for fresh vegetables on a daily basis, try shredding them and using as a coleslaw or stir-frying them with your favourite flavours – chillies, garlic, etc. The tops are edible too and apparently, by weight, they have three times the vitamin C of an orange. And look out for 'flower sprouts', a relatively new cross between Brussels sprouts and kale. It is claimed they are not shunned by children the way sprouts are. They are certainly visually attractive, looking, as they do, like mini cabbages.

Brussels sprouts 'Sanda' in Caroline's garden. For taste, select an older variety over an F1 hybrid.

SITE, SOIL, SOWING AND PLANTING

Prepare an open, sunny and well-fed site with good drainage. If you are digging, do it in the autumn to ensure a firm footing for the plants. Lime as necessary.

Sprouts require quite a long growing season, so the bed can usefully be used for accompanying catch crops as the young plants grow. You can buy varieties which crop from autumn until early spring. Grow a few of each for a succession if your conditions allow.

You can sow sprout seeds directly into the ground in late spring, but the best idea is to start them in trays then transplant into modules or sow directly into modules. Sow in mid March or earlier if you can give them a little bottom heat. After hardening off, choose the straightest seedlings to plant out in May or when your conditions allow. As with all brassicas, plant them deeply, below the level of the module soil. This helps to anchor what will generally be a rather tall and top-heavy plant. Plant in blocks at a spacing of between 75–90cm depending on the size of variety you have chosen.

Watch the plants as they grow and re-firm their stalks if they seem a bit wobbly. As they stretch, stake the plants to keep them firm in autumn and winter winds.

Brussels sprouts 'Red Rubine' contrasting with 'ordinary' green sprouts. The red variety holds most of its colour after cooking.

ROUTINE CARE, HARVESTING AND STORING

If your soil is humus-rich and fertile, your plants should need little attention. Keep weed free and water during dry spells. As the season progresses, remove any yellowing leaves to give the sprouts good air circulation and so prevent rot. They should start cropping around October or November. Pop the sprouts off when you want to eat them – cold work on a freezing winter's day! Harvest the lowest first and finish with the tops, which you can use in soups and stews. After blanching, sprouts freeze well. Remember to lift the plants and remove them from the bed after cropping to prevent pests from over-wintering.

COMMON PROBLEMS

See p. 168 for brassica problems. Watch out especially for **mealy aphids**, as they will lurk right inside the sprouts.

BRUSSELS SPROUT VARIETIES

Older varieties ripen from the bottom to the top over several weeks and you need to harvest them at the right time as they soon 'blow' or go over. There are lots of modern F1 hybrids with masses of uniform buttons which all ripen at the same time. Many of these hang on to ripe buttons for several weeks, so harvesting time is not so critical. As noted above, cold weather in November and December is believed to sweeten the sprouts.

'**Bosworth**' F1 ♀ Downy mildew and ring spot resistant.
'**Crispus**' F1 New club root-resistant variety, cropping from September to November.
'**Cronus**' F1 November–December harvesting, club root resistant.

'**Darkmar**' Dark green and productive, cropping October – December. Recommended by Jane Eastwood on Lewis.
'**Doric**' Perfect for Aberdonians, this has a strong root system and is said to be good on windy sites.
'**Igor**' F1 ♀ Mid to late season, vigorous, uniform, well-spaced sprouts.
'**Nautic**' Mid season cropping December–February, sweet flavour.
'**Peer Gynt**' Apparently the most popular variety, October/November–December harvesting.
'**Red Bull**' and '**Red Falstaff**' are new purple varieties.
'**Rubine**' or '**Red Rubine**' The red sprout can be eaten raw or cooked and the flavour is excellent. The colour fades when steamed. The *Beechgrove Garden* had reasonable results with this and we had edible sprouts until February in the hard 2010 winter.
'**Trafalgar**' Bred to be the sweetest sprout of all, seedsmen Thompson and Morgan make great claims for it!
'**Wellington**' F1 ♀ A late cropper.

Cabbage (*Brassica oleracea* var. *capitata*) H4–5 F2

Cabbage is the cultivated forerunner of many of the other brassicas. Known and eaten since classical times and valued for its health-giving properties, the Romans thought it was a cure for drunkenness. So they didn't get everything right. It is high in vitamin A and C and is said to help reduce the risk of colon cancer and to be good for the immune system. School dinners of soggy cabbage put generations of people off it, which is a great pity as, if properly cooked, it is delicious. Cut up finely and boil for three minutes or steam for six and you should have perfectly cooked leaves, ready for a seasoning of butter and pepper. The oldest cabbage varieties were 'headless' so more spring greens than cabbage. It was probably not until the Middle Ages, and possibly as a result of northern European horticultural efforts,

A savoy cabbage with its wrinkly leaves. Savoys have a long cropping season so, if you only have space for one variety, this might be a good choice.

that the headed cabbage became popular, although it never quite ousted the ubiquitous kale as the staple Scottish green. There is now a huge choice of cabbage in a range of colours from the faintest of green to the deepest of red. The textural range is broad too, from smooth to very curly or ridged. They do take up a fair amount of space and most take around 35 weeks from sowing to harvest. A careful choice of varieties will mean you can crop them all year round.

SITE, SOIL, SOWING AND PLANTING

For cabbages, choose a well-fertilised, open and sunny site with reasonable drainage. Dig, if you do, the previous autumn, incorporating compost or manure (or lay it on the surface for the worms to do their work if you are a no-digger) and then lime at least a month before planting. Leave the ground to settle to ensure the required firm footing. Scotland's first garden writer John Reid (1683) would have us sow our 'great white and red [cabbages at] the full moon in July, Plant them furth in Octob'. Try that too!

Start seed in trays or modules, under protection

if necessary (in the dining room in my case). Having hardened off the young plants, transplant only the straight-stemmed seedlings. The closer you sow or transplant cabbages, the smaller will be the heads, which you may want. For areas of Scotland with a short growing season, the prospect of cabbages cropping year round in the ground may be diminished unless you select the very hardiest of varieties (*see below*) or use a protected environment. And of course you may be able to get the cabbage variety you prefer to grow for you, no matter its ideal season, by lavishing it with extra care – always worth trying.

For spring-cropping cabbage, spring greens if cropped very early, sow in midsummer and transplant in mid autumn. Space at 30cm in a block formation – in a tunnel probably in the wilder parts of the country. You may want to top-dress with some compost come spring to give the plants a boost.

For cabbage which crops in summer to early autumn, sow in mid March in a protected environment. Harden off and plant out in late spring. Space plants in blocks at 35–45cm, depending on the size of head you are after.

For autumn cabbage, sow the seeds in late spring and transplant when ready but certainly by midsummer. Block plant to a spacing of 50cm apart.

For winter cabbage, including many of the wrinkly but beautiful savoys, sow in April/May then transplant in summer in blocks spaced at 50cm between each plant. Hardy varieties will stand in the ground until required.

ROUTINE CARE, HARVESTING AND STORING

Keep the bed well weeded. Water in dry spells or you will check the growth of the cabbages. Keep the area cleared of leaves which have dropped from the plants as they may harbour pests. Harvest as required.

It is possible to produce further rather mini

cabbages in summer and autumn if, instead of pulling up the whole plant when you harvest it, you leave the stalk in the ground and cut a cross in the top.

Cabbage will keep for a few days in the fridge or it can be finely shredded, blanched and frozen.

COMMON PROBLEMS

Cabbages are possibly the most problem prone of the brassicas and, for that reason, some people are put off trying them. I used to be a sceptic but am now converted after receiving a free packet of seeds I could not bear to waste – and on discovering the joys of fine mesh! They are really so delicious freshly picked.

CABBAGE VARIETIES

Spring cabbage

Planted in autumn for harvest in spring or early summer.

'**Duncan**' F1 ♀ Used for spring greens in early season or hearted cabbage in summer.
'**Durham Early**' Dark green, a good source of spring greens.
Offenham Group, very hardy, several strains.
'**Pixie**' ♀ Small heads with good hearts, one of the earliest to mature in spring.
'**Pyramid**' F1 ♀ Slow-growing. Suitable for sowing year round.

Summer–autumn cabbage

Usually sown in March/April, transplanted in May/June and harvested in late summer to early autumn.

'**Brunswick**' Heritage variety grown successfully on Lewis. Medwyn Williams of Anglesey, multi-times winner of a Chelsea gold medal and

Cabbage 'Minicole' is a good choice for a small plot or a small appetite!

Cabbage 'Pixie' is hearty, early and suitable for close spacing.

A red cabbage with spectacular blue outer leaves – ideal for the potager.

National Vegetable Society stalwart, suggests it can be nurtured to grow as a giant if the spirit moves you.

'**Golden Acre**' An old variety producing large heads early in the season. Good reports from Lewis.

'**Greyhound**' ♀ An old favourite, compact and quick to mature. Recommended for Shetland, Lewis (with protection) and on the machair of Benbecula with appropriate care and attention.

'**Hispi**' F1 ♀ Small, pointed heads, dark green, good flavour, earlier than 'Greyhound' and a good choice for close spacing.

'**Kalibos**' Red-leaved, ideal for coleslaw with a sweet taste. George Anderson of *Beechgrove Garden* recommends.

'**Kilaton**' F1 ♀ Club root resistant, long storage.

'**Kilaxy**' Suttons Seeds newly launched club root-resistant Dutch white cabbage.

'**Marner Lagerot**' Deep red and firm heads. Seen growing at Inverewe.

'**Minicole**' F1 ♀ Can be planted at close spacing for smaller heads.

'**Red Drumhead**' Heirloom variety with dark red, dense heads, grown successfully on Lewis.

'**Ruby Ball**' F1 ♀ Red cabbage, often pickled, found in supermarket ready meals, but not as widely grown as it could be, and the attractive blue-coloured outer foliage makes this a fine feature in potagers. Does not store well.

Winter and Savoy cabbage

Sown in April/May, transplanted in July and harvested in November to January. Often used for coleslaw.

'**Best of All**' Savoy, maturing in September.

'**Celtic**' ♀ Dr Hessayon calls this 'the crown prince of winter cabbages'. Very tough, blue-green leaves and can stand for months in good condition.

'**Holland Late Winter**' This is a good choice for coleslaw and it stores for ages.

'**January King 3**' ♀ Very tough, frost-resistant drumhead savoy cabbage. Grown with some success on Benbecula.

'**Ormskirk Late**' Savoy, one of the latest, maturing in February or March.

'**Savoy King**' F1 Pale leaves, maturing in September, highly rated.

Cauliflower (*Brassica oleracea* Botrytis Group) *H4–5 E3*

Mark Twain said that 'a cauliflower is nothing but a cabbage with a college education'. He could have added that the extra education makes it rather harder to please than its relatives. Like broccoli, a cauliflower is basically a cabbage that has started flowering but stopped at bud stage. It was probably introduced into Europe by the Arabs from Cyprus and Syria. I have to confess that, in common with many gardeners, I have had little luck with these but will keep trying. I also aspire to grow Romanesco, which has such a stunningly beautiful-looking green head – or 'curds', as the head is called – with a fine texture and delicious flavour but, again, it has not performed well. Champion vegetable exhibitor Medwyn Williams put on a superb display at the Dundee Food and Flower Show 2010, including a number of quite glorious cauliflowers – a dangerous purple, a green and a sunny yellow. And all are equally good for you, as they contain antioxidants no matter the colour.

Beyond cauliflower cheese (very good with lots of wholegrain mustard in the sauce), cauliflower cheese soup is delicious and warming, and this vegetable lends itself very well to curries too. Don't forget about piccalilli either.

SITE, SOIL, SOWING AND PLANTING

Cauliflowers are large plants which need a long growing season: 20–24 weeks for summer–autumn harvesting and much longer if overwintered. Preferring an open site and a rich, well-fertilised and moisture-retentive soil, cauliflowers remain a challenge even if you can give them their ideal situation. They hate to be checked for any reason – cold or drought – and, if this happens, they tend to bolt or produce feeble curds, if any at all. Naturally a crop happy in cooler conditions, we in Scotland should certainly have a head start! Lime the soil as necessary. A range of varieties will give you the possibility of cropping caulis over a long season if you wish. Where your growing season is short, go for the late summer/ autumn maturing type. Cauliflowers are probably best sown in modules and then transplanted when they are large enough to handle (around six leaves).

For an early summer crop, sow in autumn and overwinter in a cold frame. Harden off before planting out in spring when your conditions allow. To know if your ground is warm enough, you could try sitting on it in nothing but your undies as advised by a lady in Orkney who has never had crop failure due to cold soil. (A good story but probably apocryphal.) You could also sow seed later but you would have to use bottom heat (!) provided by a propagator to get an early summer crop. So-called winter varieties are more akin to broccoli and mature in late spring. Some of them, such as 'St Agnes', are tender and not suitable for Scotland while others are tougher. For a late summer/autumn crop, sow in spring and plant out in early summer. For a winter/spring crop, sow in late spring and plant out in midsummer.

Space plants in blocks at 55–60cm. Plant closer together if you want to grow small cauliflowers. Cauliflowers will be protected from both strong summer sun and wild winter weather by bending, draping or somehow encouraging the leaves over the curds – if they are not already there.

ROUTINE CARE, HARVESTING AND STORING

Ensure that cauliflowers always have enough moisture at their roots. Any drought is likely to result in a check in growth, which will mean inadequate development of the curds. It is worth remembering that the wider the spacing you give a plant, the more extensive will be its root run and so the better able it will be to support a lack of water. Harvest them as you need but don't leave them too long. Plants from a single sowing tend to mature all at once, but fortunately they freeze well as florets, soup or curry.

Cauliflower is the trickiest brassica to grow but a good result makes the effort worthwhile.

Coloured caulis 'Sunset' (orange), 'Graffiti' (purple) and others taste just like the white ones but look wonderful.

COMMON PROBLEMS

See under brassica introduction on p. 168. Cauliflower is sensitive to a **boron deficiency** in the soil, particularly in sandy soils where nutrients leach easily. The symptoms are brown patches on the curds. Borax can be added to soil but follow instructions carefully as too much boron is toxic to plants. Compost or well-rotted manure usually supplies boron.

CAULIFLOWER VARIETIES

'**Aalsmeer**' ♀ (early–mid) Maturing in April–May. Well-protected, medium to small cream curds, sometimes produces multiple smaller heads.

'**All the Year Round**' (early–late) Can be succession sown in a heated greenhouse in January for summer harvesting and April–May outdoors for autumn harvesting. Well-protected curds. Recommended for Lewis and by two contacts in Shetland, one of whom, Alan Crowe of Aith, plants it in a net tunnel in September for cropping in May.

'**Autumn Giant**' (mid) Long the most popular for autumn harvesting, large heads. Now being superseded by F1 hybrids.

'**Candid Charm**' F1 (early) Recommended at Broughton House in Kirkcudbright, this is a quick-growing variety that can be harvested as mini caulis. Good in Shetland.

'**Nessie**' F1 ♀ (mid–late) Medium to large, very high quality, bright white, solid curds of good weight and well protected. Can be sown up to the end of May.

'**Snowball**' (early) By far the most popular early variety. Fairly small curds.

Coloured varieties include '**Purple Goliath**' and '**Graffiti**' F1 ♀ (dark purple), '**Emeraude**' F1 ♀ (green), '**Cheddar**' F1 (yellow) and '**Sunset**' F1 (orange).

Romanesco First grown in Italy in the sixteenth century, it became popular in Britain after trials at the James Hutton Institute, near Dundee. There are various varieties – for example, '**Minaret**' ♀ Lime-green florets and beautiful peaked shape, if sown in May, it should mature in autumn, even as far north as Shetland in a good summer. '**Celio**' F1 is recommended by Jane Eastwood on Lewis.

Kale or Borecole (*Brassica oleracea acephala*) H5 E1

Probably the toughest vegetable of all, kale should be considered Scotland's national vegetable – if the Welsh can have one . . . Kale (kail in Scots), specifically curly kale or borecole, was a key part of the Scots diet of the past, initially of Lowlanders and then more widely. This is reflected in the use of the word kail as a generic term for a meal. 'Cold kail yet again' would be the description of a stale story or old sermon, and the 'Kailyard School' of late nineteenth-century Scottish writers focused on rural issues in what was regarded as a rather sentimental fashion. You'll find the ruins of walled kailyards in Caithness, Orkney and particularly on Shetland, where they are known as plantie-crubs. The stones would provide wind shelter and reflected heat as well as a sheep-free zone and the soil inside would be improved with ash and seaweed. Shetland kale, a kind of cabbage, is very slow growing, taking almost two years to mature. It was eaten in winter, used to feed animals or salted and stored in barrels. It is still grown by a few Shetlanders, fed with seaweed, peat dust and sheep manure. It appears to be resistant to club root, thriving in very acid soil. Kale, for all its lack of glamour, should now be hailed as another 'super-food', as it appears to have powerful antioxidant and anti-cancer properties and high levels of vitamins A and C.

An unpopular vegetable, it is nevertheless delicious if cooked properly. Most varieties tend towards bitterness if picked in summer before the first frosts,

Three decorative kale varieties at Inverewe, Wester Ross.

Curly kale and 'Black Tuscan' kale can be grown as cut-and-come again greens or in pots under protection to crop as salad.

Red Russian kale, also known as 'Ragged Jack'. Joy Larkcom reckons that 'Ragged Jack' is an older, more-dwarf and less-hardy variety but the two names seem to be used interchangeably.

Kale 'Redbor' is a frilly beauty which can be eaten both raw and cooked. An ideal winter vegetable.

so harvest it in winter. Growing your own is easy – you have quite a choice of cultivars and the prospect of a long harvest period at a time when little else is available. The name of the variety 'Hungry Gap' reflects its usefulness. Here is my favourite kale recipe:

> Put some caraway seeds, garlic and shallots in a small frying pan into which you have poured some olive oil. Cook until soft then add a couple of handfuls of chopped kale, rib removed, and stir-fry until it too has softened. Add some cooked pasta, a couple of beaten eggs and a handful of Parmesan. Stir, then allow to set. Carefully invert on to a plate and return to the pan to firm the other side. Fine hot or cold!

I grew 'Cavolo Nero' ('Black Tuscan' kale) for the first time in 2010 and it is fabulous, more subtle than curly kale and great when eaten with some onions 'melted' in butter for about half an hour and then poured over the cooked leaves as a sauce. And the striking foliage lends itself to potager arrangements.

SITE, SOIL, SOWING AND PLANTING

Kale, unlike many other brassicas, is happy in a relatively poor soil but does require reasonable drainage. Lime if necessary to ensure a slightly alkaline soil. Choose a sunny site and the seeds can go straight into the ground towards the end of April if your soil is warm enough or in May in colder and inland gardens. Sow sparingly in rows 1cm deep. Otherwise start in modules and then transplant once conditions allow. When large enough to handle, thin or transplant to 30cm for dwarf varieties, 35–45cm for 'Black Tuscan' varieties and between 60–75cm apart for the standard curly and broad-leaved varieties, in a block formation. Remember to plant them deeply to give a firm and lasting footing. Pigeons can strip newly planted seedlings but they tend to leave them alone later on, in our gardens at least.

ROUTINE CARE, HARVESTING AND STORING

Hoe regularly and tread around stems as they mature to prevent wind rock. Water in dry weather. You may need to stake the taller varieties to keep them upright through winter. You could cloche the dwarf varieties to keep the worst of the weather off. Kale will look bedraggled over winter, but hold faith, as you are likely to be able to continue harvesting and eating the stuff. Feed in late summer and early spring to encourage side shoots. Start harvesting from late autumn onwards. Nicking the tip from the crown will stimulate the production of tender side shoots, which you can then gather between February and May. Take a few leaves from each plant to keep them all ticking over. Kale freezes well and may taste sweeter after a spell in the freezer too. Once you see flower buds forming, stop cropping and remove the plants to the compost, except in the case of 'Pentland Brig', whose flowering shoots are delicious.

COMMON PROBLEMS

Unlike the rest of the brassicas, most kale is rarely troubled by club root and cabbage root fly but may be attacked by **mealy aphid**, **white fly** or **cabbage caterpillar**. A fine mesh cover will help prevent pest damage.

KALE VARIETIES

'**Bornick**' ♀ F1 Quick maturing curly green leaves.

'**Cavolo Nero**' or '**Black Tuscan**' Generally considered the best tasting kale with striking dark, wrinkly leaves. Not as robust as curly kale, it can be used in salads. Seen growing successfully at Inverewe, on Lewis with protection from the wind, in Orkney and in gardens all over mainland Scotland. Used as a vegetable plot edge at Mertoun.

'**Dwarf Green Curled**' A so-called 'Scotch' variety, 45cm, good for windy sites.

'**Pentland Brig**' ✉ 60cm, broad-leaved kale – harvest the crown in autumn and the side shoots and flower heads like miniature broccoli in late spring. It is not as showy as the rest, but for eating, perhaps the best choice.

'**Redbor**' F1 ♀ Purple-green leaves, attractive foliage plant for potagers. Can be used as cut-and-come-again for salads.

'**Red Russian**' Frilly grey-green with red stems, sweet taste. Eat young or mature.

'**Red Winter**' Dark-green leaved with purplish veins. Good at Inverewe. Very pretty and apparently succulent to eat.

'**Reflex**' F1 ♀ Tall, hardy, blue-green colouring.

'**Ripbor**' Tall, frilly, dark-green leaves.

'**Scarlet**' Another beautiful red variety. Stands well in winter but can be harvested young for salads.

'**Sutherland Kale**' ('*Càil Cataibh*' in Gaelic) ✉ Available from realseeds.co.uk. This was rescued from a research project by Elizabeth Woolcombe, who gardened into her 90s in Sutherland, and sent on by Vicky Schilling to Real Seeds. It can be eaten right through the spring, is pest and wind resistant and clearly is an ancient Highland landrace.

'**Thousand Headed Kale**' Harvest the side shoots in early spring. 'Pentland Brig' is probably better.

'**Westland Winter**' One of the larger varieties, very hardy and will stand well over winter, good flavour. Another seen at Inverewe.

Kohlrabi (*Brassica oleracea* Gongylodes Group) *H3 E1*

BACKGROUND

Another development of the cabbage, this is an easily grown vegetable which is high in vitamin C and potassium. Mature kohlrabi has a really interesting and unusual shape and always make me think of a sputnik (showing my age again), while Ken's children think they look like aliens. Fast maturing, edible from 8–12 weeks after sowing, it is best eaten at tennis ball size before it becomes larger and woody. It can be eaten raw if grated or cooked until soft. The taste is turnip with a touch of cauliflower – pleasant if not exciting. Try it cubed and roasted with garlic. Some recommend peeling after cooking as the best flavour is said to be just under the skin but I find this far from easy to do so I peel them first.

If you like kohlrabi, it is worth succession sowing them, as you rarely find them in the shops. There are both green and purple varieties although the flesh in both is white and the flavour is pretty much identical. The green are generally grown as earlies and the hardier purples sown and harvested later. Kohlrabi is pretty robust and we have seen it growing well in Lewis.

SITE, SOIL, SOWING AND PLANTING

Kohlrabi prefer a light, fertile soil in a sunny position. Lime the soil as necessary. They can be started off in modules or sown under protection in mid March. Transplant to block formation with plants 20–25cm apart and they should be ready to harvest by the end of June. If you sow directly into the soil from around late May onwards, then do this in drills 1cm deep with rows 30cm apart. Put two or three seeds in together (station sow), 10cm apart and then thin the weaker seedlings to leave singles. Sown in June–July (usually purple varieties), you can harvest in autumn.

ROUTINE CARE, HARVESTING AND STORING

Keep the soil weed free and water in dry weather. Mulch to help the plants grow speedily. Lift and eat when they are no larger than a tennis ball. If you want mini kohlrabi, then plant seedlings closer together. Kohlrabi does not store long once harvested but can be blanched and frozen fairly successfully. Later maturing varieties need to be lifted before any serious frost.

COMMON PROBLEMS

See p. 168 for brassica problems. These plants tend to miss the worst of the brassica ailments, in part because they are so quick to grow and crop. You may need to protect the young plants from birds, especially pigeons in my case, which delight in pulling them up.

KOHLRABI VARIETIES

'**Green Vienna**' (syn. '**White Vienna**') Green-skinned, early.

'**Lanro**' F1 ♀ Green, early, good flavour and texture.

'**Purple Vienna**' Late, purple-skinned.

'**Rowell**' F1 Green, bred to have a better, sweeter flavour and not to go woody, if allowed to get larger.

Kohlrabi is one of the fastest growing brassicas. It is virtually impossible to buy in supermarkets, so worth trying at home if you like the taste of sweet turnips.

CHAPTER 3

Cucumber Family (Cucurbits)

In Scotland the cucurbits offer quite a range of tender to relatively hardy vegetables, most of which are American in origin. The least hardy, cucumber, is most likely to have originated in India or Africa (depending on what you read) and will probably have to be grown in a greenhouse or tunnel unless you have an exceptionally warm, wind-free corner outside. Courgettes, on the other hand, are relative thugs and, with enough manure to sit on, will grow away outside through a range of potential difficulties, even marauding rabbits, producing more than you could possibly eat.

As for marrows, I have never grown them on purpose, only forgotten to harvest a courgette – they hide, you know – or rather one gives up on them after yet another surfeit. Your friends will groan when they see you coming! And then there's winter squash – I love the things. They can be grown under protection or outside but they do need quite a long season in which to ripen properly for storage, so a tunnel is good if you have one. Pumpkins are fun to grow and are now popular as Halloween lanterns, but you need a huge amount of space for a small number of them. They are certainly easier to hollow out than the swedes I used as a child, but I still find the smell of burning neep so evocative. I can't really feel enthusiastic about pumpkins as lanterns. They do make great soup, though.

The cucurbits are, nutritionally and in flavour, relatively poor, the exception being winter squash and pumpkin seeds, which are rich in unsaturated oils and many trace elements. However, all of them make great vehicles for other flavours – courgettes in an olive-oil and herby vinaigrette, winter squash in a Thai curry, cucumbers in a dill pickle and marrow stuffed then covered with a rich cheese sauce.

COMMON PROBLEMS

Disease and Fungal Problems

Don't sow your seeds too thickly and try to keep your seedlings well ventilated and well lit to discourage **damping off**, a fungal disease that may attack your tiny seedlings – pick out any mouldy ones immediately to halt spread. In the greenhouse, there are many potential pitfalls with lots of awful looking spots, rots and collapses including **root rot**, **botrytis**, **sclerotinia**, **black rot**, **neck rot** and **anthracnose** waiting to surprise you. Don't be put off as, with care, you should be able to avoid or deal with most of them. Keep your greenhouse clean, tidy and well ventilated, your plants appropriately watered and observe a rotation if you are not using pots of new compost or growbags. On mature plants, you'll need to pick off affected fruit or parts of the plant and destroy them. Sometimes you just have to cut your losses. Once planted out and cropping, you may notice **powdery mildew** on courgettes. This is very common and can be treated by spraying the leaves with a milk solution – one part milk to nine parts water. I have also read that adding baking soda helps, as it raises the pH on the leaf surfaces and so is unfriendly to the mildew spores. I haven't tried it, though. The wet summer of 2011 rotted off a good many courgettes and marrows. **Cucumber mosaic virus** affects courgettes, marrows and cucumbers. Symptoms are distorted and mottled yellow blotches on the leaves. Burn young plants. For older plants, remove and burn infected leaves and the plant may carry on, although you will get fewer fruit than normal. **Aphids** are the vector for this disease so you will want to keep them under control. This can be easier said than done if you are keen to keep your crops chemical-free.

Insect Problems

Greenfly can be prevented or reduced by spraying them off with water, squidging them between your fingers, hanging the yellow sticky cards you can buy for the job or interplanting with French marigolds. You can attract ladybirds into the greenhouse by putting a plant there that they find irresistible such as poached egg plant (*Limnanthes douglasii*) or buy and use biological controls (*see* p. 67). Cucumbers indoors can be attacked by **red spider mites** which suck sap from the leaves. See p. 75 for controls.

Courgette and Marrow (*Cucurbita pepo*) H2 E1

Every year I wonder why I have planted so many. I just can't seem to help myself. Having tried many and varied ways of using them or getting rid of them – including leaving them on Ken's doorstep when I knew he was out – I have just read of one more. It was reported in *The Herald* on 25 September 2010 that a woman in Montana, USA, repelled a bear by hurling a 35cm courgette at it. Maybe I could start a small export business?

Courgettes, or summer squash, are relative newcomers to our gardens and tables, having been introduced from Italy via France in the late nineteenth and early twentieth centuries. They gained little ground until Elizabeth David extolled their virtues in the 1950s and '60s. Quite a range of shapes, sizes and colours is available. I have found the yellow varieties especially firm and delicious. I love the patty pans that look like yellow flying saucers and have also had good success with little round ones that were perfect, stuffed, as individual portions. Not only can the fruit be eaten but the flowers too; both male and female can be stuffed, cooked and presented for a fancy supper.

SITE, SOIL, SOWING AND PLANTING

Courgettes will need a sunny site with a rich and moisture-retentive soil. They grow into large plants that are very greedy feeders and they are never happier than when on top of an outpost of your compost or dung heap. Start your courgettes inside by sowing a seed 1.25cm deep into a module or 7cm pot in compost – probably in late March at the earliest. Germinate them on a sunny windowsill. You can start them a little later than you do some of your other seeds, as they fairly romp away once they get going. Harden them off and plant them out once they have three good leaves showing – probably not until early May ideally. You may have to pot them on indoors if it is not warm enough to plant them outside.

Our soil has a good heart generally but, even so, when I plant them, I dig a hole and then put in an extra spadeful of dung. After a scattering of soil, I sit the plant right on top of this, backfill with soil and firm in. Plant the courgettes at least 90cm apart – probably more as they do wander. And try not to plant too many. You will find three is probably ample. They may be slow to get started, especially in a poorish Scottish summer. Cloche to give them a boost and if torrential rain is forecast. Courgettes are

Courgette 'Floridor' at Kellie Castle, in Fife.

Courgette rot – black rot or botrytis – is probably caused by over-watering indoors or wet summers outdoors.

Courgette mildew is very common and it is possible to ignore a mild case and still harvest a crop.

Don't forget you can eat the flowers of courgettes too – very fine stuffed and battered – or just decorate a dish with them.

one of the best vegetables for growing in containers and growbags, as you can get such a good yield from a plant or two as long as you keep feeding and watering them. The *Beechgrove Garden*'s Carole Baxter conducted trials of the so-called compact varieties in various containers. Most did well.

For marrows, just forget some of your courgettes! It is worth growing a few, although remember that, if you leave a vast fruit on a plant, all the energy is likely to go into its enlargement and little into developing new fruit. Once properly ripened, they are great storers with the thickest skin you can imagine. Probably survive a nuclear blast.

ROUTINE CARE

Your courgette plants should be kept weed free when young but are unlikely to need weeding as they mature because their canopy is so dense. Sitting on dung, they should not need too much feeding or watering and, in any case, a mulch will keep moisture in. Feed them if you don't have rich compost or soil to grow them in. Water copiously around the roots in a dry spell. Give them a liquid feed if they are not producing well (some of the seaweed-based organic feeds you can buy in garden centres are good, as is tomato food) and feed later in the season if they look like they need extra energy to continue cropping.

Courgettes will produce both male and female flowers – the male ones will have no tiny fruit forming at the base of the flowers and you can just nick them off. The male flowers tend to appear first and you may at times despair of getting a crop. Either be patient or, when they do appear, help the fertilisation process by pollinating the female flowers with the male ones. To do this, pick the latter, carefully strip the petals off and push the stamens into the centre of the female flowers. Life in the raw!

HARVESTING AND STORING

Pick them as they reach the size you prefer. Do not leave them to get too large or you will discourage further fruiting. The more you pick the more you will get. Small ones have the best texture and flavour. In a good season you will need to look for fruit daily – honestly!

Courgettes will store for a number of days in the fridge or in a cool larder. You can freeze them if you grate them first and then they can be used in soups and vegetable bakes.

COMMON PROBLEMS

See p. 182. To help prevent cucumber mosaic virus, choose resistant varieties such as 'Defender' or cover plants with a fine net to keep the aphids off.

COURGETTE AND MARROW VARIETIES

Green

'**All Green Bush**' Produces a mass of small green fruit.

'**Black Beauty**' Very dark, glossy fruits and prolific too, with the most enormous flowers.

'**Black Forest**' F1 A climbing courgette ideal for a container on the patio or for a polytunnel in wilder parts of Scotland. Compact and prolific if picked regularly. Saw it growing in a tunnel on Lewis.

'**Cavilli**' F1 Early, can set fruit without pollination so adverse weather, poor light levels and a lack of pollinating insects do not affect cropping. Indoors or out.

'**Defender**' F1 ♀ Compact, heavy cropping, resistant to mosaic virus, does not take up too much room so one of the best value for smaller spaces. Very happy in relative shelter in Orkney.

'**Endurance**' F1 Compact, the best performer in *Beechgrove Garden* trials, few spines so easier picking.

'**Green Bush**' F1 Popular marrow variety.

Yellow patty pans are very well flavoured and good to cook whole.

Marrows, which may or may not have been grown intentionally. Support off the soil on a tile or similar until harvest.

'**Parthenon**' Recommended by Dave Allan of *The Herald* as a good doer even in poor weather, as it fruits without pollination. Early and prolific. Good in Shetland.

'**Romanesco**' ♀ Sarah Raven rates this for flavour. Ribbed fruit, flowers are used in Italy for cooking.

'**Rondo di Nizza**' or '**De Nice a Fruit Rond**' A round-fruited variety with good flavour. Very pretty fruit, very productive and ideal for single portions.

Yellow

'**One Ball**' F1 Harvest when the size of tennis balls.

'**Soleil**' F1 Straight, cut thinly for a well-dressed salad.

Also look out for white or yellow patty pans – like little flying saucers.

Cucumber (*Cucumis sativus*) H1C E3

Thought to be one of the oldest cultivated vegetables, cucumbers have been known since classical times and records show that the emperor Tiberius grew them in Britain, although they later died out and were re-introduced during Henry VIII's time. Christopher Columbus reputedly introduced them to America on his travels – *quel homme*! There are varieties available for eating fresh as well as specifically for pickling, although the eating varieties can also be pickled if you have a glut. The fruit, comprising 96 per cent water, is refreshing and traditionally used in salads. It is also wonderful grated, drained and mixed with good, thick yoghurt and minced garlic as tzatziki, to be eaten with grilled meat or fish. Cucumber sandwiches should be made with *unsalted* butter.

There are two groups of cucumbers – very tender indoor varieties which need constant warmth and so-called outdoor types known as 'ridge' or 'frame' which, in warmer climes, would be grown either outdoors on a ridge of soil to give extra drainage or in a cold frame or similar. Unless you have the mildest most sheltered suntrap, in Scotland *all* cucumbers need to be grown indoors in a greenhouse or polytunnel due to cool summer night-time temperatures, which they hate. Older cultivars produced both male and female flowers and fruited on laterals. Modern cultivars, although more expensive to buy, are all-female F1 hybrids with no seeds so they don't turn bitter. They fruit on the main stem, can tolerate cooler nights and are easier all round. If you want to try the traditional types, the Real Seeds Catalogue has interesting-sounding cucumber varieties from open-pollinated seeds with a range of habits, colours and flavours.

SITE, SOIL, SOWING AND PLANTING

Cucumbers are quite tricky to grow. Disliking temperature changes, they are susceptible to damping off fungus when tiny seedlings and cucumber mosaic virus when a little older.

First sow your seeds in seed compost in modules or 7cm pots. Do not sow too many as, assuming you will have some success, you do not want a greenhouse-full. They are prolific once they get going. Pop each seed 1cm below the surface of the compost in mid March in a protected and warm environment – a pasting table set up in a sunny lobby in my case. If you use your airing cupboard, keep a careful eye on them, as they will dry quickly. Keep them reasonably warm after they have germinated and maintain moisture levels but do not over-water. Ensure good light otherwise they will stretch and become leggy.

Alternatively, most garden centres will sell you potted seedlings in April and May, which you can harden off and plant out when conditions are right.

Plant out in your greenhouse towards mid May, singly into large pots (about 25cm diameter) filled with good home-made compost or into growbags, two per bag. They should have at least two sets of true leaves (in addition to the seed leaves) by this

Productive cucumbers at Islay House Community Garden.

Cucumbers from Caroline's tunnel house which don't look as neat as shop-bought ones but taste wonderful.

time. Place the plants at the end farthest from the greenhouse door and water in.

If you want to try them outside, don't think about putting out seedlings until June, as the nights will be too cold. Space plants 45cm apart in rich soil mixed with well-rotted manure or compost, mounding them slightly above the level of the bed. Plant with the base of the stem just above soil level to help prevent rot. Water in well and proceed more or less as for greenhouse-grown fruit, using a trellis or tepee instead of a single cane for support. In cold or windy weather after planting, protect the seedlings with some sort of cloche. It will be a race against time to get ripe fruit by later summer.

ROUTINE CARE, HARVESTING AND STORING

Cucumbers like humidity more than tomatoes, which are often grown with them. Put the tomatoes nearer the door and sprinkle water on the floor around the cucumbers to keep the humidity up. Keep

well watered but not awash. If roots appear on the surface of the soil, top-dress with some soil or compost. As they grow, tie them to a cane or to a string suspended from the roof. When they reach the roof, pinch out the central growing tip. Pinch out the side shoots too, but don't remove any flower buds. (I have to say, in practice, we tend to give our cucumbers free rein and they have never let us down.) Some newer varieties set fruit low down on the stems. Jim McColl reckons that these inhibit the plants from growing to full size, so he nips the bottom fruit out.

Once the fruit are beginning to swell, feed weekly with tomato food or you can use nettle or comfrey brew. If you see any male flowers (they have no little bulge below the flower-base, which would denote fruit formation), nick them off, otherwise you might end up with bitter cukes. If any of you can grow the things outdoors, keep them weeded. And protect against slugs with a good barrier of some sort or all your efforts could be lost over night!

Pick them carefully as you need them – cutting is probably best so as not to damage the stem. Cropping encourages further fruiting. Don't leave them to become too large, as this will not improve their flavour. Discard pointy ones that have not grown well, as tends to happen towards the end of the season. They will probably be bitter.

Cucumbers will store for a few days in the fridge. It's better, if you have a glut, to pickle them. Or freeze them as a delicately flavoured summer soup (nice with some chervil on top).

COMMON PROBLEMS

See Cucurbit problems on p. 182. **Cucumber neck rot** is the most commonly reported problem for Scottish cucumber growers. Overwatering can cause this, particularly when newly planted and if the soil level is too high. To prevent it, avoiding wetting the foliage when watering and just water the soil.

CUCUMBER VARIETIES

There are many cultivars available. We have picked the most popular ones.

'Burpless Tasty Green' An outdoor ridge type, might be worth trying outdoors in a suntrap. Mildew resistant.

'Cumlaude' F1 High yielding and fine in a cool greenhouse.

'Marketmore' ♀ A ridge type, high-yielding, short fruits, said to do better than others in cool summers.

'Passandra' F1 Cucumber mosaic, powdery and downy mildew resistant. Small fruit.

'Rocky' F1 Clusters of small fruits, the top performer in the *Beechgrove Garden*'s 2008 trials of tunnel-house cucumbers, with over 70 fruit on two plants. Needs lots of warmth.

'Swing' In our polytunnel, planted in soil to which some high nitrogen fertiliser was added, we got around 240 cucumbers from three plants. Pickle anyone?

'Telegraph' F1 This has been around for years but is still popular for the cool greenhouse.

'Telegraph Improved' Very long fruit.

'Vega' Favourite in 2009 *Gardening Which?* trials. Small fruits, mildew resistant.

Pumpkin and Squash (*Cucurbita pepo, C. moschata, C. maxima*) H2 E2

BACKGROUND

The French Kokopelli seed catalogue lists over 70 varieties of pumpkin and squash in a rainbow of colours but Britain is only just waking up to their potential. Squash are great storers, versatile to cook with and delicious to eat, dense, sweet and probably the most flavourful of all the cucurbits. They are easy to grow if you can give them the right conditions, ideally a tunnel, although they will do outside if your growing season is long enough. Best to select a variety described as 'early ripening'. Pumpkins are used in both savoury and sweet dishes, the latter notably as pumpkin pie. Pumpkin seeds are worth producing too, as they provide a source of iron, magnesium, phosphorus and zinc as well as polyunsaturated fats. The trouble with pumpkins is that you need lots of room to grow a relatively small number, and one plant can cover an enormous area of garden, particularly if you want to grow really large ones. Alex West uses pumpkins at Anton's Hill near Coldstream as part of his crop rotation and as weed-suppressing ground cover, liquid feeding them through pipes directly to the roots. They are rampant enough to cover the house, garden, car . . .

SITE, SOIL, SOWING AND PLANTING

I treat these just as I would courgettes – so a rich and moisture-retentive soil in an open and sunny position. In cold and northern climates, they do well in tunnels but they do need lots of room. Sow the seeds

A great crop of winter squash and marrows from Caroline's garden after the fair summer of 2010.

inside in March in 7cm pots at 1.25cm deep and, after hardening off, transplant in May with no less than 1m between plants but up to 2.5m. If the weather is still coldish, cover with a cloche. Scotland's squash and pumpkin evangelist is Patricia Stephen at Phantassie Farm, East Lothian. She plants a range of varieties in the open through permeable membrane that has richly prepared (lots of dung and compost) planting holes cut into it. A used tyre is placed over each hole which helps to weigh down the membrane and shelter the young seedlings. Cropping starts in August and continues to first frosts.

Alec West in the pumpkin patch of his walled garden at Anton's Hill, near Coldstream.

ROUTINE CARE

Keep weed free and mulch to retain moisture. Water in a dry spell – aiming at the roots not the leaves. You may need to guide plants a little to prevent them from accidentally smothering other crops! You will get a better crop if you 'stop' the plants. Do this once you have two or three fruit developing well on a stem by nipping off the stem a couple of leaves beyond the fruit at the end. This will focus all the plant's energy on the remaining fruit and you should therefore get some good stonkers to eat and store. Towards the end of the season foliage can hamper

Winter squash growing in a tyre at Phantassie Farm, East Lothian.

The pumpkin store at Phantassie Farm, East Lothian, with a variety of winter squash on the left and butternut squash on the right.

the sun getting to the ripening fruit, so cut off some of the leaves round the fruit to let it in.

HARVESTING AND STORING

If you have grown an early-ripening variety, pick as you want to use them. For storing, leave the squash on the plants to ripen (harden) if you can, as this will ensure better storage. A fingernail pressed to the skin should hardly make a mark if the squash are properly ripe. This will not always be possible unless you have a tunnel, as they must all be lifted before the frost. If you have to lift them before they are fully ripe and they do begin to soften, make batches of soup, chut-

neys and curries and freeze. Don't let them go to waste.

Harvest the storers with a good bit of stem as this helps prevent rot setting in. Use your secateurs. They are best stored indoors, as they like a temperature higher than your average shed and they need to be dry – dampness will rot them. Patricia Stephen reckons that green-skinned ones tend to keep longer. My beautiful mixed winter squash adorn my sitting room from September. Very lifestyle-y!

COMMON PROBLEMS

See under Cucurbit problems, p. 182.

PUMPKIN AND SQUASH VARIETIES

Pumpkin

'**Baby Bear**' Successfully grown at Beechgrove, plants produce fruit of around 1kg, good for small lanterns and great in the kitchen too. Seeds good to eat. Less vigorous than most so good for smaller spaces.
'**Becky**' F1 Medium sized, good in the kitchen, high yielding.
'**Jack of All Trades**' A good big beast for a Halloween lantern.
'**Mars**' F1 Fine for soups and curries.

Squash

There are so many to choose from you might be best sowing a packet of mixed seeds.

Butternut squash 'Harrier' ♀ Bred to ripen earlier and faster than most butternut varieties, which mature too slowly for Scotland. Best indoors.
'**Celebration**' Sweet flavour and high yield.
'**Harlequin**' Green and yellow striped, good at Phantassie Farm, East Lothian.

'**Kabocha Large Fruited**' Sweet flesh, good storage.

'**Potimarron**' Medium-sized, bright-orange fruit and good storer. My top favourite.

'**Sweet Dumpling**' Small to medium, green and white.

'**Sweet Lightening**' Early ripening and good storage.

'**Turk's Turban**' Weird and wonderful looking orange, white and green fruit and good storer.

'**Vegetable Spaghetti**' Good at Phantassie Farm, East Lothian. Pale coloured, flesh stringy.

Melon *H1C E3*

Though considered fruit rather than vegetables, they belong to the same family as cucumbers and squashes so are best treated here.

Melons are one of the more challenging fruit to grow in Scotland. They really need to be grown under cover in a greenhouse or tunnel and they take up lots of room. They cannot tolerate cold temperatures so you'll need to start them off in a heated greenhouse in spring (Caroline didn't – dining room table again!) and probably not risk an unheated house until late May. They are delicate, easily overwatered and often succumb to fatal neck rot when newly planted or transplanted, which causes them to suddenly wilt. Later on they need lots of water and require feeding once or twice a week when fruit are swelling. The fruit can rot if left on the ground so are often held up in bags, with string supports and other examples of ingenuity. It can be a race to get them ripe in late summer before the light and heat levels become too low, although you can finish off ripening them after picking. If you still think they are worth the hassle, then good luck.

MELON VARIETIES

The commonly sold supermarket melons '**Galia**' and most cantaloupes need more heat than Scotland has. You'd be better off trying '**Edonis**' ♀, '**Amber**

The melon house at West Dean, Sussex, showing how rope bags can be used to support ripening fruit.

Nectar' ♀, '**Outdoor Wonder**' (not in Scotland!) or '**Sweetheart**' F1 ♀, which Caroline had a good result from in a polytunnel in a fine summer a few years back. They can be grown in growbags with plenty of liquid feeding. Annoyingly, they should not be grown with cucumbers, as they tend to pollinate one another, resulting in bitter cucumber-tasting melons! The *Beechgrove Garden* tried to grow **watermelons** in their tunnel house in 2010. They are supposed to ripen in 90 days. After 120 days (by August) they were the size of a gooseberry. Jim and Carole quite rightly came to the conclusion that Scotland just does not have the climate for them, even indoors. We agree.

CHAPTER 4

Leaf Crops and Salads

Not all of the vegetables in this section are salad vegetables as such, although all can be enjoyably eaten raw, especially if harvested young. And of course you can put more in a salad than you will find described below. Be intrepid. Lettuce isn't the only candidate. I do try to eat seasonally and I am still quite a fan of what my mother called winter salad – a cabbage-based mix with a dressing of mayonnaise. I don't feel the need to eat lettuce all winter but I know that it is the thing these days. Ken was served up a pile of bitter, inedible (in his opinion) woodland weeds as 'salad' by one gardener he visited, so clearly some people have more toler-ance than others. Many vegetables, as well as herbs, can still be grown out of season on your windowsill in trays and the young leaves (so called micro-greens) cropped and eaten raw when the plantlets show their first true leaves. Try anything you normally grow for its leaves like rocket, spinach, kale, mizuna, sorrel and land cress. You could maybe use your excess seeds for this, those that are near their use by date, and sow throughout the winter when other salad crops may be in short supply.

Other traditional 'salad' vegetables can be found as follows – radishes (p. 250), cucumbers (p. 186) and tomatoes (p. 237).

Celery germinates erratically outdoors so is best started in modules or trays.

A celery trial site at Wisley in July 2011.

Celery and Leaf Celery (*Apium graveolens* var. *dulce*) H3 E3

Celery has evolved from the original wild and rather spindly plant, smallage. Used originally as a flavouring more than a vegetable, it was also regarded as having medicinal properties. Milder-flavoured varieties were in evidence from the sixteenth century, probably originating in Italy. It was at this time that the habit of earthing up the stems to blanch them and improve their flavour began. Celery was much prized as a salad vegetable but its use in sauces, stews and soups is also well documented.

Traditional, so-called 'trench' celery takes a bit of work, as you have to earth up the stems to keep it growing, to stop it turning stringy and to blanch it. Most gardeners opt for modern varieties known as 'self-blanching', which are the varieties mainly covered here. It is not as tough as the older types, needing to be lifted before frosts come, and the flavour may not be as good, but it is easier to please. The self-blanching varieties are usually block grown so each plant helps to blanch its neighbours. Only the outer plants need covered with straw or with a small protective 'fence'.

I use celery as an essential ingredient in the vast majority of soups I make. It adds the required depth of flavour, especially if you are using vegetarian stock. It is good in salads, providing it is sliced very thinly. It goes well with a walnut oil-based vinaigrette. I also love it in a white sauce as a comforting winter veg. Sadly, Ken thinks celery stems are no more appetising than cow parsley and would not grow or eat it. Not only that but handling it brings some people out in a rash!

Leaf or cutting celery is a hardier plant and an easier-to-grow way of obtaining a celery flavour. It is grown for its leaves rather than its stems. It gives the same celery taste to soups, stews and salads and, best of all, you can go on harvesting it for months and months, even in winter in mild areas or with some protection. It can also be grown as micro leaves. (A herb called par-cel may do a similar job – half parsley, half celery, it's good in soups and salads.)

SITE, SOIL, SOWING AND PLANTING

Self-blanching celery likes a well-fed and open, sunny site with moisture-retentive soil. Sow the seeds in March indoors into a tray or modules. Germination is usually poor if sown outdoors. They

Biennial leaf celery showing its delicate flowers. Use the leaves as a flavouring in the kitchen.

Trench celery at Dundee Flower and Food Festival (photo Graham Thom).

need light to germinate, so cover the seeds only lightly with compost, keeping it moist until they germinate. For tray sown crops, prick out seedlings when they are large enough to handle and transplant into modules or buy module-grown plants in May. Once the soil is warm enough, probably by late May in most places, harden off the plants, taking a week or so to do this, and then plant out. The seedlings can bolt if they get too cold so err on the cautious side or keep them fleeced. Plant them out in a block formation. The closer you plant them, the smaller will be the stems, although they will still give a significant yield – a spacing of 20cm apart is about right. You can grow celery in large containers.

ROUTINE CARE, HARVESTING AND STORING

Protect from early slug onslaught with fleece or slug bait. Keep well watered in dry spells. Feed weekly from midsummer using a seaweed-based liquid feed or your own comfrey or nettle brew. Don't forget to make a little wall of straw around the outside of your block of plants to help the outer ones to blanch.

Dig up as required, starting with the outer plants. Self-blanching celery will have to be lifted before the frost comes. It is best eaten on the day it is harvested. If you are not using it or giving it away, then wash, chop, blanch in boiling water for four minutes and store in your freezer for up to 12 months.

COMMON PROBLEMS

Celery leaf miner may lead to leaf blisters. If this happens, remove the affected parts and burn. **Slugs** and **snails** can damage crops (*see* p. 75). You may have **celery leaf spot** if you notice small brown spots on the leaves and stems. This disease originates in seed so ensure you buy from a reliable source. There is little organically you can do if your plants have this.

Burn affected leaves and stems. Copper fungicide might help control it. **Bolting** can be a problem with celery and is most often caused by drought or cold, so ensure you keep the crop watered when conditions are dry. Celery needs warmth and a long growing season; it struggles at 300m at Chisholme, near Hawick.

CELERY AND LEAF CELERY VARIETIES

Self-blanching

'**Golden Self-blanching**' Early, harvest from August onwards.
'**Kintsai**' Delicate flavour.
'**Lathom Self-blanching Galaxy**' ♀ Vigorous, good flavour, early with crisp stems, ribbed.
'**Loretta**' ♀ Self-blanching, early, good flavour, bright white stems.
'**Victoria**' F1 ♀ Tall, vigorous, common commercial variety.

Trench Celery

'**Giant Pink**', '**Giant White**' and '**Giant Red**' Popular with competition growers.
'**Mammoth Pink**' ♀ Pink stems, also popular with competition growers.

Cutting Celery

Sold under this name or cultivar names '**Dark Green Soup**' or '**Red Soup**'. Leaf/cutting celery, aromatic, vigorous with thin stems. Very tough.

Chard, Leaf Beet and Perpetual Spinach (*Beta vulgaris* subsp. *cicla*) H4–5 E1

Closely related to beetroot but grown for leaves rather than roots, these are vegetables you must grow. They are easy, versatile and packed with vitamins A

'Rainbow Chard' and 'Swiss Chard'. Do not crop chard too close to the ground to give the plant a better chance to re-sprout.

and C. Joy Larkcom says they are ideal for absentee gardeners, as they thrive on neglect once established. They are great cooked as a side dish (with pine nuts and raisins) or as the main element of a meal and are good in frittata, quiche and in lots of things that would normally ask for spinach. The stuff stands fairly well in the winter too and, if very low temperatures 'melt' it, it comes back in the spring – at least the white variety does. I often have the next crop sown before I pull up the end of last year's.

The very popular rainbow chard adds a touch of Joseph's coat to the garden, with the colours of the stalks – scarlet, neon yellow, deep orange – making a very decorative as well as delicious addition to your patch. Some reckon that white chard has a superior taste to the coloured varieties.

Chard has long been part of Arab cuisine and was apparently known to the ancient gardeners of Babylon. The 'Swiss' epithet was possibly a marketing ploy. The *cicla* part of the plant's Latin name denotes Sicily, and it was probably there that chard was first grown, before spreading widely around the Mediterranean and beyond. So it might seem surprising that it does so well on Benbecula, for example.

SITE, SOIL, SOWING AND PLANTING

Start the seeds in modules and transplant as the soil heats up or sow directly into drills in early May or a little later, eventually thinning to about 30cm apart. Position in a very fertile and moisture-retentive soil in a sunny spot in the garden. In mild coastal gardens or under cover, you can sow in summer for winter cropping.

ROUTINE CARE, HARVESTING AND STORING

Weed and water as necessary and mulching always helps. Start to harvest when you wish. If flower heads develop, remove them to encourage fresh growth, which can reach up to 50cm in height. An occasional feed will encourage young shoots. Pick individual outside leaves from across your plants to keep them all on the go. Separate the stalks from the leaves and give them a couple of minutes head start in the saucepan.

You can blanch and freeze chard. It will keep, washed, in the fridge for two or three days.

COMMON PROBLEMS

Pretty much untroubled in my experience, if you can ignore a few insect-munched leaf holes. **Winter weather damage** may be reduced by a cloche although, even without, the plants are likely to start re-sprouting come spring. There is a **fungal leaf spot** but it does not seem to strike much.

CHARD, ETC. VARIETIES

'**Bright Lights**' ♛ Stems in bright colours – orange, red, pink, etc. The mix includes 'Rhubarb Chard' and 'Bright Yellow'.

'**Bright Yellow**' ♛ Neon-yellow stalks, resists bolting, fairly hardy, another 'ornamental'.

'**Fordhook Giant**' ♛ Puckered leaves, white stalks, recommended by Rosa Steppanova in Shetland, where it stands up to the wind and crops a second year.

'**Perpetual Spinach**' ♛ Pale green, soft texture. Cambo in Fife grow good crops in their well-drained walled garden and David Catt grows it for winter cropping near Jedburgh.

'**Rhubarb Chard**' ♛ Scarlet stems, crinkly leaves, ornamental and good for potager planting.

'**Swiss Chard**' or '**Sea Kale Beet**' Large crinkly leaves with thick white stems.

Chicory/Radicchio (*Cichorium intybus*) H4 E2

Chicory has been used as a vegetable since Greek and Roman times when the leaves of the wild plant were gathered young, so they were not bitter tasting. Cultivated forms were being developed by the sixteenth century with larger leaves and, increasingly, the bitterness being bred out.

Witloof, or forcing chicory, was developed in France and Belgium and growing it is rather a long drawn-out process – but worth it. Easier to grow, but

Radicchio 'Palla Rossa' has some frost hardiness so is a useful winter vegetable in Scotland, if you like the rather bitter flavour.

not so delicious, in my estimation, are the lettuce-like rather bitter-leaved salads – reddish 'Radicchio' or greenish 'Sugarloaf'. Both chicory types are useful for their late season, throughout autumn and winter, and both are good eaten raw or cooked. If you have tried shop-bought forced chicory and been unimpressed with its rather bitter flavour, freshly harvested home-grown varieties will be a very pleasant surprise. A classic and delicious way of eating forced chicory is parboiled, wrapped in a slice of good ham, covered in a cheese sauce and popped in the oven to bronze. Yotam Ottolenghi, in his book *Plenty*, suggests adding it raw to a mix of cooked beetroot, orange and salty black olives in a mustardy vinaigrette.

The older amongst us will remember chicory root being combined with coffee – ground, instant and liquid versions. This was the result of coffee becoming terribly expensive and cheaper alternatives being sought. I still remember drinking freshly ground coffee with added chicory – not nice! And, of course, Scotland is the home of the famous, and still available, coffee-esque delicacy Camp Coffee™ with its slogan 'Ready Aye Ready'.

Leaf Chicory

Chicory prefers well-fed and moisture-retentive soil. Sow in modules in March for planting out from May and beyond. You can succession-sow these with the 'Radicchio' types being quite hardy in the face of some frost. Plant out in blocks or rows at around 10cm apart with rows 30cm apart. You could grow these successfully in a polytunnel, if your conditions make planting outside risky. Outdoors, if you are keeping them past early autumn, you could cover them with a cloche. If you do cloche, watch out for rotting outer leaves and remove them.

Harvest individual leaves or whole hearts as required. If the stump is left in the ground, it will produce further leaves. I find leaf chicory very bitter, so mix with other salad leaves to get a balanced combination of flavours.

CHICORY/RADICCHIO VARIETIES

'**Palla Rossa**' ♀ Quite large heads, well-filled red hearts, resistant to bolting, tolerates light frost.
'**Radicchio de Treviso**' A Monty Don favourite with crimson leaves. Some of mine made it through the hard winter of 2010–11.
'**Sugarloaf**' Lettuce-like deep-green outer leaves, hearts are good for blanching, less bitter.

FORCING CHICORY

Ken reckons you need to 'get a life' to even consider going to all this trouble, but I think it worth it, so here goes. When the soil is well warmed, in mid June for me, sow the witloof seeds thinly into 1.5cm deep drills with rows 30cm apart and then thin seedlings to around 23cm apart. Avoid freshly manured ground, which can cause root forking. You may start them in modules but transplant when the roots are barely formed. Weed and water in dry weather. A mulch will help retain moisture.

'Witloof' chicory roots ready for trimming, storing and then forcing. Only the right-hand roots are suitable.

'Witloof' chicory chicons ready to harvest – one of the best winter salad vegetables.

To force chicory, lift the lovely greenery-topped roots in late autumn. Discard any that are forked or have a root-top diameter of less than 2.5cm. Leave them in your greenhouse or shed for a week to allow the moisture to move from leaf to root. Now trim the greenery to within 2.5cm of the top of the root and trim any tiny side roots. To store these before forcing, put them in sand or light soil in a box in a dark shed. Start forcing the roots when you wish through winter. Take four of them at a time and put them in a 30cm pot in soil or compost but with

2.5cm of the root top poking out. Lightly water. Take a pot of identical dimensions and cover its drainage holes so no light gets in. Invert this over the chicory roots. You may need to give them a little water again before harvesting, if they become dry. Keep the whole thing in a warm room and, in three to four weeks, your efforts will be rewarded with lovely little chicons. Cut them off about 2cm above the root top. If you wish, leave these roots in the pot and they will produce a second flush of looser but equally pale edible leaves. I keep mine in my sitting room – now a de facto annexe of my greenhouse! It is of course possible to force chicory outside or in a greenhouse or polytunnel, but it will take a little longer.

You are best to eat the chicons immediately after harvest. If you can't do this, wrap them to prevent greening and keep in the fridge. Chicory is little troubled by pests and diseases apart from the usual slugs.

Corn Salad (*Valerianella locusta*) H4–5 E1

Also called lamb's lettuce, this low-growing leafy crop fares well throughout winter in milder parts of

The ubiquitous corn salad, or lamb's lettuce, can be sown year round with some protection in the colder months. It will withstand some frost.

Scotland, maybe with a bit of protection from a cloche, making it a valuable addition to the garden, although it doesn't taste of much. Can be sown year round (indoors, if starting in winter) but, for a winter crop if you are in a milder part of Scotland, sow outdoors in August in shallow drills (1cm), 25cm apart and thin plants to about 15cm. It's reasonably happy in sun and light shade and fairly trouble free – slugs notwithstanding. Crop as you will, either pulling an entire plant or by taking a few leaves from several. To enhance your chances of a good crop, especially in the wilder parts of the country, grow your winter-cropping plants under protection, ventilating them well if you do so. Mild flavoured, it is good in salads.

Endive (*Cichorium endivia*)
H2 E1

Endive is closely related to chicory and confusingly, it is actually called *chicorée frisée* in France. There are two types – curly (or frisée) and broad-leaved varieties commonly called escarole or batavia. The broad-leaved varieties are hardier than the frisée

The rather bitter flavour of endive is improved if it is blanched by covering the centre with a plate or tile.

types and may over winter under cover. Indeed endive seems rather well suited to growing in Scotland, as it is tolerant of lower temperatures, lower light levels and higher ambient moisture than many other salad crops.

Like chicory, endive can be blanched by completely covering the developing broad-leaved plant with a flowerpot or, for the already flatter frisée, covering the centre with a tile or dinner plate to give a white heart and green edged leaves. This is done to make the leaves sweeter – although it is still too bitter for my taste. Ken thinks all the bitter varieties are only fit to feed to rabbits.

Endive leaves always have some bitterness, so they are commonly mixed with other salad leaves for a more balanced taste. It also helps to combine them with sweeter vegetables such as peeled red pepper. Endive is generally eaten raw but can be braised. It is very good for you – rich in iron, potassium, beta carotene and vitamins A and B, although blanching apparently reduces these benefits.

The broad-leaved endive is a good choice, as it is available at the start of the year when there is not an overabundance of fresh stuff to harvest from your garden.

SITE, SOIL, SOWING AND PLANTING

Endive enjoys a well-fed soil in an open sunny site. It grows best in 'cool' conditions, 10–20°C (50–68°F), so a normal Scottish summer is ideal. Sow the frisée varieties in trays, modules or directly into the soil, in drills about 1cm deep, from March to April for summer and autumn cropping, with the broad-leaved varieties going in from July for an autumn and winter crop. Thin to 23cm for the frisée and 30cm for the broad-leaved varieties. Best to grow a few at a time in succession so as to avoid a glut. The winter varieties are said to tolerate up to -10°C, so they're ideal for much of Scotland, although a hard winter will be too cold without extra protection from a tunnel house or cloche.

ROUTINE CARE

Weed regularly and water in dry conditions or the plants will bolt. Although traditionally endive was blanched to reduce bitterness, there are now modern cultivars with tight heads which don't seem to require it. However, if you are blanching, start at around 12 weeks after sowing when the heads are an adequate size. Choose a day when the leaves of the head are dry or they may rot. For the broad-leaved types, loosely tie the leaves together with thread and enclose in an upturned flowerpot, having covered its drainage hole. The endive should be blanched in around three weeks. The frisée variety can simply be all but covered with a tile or even a dinner plate. (NB you may find this encourages slugs to decamp below the plate, with its handy on-site snackerama!)

If you feel life is too short for all that, simply cut the heads at a size that suits.

HARVESTING AND STORING

Harvest the broad-leaved variety whole. The frisée variety can be harvested whole or as cut-and-come-again. It will store for a few days in the fridge but is best eaten fresh. Not suitable to freeze.

COMMON PROBLEMS

Slugs are always attracted to any sort of lettuce-type plant. Deal with them in the most dastardly way possible. **Aphids** may be a pest and companion planting might help. Try inter-planting nigella or pot marigold. **Bolting** might be a problem, as already noted. Don't let the plants dry out.

ENDIVE VARIETIES

Endive is often sold as part of salad seed mixtures, which is a good option.

'**Batavian Green**' A broad-leaved type, good to blanch.

'**Bubikopf 2**' A splendidly named escarole with a solid heart.

'**Cicoria Catalogna Pugliese**' A relatively rare curly endive from Puglia in the south-east of Italy.

'**Cornet de Bordeaux**' Broad-leaved and pretty tough.

'**Frenzy**' ♀ Posh restaurants love the fine filigree leaves. Self-blanching heart.

'**Minerva**' Curly, said to be especially hardy and good for late sowings.

Good King Henry (*Chenopodium bonus-henricus*) H4–5 E1

This is a wonderfully named tallish perennial (up to 60cm) with vitamin- and mineral-rich spinach-like leaves. It can be eaten raw but is probably better cooked. Alys Fowler suggests soaking the leaves in salt water for a while before cooking to remove some of the bitterness. Young shoots can be cooked and eaten as a 'poor man's asparagus' and the flower buds are edible too. Sow in a shallow drill (1cm) in a warm fertile soil, or earlier under protection, then transplant. Space at 30cm, although you probably won't want many. It will be fine in a container. Keep fairly well watered and feed in autumn with a dressing of well-rotted manure. Renew plants every three or four years or let it seed around.

Watercress and Land Cress (*Barbarea verna*)

Watercress ✉ *H3 E3*

A Scottish native once promoted for its medicinal properties, watercress is not all that easy to please unless you have a fairly significant body of gently moving water. Some have succeeded by planting shop-bought watercress into moist compost. Kept in a shady site, it can produce adventitious roots and grow to give you quite a crop. Beware of gathering watercress on farmland, as it can be contaminated with animal parasites. Ken visited the Peppes' commercial tunnel-house production of hydroponic watercress at Glendrynoch on Skye. The cress is grown in wide guttering in a nutrient/water solution and it does very well, cropping all summer.

Land Cress H3 E1

In the garden, land cress is easier, quick to grow and almost equally good for you. It is prolific and you may well not be able to eat the vast amounts produced from even a few seeds. It is very peppery but delicious in a mixed leaf salad. And it will make soup too and all the other things you would use watercress for.

SITE, SOIL, SOWING AND PLANTING

Land cress is best in a moist shady site and a humus-rich and well-fed soil. Succession-sow the seeds in drills of 1cm deep in short rows from mid April or

Spicy land cress is best eaten in moderation, mixed with milder salad leaves. This crop could have done with thinning.

when your ground is warm enough. Thin to 10cm, although even un-thinned it does well. You could intercrop or catch crop this plant. If you have the conditions or an unheated greenhouse or can keep a cloche on the ground, you might be able to over-winter land cress and continue cropping it. For winter cropping, continue your succession planting until September. Once you have some, it is easy to keep going. Let some of your early crop run to seed in the autumn. Gather and sow next year. Alternatively allow it to self-seed and then transplant.

ROUTINE CARE, HARVESTING AND STORING

Keep the soil moist and well weeded. You could mulch. Grab a handful of leaves as you require them to add to salads, egg sandwiches or for soups. Washed, it will store for a couple of days in the fridge. Unless pre-cooked, it will not freeze.

Land cress appears to suffer few problems. **Flea beetle** might attack but the cress certainly remains entirely edible, if a little holey.

Lettuce (*Lactuca sativa*) *H2 E1*

You could eat a different kind of lettuce every day of the summer. They are relatively easy to grow, often attractive in both form and colour and provide a range of textures and flavours from bitter to bland. Having seen a documentary about the horrors of the production of supermarket ready mixed salad leaves – covered in pesticides, cleaned with chlorine and

Lettuces showing some of the huge range of textures and colours available.

Cut-and-come-again salads from Rebekah's Veg, on show at Hampton Court Palace Flower Show.

Crisp cos or romaine lettuces are easy to grow plus they're better flavoured than icebergs and retain their crunch in a dressed salad.

Cut-and-come-again salads, including oriental greens, growing at Phantassie Farm, East Lothian.

Mixed cut-and-come-again salad leaves at Geilston in Dunbartonshire.

sorted by near slave labour – Ken says he will never buy them again. He and I grow lots of our own.

Lettuce, as those of you who are familiar with the Flopsy Bunnies will know, is a mild soporific. Indeed its initial cultivation was probably for medicinal purposes. However, it is clear from early Greek writings that it was being widely cultivated and eaten in ancient times. The Romans ate lettuce too and they combined the culinary with the medicinal by offering it at the end of meals to calm diners and encourage sleep.

It was not until the sixteenth century that the lettuces we might recognise today began to be described. Lettuce falls into two main categories – those which form a heart and are usually harvested whole, and 'heartless' varieties, known as loose leaf, which are harvested leaf by leaf. The hearting lettuces are further divided into groups such as crisphead, butterhead and cos (also called romaine).

In addition to salads, with either a cold or warm dressing, lettuce can be stir-fried or braised whole. It also makes a delicate cold soup and is central to the *petit pois à l'etuvée* vegetable dish.

Gardening Which? trialled a range of the most colourful salad leaves in 2009 in England. The five that they found best-tasting were loose-leaf 'Lollo Rossa – Assor', cos types 'Pandero' and 'Marshall', a crisphead called 'Sioux' and the butterhead 'Roxy'. And taste notwithstanding, all these lettuces look great as ornamentals.

SITE, SOIL, SOWING AND PLANTING

To be at its most succulent, lettuce needs to grow fast in moist but not soggy or heavy soil in a fairly sunny position. Mulching after planting will help retain moisture. If you let it dry out, the taste will tend to be rather bitter and it may bolt.

Lettuce is tolerant of fairly low temperatures and, indeed, may fail to germinate if the soil temperature is too high. Either sow the small seeds thinly *in situ* in drills around 1cm deep once the threat of frost is past – earlier if under cloches – or start lettuce in trays or modules and then transplant. Modules are an excellent choice as they enable you to share plants if you have been inadvertently over-enthusiastic in your initial sowing. Pop two seeds into each module and then thin to the stronger. Or you could hold back the weaker ones for a second planting. For hearted varieties, continue sowing a few seeds every two or three weeks for as long as you wish – or as long as conditions allow. For loose-leaved varieties, a couple of sowings should be adequate.

If you have planted seed *in situ*, thin out the seedlings when the first true leaves appear or certainly when they are about 5cm tall. You can try transplanting the thinned ones but do not do it in hot, dry conditions as this will likely lead to failure. Plant out module-grown seedlings when they are slightly larger. The hearting varieties are more prone to bolting than the loose-leaved. Block plant at a spacing of between 15cm for the smallest varieties to 30cm for the largest.

As well as being ideal for intercropping, lettuce can be grown in all sorts of containers under protection, including on your windowsill. 'Tom Thumb' and 'Little Gem' are popular for containers. If you are short of space, then sow every few weeks to ensure a long supply rather than a boom-or-bust cycle.

For beginners, the easiest way to grow lettuce is 'cut-and-come-again', where seed is sown directly into the soil in drills as thinly as you can, every two

to four weeks from May to midsummer. You can harvest four to six weeks after sowing. Look for seed mixes called 'oriental', 'spicy' and so on. These are ideal for raised beds or where you have limited room.

ROUTINE CARE, HARVESTING AND STORING

Keep weeded and well watered – ensuring that water is aimed at the roots of plants. Watering in the morning so that foliage dries in the daytime will help to keep rots at bay. Harvest when leaves are soft and lush: leave it too long and leaves may become coarse or bitter and once it bolts it is inedible. Washed lettuce will store in the fridge for a few days but is always best eaten straight away. It cannot be frozen.

COMMON PROBLEMS

Inevitably **slugs** and **snails** find young lettuce a magnet. Do your worst. **Birds** can also be destructive: webs of threads seem to work or cloche or fleece until they grow a little. **Root and leaf aphids** may attack but there are resistant cultivars. **Grey mould** and **mildew** can be a problem and are best prevented by cultural practice: ensure plants are thinned at the right time and are not overcrowded. Water the soil around the roots of the lettuce and not the leaves. Indoors, ventilate well. If mould appears, remove the affected leaves and burn. **Lettuce mosaic virus**, like the cucumber variety, is spread by **aphids**. If you see stunted plants with yellow mottled leaves, remove and burn them. Companion planting with French marigolds may help to minimise aphids, as will soapy water sprays. A **lack of heart**, at the risk of sounding all Wizard of Oz, may be caused by a lack of heart in your soil, so ensure you have added lots of organic matter the previous autumn before planting or feed well through the growing season.

LETTUCE VARIETIES

Seed companies sell mixed packets of lettuce seeds which give you lots of variation and they can be grown as 'cut-and-come-again' or as individual plants.

Butterhead

The most popular group for gardeners, soft and succulent leaves, quick growing, for summer cultivation only and they tend to bolt if they dry out. Also called 'bibb' lettuce.

'**All the Year Round**' Very popular, flavourful.
'**Cassandra**' ♀ Pale green and well flavoured. Mildew resistant.
'**Grandpa Admire's Lettuce**' Pale green leaves with a beautiful reddish blush.
'**Marvel of Four Seasons**' French heirloom variety, green leaves with a wash of red.
'**Roxy**'♀ Plump, dense and outer leaves attractively red. *Gardening Which?* recommends.

Cos (Romaine)

These need rich, moist soil and are slower to mature. They are a good choice for late sowing to extend your salad season.

'**Corsair**' ♀ Open but dense heads.
'**Little Gem**' ♀ Quick maturing and very sweet, small compact heads, very popular and a good choice for containers.
'**Marshall**' ♀ Crisp, deep-purple leaves. Sweet. Recommended by *Gardening Which?*.
'**Nymans**' ♀ Beautiful red leaves with green base, slow to bolt.
'**Pandero**' ♀ 'Little Gem'-sized with dense heads. Outer leaves dark purplish to green. Crisp and sweet. Recommended by *Gardening Which?*.
'**Parris Island**' ♀ In a comparative test, this heritage variety beat the newer '**Chartwell**' on taste.

'**Pinokkio**' ♀ Dense with a crispy heart.
'**Rubens Red Cos**' Green leaves overlaid with red, crunchy.
'**Tom Thumb**' Small lettuce with a good tight heart.
'**Winter Density**' Sweet tasting and a good choice for late sowing for autumn and winter.

Crisphead

Tight, round and crunchy-leaved.

'**Iceberg**' The classic supermarket and prawn cocktail variety. There is now a red-leaved version, '**Red Iceberg**'.
'**Lakeland**' ♀ Later maturing, good in RHS trials.
'**Sioux**' ♀ Crisp and sweet with a pretty blush on the leaf edges. *Gardening Which?* recommends.
'**Webb's Wonderful**' Very popular, frilly leaves.

Loose-leaved or leaf lettuce

Heartless, can be harvested over several weeks and, in theory, can be kept growing well into autumn or winter with some protection.

'**Bionda Foglia**' Narrow, deeply-lobed leaves.
'**Lollo Rossa**' ♀ Frilly red-edged leaves, popular supermarket variety. '**Lollo Rossa – Assor**' ♀ is recommended by *Gardening Which?*
'**Red Salad Bowl**' ♀ Oak-shaped leaves with red margins, very popular and ornamental.
'**Salad Bowl**' ♀ Classic green lettuce, can be harvested over a long period.

Oriental Greens – Mizuna, Komatsuna, etc. *H3–4 E1*

Becoming popular in recent years, they can provide fresh greens in the autumn and winter months. Joy Larkcom, who championed them, recommends sowing in summer, probably July, for an autumn crop in the north. You could try sowing them

Above. Oriental greens including komatsuna, pak choi and mizuna, grown as cut-and-come-again leaves.

Left. Oriental green, mizuna, can be eaten raw or in a stir-fry – and it looks attractive in the plot.

outdoors and then cloching them in September or grow them in a tunnel. Seed companies offer mixed packets, which is a good place to start. Some of the best for Scotland are:

- **mustard spinach** (komatsuna) – mild and slightly peppery, tough and vigorous, a good crop with a long season at Phantassie Farm, East Lothian. I felt it tasted of little and was very coarse textured so won't grow it again.
- **mibuna** – strap-like leaves and a medium mustardy taste.
- **mizuna** – attractive serrated foliage in green or red forms and mustard-like flavour. We saw this growing successfully with some shelter on Lewis.
- **mustard greens** – coloured leaves and a spicy taste.
- **pak choi** – Scotland is not ideal for producing the large leaves you find offered in supermarkets but Phantassie Farm, East Lothian, find them excellent as a cut-and-come-again salad outdoors in summer and in tunnels in autumn and winter. They also plant out seedlings in the field in

October and November, covered with mesh to keep off pigeons, for early spring cropping.
- **tatsoi** (a variety of pak choi) – a good performer in a tunnel house at Chisholme in the hills near Hawick.

SOWING, ROUTINE CARE AND HARVESTING

Oriental greens are shallow rooted and rather greedy so they may need to be fed. Grow in situ or in tunnels, if needs be, as a cut-and-come-again crop, in shallow drills or broadcast, or space out 15–25cm apart to grow larger leaves.

COMMON PROBLEMS

Most oriental greens are theoretically susceptible to all the usual brassica pests and diseases. A fine mesh should keep flying problems from the crop, including flea beetle.

Rocket (*Eruca sativa*) *H3 E1*

A plant with a delicious tangy taste, both the leaves and the flowers can be eaten. Native to Asia and the Mediterranean area, in Roman times the seeds were also used as a flavouring. There are two types. Annual rocket is milder, vigorous and very quick to grow – 4–12 weeks from seed to harvest. Varieties include '**Esmee**' with lobed leaves and '**Serrata**' with jagged leaf edges. Wild rocket is perennial, slower growing, less productive and sharper in flavour. Both will self-seed if allowed. Ken tried sowing it on potato drills in April and got a crop before the potato foliage covered the ground. Rocket will support a hint of frost. A crucial ingredient of a mixed green salad, rocket can be cooked quite successfully too and added to an omelette, for example. It also makes the basis of an excellent pesto.

SITE, SOIL, SOWING AND PLANTING

Sow directly into the ground from mid April in a sunny, open position with a fertile but well-drained soil. Rocket will be happy in slight shade in high summer. You will have to succession-sow the seeds to ensure you have a supply all summer. Sprinkle them into a shallow drill 0.5cm deep and lightly covered with soil. Thin to 15cm apart.

For a year-round supply, plant out of season in pots in the house or greenhouse or in your polytunnel and eat young.

ROUTINE CARE, HARVESTING AND STORING

Keep weeded and well watered. Pick individual leaves from the plants as you need them. Use the flowers too in salads. Washed and bagged, rocket will store for a few days in the fridge. As pesto, it will store in its jar in the fridge for more than a week. Don't freeze.

COMMON PROBLEMS

Flea beetle can make leaf holes – it's best prevented with fine mesh covering. Bolting may occur in hot and dry conditions – hence the requirement for a little shade at the height of summer.

Spinach (*Spinacia oleracea*) *H3–4 E1* and Spinach-like Vegetables

Popeye's favourite is good for you – high in fibre, vitamins A and C, beta carotene and lutein. True spinach, perpetual spinach (*Beta vulgaris* subsp. *cicla*), New Zealand spinach (*Tetragonia expansa*) and mountain spinach or orache (*Atriplex hortensis*) can all be used in similar ways. Perpetual spinach is similar to chard and is covered on p. 194. By sowing all four types, you can have spinach almost all year round.

Spinach is a native of Persia and its name comes to us from that language via Arabic – *aspanakh*. It probably reached Europe through Spain thanks to

Peppery rocket showing its edible flowers.

Left to right: perpetual spinach, orach 'Magenta' and true spinach. All can be eaten raw when young or cooked.

the Moors and was known in Britain by the sixteenth century, although it was used initially for medicinal rather than culinary purposes. In those early days, it formed the basis of sweet recipes – something I can't really imagine. However, the common habit of adding a little nutmeg to flavour our spinach is probably a hangover from this time.

With its impressive nutritional credentials, beautiful colour and flexible nature, it is an absolute must in the vegetable patch. Varieties used to be divided into summer and winter types but, these days, most hardier varieties can be used for both and, although it may stop growing in midwinter, it will come back for a while in the spring. And it can be used in so many ways in the kitchen, from pasta sauces and fillings for quiches, to soups and saag aloo. Spinach will store in the fridge for a couple of days and it freezes very well.

SITE, SOIL, SOWING AND PLANTING

Spinach likes rich and hearty, moisture-retentive soil in sun or partial shade at the height of summer. It will bolt if conditions are too hot and dry or if planted too early and checked by cold. Succession-sow for lasting cropping.

Sow spinach *in situ* in spring in 2cm deep drills, thinning to 15cm, and protect with a cloche or fleece until the seedlings gather strength. Eat any succulent thinnings. Sow *in situ* in summer and, with a cover in autumn, you may well be cropping into winter. You can sow under cover in early autumn to get a crop in very early spring. If you start sowing too early, spinach will tend to bolt; too late, and seedlings are too small to overwinter. Trial and error is the best advice, to suit your local climate. Alternatively, all of the spinach and spinach-type plants can be started early in modules and then hardened off and transplanted.

ROUTINE CARE, HARVESTING AND STORING

Keep weeded and well watered. Protect seedlings from birds in the usual way. Remove any potential flowering shoots if you are still cropping it. It can run out of puff in late summer without a dose of nitrogen fertiliser.

Harvest the outer leaves in a cut-and-come-again way when they reach the desired size. You can even cut the whole plant down to near the ground, as it will often re-sprout. Keep picking to encourage new growth. Small leaves are currently fashionable and always most delicious eaten raw but, such is their reduction in bulk on cooking, you may wish larger ones if you have a recipe in mind.

COMMON PROBLEMS

Many potential spinach difficulties will be avoided by keeping your rotation going. Keep an eye on **slugs**. **Birds** love young spinach seedlings, so net them. **Bolting** is a bit of a problem and may occur in hot, dry weather and if the plants are short of water or food, so plant in rich soil and keep well watered. Look out for bolt-resistant cultivars. **Mildew** can be kept at bay by thinning plants appropriately and cropping regularly. Remove and burn any mildew-damaged leaves. If the young leaves start to curl inwards, you may have **cucumber mosaic virus**. Remove and destroy infected plants. To prevent this, don't grow cucumbers near spinach.

SPINACH VARIETIES

'**Atlanta**' ♀ Hardy, good for overwintering.
'**Long Standing**' A popular older variety.
'**Medania**' ♀ Easy to grow, long-lasting as long as it does not dry out. A favourite of *Beechgrove Garden*'s George Anderson.
'**Mikado**' F1 ♀ So-called oriental spinach with mildew resistance and some hardiness.
'**Scenic**' F1 ♀ The most mildew-resistant variety, good in baby salads.

New Zealand Spinach H2 E1

New Zealand spinach is generally eaten cooked. It is really worth growing as it is easier to please than traditional spinach as a summer crop – if you can give it reasonable shelter. One sowing after all danger of frost is past will last you the summer. Soak the seeds for 24 hours before planting. You can start it off in modules and plant out when conditions allow or sow direct in rows 30–50cm apart. It will not over-winter due to cold sensitivity. Crop by taking some of the young shoots and the growing tips. In my experience, such is their vigour, I take entire branches of the thing and strip the leaves straight into the sink – and there's always plenty left in the ground. I actually had an accidental, and very welcome, crop of the stuff this past year growing from my compost heap. It does seem to set seed with great alacrity. There don't appear to be named forms, just seed strains.

Orach/Mountain Spinach H2–3 E1

Orache is a tall, attractive plant whose smallish, arrowhead leaves, red or greenish-yellow in colour, taste similar to spinach. Sow in rows up to 20–25cm apart. It can be eaten raw or cooked and is best grown to be harvested very young, once the plant reaches 10cm, unless you are using it as a back of border architectural statement. Nip out the growing tip to encourage it to bush. Very pretty in salad.

A new red-purple leaved variety, '**Magenta Magic**', is available from Real Seeds. It looks great from the small seedling stage onwards.

Sprouting Seeds *H1C E1*

Sprouting seeds are a quick, nutritious crop, high in vitamin A and C, which can be grown all year round. Many common vegetable seeds can be sprouted and eaten but one or two are indigestible so check first. They are excellent in salads and stir fries. They are germinated in a jar and swell with water to produce a growing tip. Some sprouting seeds can be eaten after as few as two days, with the longest taking around two weeks.

The simplest way to grow them is to use a clean and sterilised (with boiling water) jar covered with muslin instead of a lid. The muslin acts as a sieve to reduce the water in the jar. The seeds need to be kept moist and warm. Sprouting seeds will increase dramatically in size, so don't grow too many at once. Overcrowding leads to mould, which tastes foul. Most, but not all, require greening and so need some light after germination. Indirect light from a north-facing window in a reasonably warm room is ideal. Soak seeds for eight hours or overnight, then drain the water away. Keep the jar upside down to keep seeds drained. Rinse well twice a day. This both cleans away any possible fungi and keeps the humidity up. Once the seeds have germinated, rinse gently so you don't knock off the sprouts. After 'harvest', keep them in the fridge for no more than two days. There have been reports in the press about E. coli outbreaks in France and Germany from sprouting seeds. These are more likely to be caused by contaminated water than the seeds themselves. There have been no problems the UK. Keen sprout fans can buy a bespoke propagator.

Pulses and Grains

These can be used in soups and salads as cooked beans would be. Light cooking is advised for regular use, as they can be somewhat indigestible raw.

Adzuki beans Crispy, nutty flavour – ready in 4–8 days.

Chickpeas Crunchy and mild and can be cooked in soups – harvest in 2–4 days.

Lentils Very easy to grow. Steam them or eat sparingly on salads – ready in 5 days.

Mung beans The Chinese sprout, high in vitamin C – harvest after 4–8 days.

Sprouting seeds give you an incredibly nutritious micro-crop with no garden at all! Ensure you buy reputable seeds – possibly safer to choose organic in this instance at least.

Vegetable Seeds

You can sprout many common vegetables such as cabbage, beet, peas and radish. The seeds tend to remain small and it is mainly the shoots you eat. All below require greening.

Alfalfa 'Father of all foods' in Arabic, mild tasting – 2–7 days to harvest.

Cress Almost everyone has tried growing this as a child on blotting paper. Easy on wet kitchen towel – harvest in 6–8 days.

Fenugreek Vigorous and somewhat bitter so best mixed with other sprouts – harvest in 3–5 days.

Mustard Spicy, can be raised on damp kitchen towel on a plate – 5–6 days to harvest.

CHAPTER 5

Onion Family (Alliums)

The various members of the allium tribe – onions, shallots, garlic, leeks, chives and spring onions – lie at the heart of present-day cookery. This was always so to some extent, although the use of garlic in the UK has increased dramatically since I was a child, with access to foreign summer holidays leading to an interest in Mediterranean cooking. All these vegetables are relatively easy to grow in all parts of Scotland in reasonably well-drained soil – however, they mostly need a longish growing season so may need to be started in modules under protection in the wilder parts. Alliums dislike acid soil so, in most of Scotland, lime your beds before planting. Allotments and other intensively cultivated vegetable growing areas often suffer from a gradual build up of allium pests and diseases such as leek rust and onion rots. The spores are spread from plot to plot, even when rotation is practised. Some people feel that, such is the ubiquity of onions in shops, there is little point in taking up space in the garden with them. I disagree. I grow all the members of this family and, although they do present challenges, it is such fun when you get it right and you have lovely pleated strings of the things in your shed, still firm and succulent, waiting to be used.

Garlic (*Allium sativum*) *H4–5 E1*

Garlic grows well in many parts of Scotland, including Orkney and Shetland, and, indeed, there is a very successful company near Nairn growing and selling

Garlic being started off under protection in modules at Carloway on Lewis. Grow plenty, if you have the space, as you will use it.

Garlic 'Cristo' and 'Arno' from Ken's garden hanging up to dry. Both are soft-neck varieties, easy to grow and store well.

Garlic hung to store in the traditional manner. It must be kept very dry or rot will set in.

Roast whole bulbs having sliced their tops off and drizzled them with a good olive oil. Cook in a muffin tin to keep the bulbs upright. Squidge the cooked cloves over whatever you want – toast, meat, roast veg. Pungent-smelling wild garlic (*Allium ursinum*) or ramsons grows rampantly in parts of Scotland, much to the dismay of many gardeners who can't get rid of it. The bulbs, leaves and flowers are all edible.

SITE, SOIL, SOWING AND PLANTING

An open, sunny spot with fertile and relatively light soil is desirable. It may need to be limed. Garlic needs a long growing season and, traditionally, was planted on the shortest day and harvested on the longest. Given that you are likely to have significant Christmas-related duties to perform on 21 December, I would advise that you plant the individual garlic cloves – bottom-side down! – in November, if you have well drained soil and a relatively mild climate. However, garlic cloves can be frosted to mush in cold and wet soils so, for such gardens, I'd hold off planting until the early spring. Alternatively, do what my stepfather does and lay individual cloves on damp peat under the greenhouse bench in November, planting them out carefully at the end of winter. I have had success planting them in both autumn and spring, and Ken has planted as late as the end of March and had good results, particularly with 'Cristo', which grew the largest by late summer. Garlic does need a period of chilling so, if you plan to plant late, it might be worth popping the cloves in the fridge for a couple of weeks beforehand. If your soil is damp or heavy, try making low ridges to help drainage and plant on these. And you could pop a handful of sand under each clove as you plant it to improve drainage too. Alternatively, plant the cloves into modules or small pots in autumn or early spring (February) and keep in a cold frame or unheated greenhouse. Carole Baxter recommends this for Aberdeenshire and I am doing this in addition to planting out directly. We have a mouse

the stuff across the UK – the Really Garlicky Company ('It's Chic to Reek!'). Garlic is now an essential in the kitchen, though back in the 1960s and 1970s it was regarded as continental and therefore subversive to eat it at all. Just read what Dr Hessayon says about it in his *The Vegetable Expert* to see the sort of terror that it used to induce: 'If you are a beginner with garlic, you must use it very sparingly or you will be put off for ever.' It is known to have been in use since the time of the Ancient Egyptians and has a broad array of health benefits – antifungal, antibacterial (including MRSA), good for digestive complaints and great for keeping vampires at bay.

There are two categories of garlic. **Hardneck** varieties have fewer but larger cloves and are probably better for autumn planting. They produce coiling flower stalks (scapes), which are best removed to encourage large bulbs. Don't wait until the flowers open. The scapes are a delicacy that can be eaten raw or cooked. **Softneck** varieties have smaller cloves and flexible stalks that can be pleated for keeping and they store for longer.

Try cooking your garlic 'in the wet' – that is, straight from the ground. It is absolutely delicious.

problem, so I will cover each 7cm pot with an old pop bottle 'greenhouse' in the hope the critters will not gnaw through them. In North Uist and in Lewis, we observed great garlic which had been planted in polytunnels in September. On Shetland, Alan Crowe grows good garlic in Aith, and on Unst they plant in fish boxes under protection; but Jamie MacKenzie, north of Lerwick on Mainland, says that his soil is too heavy.

Choose only the firmest heads. Break them into individual cloves and block plant them 15cm apart, pushing or dibbing them into the ground and covering them with around 3cm of soil if your soil is well drained or pushing just below the surface if not. It is advisable to buy garlic which is certified as disease free. I have to admit that I have at times, successfully, simply planted garlic I liked the look of in the supermarket. I have also planted garlic I had previously harvested and stored.

ROUTINE CARE, HARVESTING AND STORING

Another fairly easy-to-manage crop. Keep it well weeded. Harvest as the leaves begin to change colour, around mid to late summer. Don't leave this too long or the bulbs will start to split and re-sprout. Dig up carefully so that you do no damage to the bulbs, which may lead to rot. Dry outside for a week if the weather is good or in a ventilated shed or greenhouse if conditions are damp. Hang in a dry and frost-free shed or store there, with the leaves cut back to 5cm, in a plastic 'open-weave' box.

COMMON PROBLEMS

Garlic can suffer from the same problems as onions (*see* p. 210).

GARLIC VARIETIES

'**Arno**' ♥ Softneck, pink-skinned.
'**Cristo**' ♥ Softneck, large, up to 15 cloves per bulb, a good performer for Ken in his trials.
'**Early Wight**' ♥ Softneck, fast maturing – if planted in autumn, can be ready by midsummer.
Elephant garlic (*Allium ampeloprasum*) A type of leek really, it has a mild flavour and you can eat the whole stem. Space the cloves at 20cm.

Leek seedlings ready to plant out (left) and planted out in holes (right) then watered in.

'**Music**' Hardneck. More than 10 acres grown by the Really Garlicky Company, Nairn, Moray.

'**Purple Moldovan**' A hardneck variety, aromatic and apparently perfect for garlic bread. Performed well in *Gardening Which?* trials.

'**Solent Wight**' ♀ Softneck, purple-skinned, high yield and keeps well. Good in RHS trials in Yorkshire. Recommended as the best buy after both Scottish and English trials by *Gardening Which?*.

Leek (*Allium porrum*) H4–5 E2

Despite the claims of Wales, leeks are a quintessentially Scottish vegetable. Indeed, the long-time most popular variety 'Musselburgh' was raised on the Firth of Forth around 200 years ago, possibly from imported Dutch stock. Leeks are great for Scotland because they will stand in the ground throughout most winters, providing fresh vegetables at a relatively barren time of year. They are an important element in our traditional and hearty stews and tattie and leek soup. Leeks are deliciously sweet and mild too and lovely to eat as a main course ingredient in tarts and patties. And little, early picked leeks are great steamed and then served warm or cold with a vinaigrette.

I love to have flowers growing amongst my vegetables and I have recently discovered how great the purple of self-sown *Verbena bonariensis* looks amongst the pinky-blue leaves of leeks. And, as Ian Crisp, gardener at Dunrobin Castle mentioned, leeks themselves turn into rather impressive cut flowers if left to grow on.

SITE, SOIL, SOWING AND PLANTING

Leeks prefer a sunny, open site with a well-fed, moist and humus-rich soil. Varieties are divided into early, mid and late or maincrop, depending on when they mature (autumn, winter, spring). Leeks can be sown

Leeks in a raised bed at Malleny, Balerno outside Edinburgh. A large leek crop can be grown in a relatively small space.

Leeks harvested and ready for the kitchen. If your leeks do shoot, lift them speedily, cut them in half longways and remove the flower shoot. The remains should be fine in soup.

directly into the soil as farmers do, but they tend to be more successfully grown from seed sown indoors, where germination is more even. This is especially true if you are growing in the more challenging parts of Scotland, including the Outer Hebrides and the Northern Isles. They get a good, strong start this way and it also enables you to plant them deeply outdoors which helps with the blanching of the stems.

Sow in seed trays in late winter to early spring indoors, in a propagator or in a warm greenhouse.

Broadcast them on to moist seed compost and cover lightly with a little more. Once they are about 15cm tall, either pot on into modules or 7cm pots and grow on or plant out at this stage if conditions allow, having hardened the plants off first. Plant once the ground is warm enough, probably towards the end of May and into June. Jim McColl suggests knocking out all the seedlings, discarding the smallest ones, shaking out the roots and trimming them (to 2.5cm) to stop them tangling up when they are planted. Root trimming also makes it easier to get them down to the bottom of the planting holes. The tops can be trimmed a little too.

Plant them about 23cm apart in blocks or in rows 30cm apart spaced at 15cm. Use a dibber (or the broken end of a wooden-shafted spade which has been formed into a bit of a point) to make a 15cm deep hole for each leeklet and then plop the plant in and water it. Do not backfill with earth. The initial watering will start this process and the weather will complete the filling of the hole. As the plant grows and strengthens, you can earth up the plants above the level of the soil to create even more of a blanched stem, the white flesh being more succulent that the coarser green part.

ROUTINE CARE, HARVESTING AND STORING

Keep the leeks well watered until they are established. If you want to grow giants, maybe to show, then you will need to carry on watering all summer but otherwise they'll be fairly happy only to be watered when really dry. An occasional feed is helpful. Keep weeded. Succession sowing should provide harvestable leeks from late summer until spring. If you need the ground to prepare for the forthcoming season, then dig them up and heel them into the same depth they were growing, in a spare piece of soil. At Glendoick, leeks came though the extreme and prolonged frost and snow of winter 2010–11 without turning a hair – clearly a tough crop.

COMMON PROBLEMS

Leeks are fairly problem free. **Slugs** may go for them and **cutworm grubs** may attack the roots if they are dry for long periods. **Rust** can strike in hot weather. It is best to remove and destroy the infected plants, although rust-infected plants are still quite edible. If leeks are checked or dried out it can cause **bolting** which makes them inedible with a solid central core. All is not lost as leek flowers are pretty and you can collect seed to sow the following season.

LEEK VARIETIES

'Atlanta' ♀ High yielding, late-season, cold hardy and beautiful blue/green colour. Seen growing at Inverewe.

'Autumn Giant' These are tough mid-season varieties: 'Autumn Giant 2 Argenta' – very hardy with long, thick stems and a mild flavour. 'Autumn Giant 3 Albana' – high yielding and stands very well over winter.

'Bandit' F1 ♀ Very dark coloured, late-season, stands well in winter and good resistance to rust and bolting. Seen growing at Inverewe.

'Below Zero' F1 A new Thompson and Morgan late-season variety which claims extreme cold tolerance. Bolt resistant.

'Longbow' ♀ A Medwyn Williams choice, mid-season, medium length.

'Musselburgh' ✉ Mid-season, very winter hardy, raised in the early nineteenth century. Thick stems but not too tall, so a good choice for windy sites. Happy in Lewis and Shetland (started off indoors in January/February).

'Oarsman' F1 ♀ Erect, very smooth, mid-season, resistant to rust and bolting.

'Pandora' Productive and early so quick to mature. Good rust resistance. A good doer in Wester Ross.

'Toledo' ♀ Another Medwyn Williams choice, rust resistant, a mid-season leek.

'**Winter Crop**' Dr Hessayon's choice as the hardiest variety, late-season so should be good in the north.

For mini leeks, try '**King Richard**' ♈ or '**Zermatt**' – both are early-season.

Onion and Shallot (*Allium cepa*) H3 E2

The ancestor of the onion probably has its origins in Central Asia. The onion is recorded in Palestine around 5000 BC and in Egypt *c.* 3000 BC and was spread around the Mediterranean area by the Greeks and Romans. Scotland's role in onion development centres on the giant Kelsae onion raised at the nursery of seedsmen Laing and Mather in Kelso. Launched in the 1950s and seen each autumn in the many vegetable shows across the country, the current record is just over seven kilos.

Increasingly popular are autumn-planted varieties, once known as Japanese onions. These come as sets available in autumn and, with a reasonable winter, you can get an early crop from them. There are so many culinary uses for onions that I really don't need to rehearse them here. I can't imagine life without them. And, if weeping on to your chopping board is an irritation, then pop the onions in the fridge for a while before chopping as this reduces the volatility of the substances that prick the eyes.

Shallots are smaller than onions. It is another form of magic to watch the one planted bulbil morph itself into a bunch of eight or more shallots. I find them easy to grow and they generally store well until at least March. The flavour is milder than onions and they can often be eaten by people who shy away from eating onions for various reasons. They can be made into a 'marmalade' with olive oil, butter and thyme, and joined by goat cheese, as the flavours do well together. Cooked whole they look and taste good in stews or with mixed roast veg. Grow as many as you can. Shallots come in a range of sizes, shapes and colours. With my lazy tenden-

Onions bent over ready for lifting – although not all experts agree with this practice.

Some ways to dry onions – against walls at Kellie Castle and on old pallets at Islay House Community Garden.

cies, I favour the larger ones, as they are so much easier to deal with in the kitchen.

Finally, don't forget growing onions to pickle. The best varieties for this include '**Paris Silver Skin**'. So keen was my sister on these things that she used to drink the vinegar too!

Shallots in Caroline's garden – a great yield from a single set. Use the larger ones in the kitchen and the smaller for pickling.

Show onions at Dundee Flower and Food Festival. The large ones at the back are the famous 'Kelsae' variety.

Freshly harvested shallots at Islay House Community Garden.

SITE, SOIL, SOWING AND PLANTING

Onions and shallots can be grown from seeds or sets, the latter being little onion 'bulbs'. I have used both with reasonable success. Seeds are cheaper to buy and less prone to bolting but they do need a longer season and may be more susceptible to pests and diseases. Sets cost a little more but shorten the planting-to-cropping time by two to four weeks. This head start can be significant in relatively poor soil or cold and northern gardens. Eric Hutchison of Orkney commented on the challenge of ripening onions in a very short growing season. On Unst they plant them in fish boxes to give them shelter and then move them outside in summer.

Choose an open site with fertile soil manured the previous autumn. A damp site will not do, as this is likely to lead to bulb rot. Your chances of a good crop may be enhanced if you add a little lime to your soil (at least one month before sowing or planting out), as onions and shallots do not like too acid a root environment.

Onion seeds

Sow *in situ* in mid April for a crop ready in late summer. Spread the seeds thinly in a drill 1cm deep. Space rows at 30cm apart. Thin the onions gradually. Remove all thinnings to deter onion fly – eat them as 'spring onions' if you like. Aim to achieve a spacing of 10cm between each bulb. In cold or wet gardens try sowing the seeds in trays or modules indoors in late winter to germinate before pricking them out at around 5cm tall. Grow them on and then harden off for at least a week before planting into their cropping bed when the soil is warm enough. Jane Eastwood from Lewis noted that results were much better starting both seeds and sets indoors. Space your onions out in blocks at 15cm apart or in rows 30cm apart, spacing the plants at 10cm minimum. To some extent, the more space you give an onion, the larger it will be inclined to grow. We have seen gardeners in the Borders, the north and the west grow their onions through slits/circles cut in black horticultural fabric. This serves both to warm the earth and to keep weeds at bay.

Onion sets

Make sure your sets are nice and firm and the right size. Reject the giants (likely to bolt) and the runts and any that feel soft. Planting times *in situ* as for seeds. Pop the sets into the soil, leaving just the tips showing above ground level. Space them at least 10cm apart in rows 30cm apart or block plant at 15cm all round. Ensure the soil is friable enough otherwise root growth will cause them to pop out of the ground. Birds may pull them from the ground, so make some sort of protective arrangement with thread and small canes or some other form of bird scarer. If birds attack, dig the onions back in, taking care not to damage the young roots.

Autumn-planted varieties such as 'Senshyu Yellow' can be sown as seed in August or planted as sets in September–October. These have been heat treated to encourage them to grow in autumn. They tend to rot off in winter in wet and cold climates, so here you would be better off planting in modules and keeping them in a cold frame or unheated greenhouse until planting out in April, or whenever your ground is warm enough. I visited Lewis in late September and noted sets of 'Radar' and 'Shakespeare' already planted in small pots in a cold frame. *Beechgrove Garden*'s Jim McColl suggests sowing spring onion seed in autumn and early spring under cover for cold weather harvesting.

ROUTINE CARE, HARVESTING AND STORING

If your soil is in good condition, you should not need to water onions much. Do keep them weed free, though, and do this by hand and not hoe so as not to damage the developing bulbs. Onions and shallots should be lifted when the foliage yellows and begins to keel over, probably around August. Jim McColl and many other authorities recommend bending the stalks over at the neck but Joy Larkcom thinks that this encourages storage rots and advises waiting until they bend over naturally. Carefully pull the bulbs from the ground by forking underneath and, if the weather is good, leave them on the surface for about a week to ripen. In wet weather, you are better off taking them into the greenhouse to dry, as they will tend to rot if left on damp soil. At Kellie Castle, the onions are hung on the walls or laid on chicken wire suspended above the soil on small posts, while at Islay House Community Gardens onions are dried in layers in/on piles of old pallets. If you are not planning to store the onions, lift and use them when you feel they are big enough but certainly lift them all before the first frosts. When the skins start to crackle or rustle as you peel them, they are dry enough to store. Do not store any with really wide necks. A well-ventilated shed or greenhouse is ideal. Onions can be stored hung by their pleated leaves, hung in nets or placed in slatted wooden trays. Keep an eye on them in case some begin to rot. Onions need to be stored over winter in cool but frost-free conditions. Not all onions store well. Some popular varieties such as 'Ailsa Craig' are not recommended for long storage. Varieties which store well include 'Stuttgarter Giant' and 'Red Baron'. Check the advice on the seed or sets packet when you buy them. Winter onions will not store terribly well but you might get a couple of months from them.

COMMON PROBLEMS

A number of factors can cause onions and their relatives to **bolt**. These include cold and wet soil at planting time or bulbs which are planted when they have already begun to shoot. Some varieties have bolt resistance. **Onion eel worm**, a nematode, will lead to swollen leaves, stems and roots. Infected plants should be lifted and destroyed. Rotate your onions assiduously to prevent a build-up of this pest. **Onion fly** lays its eggs in the soil around onion plants. The white maggots hatch out and burrow into the base of the onions. Usually the first you know about it are the yellowish drooping leaves. If you get this, dig up and burn all affected bulbs. If you act quickly, you may be able to save the remaining ones. They tend to attack young seedlings in June or July but can strike as late as September. You can use a fine mesh covering over the onions to prevent the fly from laying its eggs. Onion sets are not as susceptible. Onions are very prone to damp, leading to **rot**, particularly in wet summers and heavy soils. **Onion white rot**, a soil-borne fungal disease, can remain in the soil for 20 years and, if you get it, you'll need to change or sterilise the soil or move cultivation of the allium family to another part of the garden. Good crop rotation is the best way to avoid the problem. Destroy affected plants.

ONION AND SHALLOT VARIETIES

Onion

'**Ailsa Craig**' ✉ Named after the Scottish island and raised in the walled garden at Culzean in Ayrshire by David Murray. Does not store well so best used quickly.

'**Autumn Gold**' Plant in spring. Good yield, great storer and well flavoured. Does well from sets in Orkney.

'**Bedfordshire Champion**' Over 100 years old. Stores well. Good reports from North Uist.

'**Centurian**' ♔ Straw-coloured skins, a consistent performer.

'**Hytec**' F1 A good cropper and storer. For really large onions, start them in modules under protection in December/January. Good in Orkney.

'**Kelsae**' ✉ Raised by Laing and Mather, Kelso, this is the giant competition onion. It tastes good too.

'**Marco**' ♔ Very long storing, good disease resistance.

'**New Fen Globe**' A heavy cropper and good storer. Mild flavoured. Good in Orkney.

'**Paris Silver Skin**' Harvested in July and August and recommended for pickling.

'**Red Baron**' ♔ The most popular red-skinned variety, early ripening, stores well.

'**Red Spark**' ♔ A medium-sized red-skinned onion.

'**Santero**' F1 Resistant to downy mildew. Large bulbs and stores well.

'**Setton**' ♔ Some consider this an improvement on 'Sturon', with higher yields and better storage potential. Recommended for Lewis.

'**Sturon**' ♔ Very popular, resistant to bolting and high yielding. This does well all over Scotland, with good reports from the Western Isles, Inverness, Sutherland, the Borders and Perth.

'**Stuttgarter Giant**' Mild flavour, very popular and resistant to bolting. Keeps well.

Over-wintering onion

Plant in autumn for an early crop and protect in cold and wet gardens to avoid them rotting off. Good in cold frames.

'**Electric**' A *Gardening Which?* best buy. A red variety producing good-sized onions. Not a good keeper.

'**Hi Keeper**' Sow seed in autumn for overwintering, good hardiness. Can be sown in spring too.

'**Radar**' Mild flavour and crunchy texture. Hardy. Stuart Oakley on Lewis overwinters them in cold frames, as do gardeners on Shetland. A *Gardening Which?* trial based in Central Scotland recommended this variety.

'**Senshyu Yellow**' A *Gardening Which?* best buy. Planted in autumn and ripening in midsummer. Ken's crop did not make it through the harsh winter of 2010 but in milder winters and well-drained soil it should be OK.

'**Shakespeare**' A very dark brown-skinned variety, good keeper. Grown by Stuart Oakley on Lewis.

'**Troy**' A *Gardening Which?* best buy, producing large bulbs that store well.

'**Turbo**' ♔ Heavy cropper and good keeper.

Shallot

'**Aristocrat**' A long-bulbed French variety of long-standing. Looking good in Orkney.

'**Banana**' A good keeper. Single bulbs mean easier handling in the kitchen.

'**Golden Gourmet**' ♔ The most widely planted shallot, with resistance to bolting and large bulbs.

'**Jermor**' ♔ A popular French variety, needs a warm and sunny site for best results.

'**Red Sun**' Red-skinned, white-fleshed and mild-flavoured.

Spring Onion (*Allium cepa*) H3 E1

Spring onions are essentially immature 'ordinary' onions grown very close together, although there are specific varieties grown for salad/spring use. They are generally eaten raw but can be cooked if desired – and this is a good idea if you have forgotten to harvest them and they have grown unintentionally chunky.

Japanese onion 'Shimonita' at Phantassie Farm, East Lothian. This is a fairly hardy vegetable that can be harvested as a spring onion when young and as a leek-like onion when it is more mature. Very good value.

Spring onions from the supermarket looking like they could do with a good feed!

Welsh onions, which can be used as an alternative to chives or spring onions.

CULTIVATION AND HARVESTING

Sow *in situ* every three to four weeks from April onwards and as late as July if you can protect the onions from early frosts. They are a good catch crop and can be intercropped, as they are so quick growing – 10–12 weeks. Space rows about 10cm apart with seeds 2cm apart. Grow them under cover if necessary. Keep weeded. Water if conditions become very dry. Pull them as you want to use them once they reach a good size. They will store in the fridge for a few days. They are little troubled by pests and diseases, being so quick growing and speedily cropped.

SPRING ONION VARIETIES

'**Crimson Forest**' This looks great in salads as it has rich red stems.

'**Guardsman**' F1 ♀ A good performer in RHS trials at Harlow Carr, Yorkshire. Very vigorous.

'**Ishikura**' ♀ A Japanese bunching onion with long white stalks and a mild flavour. Good for salads and stir-fries. Alan Romans, Fife-based seedsman and potato guru, recommends.

'**Ramrod**' ♀ Tough and suitable for autumn sowing and early cropping in reasonable conditions. Good reports in east Central Scotland.

'**Shimonita**' A versatile fast-growing salad onion which, if left until late summer, forms a leek-like vegetable. Recommended by Patricia Stephen of Earthy Foods.

'**White Lisbon**' ♀ Long the most popular variety, fast-growing, sown regularly will crop all summer and can be sown in September in relatively mild gardens or under protection for an early crop the following year.

Welsh Onion (*Allium fistulosum*) H4 E1

With a flavour stronger than chives but not so nippy as raw onion, this is a useful source of onion 'greens' all year. Cultivate this hardy perennial from seed or find a friend with a clump then divide and replant young pieces from the plant edges. Replace clumps every couple of years by division and replant in a new place. It will flower in its second year and flowers are edible – and very attractive to bees. Some authorities suggest that Welsh onions and Japanese bunching onions are synonymous but Joy Larkcom notes that the latter are finer flavoured and tend to be cultivated as annuals. The hollow stems are harvested as you need them and are eaten both raw and cooked. The 'Welsh', by the way, alludes not to the country but is the anglicisation of a word that meant foreign.

CHAPTER 6

Potato Family (Solanaceae)

Ken Cox

As well as potatoes, a Scottish staple of longstanding, this family includes tomatoes, chillies, peppers and aubergines. With the exception of potatoes, for most of Scotland, these are best grown as indoor or protected crops, which is not surprising considering the origins of the plants – aubergines from India and peppers, chillies and tomatoes from Central and South America. They all need warmth to germinate, so an electric propagator or a shelf in an airing cupboard near the hot-water cylinder will be ideal.

Aubergine (*Solanum melongena*)
H1C, E2-3

From India, this tender, tropical vegetable, delicious only if well cooked, is used to make moussaka, ratatouille and many other dishes. It is an indoor crop for all of Scotland and is probably best grown in tunnel houses, as the plants need quite a lot of space. It takes five to six months between sowing and harvesting, so you are in for the long haul to get a decent crop. Like most of the potato family, this vegetable had a bad press when it was first introduced into Europe. Known as 'mad apples', it was believed that Muslims could eat them but that they would kill Christians or render them mad. They were introduced to southern Europe from North Africa but only recently have they become a popular garden and greenhouse crop in the UK.

Aubergines growing in a pot under protection. Four or so aubergines per plant are more than enough if you want them to grow to a decent size.

Aubergines 'Hansel' and 'Gretel' (white) on Medwyn Williams' display at Dundee Food and Flower Festival, 2010.

221

SITE, SOIL, SOWING AND PLANTING

Most people are familiar with the dark, shiny black varieties available in supermarkets but more adventurous gardeners can try varieties with white, yellow, red and striped fruits. Sow in March or April in 7cm pots. Seeds require warmth, 21–30°C (70–86°F), to germinate and soaking the seeds in warm water for a few days beforehand may help the process too. Once germinated, they like to be kept warm, between 16–18°C (60–64°F), and a heated greenhouse or warm windowsill is therefore required. If the expense of keeping them warm does not appeal, buy plants in May–June which are ready to plant out in your tunnel or glasshouse. Once the seedlings grow to 7cm or so, plant in soil/compost, 40–45cm apart, in pots at least 20cm in diameter, or two to three plants per growbag. Each bush should produce four to six aubergines.

ROUTINE CARE, HARVESTING AND STORING

Once plants reach 25cm or so, begin pinching out the growing tips to encourage bushiness. The purple flowers are attractive. When fruits forms, thin them out to no more than four to six per plant and remove all new side shoots and new flowers as all the energy of the plant needs to go to fruit ripening. Keep the plants moist but not soaking and feed with tomato feed or seaweed extract. Aubergines like a humid atmosphere, with misting on hot days, and Joy Larkcom recommends that shallow trays of water should be left to evaporate into the surrounding air. Harvest fruit in late summer when they reach a rich colour. If you leave them too long (the shine starts to dull), they become dry, tough and bitter. They will keep in the fridge for a few days and can be frozen after a short blanch, although they are quite soggy on defrosting.

COMMON PROBLEMS

Even indoors, **cold sensitivity** is the most common problem. Wind, chilly nights and dropping autumn temperatures can all take their toll. Most authorities claim that aubergines dislike temperatures below 20°C (68°F) but Scottish nights, even indoors, are colder than this and gardeners manage to grow ripe fruit in good summers. **Aphids, red spider, whitefly** and other insects can strike; misting the leaves helps discourage them. Caroline urges you not to but, if you must, you can use insecticides such as pyrethrins or rapeseed oil before fruit starts to colour up. Interplanting with French marigolds should discourage whitefly. **Blossom end rot** and **botrytis** are caused by irregular watering and damp foliage on cool nights.

AUBERGINE VARIETIES

For Scotland, it is best to go for early-ripening varieties to beat the onset of cold autumns. '**Black Beauty**', '**Bonica**' ♀, '**Falcon**' ♀ and '**Moneymaker**' have all been recommended. The old favourite '**Long Purple**' is still popular. '**Ova**' has dramatic white fruit. Or try '**Hansel**' F1 and '**Gretel**' F1, dark purple and white respectively. Both can be harvested as young/immature mini-aubergines.

Sweet Pepper and Chilli Pepper (*Capsicum*) H1C, E2–3

Sweet peppers and chillies are both forms of *Capsicum* and are native to South and Central America. Though discovered by Christopher Columbus, Britain's love of chillies is a fairly recent trend, coinciding with a newfound love of hot and spicy food from Asia, Mexico and elsewhere. You might be amused by the normally calm authority on gardening matters, Dr Hessayon, who is clearly as terrified of chillies as he is of garlic: 'take care . . .

'Yolo Wonder' sweet peppers from the Walled Garden in Perth. Rather neatly sized but they did struggle successfully through the poor summer of 2011.

The chilli collection at West Dean Gardens, Sussex, where an annual chilli festival is held.

these can make your throat burn ... Don't eat them raw ... don't even try a small piece.' Now they are so popular that West Dean Gardens in West Sussex have an annual chilli festival showcasing over 300 varieties. If you have a warm place to grow them, they are well worth trying, as they don't take up much space. You can freeze the fruits, and chillies dry well too, as long as they are fully ripened. Sweet peppers produce fewer, larger fruits per plant and they are generally considered to be rather hard work – by the time they fruit they tend to look bedraggled and often ravaged by insects. Don't bother trying to get any of the pepper family to grow outdoors in Scotland unless you are ripening plants bought in from further south, as it just is not hot enough. You need a tunnel or greenhouse. The challenge in Scotland is getting them to flower and ripen before the light and heat levels start to drop in autumn. The *Beechgrove Garden* grow good crops of several varieties in their 6x8 greenhouse while Chip Lima in Larbert grows his successful chillies on a west-facing window ledge. Mary Kennedy and Ursula Fearn in Haddington grew small plants which they overwintered and which fruited well the following year. Chillies can produce a succession of fruit over several weeks, even months, if they get an early start. Really keen chilli growers use artificial lights for an early start in germinating and to help ripen the last fruit of autumn. You can use ordinary florescent tubes for this – you don't need the more expensive grow lights.

SITE, SOIL, SOWING AND PLANTING

Peppers and chillies are usually grown as annuals, although some chillies such as *C. baccatum* and *C. pubescens* can be grown as perennials if you can keep them frost free. Selected forms of annual chillies, *Capsicum annuum*, can ripen in 20–26 weeks from sowing in Scotland and are generally the best performers in more northerly climates. You'll need to sow at the end of February or early March to ensure that you have enough time to ripen fruits. Peppers need plenty of warmth and can be slow to germinate, requiring 18–21°C (64–70°F). Most authorities recommend a heated propagator but Caroline germinates them fine on a sunny windowsill. Prick out at the four-leaf stage. Most experts recommend keeping them at 16–18°C (60–64°F), which means you can have considerable heating bills. Again, Caroline has kept them in an unheated porch in late spring at cooler temperatures without problems. For shop-bought plants or

Chillies clockwise from top left: 'Stumpy', 'Padron', 'Cayenne', 'Santa Fe', 'Super Chili' F1 and 'Jalapeno'.

home-raised ones, once they reach 10cm or so and/or look like starting to flower, transplant into a container or the ground. *Capsicum* like a pH of 6.5, so ordinary potting compost is ideal. Don't over-feed with nitrogen, as this encourages masses of foliage at the expense of fruit. As with other tender vegetables, you could consider buying young plants, or even flowering-sized pepper or chilli bushes in early summer, as these will have been grown in warmer climates and brought north.

blane, showed me his tunnel housing around eight varieties with different uses and degrees of heat. Mark admitted that his success varied from year to year, depending on the weather. Gloom and rain meant poor crops and late ripening. He also suggested that, at the end of the season, you can uproot plants and hang them upside down in a greenhouse or tunnel to finish ripening for a few weeks. Peppers and chillies do fine in the fridge for a few days and both can be chopped and frozen, although chillies are slightly more successful than peppers.

ROUTINE CARE, HARVESTING AND STORING

Peppers need as much light and sun as possible but don't let them dry out. Keep compost moist but not wet. Misting plants in flower can help pollination. Sweet peppers will naturally branch, forming bushy plants. Commercial growers remove side shoots and train the main shoot for large fruit production. Keen chilli grower Mark Grindle, from just outside Dun-

COMMON PROBLEMS

Watch out for **slugs**, as they can demolish small plants. **Cold weather** and a **short growing season** are the main challenges to chilli and pepper growing; they can suffer from **blossom drop** if subject to cold nights at flowering time, much below 12–15°C. **Aphids** are often a problem, as are most of the problems listed for aubergines on p. 222.

PEPPER AND CHILLI VARIETIES

The choice can be bewildering: one chilli website lists more than 3,000 varieties. Some varieties will grow quite large, to at least 1m, while others are more bushy and compact. The main groups are covered below but it is worth experimenting with other varieties too. Some companies sell packets of mixed seed. Chilli heat is contained in the alkaloid capsaicin, the strength of which is measured in Scoville units. The hottest are 1,000,000 and the mildest 100, with those below 50,000 sensible for normal use. The hottest is the utterly lethal 'Bhut Jalokia', which the Indian Army is using to make anti-terrorist smoke grenades. You have been warned. Scoville heat units are given in brackets.

Sweet Peppers – no culinary heat

'**Bell Boy**' F1 ♀ Said to be tolerant of relatively cool conditions. Green to red.

'**Big Bertha**' This has the biggest fruit and is said to be good in cool climates.

'**Californian Wonder**' Good in *Beechgrove Garden* trials. Green turning red.

'**Gypsy**' F1 ♀ An early-maturing variety so ought to be a good choice for Scotland.

'**King of the North**' A short-summer pepper recommended by Stuart Oakley on Lewis

'**Mowhawk**' F1 ♀ Said to be a good variety for patio or windowsill.

'**New Ace**' Another good choice for us, as relatively tolerant of cool conditions.

'**Redskin**' F1 ♀ A patio or windowsill variety.

Chillies – Mild to Medium Hot
(SHU = Scoville Heat Units)

'**Cherry Bomb**' Rounded in shape, green, turning red as it ripens. (6,000 SHU)

'**Cheyenne**' Produces medium-sized orange fruit. (30–50,000 SHU)

'**Hungarian Hot Wax**' ♀ Mild if eaten green, medium hot if matured to orange-red. (5–15,000 SHU)

'**Jalepeno**' Mid-sized and medium hot, green or red, used in nachos and on pizzas. Not easy to dry so usually smoked. (10–50,000 SHU)

'**Padron**' Offers Russian roulette for you and your dinner guests. One in five to ten of these is very hot – the rest are mild and green like small peppers. (up to 5,000 SHU)

'**Santa Fe**' Grows to 8cm long, yellow turning orange, medium hot, melon flavour, free fruiting. (6,000 SHU)

'**Serrano**' A variable variety from highland Mexico with pendent, blunt fruit. Usually a little hotter than 'Jalapeno'. (10–20,000 SHU)

Chillies – Hot

'**Apache**' ♀ Dwarf with small medium-hot, bullet-shaped fruits. Long season of fruiting if you get them going early enough. (70–80,000 SHU)

'**Cayenne**' Produces long, narrow, red or green fruit, often wrinkled and curled at end, variable in heat but usually hot. (30–50,000 SHU)

'**Habanero**' ♀ Probably the most widely grown really hot chillies, they come in several colours, forms and shapes. Described as 'dangerously hot'. (100–350,000 SHU)

'**Masquerade**' Produces hot, multicoloured-effect fruit in clusters of chillies that change from green through purple to red. Said to ripen early, so a good one to try. (*c.* 100,000 SHU)

'**Ring of Fire**' Relatively quick-growing from sowing to harvest, this chilli is small and very hot. It is recommended by Nick Hoskins, gardener of Broughton House in Kirkcudbright. (70–85,000 SHU)

'**Scots Bonnet**' Named after its tam-o'-shanter-like shape. There are several colour forms. (150–300,000 SHU)

'**Tabasco**' Used to make the famous sauce, probably not the best choice in Scotland, as it likes high heat and humidity. (30–50,000 SHU)

Potato (*Solanum tuberosum*) *H3 E2*

Scots love potatoes and potatoes love Scotland. The humble potato tuber has been our most popular vegetable for 250 years and this shows no sign of abating. As far as I know, no other country still has 'tattie holidays' in October, programmed so school-children could pick potatoes from the fields. How did this tender crop from the Andes of South America become such a significant part of Scotland's history? Spanish conquistadors discovered the Incas cultivating the potato around Lake Titicaca in Bolivia and their collections of tubers reached Spain around 1570, shipped with a cargo of silver and gold. From Spain, probably via France, the potato is believed to have reached England in 1586 and Walter Raleigh is said to have taken it to Ireland.

The potato is a member of the family Solanaceae, which also includes tomatoes as well as deadly nightshade. Most members of Solanaceae are poisonous to eat and, indeed, this is the case with the foliage of potatoes. It is only the swollen tubers which can be cooked and eaten. Perhaps fear of any plant with the characteristic potato flower was what made many countries slow to adopt this most nour-ishing vegetable. The first potato introductions from South America were not ideally suited for cultivation in colder and more northerly regions, but the mild climate of Ireland was better adapted and potatoes had taken off there as a significant food crop by 1600. John Reid records the potato as being grown in the Edinburgh Physic Garden in his 1683 book *The Scots Gard'ner*, but it took another 100 years before the Scots adopted the potato in significant numbers. The French actually banned eating pota-toes in 1748 for fear they might damage the nation's health and the law was only repealed when early adopter Marie Antoinette became a fan, inspired by potato proselytiser Antoine-Augustin Parmentier. In Britain, potatoes even became a symbol of religious bigotry. Potatoes were associated with Catholics, so Protestants refused to eat them, with an election candidate in Lewes, Sussex, declaring, 'No potatoes, no popery!'

Most Scots were suspicious of the new vegetable at first – famously, in North Uist, clansmen were jailed for refusing to plant it. Gradually, through the eighteenth century, crofters began to appreciate that

The amazing 'Three Counties' potato display at Dundee Flower and Food Festival 2010.

The blight-susceptible 'Lumper' potato, the failure of which was responsible for the Irish and Scottish potato famines.

this crop could be grown in poor soil and stored for much of the winter, so alleviating the all too common nightmare of starvation. An acre of potatoes could feed four times as many people as an acre of wheat. By 1811, some Hebridean crofters were getting 80 per cent of their nutrition from potatoes and, moreover, for the first time, a Highland farmer could grow a significant amount of excess food to sell. This potato-driven improvement in nutrition caused a significant population explosion throughout Europe and Ireland's population quadrupled in the 100 years from 1730, largely due to the potato, leaving the population virtually dependent on it. When the potato harvest was wiped out by disastrous potato blight in the 1840s, the effect was immediate – almost half the population died or left Ireland's shores in the years that followed. Potato blight soon spread throughout Britain and the resulting starvation caused significant emigration from Scotland too. Ironically the blight-susceptible knobbly potato grown all over Ireland, the 'Lumper', is believed to have been raised in Scotland. Potato seed merchant WCF-Phoenix's John Marshall gave me some 'Lumpers' to try. They look odd but taste fine.

In the last 150 years, potatoes have become a major farming crop in Scotland, both for food and for seed potatoes, which are sold to farmers and gardeners throughout Europe. Scotland's cool climate is not conducive to potato aphids, which spread damaging potato viruses, so our seed potatoes have acquired a reputation for consistent quality. Scotland's potato industry is worth over £180 million per year.

Scotland has played a hugely significant but largely unsung role in the breeding of important commercial varieties. Scottish breeders have concentrated on raising varieties which ripen quickly in cool summers and which show resistance to the major pests and diseases which can afflict them – blight, virus, eel worm, wart and others. William Paterson was a determined amateur breeder who spent £7,000 (a small fortune in the mid nineteenth

Important early Scottish potato breeder Archibald Findlay of Auchtermuchty.

century) having potatoes sent to Scotland from around the world to use in his breeding programme. He raised 'Victoria', which has been used extensively by potato breeders ever since, producing many excellent offspring. 'Up-to-Date', released in 1893, was bred by Archibald Findlay from Auchtermuchty, a breeder whose new potato varieties were traded as if they were stocks and shares. A mini boom-and-bust cycle occurred in 1903–4 as speculators bought up tubers of Findlay's much-trumpeted 'Eldorado' at vast expense, losing all their money when the variety turned out to be worthless. Findlay gets a bad press in some quarters but Alan Romans, Scotland's Fife-based potato guru and historian, rates him as one of the most important breeders of all time. Findlay varieties fed Britain during two world wars. His 'British Queen', 'Catriona' and 'Majestic' are still grown today and their descendants are the modern varieties of today. William Sim, from Fyvie in Aberdeenshire, raised the best-seller 'Duke of York' in 1891 before moving to the USA, where he subse-

The Commonwealth Potato Collection at the James Hutton Institute, with curator Gavin Ramsay.

Scottish potato expert and enthusiast Alan Romans at Glendoick Garden Centre.

quently bred carnations. The 1930s saw the fruition of the work of Donald MacKelvie, who named his best-selling potatoes after his home on the Isle of Arran. The best known, 'Arran Pilot', is still widely grown today. 'Golden Wonder' was discovered as a sport in a field near Arbroath in 1906; 'Kerr's Pink' (1917) was raised in Banff, though not by Mr Kerr, who bought it from the emigrating breeder James Henry; 'Home Guard' was named in Ayrshire in the 1940s. Agricultural research centre Pentlandfield Station, Edinburgh, was the origin of very successful varieties such as 'Pentland Javelin'. Jack Dunnet worked at Pentlandfield before moving north to Caithness, where he has bred further important commercial potatoes such as 'Nadine' and several birds of prey varieties, such as 'Kestrel' and 'Osprey'. The James Hutton Institute in Invergowrie has bred the 'Mayan' series by going back to South America for new parent species such as *Solanum phureja* to add to the breeding mix, while Cygnet PBI, based in Milnathort, took over PBI Cambridge and now runs the largest UK potato-breeding programme.

Southern England-based potato expert Redcliffe Salaman raised blight-resistant cultivars by introducing a Mexican potato species into breeding lines in 1911–14. This encouraged breeders to return to the Andes in search of hitherto unexploited potatoes, most significantly the intrepid Russian Nicolai Vavilov, who eventually ended up in the Gulag for displeasing Stalin. The Russians inspired parallel British expeditions to Latin America and their South American spoils eventually led to the setting up of the Commonwealth Potato Collection, now held at the James Hutton Institute in Invergowrie. It is used to study the evolution and further breeding potential of the fascinating and complex potato genus. The keeper of the collection, Gavin Ramsay, showed me round the greenhouse of 80 potato ancestors and relatives, many with spectacular purple, blue or white flowers, pointing out which ones had provided genes for insect and blight resistance and other desirable characters. Each one is carefully pollinated annually to maintain the stock. Restrictions on GM research in Europe limits the experimental work that can be done but breeding goes on apace and I was shown some of the new cultivars being tested. NASA is convinced that growing potatoes on board spaceships will sustain humans on the three- to four-year journey required to send a space flight to Mars.

SEED POTATOES

Britain's tatties are usually cultivated from certified seed potatoes, most of which are grown and packed in Scotland. The concept of certified seed potatoes was invented in Scotland in the early twentieth century and this system is now followed worldwide. Certified seed is checked for virus and other disease and then carefully stored until spring, when it is available from garden centres and by mail order from Scottish suppliers such as Alan Romans (www.alanromans.com), Jamieson Brothers Seed Potatoes in Dumfries (JBA – www.jbaseedpotatoes. co.uk) and garden centre suppliers WCF-Phoenix (www.wcf-phoenix.co.uk). Bridgend Garden Centre in Freuchie, Fife, stocks over 100 varieties and you can choose as many of each variety as you like from big sacks.

Earlies come in from January onwards but February is early enough to acquire them. Potatoes should yield 10–20 times the weight of the tubers, so 1kg should yield 10–20kg or even 30kg in perfect conditions. Potatoes are not frost hardy so must not be planted out too early. Many growers 'chit' their early potatoes – encouraging small shoots to grow by placing them in a light, frost-free place away from strong sunlight. Try placing the tubers, most eyes pointing upwards, in seed trays or egg containers. Once they start to grow, show growers mist the tubers with water or even dilute liquid feed. Potatoes are usually planted once the sprouts reach 2cm (1in). They can be allowed to grow longer but be careful not to knock off the delicate young shoots. If your potatoes are already beginning to sprout when they are in their packaging, carefully untangle them without breaking off the young shoots and then plant them, as they won't need any more chitting. Experts differ in their support for chitting. WCF-Phoenix's John Marshall is an advocate. He explained that encouraging one very strong sprout produces an exceptionally early crop. Alternatively, multiple sprouting of all the eyes will gain a crop which is ten days earlier than it would be without chitting. In warm, wet years, when blight is bad, this ten-day advantage can make the difference between a good yield and a poor one. Alan Romans reckons that chitting is overrated and can reduce yields. He advocates chitting a few tubers to give an early crop

Borders Organic Gardeners' Potato Day, 2011. Buyers can choose from hundreds of varieties.

but leaving the remainder to develop naturally. The challenge is often keeping seed potatoes cool enough in early spring so that they don't sprout too early in the season. Most garden centres keep their potatoes too warm, so they tend to sprout early.

SITE, SOIL AND PLANTING

A 2kg or 3kg bag of potatoes should be enough for a 10–12m row, planted at three to four potatoes per metre. There are several alternative potato soil preparation regimes. If you are fit and strong, dig plenty of manure into the potato bed in autumn. Alan Romans's suggestion for the less fit is to dig a spade-depth trench in spring into which can go some fertiliser, a little manure, wilted comfrey leaves, compost or seaweed with a subsequent layer of soil. The potatoes are planted on top of this. Alternatively, if your soil is good for growing, plant with a trowel in individual holes about 10cm deep and earth up as the haulms grow. If your soil is friable and not too heavy, you can just place tubers on the surface of the soil with some fertiliser and cover with a thick layer of straw. Patricia Stephen at Phantassie Farm, East Lothian, puts grass cuttings on top of the straw as the season progresses. Potatoes don't like cold, wet soil and can easily rot. Joy Larkcom recommends a minimum of +6°C for three consecutive days before planting but Scots gardeners should not rely on this, knowing how fickle spring weather is. One solution is to plant through black plastic or membrane. Loosely cover the soil with the plastic to warm it up and keep it dry before planting. Plant the potatoes and place the polythene back on top. As the potatoes emerge and push against the film, cut holes in it so the haulms can poke through. The polythene can act as a mulch for the rest of the season. At Chisholme, near Hawick, at 300m, Richard Owen cuts holes in woven polypropylene membrane and plants through this. At harvest time, he cuts back haulms and peels back the cover to dig the crop. The membrane can be reused the next year in another bed. Beware of slugs under the polythene.

Potatoes can be grown in containers but do tend to give rather modest yields. A single potato planted in a 7.5 litre container should provide a meal or two of potatoes. You can plant two to five tubers in a pot but the more you plant the smaller the resulting potatoes tend to be. Make sure the drainage is adequate, the compost is reasonably open and the pot is protected from frost. This same advice applies to growing potatoes in barrels and any other form of container – for example, a compost bag turned inside-out and with drainage holes slit in the base. If the soil becomes compacted and stagnant, the potatoes will probably rot. For this reason, the commonly advocated idea of planting layers of potatoes in a barrel seldom works well and you'd be better off with two smaller pots than one deep barrel. Feed potatoes in containers with high potash tomato food or seaweed extract. If you overfeed potatoes with nitrogen, you tend to create excess disease-vulnerable top growth at the expense of tubers. Alan Romans's suggestions for container growing are 'Charlotte', 'Duke of York', 'Maris Peer', 'Rocket' and 'Swift'.

Like most vegetables, potatoes need a sunny site for at least some of the day. Potato diseases build up in soil, with eelworm being one of the most persistent, and so it is advisable to rotate the potato patch and not replant in the same soil for four seasons. You can grow a reasonable crop in poor soil, but a plot with friable soil, well dug over and manured – or mulched with manure in autumn, if you are not into digging – will give the best yields. Soil which is not well prepared is hard to use for earthing up the stems as they grow. Earthing up both protects the plants from frost and ensures that maturing potatoes stay underground. It involves pulling more soil over the greenery, most easily with a draw hoe. It can be done gradually but Dr Hessayon is convinced that just doing it once gives the same result. If soft shoots do protrude out of the ground when late frosts are forecast, then you'll need to protect with fleece or cloche.

Potatoes planted by Dave MacDonald of Glendoick using the traditional ridge and furrow method.

ROUTINE CARE, HARVESTING AND STORING

Potatoes need plenty of water. When the earlies start to flower, you can think about harvesting. This is likely to be around July and August for first and second earlies respectively. Check at the side of the ridge with your hands or a flat-tined fork to see what size the tubers are. For maincrops, wait until after flowering and you can leave them in the ground for several weeks, as long as you don't get an attack of blight. If blight does strike, you should cut all the foliage away and remove it. You can compost it, as the blight spores quickly die off. Unless it is frosty, leave the potatoes in the ground for a few weeks to help develop a thick skin, which allows them to be stored. Do watch out for slugs and wireworms. Potatoes which turn green from light exposure should not be eaten as they are poisonous. Each year, try to ensure that you lift all the potatoes from the soil, probably in September, as you don't want any 'volunteers' left to re-sprout the following year. Leave them on the soil to dry for a few hours before storing. Wooden boxes, jute or paper sacks in a dark, cool but frost-free shed should allow storage for much of the winter. The traditional potato clamp involves piling potatoes on the ground, covering them with straw and then loading as much soil as possible on top but leaving a 'chimney' of straw for ventilation. Beware of rats and mice finding a winter feast.

Potato blight is worst in warm and wet years. It's best to cut back the shaws as soon as you see it.

COMMON PROBLEMS

As you might be aware, for such a commonly grown crop, there are several pests and diseases which can affect potatoes. Crop rotation will reduce the incidence of most of these. The most serious is **potato blight** (*Phytophthora infestans*), which predominantly affects maincrop potatoes and which tends to strike in warm and wet weather in August and September. Blight is predicted in so-called 'Smith periods', which are 48 hours of wet weather during July to September when the temperature remains above 10°C. Blight alerts are available on the Internet at www.potato.org.uk/blight and www.blightwatch. co.uk. Symptoms are leaves with brown patches and mouldy fringes, leading to quick collapse of foliage. If it spreads to the tubers, it forms brown patches under the skin and quickly spoils the flesh. The key to chemical blight prevention is to spray before the symptoms appear. Long used to prevent blight, dithane (mancozeb) has been removed from the market. Copper oxychloride (Bayer Fruit & Vegetable Disease Control) and copper fungicides

such as Bordeaux mixture are still available and are acceptable for organic growing, though hardly desirable with an EIQ of 67 (*see* p. 66). They will slow the spread of blight but probably not completely control it. If you get an attack of blight and have not sprayed, cut off and burn or compost all the affected shaws. This should protect the potatoes underground. There are several so-called blight-resistant cultivars such as 'Cara' and 'Record' but combating blight is an ongoing battle for breeders as the strains keep mutating. The worst of the newer blight strains, 'Blue 13', seems to affect almost all previously resistant varieties. The most resistant maincrop variety is the Hungarian 'Sárpo Mira'. Although it can show symptoms on the leaves, the potatoes beneath remain unaffected.

If your seed potatoes fail to sprout, check if **frost damage** or **poor drainage** has caused them to rot. In heavy, wet soils it is best to make raised beds or plant on a base of straw. Other serious problems which can occur include **slugs** and **wireworms** (orange yellow worms), which can burrow through the potatoes. Ordinary **slugs** eat the emerging spring foliage while keel slugs burrow into mature tubers. Select slug-resistant varieties (*see below*). The two forms of **scab**, with irregular dark brown patches, can be a problem in some areas. It is a cosmetic problem and you can still eat the potatoes, usually peeled. There is no cure, so it's best to select scab-resistant varieties and to avoid over liming the soil. **Black leg** tends to strike in early summer. It is easily recognised, as the base of the stem goes black and the stem collapses. **Eelworm** (potato cyst nematode) builds up in the soil and is one of the main reasons why potatoes should be rotated, with at least four years between crops. The microscopic eelworm causes weakened and stunted plants, and infected areas should not be used for potatoes again for, if possible, six to ten years. **Spraing** shows up as brown, curved marks in the potato flesh. It can be caused by a virus, deficiency of a trace element or drought. Destroy infected spuds and keep rotating. Scotland's cool climate means low incidences of the aphid-spread **potato virus**.

POTATOES WITH DISEASE RESISTANCE

Slug (keel) resistant: 'Arran Pilot', 'Cara', 'Desiree', 'Epicure', 'Golden Wonder', 'Kestrel', 'King Edward', 'Nadine', 'Pentland Dell', 'Romano'.
Eelworm resistant: 'Cara', 'Kestrel', 'Maris Piper', 'Nadine', 'Pentland Javelin', 'Picasso', 'Rocket' (most modern varieties are bred for it).
Scab resistant: 'King Edward', 'Sentanta', 'Wilja'.
Blight resistant: 'Cara', 'Sárpo Mira', 'Sentanta'.

CHOOSING POTATO VARIETIES

As noted above, Scotland is one of the best places to grow potatoes and almost any of those offered will probably grow well enough. Alan Romans lists 150 varieties in his famous book *The Potato* but there are over 500 varieties grown in the UK, most of which are held *in vitro* at the UK national potato collection at Science and Advice for Scottish Agriculture (SASA) in Edinburgh. For those of us with a more general interest, there have been magnificent displays of potato varieties at the Dundee Flower and Food Festival in recent years.

If you have space, grow some earlies and some main crops and try to grow the less common varieties which you won't find in the supermarkets. Ian Barbour of JBA told me that the most popular garden potatoes in Scotland are 'Arran Pilot', 'Charlotte', 'Desirée', 'Epicure', 'Kestrel', 'King Edward', 'Maris Piper', 'Pentland Javelin' and 'Wilja'. At Glendoick, we sell more 'Duke of York' than any other. Some of the most rewarding to grow are Scottish heritage varieties, particularly those with coloured skins and flesh. With a 2kg or 3kg sack containing about 30–60 tubers to be planted 35–40cm apart, you should get a 10–20m row of potatoes. If you are short of space, earlies take up less room but have a smaller yield. You can buy taster packs of a small number of potatoes which are ideal for containers or limited planting space. For a wider choice of varieties, try mail order. There are several suppliers noted on p. 229.

WAXY VERSUS FLOURY?

These two terms are commonly used to describe the texture of potato flesh. **Waxy potatoes** are translucent and moist. They are firmer and keep their shape when cooked, so are the best choice for boiling and salads. **Floury potatoes** have a more granular and drier fluffy flesh – you'll feel that they need butter added! They are best for chips, roasting, baking and mashing and for when you want to soak up sauces and gravy. Some, like 'Golden Wonder', are so dry and floury you need to add a huge amount of butter. For taste alone, I'd choose floury 'Golden Wonder' and waxy 'Pink Fir Apple'. The layer of flesh right below the skin contains most of the vitamin C and, according to Alan Davidson, most of the flavour too, so I'm a firm believer in cooking and eating most potatoes in their skins – even when they're to be mashed – although my wife Jane does not agree. And, on the subject of eating the things, Laura

Potatoes, first early varieties: 'Bonnie Dundee', 'Swift' and 'Red Duke of York'.

Potato type	Planting time	Space between potatoes	Space between rows	Time between planting and harvesting	When to harvest	Harvest time
First Early	March–April	25–30cm	35–50cm	3+ months – 100 days	in flower	July
Second Early	Late March–April	25–35cm	35–50cm	4 months – 110–120 days	in flower	July–August
Main crop	April	30–40cm	75cm	up to 5 months – 125–140 days	any time after flowering	September–October

Donkers of North Uist suggests that machair-grown potatoes need little or no added salt, as they take it up from the sand.

POTATO VARIETIES

First Earlies

These can be harvested in flower.

'**Arran Pilot**' ✉ Launched in 1930 and still one of the most popular Scottish-bred potatoes. A great taste and high yielding, with white skins and pure white waxy flesh. Not so good in heavy soils. Good for boiling and chipping. Scab and spraing resistant. Does in Lewis.

'**Bonnie Dundee**' ✉ Deep-red skin, round with creamy flesh, this potato is ideal for boiling and salads. Blight and scab resistant. Caroline grew these and we all thought they were delicious and great to look at. We'll definitely grow them again.

'**Duke of York**' The best-selling first early at Glendoick with good flavour and a dry, mealy texture. Oval with yellow flesh and versatile in the kitchen. '**Red Duke of York**' ♀ differs in its red skin and greater vigour. This latter is Alan Romans' choice as his 'desert island potato'. It is much favoured in Orkney too.

'**Epicure**' Also known as 'Ayrshires', as it's much grown there. For cold areas, this is a good choice as it can recover from a bit of damage after late spring frosts. White-fleshed and floury in texture.

'**Foremost**' ♀ ✉ Has a good flavour and holds its shape when boiled. Oval with white skin and flesh. Yield below average and only moderately disease resistant but 'a gardeners' favourite', according to Alan Romans.

'**Home Guard**' Introduced in 1942 and an important crop immediately post-Second World War. White, short, oval tubers with good resistance to all forms of scab and spraing.

'**Maris Bard**' One of the earliest 'earlies' with white skin and flesh. Excellent choice for salad and boiling, with good scab resistance.

'**Pentland Javelin**' ✉ A very popular white Scottish potato with good yield, flavour and disease resistance.

'**Rocket**' Very high yielding and so widely grown but the taste is bland. Resistant to blackleg, common scab and spraing. Lift quickly to avoid splitting.

'**Sharpe's Express**' Long and oval in shape with white skin, good flavour and dry, mealy texture, so one of the best earlies for boiling, roasting and chipping. Good resistance to common scab. Good reports from Sutherland and popular in Orkney.

'**Swift**' White, very early and one of the fastest growing. Short foliage so good for containers. Good disease resistance.

Second Earlies

These can be harvested in July and August and include a lot of good performers for Scotland. In recent times, some second earlies including 'Carlingford', 'Charlotte' and 'Maris Peer' have been supplied from cold storage in early August for planting with a view to harvesting towards Christmas. In Scotland, this is for relatively mild, southern coastal gardens only or for under some protection in tunnels or cloches. The *Beechgrove Garden* tried this in Aber-

Potatoes, second early varieties clockwise from top left: 'Kestrel', 'Anya', 'Charlotte', 'Maris Peer', 'Edzell Blue' and 'Carlingford'.

deenshire but Jim McColl admitted that, without a heated greenhouse, the potatoes stopped growing too early to make it worthwhile.

'Anya' ✉ Bred at the James Hutton Institute, it looks like a smoother, less knobbly version of its parent, the 'Pink Fir Apple'. It is better yielding, scab resistant but not quite as tasty.

'Carlingford' A high-yielding salad potato with white skin and flesh and a firm, waxy texture. Resistant to common scab and potato virus.

'Catriona' ✉ Oval with a white skin and striking purple eyes. Pale yellow, dry, floury flesh. 'Archibald Findlay's swansong', says Alan Romans.

'Charlotte' ♀ Britain's most popular salad potato, with good flavour, a yellow skin and firm yellow, waxy flesh. Excellent resistance to foliage and tuber blight. Does on Lewis and Unst.

'Estima' A very popular commercial potato, good for boiling and baking.

'Ezdell Blue' ✉ Blue-skinned with white, floury flesh. Good flavour and very dry but hard to boil without disintegration. 'The test of a good cook,' says Alan Romans. Prone to eelworm.

'Kestrel' ✉ For flavour, the best of Jack Dunnet of Caithness's cultivars, according to Alan Romans. A handsome specimen with blue eyes and good disease and slug resistance.

'Lady Balfour' A good performer in poorer or peaty soils, best boiled or roasted. Rosa Steppanova reports that this is a good doer in Shetland. Scab and eelworm resistant. A good choice for organic growing.

'Marfona' A high-yielding, large, creamy, waxy potato. Prone to slug damage.

'Maris Peer' Dramatic foliage and scented, purple flowers. Oval with firm, creamy texture and white skin. A good choice for containers and good disease and slug resistance.

'Nadine' ♀ ✉ High yielding, round with white skin and waxy, cream flesh. Good disease resistance.

'Shetland Black' ✉ Dark blue skin with pale yellow, floury flesh. Short, dark, wind-resistant stems. Boiled, they tend to fall apart and don't have much flavour. Baking or steaming is the best way to cook them.

'Wilja' A versatile Dutch variety with quick maturing, white-fleshed tubers which are neither waxy nor floury but somewhere in the middle.

Main Crop

'Arran Victory' High-yielding in a long season. Blue/purple skin and white, floury flesh.

'Cara' Round, with creamy flesh and a mild flavour. Late maturing and stores well with good disease resistance, including blight. Does on mainland Shetland. 'Red Cara' is a red-skinned version.

'Desirée' Oval, red-skinned with pale yellow, waxy flesh, good flavour and good in most soils, though prone to scab in sandy ones.

'Golden Wonder' ✉ Long with a very dry, floury texture, thick skins and needs tons of butter but the taste is excellent. A bit fussy as to soils, sensitive to drought and seems to be particularly attractive to slugs.

'King Edward' Oval with creamy flesh, very popular, good flavour. Scab resistant. Early main crop.

'Majestic' ✉ Long, with white flesh, one of the best for making chips. Once was the most popular potato in the UK and it fed the population during the Second World War.

'Maris Piper' Oval with creamy flesh, good yields and excellent for all styles of cooking – said to be the best variety for chips and for Christmas roasts. Some susceptibility to scab and slug damage but eelworm resistant.

'Mayan Gold' ✉ Bred at the James Hutton Institute in Invergowrie by crossing Andean potatoes. Small and dry with good taste but boils to a puree. Slug resistant. Happy in Orkney – like Caroline!

'Pentland Crown' ✉ Oval with white flesh. It is late and dislikes cold soil so best avoided in severe climates. Taste is bland; becoming less popular.

Potatoes, maincrop varieties, clockwise from top left: 'Arran Victory', 'Mayan Gold', 'Desiree', 'Sárpo Mira', 'Pink Fir Apple' and 'Sárpo Axona'.

'**Pink Fir Apple**' ♀ A long narrow, knobbly curiosity which tastes great, even if cleaning off the soil is a fiddle. Straggly foliage, low yields and prone to blight but delicious hot or in salads. Many growers moan about it but admit that it is worth the extra effort. Caroline loves it.

'**Romano**' Red-skinned, a good storer and cooks well – midway between waxy and floury. Don't let it dry out. Good disease resistance.

'**Rooster**' A late-maturing, red-skinned, versatile variety with pale yellow flesh and purple-tinged foliage. Good reports from all over Scotland, including mainland Shetland. Caroline sometimes grows it but finds it a little too attractive to slugs.

'**Salad Blue**' ✉ Blue skin, blue flesh and remains blue after cooking. Tastes good too. Not worth boiling, as it tends to falls to bits. Alan Romans recommends making 'deep blue novelty crisps, chips'. He also comments on the distinctive flowers. Mashed it looks an odd blue-grey colour.

'**Sárpo Axona**' Pale-pink tubers, not as blight resistant as Mira but almost as good.

'**Sárpo Mira**' Hungarian, red-skinned and the most blight-resistant potato ever raised. Even if blight appears on the leaves, it won't spread to the tubers. The growth habit is curiously horizontal and the favour is not to everyone's taste. The tubers can be hollow inside and Ken grew some monsters. Said to be good in less than ideal soils and it stores for ages if you can keep it frost free. Other Sárpo varieties are becoming available via Thompson and Morgan.

'**Sentanta**' Boasting some scab and blight resistance and drought tolerant into the bargain, this oval, red-skinned potato is a good storer. Its flesh is yellow and floury. It does well for National Trust gardener Nick Hoskins in Kirkcudbright.

'Valor' ✉ Good grown organically because of disease resistance. Good in poor soil. It does not taste of much.

Tomato (*Lycopersicum esculentum*) H1C E3

'Deemed bizarre, exotic and quite possibly deadly,' recounts Christopher Stocks in his excellent vegetable history *Forgotten Fruits*, describing the early European reaction to the now ubiquitous tomato. Originating in Peru and Ecuador, tomatoes were introduced to Europe by the conquistadors, who brought them back to Spain in the sixteenth century. Italy and Spain were early adopters of tomatoes as a foodstuff but, recognised as a relative of deadly nightshade, they did not find favour in the cuisines of northern Europe until relatively recently and were grown first as an ornamental. French cooks decided that tomatoes had qualities as an aphrodisiac, calling them '*pommes d'amour*'. Italian immigrants took their tomatoes to the USA during the nineteenth century and gradually they conquered the world – we now eat 130 million tonnes per year, with China currently the leading producer. Tomatoes are very good for you – full of vitamin C and the antioxidant lycopene.

Tomatoes are a hugely popular, tender annual garden crop but they are not the easiest of plants to please and they are mainly grown indoors in Scotland. Even if they suffer from some of the many tomato afflictions, they usually manage to produce some edible fruit. The Fison growbag seems to have brought about a massive interest in growing tomatoes in the 1970s, which has never really waned. Scotland used to have a huge commercial tomato industry in the Clyde Valley but the greenhouses mostly grow bedding plants these days and many nurseries were converted into garden centres years ago. One of the last Lanarkshire tomato producers is Jim Craig at Briarneuk Nursery, Carluke, who sells his tomatoes at farmers' markets and through local garden centres and delis. Jim sows tomatoes in January in heated greenhouses and crops from April onwards. Jim reckons that he'll be the last of a dying breed unless a sustainable local food economy is created. Bob Nelson from Birsay in Orkney continues to supply the wholesaler in Stromness, although this is an increasing challenge given the impact of supermarket growth on the islands.

Most vegetable guides discuss indoor and outdoor tomatoes but, in Scotland, it is best to consider them all as indoor crops with at least some protection. This is because tomatoes need a minimum night-time temperature of 12°C (55°F) to set fruit and that is rarely achieved outdoors in Scotland. Once fruit has set, you can move them out if you have a sheltered garden and, in a warm summer, you should get reasonable results, particularly if you grow them on a south or west wall. An East Neuk of Fife sheltered seaside courtyard provided an ideal

A selection of tomatoes, showing some of the range available – excellent for eating raw . . . and straight from the plant.

site for a good crop of dwarf cherry tomatoes for us, but the plants had spent May in tunnels where they flowered and were pollinated. Caroline saw a number of plants growing on outside in a very sheltered and sunny corner in Orkney.

One problem with growing tomatoes indoors is that pests, diseases and mineral deficiencies soon build up in the soil of a greenhouse if tomatoes are grown year after year. Joy Larkcom reckons that, after three or four years, the problems are significant. You can rotate the indoor beds or replace or sterilise the greenhouse soil but, for most people, it is easier to use containers or growbags to avoid this problem. You can add the compost to your patch outside once the tomatoes are done. Another option is to plant into straw bales which are liquid fed. I saw this method used effectively in the greenhouses at

Cambo in Fife. A traditional way of growing indoor tomatoes in the soil is 'ring culture' where they are grown in bottomless pots placed on or sunk into a bed of aggregate. The roots are allowed to grow out of the bottom of the pot and they can be fed and watered by soaking the aggregate. This method is not as popular as it was but it does work well.

SITE, SOIL, SOWING AND PLANTING

If you are lucky enough to have a heated greenhouse, sow your tomato seed in January (and transplant in March). Otherwise, you'd be best to hold off sowing tomatoes in Scotland until March–April. They need a daytime temperature of 16°C (60°F) to germinate, so you may need a heated propagator. They can take

Tomato culture using straw bales at Cambo in Fife. Use wheat straw for preference as it rots relatively slowly and produces heat and CO_2 in the process. Water and feed the bales well before planting.

Cordon tomatoes supported by strings from the greenhouse roof, at Mertoun in the Borders.

cooler nights. Sow seeds in trays or pots on the compost surface. You can sow two seeds per pot and keep the stronger seedling. Many advise covering seeds with a layer of vermiculite but Caroline uses compost. If you don't have a heated greenhouse, you can grow the small plants on a sunny windowsill. If kept too cold or dark, they tend to become leggy. Turn them regularly. Alternatively buy tomato plants from garden centres in April and May. If the plants are spindly, as they tend to be, plant them deeply to encourage roots to form further up the stems.

Tomatoes hate the cold and it is not simply a case of keeping them frost free, as they suffer if temperatures drop below +5–7°C. As this is common in much of Scotland right into June, they can easily be damaged – even indoors in an unheated greenhouse. Plant too early and they'll die of cold. Plant too late and they won't ripen in time – such are the challenges of the Scottish tomato grower. It generally takes about five months from sowing to harvesting. Caroline puts hers out in an unheated greenhouse in May and this seems to work.

Tomatoes like fertile, well-drained soil with lots of organic matter such as home-made compost. A bit of poultry manure or Growmore before planting will give a boost. If growing in containers or grow-bags, go for something as large as possible. The standard growbag is too small to supply a decent reservoir of soil or feed for tomatoes. Pay the extra to get the larger version, which will sustain better plants. Alternatively, plant the tomatoes in large pots (about 25cm diameter) and plunge the base of these pots, three at a time, into a growbag. Caroline has tried this and reports that it not only maximises the amount of substrate available to the plants but also really helps to regulate soil moisture. This may lead to you having to water slightly less often and might help to avoid blossom end rot too.

Do not grow plants too close together, as it encourages rotting and disease – aim for 35–50cm apart for cordons and 50–90cm for bush tomatoes. You can spray the plants with water or shake them gently to dislodge pollen and improve pollination.

ROUTINE CARE, HARVESTING AND STORING

Keep the soil moist but not over-wet. A dry and wet cycle tends to yellow the foliage, split the fruit and cause blossom end rot. Tomatoes are greedy and you can liquid feed them every time you water once the fruit are setting – but certainly do it at least once a week. Use a liquid seaweed feed or a tomato feed high in potash. The temperature should be kept below 25°C (75°F) if possible, as high temperatures can cause fruit to drop. Moderation of temperature is often hard to achieve in tunnel houses. Ensure that ventilation is good. For cordons, it is best to pinch out the growing tip after two to four fruit trusses have formed to obtain the ripest fruit. Letting too much fruit form can delay or prevent ripening, particularly in a poor summer. Most authorities advise removing leaves below the lowest ripening truss on a cordon/vine tomato to reduce disease. If tomatoes are still green at the end of the season, they can be picked and ripened in a warm sunny site or you can cut the whole vine and hang it up in the greenhouse. Putting them into a brown paper bag with a banana is said to speed ripening. And you can always make chutney or relish.

COMMON PROBLEMS

Tomatoes are prone to a long list of pests and diseases. In addition, if you don't get the watering right, fruit will tend to suffer **blossom end rot, splitting**, **ghost spotting** or **uneven ripening**. Investing in a self-watering kit will give you more even results. If you forget to water or let the temperature rise too much, fruit can suffer **greenback**, with hard green patches near the stalk. Temperature fluctuations tend to cause the leaves to roll up, although they'll usually recover. **Aphids, whitefly** and **red spider** can all suck the leaves dry, while **mould (botrytis)**, **virus** and **eelworm** can cause crops to fail. The most common and often fatal problem is **blight** – the same disease which affects potatoes. Blight is less of a problem on indoor tomatoes but outdoor tomatoes may be affected in Scotland's typically cool, wet summers. Some tomato varieties have blight resistance. There is not much you can do if blight strikes, as the plants develop brown patches on leaves and fruit and then quickly collapse. It's best to dig everything up and burn it. Blight apart, you'll usually manage to get a reasonable crop of tomatoes, even if the plants end up looking a bit sorry for themselves.

CHOOSING TOMATO VARIETIES

There are hundreds of named varieties and the choice can be bewildering. Almost everyone we spoke to favoured different varieties, so clearly there are many that do well. However, the two with the most recommendations are 'Shirley' and 'Sungold'. Grafted tomatoes, pioneered by Suttons, are coming on to the market. These cost three times as much as a seedling tomato but they are said to be more disease resistant and, with a stronger root system, they are higher yielding at lower temperatures so, for Scotland, they might well be worth considering. The

2010 *Beechgrove Garden* trials were inconclusive but Caroline tried some this year and has never had such beautiful-looking plants at the season's end – and they were productive and delicious too. She grew 'Felicia' and 'Sungold'. Having said that, the control plants on their own roots yielded almost as well. Professional growers mostly grow grafted plants.

TOMATO VARIETIES

There are two tomato types:

1. Bush (or determinate) plants have a spreading, lower-growing habit with smaller fruit. Don't remove side shoots, as these will bear fruit. Some varieties are intermediate between bush and cordon types and these will need some support – a one-metre cane is usually enough. Dwarf bush varieties are suitable for containers, window boxes and hanging baskets. They yield lots of small fruit.

'**100s and 1000s**' Masses of tiny fruit, cascading downwards. Try in a hanging basket.
'**Golden Sunrise**' ♀ Small yellow fruit.

A bush tomato in a hanging basket at Scotlandwell Allotments, near Kinross – an ideal space-saver if conditions mean you are gardening in a greenhouse.

Tomato fruit splitting caused by erratic watering.

'**Latah**' A super-early variety that tolerates short or cool summers. Small red fruit. Recommended by Alan Crowe on mainland Shetland.

'**Polar Baby**' Grows outside successfully on Lewis, according to Cris Stubbington and indoors on Unst, Shetland. Bred in Alaska for low light levels, so should be good in Scotland. Prolific with small red fruit.

'**Red Alert**' Produces small tomatoes, interestingly shaped and very flavourful, worth a try outside in some parts of Scotland. Caroline put some outside in June and the plants ended up looking awful but they cropped really well.

'**Sungold**' F1 ♀ The most popular orange-yellow cherry tomato, sweet flavoured, good in *Beechgrove Garden* trials and a Jim McColl pick. It ripens early and gets an excellent press from most growers, including Kirsty Macdonald on Lewis.

'**Supersweet 100**' Produces cherry-sized fruit, prolific.

'**Sweet Olive**' F1 ♀ Olive-shaped fruits, support with a small stake, cascading trusses.

'**Tiny Tim**' Very dwarf plant with small fruit, good for window boxes.

'**Tumbling Tom**' A yellow and red trailing variety.

2. Tall/cordon/vine (or indeterminate) varieties are grown as single stems trained up canes or strings attached to the greenhouse roof until, at around three or four feet tall, the growing tip is pinched or stopped. Side shoots are pinched out. Use your fingers rather than a knife or secateurs. Expect 2–4kg of fruit per plant indoors. These require some skill and regular attention to get good results. Beginners might be advised to start with the bush varieties.

'**Ailsa Craig**' ✉ An old favourite, early and Scottish-raised, not too highly rated in a 2009 *Gardening Which?* trial.

'**Alicante**' ♀ A good flavour and resistant to greenback. Taste not rated highly in a *Gardening Which?* 2009 tomato tasting.

'**Black Russian**' Dark mahogany-brown fruit – great colour.

'**Brandywine**' A heritage variety which, in a *Gardening Which?* comparison, beat the newer '**Country Taste**' F1 on taste if not looks. You choose which is the more important!

'**Gardener's Delight**' ♀ Long trusses of cherry tomatoes. Ripens well even in poor summers.

'**Marmande**' ♀ A red beefsteak tomato, high yielding and well flavoured.

'**Moneymaker**' A heavy cropper, medium sized, very popular in Scotland. Flavour average.

'**Outdoor Girl**' ♀ Probably not outdoors in Scotland! Medium-sized fruits.

'**Red Zebra**' Slightly stripy, especially when unripe, with great flavour. A *Gardening Which?* 2009 tomato-tasting trial recommendation.

'**Shirley**' F1 ♀ Great disease resistance, good yields and some cold resistance, so a good choice for Scotland, especially if you try to grow organically. If you want to try one larger-growing variety, everyone we surveyed seemed to rate it highly.

'**Sioux**' Not great to look at but has an excellent flavour. Good yield. Winner of *Gardening Which?* 2009 tomato-tasting trial.

'**Sweet Million**' F1 ♀ Cherry tomato with small red fruit, worth a try outside.

'**Tigerella**' ♀ Early with orange stripes on the fruit, tangy flavour.

CHAPTER 7

Root Vegetables

Roots are staples for most Scottish growers. We wouldn't manage to cook without carrots; parsnips are great keepers in the soil over winter, which makes them valuable, and beetroot is so versatile, with the tops eaten green, mini-beets to pickle and fully-fledged adult roots to boil and eat with a dill-flavoured white sauce or to roast in individual foil parcels in a hot oven with butter and thyme. The **skirret** (*Sium sisarum*) – or crummock in Scots – is a root vegetable once widely grown in Scotland and now virtually unknown. It looks like clusters of small parsnips, tastes a bit like celeriac (or sweet potato, according to some) and is still widely used in Asia. Tough and resistant to pests and disease, it grows from small parts of roots left from year to year. Perhaps it is time for a skirret comeback, as it clearly grows easily in Scotland. You'll find seeds available online. Scottish historian Forbes Robertson reckons that the coming of the potato was responsible for its decline.

Beetroot (*Beta vulgaris*) H3–4 E1

This is one of the vegetable plot's great 'doers'. It is easy to grow in all parts of Scotland, is troubled by few pests and diseases, is very easy to harvest and is a good storer. As with chard (*Beta vulgaris* ssp. *cicla*), beetroot is descended from the sea beet (*Beta vulgaris* ssp. *maritima*) – which grows wild along many Scot-

tish shorelines. The Greeks and Romans selected and ate it in quantity but the beetroot as we know it, globe-shaped and red, was probably introduced to Britain in the seventeenth century, when it began to appear in recipe books. What was eaten before that was long, slim and fairly pale in colour. You can now choose from a huge range of varieties, both round and elongated, in a colour palette from almost white through golden yellow to the deepest red. It has been suggested to me that the red are best eaten cold and pickled and the golden, hot. Significant health claims are being made for beetroot and beetroot juice, in connection with both circulation and dementia.

SITE, SOIL, SOWING AND PLANTING

Beetroots need an open sunny site. The soil, ideally on the light side, should be well prepared and the surface raked to a fine tilth. Very acid soils should be limed a number of weeks before planting (*see* p. 33).

Most beetroot seeds are in fact little multi-seed clusters. Create a drill 1.5cm deep, with rows 30cm apart – a little closer if you are block planting. Dr Hessayon recommends soaking seeds in warm water for a few hours before sowing. Sow them every 7cm initially. If the soil is dry, water the drill before sowing rather than after. Start around mid April and you can succession-sow until early summer to give a continuous supply. Once the seedlings reach about

Left. Beetroot at Mertoun in the Borders, large enough to crop and store. Don't forget to use the tops as a spinach substitute too.

Right. Beetroot 'Boltardy' is a popular and easy-to-grow variety that eats and stores well. Its resistance to bolting makes it a reliable choice for Scottish gardeners.

3cm, thin out and discard the weakest, leaving only one at each 'station', firming up the remaining seedling as thinning tends to loosen the soil. When the beetroots are about the size of a golf ball, thin out every second root and use these in the kitchen. As with most roots, beetroots prefer not to be transplanted and so should be sown directly into the ground. The round type is, however, fairly successful if sown initially in modules and this may be an ideal approach in cold, inland gardens or where strong winds and short seasons combine to give challenging growing conditions. Plants will have a good and early start before facing life outside.

ROUTINE CARE, HARVESTING AND STORING

Keep weeded, taking care not to damage the developing roots. Beetroots do best with an even availability of moisture – if it is too dry, they can turn woody; too wet can cause splitting. Otherwise little needs to be done to this least demanding of vegetables. Beetroots can be harvested when they are the size you like. If you want to pickle them, gather them as 'baby beets'.

For storing, harvest in September. The globe-shaped ones pull easily from the soil, the elongated varieties may need a little help with the garden fork. Generally, Scotland does not experience the kind of climate which would allow them to overwinter in the ground, although you could create a 'clamp' or experiment with a thick mulch of straw if you have nowhere to store them. Only store perfect specimens. Cut off the leaves 2.5cm from the beetroot top. Gently rub off any remaining soil and pack, ensuring they do not touch, in light soil or sand in a box in a dark, frost-free shed. They should last for several months but they will lose a little firmness as time goes on. Watch out for mice. Some say that the longer-rooted varieties store most successfully.

COMMON PROBLEMS

Beetroot is liable to **bolt** if sown too early in cold soil. For cold inland gardens, select a variety with bolt resistance such as 'Boltardy'. Sow under cloches for an early crop. **Birds** may be attracted to the young seedlings, although I have not had this problem. Take some protective measure until the plants are well established – fine mesh pinned round the crop or some twigs formed into a shallow tunnel, for example.

BEETROOT VARIETIES

'**Alto**' F1 ♀ Red, cylindrical and very sweet. Good in Orkney.

'**Boltardy**' ♀ Globe-shaped, red, smooth skinned, resistant to bolting, good in containers, the most popular variety for Scotland – including the Western Isles. Most of our contacts recommend it.

'**Bulls Blood**' Amazing deep reddish-purple leaves, great for the potager. More ornamental than edible but does produce small beets.

'**Burpees Golden**' A Victorian variety, orange-yellow. Best eaten fairly small. Young tops good in salad.

'**Cheltenham Green Top**' ♀ A heritage variety. Tapering, red, smooth skinned, good flavour. Tops can be eaten as spinach.

'**Cylindra**' Oval in shape, dark-red flesh and stores well. The most popular of the cylindrical varieties, with good disease resistance.

'**Detriot**' Red, round and a heavy cropper. Good in Orkney.

'**Golden**' A yellow beetroot with tops that are good eaten as spinach.

'**Golden Detroit**' A yellow-orange beetroot with edible, spinach-like tops.

'**Moneta**' Monogerm (single seeded), so requiring less thinning. Rounded, deep-crimson beets.

'**Pablo**' F1 ♀ Rich red, smooth skin, good at the Beechgrove Garden and does in Orkney. Slow to become woody so can be left in the ground longer than most.

'**Red Ace**' F1 ♀ Very good in a range of conditions and excellent in the kitchen.

Carrots (*Daucus carota*) H3 E2

Some people sensibly suggest that it is barely worth growing what is cheap to buy in the shops and that one should concentrate on the more expensive and unusual vegetables. If you followed that advice, you might never experience the taste of carrots har-vested, cooked and eaten all within the hour. We defy anyone not to taste the difference between shop-bought carrots, which often look like they have been fed on steroids, and smaller, freshly-picked, home-grown carrots.

The carrot that we now know is a highly culti-vated form of the wild carrot native of west Asia and Europe. In its earliest incarnation, it was most prob-ably grow as a herb, with its seeds and leaves finding favour rather than its roots. It arrived in Britain around the fifteenth century, probably brought in by Dutch Protestants fleeing persecution who settled in Kent, with its ideal soils for carrot growing. Edin-burgh seed merchants were offering carrot seed in 1691. Dutch breeders came up with 'Long Orange', said to be the origin of most modern carrots, and they also grew both pale yellow and purple varieties.

Used as the basis for many soups and stews, carrots are excellent in their own right, delicious raw with vinaigrette or cooked with butter and a touch of sugar or parsley or fennel. And, of course, it is the main ingredient in the eponymous sweet treat, carrot cake. Carrots did their bit during the Second World War too, for the nation's eyesight (propa-ganda mainly) and in the making of carrot jam. I tried making this – the results were incredibly orange, perfectly edible but somehow tinged with worthy desperation. It is still languishing in the fridge. However you eat them, carrots are a great source of vitamin A.

SITE, SOIL, SOWING AND PLANTING

Choose a sunny site. As a root, carrots need a well-fed, light and stone-free soil to allow for a long taproot. They grow best in a sandy loam so, if your soil is on the heavy side, you can either use raised beds or containers or select one of the many short or 'golf ball' varieties. For early crops in the wilder areas of the west and the north of Scotland, these round cultivars can be grown two or three to a module then, after hardening off, they can be

Carrots come in a variety of shapes, sizes and colours. Short carrots (top left) are good for containers and shallow soils.

planted into their cropping space. Long carrots can also be started, singly, in modules but they must be transplanted before the taproot starts to develop. Carrots need a temperature of 7.5°C (45°F) to germinate so there is little point in sowing them too early in cold ground. They are ready to eat 12–16 weeks after sowing and you can sow every few weeks to ensure a long harvest season.

For early crops, sown in March–April, probably under cloches, and harvested as early as June, the most popular varieties are 'Early Nantes' and 'Amsterdam Forcing'. Either broadcast or sow thinly on a very fine tilth in 1cm drills, 15cm apart. For the maincrop carrot, sow the tiny seeds directly into the ground. In relatively mild gardens, you can start outside in mid April. For cold, windy and northern gardens, you'd be advised to wait 3–4 weeks or plant under cloches or in a polytunnel. If you have to, thin when large enough to handle, allowing about 5cm between each plant.

ROUTINE CARE

Keep your carrots well weeded. It's best to weed on a damp and still day if possible so as not to alert

Carrots ravaged by carrot root fly. They burrow into the flesh and render the vegetables more or less inedible.

Carrots in a bespoke raised trough in an attempt to avoid carrot root fly, Kirkwall Allotments, Orkney.

carrot root flies. Keep reasonably well watered but not so much that the leaves grow instead of the root. You could mulch them to keep moisture in.

HARVESTING AND STORING

Maincrop carrots can be harvested at the season's end in September. You might want to use a fork to harvest larger carrots so they do not break. Select the perfect ones, cut the leaves to within 1 cm of the root top and store in dry sand or light soil in a dark shed, ensuring the roots are not touching. But, of course, they can be pulled whenever they are the size you like. The smaller cultivars are grown to be eaten right away, so simply pick them as you need them. You can leave them in the ground for some time but lift before severe frosts.

COMMON PROBLEMS

All carrot growers need to deal with the dreaded **carrot root fly**, which can devastate your crop. The flies lay eggs in the soil and the small white larvae feast on the carrot flesh. Chemical controls are now banned so there are various alternative strategies for avoiding this serious pest.

1. Carrot flies tend to fly low to the ground, so plant carrots above their low-level flight path in raised beds or deep containers only half filled. We tried both these methods with good results, although I would say that the damage was minimal rather than entirely absent. You can also make fine mesh surrounds, which the carrot flies tend not to fly over.
2. A complete cover of fine mesh or fleece is extremely effective at keeping the flies off. Garden centres stock this specifically for carrot protection.
3. Carrot flies tend to hatch in May and in late summer (August–September) so, by sowing late (in June) and harvesting early (in August), they

may be outmanoeuvred. When you first see cow parsley flowering in the hedgerows, then you can be sure carrot flies are around.

4. Sow seed sparsely so as to avoid thinning. If you do need to thin, take care, as carrot root flies can smell the crushed leaves at a great distance and will head straight for your beds. Thin them in the evening in still weather if possible and then take the thinnings away from the garden. Don't put them on the compost heap unless it is some distance away from your crop.
5. There are some resistant cultivars, the best known of which is 'Flyaway'. This did not prove resistant in the *Beechgrove Garden* trials and Joy Larkcom says they are only about 50 per cent effective.
6. Companion plants may help deter them – French marigolds or nigella are commonly used. Garden Organic suggests sowing with red flax (*Linum rubrum*). They also mentioned mulching with grass mowings, adding 1cm or so each time you mow (as long as you have not used weed killer on the lawn).

Cut worm can damage young roots but a good watering should kill the larvae. **Viruses** and **aphids** may cause the foliage to yellow and the plants need to be destroyed. Practise crop rotation to reduce the incidence. A **green top** to the roots is simply the work of the sun on the exposed crown. Unlike green potatoes, green carrots are entirely edible. **Forked roots** can be caused by stony soil or by manure added too late, just before planting, while **split carrots** may be the result of too much water. These can't be stored but are still quite edible. **Slugs** will attack too.

CARROT VARIETIES

Early, short-rooted varieties

'**Amsterdam Forcing**' ♚ Very popular early variety, good for forcing for early crops and good for freezing.

'**Early Nantes 2**' Slightly longer roots than the above, fast maturing, equally good.

'**Rondo**' Almost round, good for shallow soils and containers.

Main Crop

'**Autumn King 2**' ♚ Tough, can be left in the ground and has some resistance to carrot fly. Stump-rooted in shape.

'**Eskimo**' F1 ♚ Said to be the most cold tolerant and can be left in the soil (if well-drained) until late in the year. Stores well.

'**Flyaway**' F1 ♚ and '**Resistafly**' F1 Some resistance to carrot fly, sweet flavour. 'Resistafly' does well in Lewis.

'**Sugarsnax 54**' F1 ♚ Long, smooth carrots best in well-drained light soil.

If you want colours other than orange, try '**Yellowstone**' (yellow), '**Rainbow**' F1 (multicoloured) or '**Purple Haze**' F1 (reddish purple).

Celeriac (*Apium graveolens* var. *rapaceum*) H4 E3

With a reputation as the world's ugliest vegetable, celeriac, also known as turnip-rooted celery, looks most unprepossessing. It can be a bit of a fiddle to peel but it is absolutely delicious. It was a complete revelation to me when I first ate it and is ideal for those of us not too keen on the full-frontal taste hit of celery. The mild and sweet flavour is great cooked in creamy bakes or raw and grated in a winter salad. Makes a grand addition to soups and stews too. Try it pureed on its own, or mixed with mashed potato as a bed for a grilled mackerel. Remoulade is probably the best-known vehicle for this vegetable and is, of course, a great excuse to eat lots of home-made mustardy mayonnaise. The leaves of the celeriac can be used sparingly to flavour soups and stews.

As with celery, celeriac has its origins in wild

Celeriac in rows with the swelling vegetable just visible above the surface of the soil.

Achieving celeriac this large is a challenge in Scotland – but it can be done.

celery or smallage. The development of celeriac may well have been inspired by the Arab world, where people ate the roots of wild celery as a delicacy. Celeriac has never been as popular in Britain as it is in Europe, but it is hardier, easier to grow and less prone to problems than celery.

SITE, SOIL, SOWING AND PLANTING

This is a crop that needs patience and a combination of skill and luck to succeed. It takes eight months to mature. Celeriac will do well on a sunny well-fed site in soil with moisture-retentive tendencies. It will

247

even tolerate a bit of shade. You are probably best to sow celeriac in modules. Sow two seeds per module then thin out the weaker of them. Do this inside in February or early March. Harden off ready to plant out around mid May but do wait until the ground has warmed or they may bolt. Plant in rows if you like, but I prefer to block plant. In rows, plant seedlings 30cm apart with rows 45cm apart. In blocks, the plants should be spaced at 30cm. Plant out no deeper than they were in their pots but, as they like to be moist, it may be worth planting them in a slight depression to catch moisture.

ROUTINE CARE

Keep the bed well weeded and water very well in dry conditions. Mulching will help to retain moisture. As summer wears on, remove the celery-like leaves from the 'edges' of the plants to expose the increasingly bulbous root to the sun. Be careful to hold the root as you do this so as not to dislodge it. A weekly feed from midsummer on will help.

HARVESTING AND STORING

Celeriac can be harvested when you feel the roots are large enough – in practice, this will be from autumn onwards. It can be left in the ground until needed and can take -10°C, as long as it is not too wet. To be on the safe side, mulch with compost or straw to give some protection. Frost-proofing fleece is also an option. In the coldest and wettest climates, you may be better to lift them, removing the central cluster of leaves, and store as for other roots.

COMMON PROBLEMS

Poorly-sized or **non-swollen roots** seem to be a common problem. Both Ken and I have suffered from this and many Scottish growers have reported similar issues. Down south, the things seem to grow much better. Clearly there is a need to start celeriac as early as possible and, through the eight months it takes to mature, keep it well fed and watered. The Beechgrove Garden has managed to grow crops. Celeriac is relatively pest free but can be affected by **celery leaf miners**. If you notice the leaves blistering, remove and burn them. A covering of fine mesh may prevent attack by this wee beastie. **Slugs** may attack when the plants are young so bring your usual anti-slug armoury to bear.

CELERIAC VARIETIES

'**Giant Prague**' Long the most popular variety but probably superseded by the two below.
'**Monarch**' ♚ Large roots with firm white flesh. Smooth skinned so easy to peel and resistant to celery virus.
'**Prinz**' ♚ Early, large, smooth bulbs. The only one worth trying in Shetland, says Rosa Steppanova.

Parsnip (*Pastinaca sativa*) H5 E2

I have just discovered that poor old Boris Pasternak would be Boris Parsnip if he lived in an English-speaking country.

The name parsnip comes from the Latin, through the French, with the 'nip' ending to denote a supposed similarity to the turnip. Prized in the kitchen before the introduction of the potato because of its starchiness, it was also valued as an inexpensive sweetener and so was included in both savoury and sweet dishes, as well as being used for making wine and beer. Its popularity faded as the potato grew in ubiquity and sugar became less expensive. Some growers are put off, as they take a long time to mature – 35 weeks on average – but parsnips are an ideal vegetable in many parts of Scotland, as they can be happily left in the ground during winter. And they positively improve after a bit of frost, many say, as this turns more of the starch to sugar. Much of the flavour lies just below the skin and so they are best left unpeeled or very thinly peeled. Mashed with butter, on their own or mixed with potato, they are delicious, quick and easy. And curried parsnip soup, with or without crab apples or cookers, is just the thing for a freezing winter's day. Ken reckons the only way to eat them is parboiled and then roasted until caramelised, with chicken and roast potatoes.

SITE, SOIL, SOWING AND PLANTING

Parsnips need a sunny position and a deep but light soil manured the previous year or even the year before that. If your soil is not deep, then look for shorter-growing cultivars. As mentioned, parsnips need quite a long growing season so sow them in April or May as the soil warms. Do be warned, though, they are fickle germinators – in cold soils, they can take up to a month to appear above ground. Do not be tempted to pop them in early to give them a good start without heating your soil first with fleece or a cloche and leave this on after sowing until the seedlings appear. Stuart Oakley on Lewis has tried germinating parsnip seeds on cotton wool or blotting paper to give them an early start and to make monitoring germination easier. They are then quickly planted into modules and subsequently out into the soil once it has heated, which is May-ish in his part of Scotland.

Parsnip seeds are large, flat, very light and can be sown directly into drills 2.5cm deep with rows 30cm apart. Thin to roughly 15cm and do not attempt to transplant. Alternatively, sow in blocks at a spacing of 20cm between each plant. As with many vegetables, if you plant them closer together you can get a smaller, often sweeter, early cropping result. Since they take ages to mature, the rows can easily be used for the intercropping of salad leaves, radishes and other quick maturing crops. For containers, select large, deep pots with good drainage and plant the shorter varieties such as 'White Gem'.

Parsnip 'Tender and True' at Fyvie Castle, in Aberdeenshire. This is a very long-rooted variety so you will need deep soil.

Parsnips trimmed, cleaned and ready for the kitchen. It's best to store them where they grow rather than harvest more than you need.

Rather revolting-looking parsnip canker. Select canker-resistant varieties to help avoid this common problem.

Parsnips should not, in a normal year, need much irrigation. Water occasionally but well in a dry summer. Keep well weeded, taking care not to damage the top of the root.

HARVESTING AND STORING

Parsnips are best harvested when needed and eaten straight away. This is likely to be from November onwards for the long-rooted varieties. They may, however, be all but impossible to dig out in a hard frost – unless you have covered them with a mulch of straw or similar. They can be harvested and, with the leaves trimmed just above the root, stored in dry sand in your shed. If you are leaving them in the ground, you may be best to mark the rows, otherwise, when the leaves die down over winter, you may find them tricky to spot! Remember to dig deeply, with a long-tined fork, if you have one, to extricate them from the soil – or you will leave part of the delicious root behind! If you need to move them in early spring to prepare their patch for another crop, they can be lifted and heeled in elsewhere in your garden for a while.

COMMON PROBLEMS

Parsnips are susceptible to **carrot root fly** damage but, compared to carrots, we hear relatively few reports of serious problems. Companion planting with flowers or fleecing when the flies are about would both help to give protection. Don't plant them next to carrots, if you can help it. **Celery fly** can attack the leaves; simply remove any damaged leaves and destroy them. **Canker** (rotten brown patches in the flesh) is probably the most common problem our parsnips have suffered from. Rough hoeing can damage the root tops, letting the canker spores into the plant, so go canny with the tools. Liming soil to achieve a pH of 6.5–7 helps prevent it. Some authorities say that manured ground encourages canker but veg guru Joy Larkcom reckons that research does not bear this out. Although it is unsightly, canker can be cut out and the remains of the root used. There are canker-resistant varieties.

PARSNIP VARIETIES

Unless you want to produce show vegetables or you have perfect growing conditions, avoid the long varieties such as 'Hollow Crown Improved', as they need a huge depth of fertile, stone-free soil.

'**Albion**' ♀ Smooth with long tapering roots, resistant to canker.
'**Avonresister**' Good in less than ideal soils, short, resistant to canker and bruising. Patrick Kelsey recommends it for Sutherland and Rosa Steppanova for Shetland.
'**Gladiator**' F1 ♀ Wedge-shaped and resistant to canker. Medwyn Williams' choice as the most reliable variety – and does well on the Western Isles.
'**Tender and True**' ♀ Great flavour, roots of variable depth, resistant to canker. Happy on Lewis.
'**White Gem**' Quite short rooted, easily harvested, great flavour and resistant to canker. Tolerant of heavier soils.

Radish (*Raphinus sativus*) H3 E1

To encourage gardening in children, this is the vegetable that we often start them growing, not because they like to eat it, as they almost certainly won't, but because it is so very easy to sow and quick to appear (4–6 weeks) so demands little deferred gratification. It can be grown throughout the season and is a great catch crop, popped in a bed between the harvesting of one thing and the planting of the next, or can intercrop/partner slower-growing vegetables such as parsnips, thereby maximising the yield of your plot.

I was not a great fan of radishes until a stay in France as an au pair girl a lifetime ago taught me to love them served as a starter with unsalted butter and a piece of baguette. And of course I remember helping my mum to prepare little radish 'flowers' to grace her 1960s dinner parties. There are now many radish varieties available to grow and not just the little peppery red-and-white root of fond memory.

Winter radish is interesting. Grown to be cooked, it turns mild and delicious in stews, soups or stir-fries. Mooli radish (Hindu name) is also known by its Japanese name, daikon, and sometimes called Chinese radish just to confuse the issue. These are large and long but still quick-growing roots.

Radishes have been around for so long that their origins are all but lost. They were probably introduced into Britain, the Romans notwithstanding, in the sixteenth century. They come in a variety of shapes and colours ranging from white through red to nearly black. They were commonly used as an appetite stimulant. The summer variety is the small pop-in-the-mouth salad plant. The winter type, weighing in at up to 250g, is more like a small turnip.

SITE, SOIL, SOWING AND PLANTING

Radishes are pretty forgiving and, sown in any soil, as long as it is moist enough, will give a good crop. From choice, they would select a rich, moist soil raked to a fine tilth in which to give of their best. Sow a few seeds at a time for a long cropping period, in a sunny position, from April (with protection if cold) or May to June or July. They can bolt or turn so hard as to be inedible if they get too dry in summer. If the garden is very warm and sunny, look for partial shade for later sowings.

If you sow them carefully, spacing them to about 2.5cm, you should have little need to thin. But do thin if necessary, as overcrowding may lead to a poor crop.

Winter radish is fairly rare in the kitchen garden but it is not hard to grow. It should be sown in mid to

Multicoloured summer radishes are very quick growing, so pop them in amongst other crops from spring through summer.

Mooli radish from Caroline's garden. 'Mino early' is a popular and mild-tasting variety and fairly jumps out of the ground.

late summer in drills about 1cm deep and in rows 30 cm apart. Thin to 13–15cm. You can leave these in the ground and harvest them as needed, best under a protective mulch of straw or fleece.

ROUTINE CARE, HARVESTING AND STORING

Keep radishes well watered and weed free. Be sure to thin appropriately and harvest as soon as they are ready or they will quickly run to seed and become woody.

The small summer radishes are harvested and used fresh. They are not stored. However, the larger winter varieties can be lifted and stored in sand or light soil in your shed.

COMMON PROBLEMS

Radishes are actually brassicas so may suffer from the usual brassica problems, although the short space of time between sowing and harvesting means this is unlikely. Radish failure is usually due to cultural issues – **overcrowding** or **lack of water** leading to small inedible roots. You may be unlucky enough to suffer from **flea beetle**, which will leave the radish leaves spattered with little round holes. This happens in April/May time. It may weaken the plants, especially if still at the seedling stage. A very fine mesh covering will prevent it.

RADISH VARIETIES

Summer Radishes

'**Amethyst**' ♀ Purple, flattened, round shape, distinctive leaves.

'**Cherry Belle**' ♀ Very popular, red with white centre, can remain in the ground for some time without going pithy.

'**French Breakfast**' ♀ Red and white, hot if not harvested young.

'**Rougette**' ♀ Very fast growing, short tops, rounded, uniform shape.

'**Scarlet Globe**' ♀ Globe shaped, red skinned, quick maturing and good for forcing in early spring.

'**Red Prince**' Globe shaped, all red, grows larger than most without becoming woody.

'**Saxerre**' Red, globe shaped, good for early sowing under cloches.

'**Sparkler**' ♀ Red roots with a white base.

Winter Radishes

'**Black Spanish Round**' Dark skin, white inside, recommended by Patricia Stephens at Phantassie Farm, East Lothian, and Stuart Oakley of Lewis. Eaten raw (very spicy) or cooked.

'**Mino Early**' (mooli) 30cm-long, cylindrical roots with a flavour which is milder and perhaps more acceptable for salads than the other winter varieties.

'**Neptune**' F1 (mooli) Produces a 25cm root, pure white and mild tasting. Grows on Lewis.

'**China Rose**' Tapering, pink root, peppery. Grows well at Phantassie Farm.

Salsify (*Tragopogon porrifolius*) and Scorzonera (*Scorzonera hispanica*) *H4-5 E1*

Salsify was probably eaten by the Greeks and Romans but was first cultivated in Italy and France in the sixteenth century. In Britain, it was initially grown for its edible flowers. Scorzonera was originally known as black or Spanish salsify. Its early cultivation was for medical purposes, with its culinary uses not documented until the late seventeenth century. The flavour of scorzonera is reckoned to be better than that of salsify and it is high in vitamin C and potassium.

Rarely available in the shops and quite easy to

please in Scotland, salsify is biennial and scorzonera perennial but both can be grown as annuals. I have had great success with them and they are grown for the vegetable boxes at Phantassie Farm, East Lothian. Although the flower buds, flower petals and young shoots are edible, they are now rarely used. The roots have a delicate flavour that some (but not me) liken to oyster or to artichoke, which is a little nearer the mark.

To cook them, clean and peel the dark roots, dropping them straight into water with a little added lemon juice to prevent browning. Note that some reckon that peeling *after* cooking affords the best flavour. Cut into reasonable-sized pieces and boil in a little water until soft. Serve with butter and lemon juice.

SITE, SOIL, SOWING, HARVESTING AND STORING

As with most root crops, they prefer a stone-free site, a light soil and a bed manured the previous year. Sow the seeds in mid to late April, or later in cooler parts of the country, directly into the ground in drills 1.5cm deep with rows 30cm apart. Thin to 12cm – and don't be tempted to transplant. Block planting is fine and, in this case, space at 20cm apart all round. Keep the weeds at bay, being careful not to damage the root crowns, and water during dry spells. A mulch will help to keep the soil moist.

Both salsify and scorzonera take 26–30 weeks to mature. The roots will be ready by late autumn and can be harvested until spring, lifting them as you need them – frost permitting. They are delicate and easily broken so ease them out carefully to waste none of the delicious flesh. You may want to mulch them with straw if you are leaving them in the soil, and leaving them there apparently improves their flavour. If you do lift them, store in the shed in boxes of dry soil. Thin scorzonera roots can be left in the ground for a further year to enlarge.

COMMON PROBLEMS

Salsify and scorzonera are rarely troubled by pests and diseases and, planted next to carrots, scorzonera apparently discourages carrot fly.

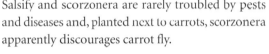

Scorzonera flowers and the rather rustic-looking roots which, if fiddly to prepare, taste great.

SALSIFY AND SCORZONERA VARIETIES

In practice, you may have little choice in the seed available to you and not all of them will be named varieties. I think all are fine.

Swede and Turnip

Though they are brassicas, swedes and turnips are usually counted as roots and have been part of the Scottish diet for 200 years, eaten as vegetables as well as used to feed animals through the long winter months. Without them, both humans and animals would have starved. You won't find many fancy recipes for them, though, as they are not considered gourmet by most food writers. Like many Scots, I have spent my whole life *not* using the word 'swede' and I am not sure if that is through ignorance or culture. The big orange things we spent hours making into lanterns for Halloween we called turnips (or neeps) and we also grew snowball turnips – the wee white things that I loved to eat with mince. But it seems that botanically this is not correct. Turnips have white flesh and tend to be smaller, while swedes are usually larger, hardier, with purple skin and yellow flesh. And it is swede that we eat as 'neeps' with tatties and haggis.

Turnips and swede are related, of course. The swede (or neep!) is probably European in origin and arrived in Britain in the seventeenth century from Sweden – hence the name, which is short for 'Swedish turnip'. Thought to be a turnip–cabbage hybrid, it is hardier and gives a heavier yield than turnip and it has a longer growing season. We Scots have adopted swedes as one of our national vegetables, mashed with lots of butter and pepper, and don't take nearly so much interest in turnips. The James Hutton Institute in Invergowrie has bred several important commercial swede varieties such as 'Gowrie', as well as the popular garden variety 'Invitation'.

The turnip, smaller and sharper flavoured, is thought to be one of the oldest cultivated vegetables.

In classical times, the root – actually the swollen base of the stem – was eaten roasted whole, which intensified its natural sweetness. It was popularised in Britain in the eighteenth century by landowner Viscount 'Turnip' Townshend from Norfolk. In Scotland, we still tend to eat them plain boiled but in some countries they are pickled and preserved.

Turnip and swede tops (foliage) are, according to Joy Larkcom, worth trying. They are available in early spring when other vegetables are thin on the ground and are said to be healthier even than spinach.

Swede (*Brassica napus ssp. rapifera*) H5 E1

SITE, SOIL, SOWING AND PLANTING

An open site is the best but avoid anywhere too dry. As with all brassicas, swedes like a nitrogen-rich, firm soil with a tendency towards the alkaline. So liming at least a month before planting is a good idea. If manuring, do it the previous autumn. Swedes are not especially hungry so do not require a very high level of soil fertility. They are one of the easiest vegetables to grow – sow, thin, wait and harvest.

Sow the small seeds directly and thinly into the soil in a drill 1cm deep. Rows should be 43cm apart. If planting in blocks, space 30cm apart. Sow in mid April in areas where the ground is warm enough or a little later where it warms more slowly. Thin the seedlings when they are large enough to handle. They should eventually be thinned to 20–25cm apart.

ROUTINE CARE, HARVESTING
AND STORING

Keep the ground weeded and water well in dry weather. Rain after a dry spell may split the roots. Start to harvest when you feel the roots are large enough for your purposes, which is likely to be from autumn. They can be left in the ground for a while but you are probably best to lift them by Christmas as the roots will begin to get woody if left much longer. Store in a dark and frost-free shed in boxes of dry sand or light soil. Will keep for ages in the fridge, although the quality and flavour diminish.

COMMON PROBLEMS

Root brassicas are generally not as prone to diseases as the leafy kinds, but you may be particularly troubled with **club root** and **cabbage root fly** (*see* p. 168 for details on these). For the former, there is not much to be done once it is in evidence but to remove the plant and destroy it away from the garden. As preventative measures, ensure the soil is well limed and well drained. And remember to keep a rotation going so pests and diseases do not build up. For the cabbage root fly, a covering of fine mesh or fleece will sort the problem. **Mildew** can be a problem on foliage if sown early. If you sow in May, you should avoid it. **Flea beetle** can attack the young foliage on seedlings but mesh will offer protection.

SWEDE VARIETIES

'**Brora**' ♀ ✉ Bred at the James Hutton Institute, good sweet flavour.

'**Champion Purple Top**' Tough, large growing and still popular after 150 years.

'**Invitation**' ✉ Dundee raised, vigorous, club-root and mildew resistant and said to be the hardiest variety. Freezes well. A good choice for the Western Isles.

'**Joan**' Reddish-purple skin, looked fine at Dundonnell in Wester Ross.

'**Marian**' Dr Hessayon's choice, club-root resistant and high yielding with good flavour. Does on Lewis and Rosa Steppanova rates it for Shetland.

'**Ruby**' ♀ Very sweet and with good overwintering hardiness. Dark-purple skin. Good in Orkney.

Swede seems less popular now than it was but is worth growing as a hardy and hearty winter root.

Turnip (*Brassica rapa*) H4–5 E1

SITE, SOIL, SOWING AND PLANTING

Site and soil are as for swedes above, although turnips are hungry so ensure the soil is hearty. Turnips are fast growing so are good as a catch crop or for intercropping. For a very early crop, start the seeds in a cold greenhouse in modules or sow them *in situ* under cloches. Otherwise, sow the small seeds directly into the ground in a drill 1cm deep. Rows should be 20–25cm apart for the smaller, early varieties and 30cm apart for the larger maincrop varieties. Start to sow in mid April in areas where the ground has warmed, although May is time enough and helps to avoid mildew on the foliage. Succession-sow as you wish. Where conditions are less

Turnip 'Purple Top Milan' is a very early, flattish variety. In addition to the roots, you can eat a picking of the very young leaves in a mixed salad.

Turnip 'Snowball' is a quick-growing and mild variety which can be sown as a catch crop. Try eating them small, thinly peeled, boiled whole and with lots of butter.

conducive – in the windswept Western Isles, for example – you can grow turnips in a polytunnel. And there is even a variety now being promoted as suitable as a 'patio vegetable' – 'Primera', an F1 hybrid.

Thin the seedlings when they are large enough to handle. They grow quickly, so keep an eye on them. The earlier varieties should eventually be thinned to 10cm, the main crop to 15cm.

Sow turnips you are growing for greens in the autumn to overwinter. They should be sown in rows 10cm apart and will not need to be thinned.

ROUTINE CARE, HARVESTING AND STORING

Keep the ground weeded and water well in dry weather. Rain after a dry spell may split the roots. Harvest early varieties small and eat raw or cooked. Harvest maincrop turnips in early autumn or before – don't let them get hot and woody. Unlike the small earlies, they may need the help of a garden fork to lift them. Also unlike the earlies, they can be stored in your increasingly full garden shed in dry sand or light soil.

COMMON PROBLEMS

As for swedes.

TURNIP VARIETIES

'**Atlantic**' ♛ Early to mid season, quick maturing, purple top. Rosa Steppanova's pick for Shetland.

'**Golden Ball**' Flesh yellowish, rounded shape, good storage.

'**Invitation**' ♛ Mildew and club-root resistant variety.

'**Oasis**' ♛ Thompson and Morgan claim this is the turnip for those who don't like turnips. Sweet, juicy flavour, can be eaten raw in salads. Ken grew this in 2011 and, though it did not really taste like melon, as claimed, it made good salads.

'**Primera**' F1 ♛ For patio growing – small, sweet and used raw or cooked.

'**Purple Top Milan**' Purple with white roots, frost tolerant, stores well and good under cover.

'**Snowball**' Very popular, quick growing and can be harvested in as little as 4–6 weeks from sowing, rounded in shape, creamy white skin and mild flavour. Happy even in the Western Isles.

CHAPTER 8

Other Vegetables

Asparagus (*Asparagus officinalis*) H4–5 E3

Prized by the Greeks and Romans, this vegetable still has a slight frisson of exclusivity. That is no doubt helped by the fact that its local season is so very short and, unless you are eating the stuff flown in from Peru, you will only have access to it in Scotland for six or so weeks a year. Asparagus also has attached to it some alleged medicinal uses, including increasing libido, acting as a laxative and, recently, as an aid to sufferers of cancer, although the research on the latter appears less convincing. Whether it does all these things or not, it is incontrovertibly good for you – full of folic acid, various other vitamins and lots of fibre. Asparagus is grown commercially in Angus by the Pattullos and in East Lothian, and top Scottish chefs rave about the quality.

Asparagus growing requires both patience (three years from seed) and self-denial (the more you harvest, the less you'll have next year). And, although we have observed successful growers in many parts of the country, from Mertoun in the Borders and Lewis out west to as far north as Shetland by way of Dunrobin Castle in Golspie, many gardeners have given up in frustration. If you have the space, it is worth all the extra effort. Ken's mother religiously divides up the smallish crop every year so all the family get the same tiny number of spears! The flavour of asparagus freshly cut from your garden, steamed for a few minutes and then dipped in melted butter and eaten in your fingers is just unmatchable.

SITE, SOIL, SOWING AND PLANTING

As a perennial vegetable, you will need a garden large enough or want the vegetable enough to devote a decent-sized bed to the growing of it. An asparagus bed should remain productive for up to 20 years if it is well tended.

Well-drained soil is key to successful asparagus. Choose a light soil, if possible, with good organic

Rora Paglieri at Carestown Steading, near Buckie, beside her deep raised bed of asparagus, past harvest time.

content. A sunny, sheltered spot is ideal. Ensure the patch is free of perennial weeds. Dig in well-rotted manure the previous autumn. To keep pests and diseases at bay, do not seek to establish an asparagus bed on ground that has already been used for that purpose or for potatoes. We'd recommend purchasing one-year-old crowns from a reputable source. The Pattullos of Eassie (pattulloeassie@btinternet.com) will supply. A crown is a stump with finger-like roots. To plant crowns, make a trench 30cm wide and 20cm deep. Next make a little mound of soil about 7cm high along the middle of the trench. Now place your rooty pieces on top of the mound and arrange the roots down the sides. Space them at least 30cm apart. Carefully begin to fill the trench with soil. Do this gradually, starting with 5cm on planting and finishing with a level site in autumn. Plant them as soon as possible after purchase, as they dry out very quickly – around mid April is a reasonable time. Once planted, you will have to wait until the third year before you start a (modest) harvest – difficult but possible! To save money, you can grow from seed. Sow seeds in early spring in modules under protection and, after hardening off, plant out in early summer in a little furrow. Fill the furrow at season's end.

You can grow asparagus indoors in polytunnels, as the Beechgrove Garden proved with the variety 'Cito'. But the plants don't like being hot and dry so you may need to invest in good irrigation and ventilation.

Asparagus produces the beautiful ferny fronds beloved of flower arrangers but don't let them cut too many, as this simply reduces next year's yield. Once the fronds turn brown in early autumn, cut them back to 10cm.

ROUTINE CARE

In 1683, John Reid noted that 'weeds will quyt destroy them' (*The Scots Gard'ner*) and this remains true. Keep the beds clean, probably by hand not hoe so as not to damage the developing tips. Joy Larkcom suggests under-planting asparagus with parsley and letting it self-seed. Presumably this may eventually push out weeds. Beyond keeping the bed well weeded, an annual mulch of compost or manure at the end of the year will nourish the crop. Manure, if you have access to it, acts both as feed and weed-suppressing mulch. Ian Crisp, gardener at Dunrobin Castle, loads five tons of seaweed on to his large asparagus bed every year. I put some on our asparagus bed and it certainly acted as an impenetrable weed barrier. Salt is often mentioned in connection with the growing of asparagus. Maybe both the salt and the seaweed connections link back to the plant's coastal heritage. Sandy Pattullo used to spread salt and reckoned that it did help to keep soil-borne diseases at bay. Too expensive to do now!

You may need to support the ferns with canes later in the season before they need to be cut back, as wind rock can lead to rot entering plants. Watch not to damage the crowns as you do this. You will only have to water in the driest of summers. Ken noted that, on German asparagus farms, most of the crop was blanched. He thought the flavour and texture were reduced somewhat.

HARVESTING AND STORING

After establishing your asparagus bed, remember not to crop it until the third year. This takes some self-control. And, to nurture a sustainable crop, you must only harvest the asparagus for around six weeks of the year – approximately late May to early July. Make that only four weeks for your first harvest and stop around midsummer. Later harvesting will weaken the crowns and next year's crop will tend to be poor.

Take them whilst the heads are still firm and tight, probably at around 13cm to 18cm long, cutting them with a very sharp knife level with the soil. The fatter stalks are likely to be more succulent than the pencil-thin ones. In season, you may have to harvest daily – life's tough!

Store in the fridge for a couple of days if you must but do try to eat them within an hour of picking. Asparagus freezes well but is not the same as when fresh. After freezing, it's best used for soups, soufflés and quiches.

COMMON PROBLEMS

The Beechgrove Garden's once flourishing bed seemed to become infected with **fungal disease fusarium** or **phytophthora**, probably due to a drainage issue. Also caused by poor drainage is **violet crown rot**. For any of these problems, you probably need to dig everything up and start again in a raised bed. **Orange-spotted asparagus beetle** can attack foliage. Squidge them if you can. **Slugs** may attack the fresh spears – at their peril. In cold inland gardens, **late frosts** can destroy your just-about-ready-to-pick crop, so keep some fleece handy. **Rabbits** and **hares** will also help themselves.

ASPARAGUS VARIETIES

The all-male cultivars listed below don't self-sow and are the most widely planted varieties these days. They are said to produce more succulent spears and be higher yielding. Dutch or French varieties are reckoned by Sandy Pattullo to be the very best for Scotland – better than the American or New Zealand crowns on offer.

'**Backlim**' F1 ⚥ A Dutch variety, high yielding.
'**Cito**' Not very commonly offered but did well in *Beechgrove Garden* trials. Spear tips tend to open quickly in very warm weather so may need quick picking. The Pattullos reckon this has the best flavour.
'**Conover's Collosal**' ⚥ Early, heavy yielding, a Bob Flowerdew favourite. Rora Paglieri from Carestown Steading near Buckie has grown this very successfully.

'**Gijnlim**' F1 ⚥ Another Dutch variety, good yields of green spears with purple tips.
'**Stewart's Purple**' A New Zealand variety, tender with purple spears, very sweet.

Florence Fennel (*Foeniculum vulgare* var. *azoricum*) H2 E3

I can't get enough of this delicious aniseed-flavoured vegetable, rich in potassium and folic acid. I have found it quite a challenge to grow well, but I like it too much to give up! Probably developed in Italy in the seventeenth century, it is grown for its swollen bulb-like base. Its feathery leaves are delicious too and my father dries these every year and uses them for his home-made gravadlax instead of dill.

Extremely thinly sliced, using a mandolin if you have one, and then dropped into a bowl of iced water for a while, fennel is a sophisticated and subtle salad ingredient. It can be cooked in a number of ways, including griddled, roasted with other vegetables in the oven or poached with just enough water and olive oil to cook it, then finished with a little butter and grated parmesan cheese.

Florence fennel at Castle Fraser, in Aberdeenshire, ready to harvest.

SITE, SOIL, SOWING AND PLANTING

Deciding when to sow your seeds is the first challenge. They are originally Mediterranean marsh plants and, if you plant them too early, the cold is likely to cause them to bolt. Expose them to a dry spell and this will make them bolt too. Plant them too late and they may not have time to fatten up. You see the problem. Fennel needs a humus-rich, moisture-retentive, well-drained soil in a warm and sunny position. Sow the seeds in short and shallow 1cm drills in a block formation, with the drills 30cm apart. Thin the seedlings, which will not happily transplant, to 30cm apart. I generally sow my fennel seeds outside at the start of June.

If your soil is late in warming, fennel can be very successfully started in modules and then planted out when the ground is warm enough. Start it in late March. It can also be grown to maturity in 13cm pots.

ROUTINE CARE

Keep the plants well watered to prevent them from bolting. Mulching helps. Though not all experts agree, once the bulb is the size of a golf ball, earth it up to cover half the swelling. This blanches the plants. Continue this earthing up until the fennel bulb is the required size.

HARVESTING, STORING
AND COMMON PROBLEMS

Once the fennel is a good size, cut it at the base with a sharp knife. This is likely to be late summer or very early autumn. Certainly harvest before hard frosts. If you leave the roots in the ground, they will resprout and you can use these greens in salad. You can blanch and freeze fennel but it is probably at its best eaten fresh. Apart from a powerful tendency to **bolt**, fennel is not very troubled with pests and diseases. Watch out for **slugs** early on.

FLORENCE FENNEL VARIETIES

'**Colossal**' Grows well, bolt resistant.
'**Finale**' Bolt resistant, large bulbs.
'**Romanesco**' Large, round bulbs, bolt resistant.
'**Sirio**' Large, white bulbs of sweet flavour.
'**Sweet Florence**' Traditional variety, high yielding.
'**Victorio**' F1 ♀ Greenish-white, uniform shape.

Globe Artichoke (*Cynara scolymus*) and Cardoon (*Cynara cardunculus*) H4–5 E2

The statuesque globe artichoke produces one of the finest vegetables for my money. Ken is a big fan too. Even if you don't like the taste, the giant thistles and jagged leaves look so good in the border. I have found it relatively easy to grow. When small, once cooked, nearly the whole flower bud can be eaten. If left to swell before harvesting and boiling, the pointed bracts of the flower can be pulled one by one, dipped in a sharp vinaigrette (me) or melted salted butter (Ken) and the bottom edge nibbled to get a tiny hint of what is to come – the heart in the centre. The epitome of slow food too! The heart itself can be added to a mixed salad and to a range of other dishes. It always seems wonderfully fancy to me. Unharvested, the flower head that develops is most beautiful and can be dried and kept. They seem to grow well across Scotland – in the Borders, Perthshire, Ayrshire, a sheltered spot on Lewis, in the walled garden at Castle of Mey, Caithness, and they seem very at home indeed in many parts of Orkney mainland.

The **cardoon** is a cousin of the globe artichoke, standing up to 2m tall, with its large flower heads providing visual excitement as well as a rather hard-won food crop. The small flower hearts can be cooked and eaten like artichokes – although the taste is not so good. You can also apparently blanch the stalks and eat them boiled as the Romans used to do. I haven't tried this and, since Dr Hessayon suggests that the result is like 'tough and stringy celery', I don't think I'll bother. For most gardeners the cardoon is a striking ornamental rather than edible plant.

SITE, SOIL, SOWING AND PLANTING

Both John Reid (1685) and Joy Larkcom (2002) recommend growing artichokes from offsets which can be bought from the garden centre or taken from the outside of an established plant. Do this in late spring in Scotland, just as the plant is about to sprout. Carefully scrape away the soil from the roots on one side of the plant and use a spade to cut off a section or sections with some roots attached. Choose those that are around 20cm high. It is best to leave at least three shoots on the mother plants and, if your offsets are small, then plant several as a clump. Plant them deeper than they were originally, as they tend to be pushed out of the soil by the roots later on. You might also remove the leaf tips to decrease transpiration and to give the roots a chance to develop. The offsets need wind shelter and protection from frost and drying out until they get going.

Having said all that, and in my usual state of ignorant enthusiasm, I started my plants many years back from seed and have had great success (luck) with them. You'd be advised to raise seedlings in modules undercover and plant out once hardened off, when frost danger has passed.

Artichokes need a rich but well-drained soil in a sunny, sheltered position. They are very tall, so do not do well in wind and they may need a little protection over winter in colder gardens. Before planting, dig in plenty of compost or well-rotted manure, ideally the previous autumn. If trying seed, sow in spring in drills 2.5cm deep or start indoors in late winter in modules. Thin outdoor-raised seedlings to 25cm apart and transplant the strongest-looking specimens the following spring into their permanent position at spacings of 90cm at the back of a border, or at least in a position where they will not crowd or shade neighbours. They are a semi-permanent planting, so bear that in mind too, as you

Globe artichokes at Fyvie Castle, in Aberdeenshire. Inland, you may need to protect the crown of plants to get them through a Scottish winter.

select a site. They should last five to ten years before needing to be replaced, so continue to take offsets to keep a succession going.

ROUTINE CARE, HARVESTING AND STORING

Keep well watered, especially in dry spells. Mulch with well-rotted manure in late spring to feed and to retain soil moisture. Keep weeds down. Protect over winter by mulching with leaves or straw or even a piece of frost-grade fleece.

For new plants, you will get a better and longer-lasting result if you shun the probably small harvest in the first year. Cut the developing buds off and discard them. For plants in their second year and beyond, remove the first couple of small heads that develop in spring (then boil and eat them!), as this will encourage more buds to develop and therefore more delicious artichoke hearts will be available to you – and to friends, if you are more generous than I am. Start cropping with the top bud first – what Dr Hessayon calls the 'king head'. Take about 5cm of stalk too, as this is also quite edible when cooked. Remember to pick the heads before they begin to open up. You can eat the 'choke' or hairy part at the heart when very young (as it is virtually non-existent) but older heads should have the choke scraped off and discarded. Artichokes will last a few days in the fridge raw and two days once boiled. You can preserve the hearts in oil and there are plenty of recipes around to show you how this is done.

COMMON PROBLEMS

Slugs may attack succulent new shoots in spring. The most likely problem is a flower-head **blackfly** infestation. Soak harvested heads in salted water before cooking and this will get rid of most of them. Where they appear, I try to spray them away with water – not always successfully! Plant some ladybird-attractive plant beside the artichokes to encourage their natural predators. Mine are under-planted with *Limnanthes douglasii* (poached egg plant), for example.

GLOBE ARTICHOKE VARIETIES

'**Green Globe**' and '**Green Globe Improved**' The best-known green varieties.

'**Vert de Laon**' Said to be relatively hardy.

'**Violeta di Chioggia**' Vegetable-hater the late John Cushnie, gardener and *Gardeners' Question Time* panellist, loved this as it is so ornamental. The flower heads are a rich purple colour. '**Purple Globe**' is similar.

Jerusalem Artichoke (*Helianthus tuberosus*) H5 E1

A curiously named plant that has nothing to do with Jerusalem or artichokes – that name possibly comes from the anglicisation of the Italian word *girasole*,

Freshly harvested Jerusalem artichokes.

meaning sunflower, and the taste was once likened to globe artichoke hearts. It is, in fact, a North American plant and a member of the sunflower family, with edible tubers. It was much favoured by Native Americans in Canada.

Jerusalem artichokes probably arrived in Britain via Holland in the early seventeenth century and, like spinach, were initially used in sweetened dishes. They quickly lost favour, not least because of their infamous capacity to cause wind – this tendency resulting in their being renamed 'fartichokes' in recent times.

We have seen – in West Lothian, Dundee, Lewis and Torridon – Jerusalem artichokes used in gardens and allotments as an internal boundary, windbreak (oh, the irony) or screen, with the tubers seldom or never harvested. They are very effective in this role, growing in excess of 2m high and attractive into the bargain, with their large yellow flowers. In really windy sites, you'll need to shelter them when newly planted, as wind rock will cause small and very knobbly tubers to form. Once you plant them it is quite hard to get rid of them, as you have to find and remove every vestige of tuber or they sprout again in spring. We have them planted in a piece of spare ground just outside our vegetable garden and they grow away there quite happily.

Jerusalem artichokes are probably best scrubbed and cooked in their skins to be peeled after or not at all. If you are peeling the knobbly things raw, put them into a bowl of water with a drop of lemon juice or vinegar to prevent them turning grey. They make good soup and are fine pureed and mixed with mashed potato or used as a bed for scallops, with which they go well. Nigel Slater loves them roasted in olive oil, mixed with potatoes and lemon wedges. He eats them skin and all. They can also be eaten raw, thinly sliced or grated into salads. I have tried this and they are rather tasteless but very crunchy.

SITE, SOIL, SOWING AND PLANTING

If you need huge quantities, Jerusalem artichokes produce a better crop if they are started afresh each year in a different patch. But, as a small amount is enough for most people, this is not usually a consideration. They are tolerant of most conditions except a waterlogged soil and so can be popped in anywhere that allows them to express their full size without compromising other crops. Dig in some compost or well-rotted manure the autumn before planting. Tubers are available from garden centres in early spring or you can plant those bought from a grocer or begged from a friend who has plenty. Plant them in early spring 10cm to 15cm deep and around 30cm apart, with rows 90cm apart. Once the plants are 30cm tall, earth them up to give them a little more support.

ROUTINE CARE

Keep watered in dry spells and weeded, although weeds won't stand much of a chance once these large plants get going. If you are planning to harvest the artichokes, nip out the growing tip of the plants when they are no more than 2m tall, possibly less if you are shorter yourself, and remove any flower buds that develop too. This will help concentrate growing effort towards tuber production. Stake the plants later in the season to support them against inclement weather. Or, if you have them in a block, surround the block with a fence of chicken wire and sturdy canes or similar. When the plants start dying back, cut the stems down to about 25cm.

HARVESTING AND STORING

Leave the artichokes in the soil and harvest as you need them – generally from late October onwards. Dig carefully so as not to damage the tubers. You may want to protect them from bad frosts with a covering of straw or earth them up so they are covered with a good depth of soil. If you are rotating, at the end of the season, remove all trace of tubers or they will, like potatoes, continue to produce just where they are not wanted – but save some good specimens to replant next year.

You can store artichokes in the fridge for a week or so, if you have to, and you can freeze them cooked. **Slugs** are the only problem we have encountered, but we have so many tubers I can afford to sacrifice a few to them. Everyone seems to grow the same variety, '**Fuseau**'.

Sea Kale (*Crambe maritima*) ✉ *H5 E2*

Quite different from kale, this hardy perennial British native is drought tolerant and can be forced and harvested in early spring when little else is available in the garden. Small plants called 'thongs', raised from root cuttings, should be planted and spaced at 45cm. Allow them to grow for the first season, then remove all yellow foliage in the autumn. To blanch the stems *in situ*, the dormant crown of the plants must be forced by covering them in late winter with a 7cm pile of dry leaves and then a bucket or large flowerpot with the hole blocked to exclude all light. A rhubarb forcer is ideal. Cut the blanched stems when they are about 20cm tall. Dunrobin Castle has

Sea kale is eaten in the winter months as forced shoots and then allowed to grow away. Leaves can be eaten too, raw or cooked.

rustic little bespoke terracotta sea kale forcers to encourage these succulent sprouts to develop. Plants will need replaced every seven years or so. It is little troubled by pests and diseases.

As well as their famous asparagus, the Pattullos of Eassie grow sea kale and, as probably the only commercial supplier in the UK, their produce is much sought after. Indeed, Rowley Leigh of Le Café Anglais in London has told Sandy Pattullo he is 'heroic' and 'a saint' for growing it. Such passions vegetables stir! You can sometimes find this to buy in garden centres as an ornamental or you can buy plants from the Pattullos – or try some of their harvested sea kale, available from January to March (pattulloeassie@btinternet.com). The flavour is faint celery, maybe a little nutty, but succulent and sweet. It is good raw, steamed or stir-fried.

Sweetcorn (*Zea mays*) H1C E3

No one knows exactly where maize comes from, as it has never been found as a wild plant. Essentially a giant mutant grass, the staple food of much of Central America and the South American Andes, it is often grown with beans climbing up it and squash scrambling at its base. Scotland's relative lack of heat and sun and the short growing season mean that, if you want to ripen it outdoors, you need a warm site, early maturing supersweet varieties, a good start in the spring and at least some decent summer weather. We saw fine beds of corn growing all round the country from Fyvie in Aberdeenshire and Mertoun in the Borders to Culzean in Ayrshire. It will grow well in a greenhouse or tunnel too and the *Beechgrove Garden* grew it under a temporary greenhouse which was removed in late summer.

Although Columbus is reputed to have brought the cobs to Europe, there exists an alternative view suggesting that maize actually made its way to Europe around the world westwards from America via Asia, and did so long before Columbus's voyage. That would certainly explain the presence of stone carvings of corncobs in the chapel at Rosslyn in Midlothian, which was built 50 years before Columbus set sail.

Corn grows with both the male and female flowers on the same stem. The male flowers sit above and produce a tassel that will hopefully shower pollen on to the female flowers. They then produce the cobs of immature seeds that we eat. Interestingly, the seeds are enveloped by modified leaves which, if not removed, cause the whole cob to rot on the stem. So maize is now co-dependent on humans for its survival, as it needs to be carefully unwrapped.

Corn is a statuesque plant, not out of place at the back of a flower border although, as pollination occurs most efficiently when corn is block planted, you may need to hand pollinate if you plant them singly.

Corn on the cob can be used for a range of purposes but the best remains as a succulent vehicle for lashings of melted butter, sea salt and freshly ground pepper. When you get it right and the sun shines sufficiently to ripen the cobs well, the flavour of newly harvested home-grown corn is impressive. It is suggested that, for maximum succulence, you should add salt after cooking and not before.

SITE, SOIL, SOWING AND PLANTING

As already stated, sweetcorn needs warmth, shelter and a fairly long growing season in a suntrap. For most of the country, but certainly for northern and cold inland areas and the Western Isles, you will need a greenhouse or polytunnel. Growing in tunnels is easy and the same method is used both inside and out – plant in a block in moisture-retentive soil which is carefully watered and regularly fed.

Start the seeds off under protection in April, as they won't germinate outdoors in soils colder than 13°C (55°F). You can pre-germinate them on damp tissue paper in a polythene bag kept in an airing cupboard and pot them up when you see the first tiny sprout. Or sow in deep modules or 7cm pots 2cm deep. For transplanting outdoors, harden off well and wait until any danger of frost is past, unless you can cover them. Planting next to a south wall or greenhouse will give extra reflected heat to ripen them. They need to be transplanted when quite small and handled carefully so as not to damage the roots. Once pot bound, corn plants seldom flourish. Space your plants at 45cm apart all round in a block formation to help the pollination process. Under protection, without the help of a breeze, pollination is encouraged by tapping the tassels (male flowers) at the top of the plants. Sweetcorn varieties tend to cross-pollinate readily, which can cause disappointing cobs, so it is best to stick to a single variety. You can grow corn in growbags or large containers. It is probably advisable in this case to go for the more dwarf forms such as 'Snobaby' or 'Minor'.

ROUTINE CARE, HARVESTING AND STORING

Corn is shallow rooted and easily damaged by careless hoeing. This can be avoided by under-planting with some kind of squash to keep the weeds down. At Castle Fraser, Aberdeenshire, a crop of salads was

Sweetcorn seedlings nearly ready for planting out in the polytunnel.

Sweetcorn inter-planted with lettuce at Fyvie Castle, Aberdeenshire.

Supersweet (and it was) sweetcorn 'Conqueror' F1 from Caroline's tunnel. The white nibs are due to poor pollination.

successfully grown under the corn – a good idea if you are short of space. Water well while the cobs are swelling. A little liquid feed at this stage will do no harm either. Staking will not be needed under protection but may be required if you are trying corn outside. If roots appear at the base of the stems, cover with a mulch of compost. You should expect no more than two cobs from each plant. Inspect your cobs once the silks at the cob tips start to turn brown, earlier with dwarf varieties. Expose an edge of the cob and push your nail into one of the kernels. If a milky liquid appears, then the cob is ready. A clear liquid suggests it is not quite ripe. A very thick milky liquid means you may have left it too late. Do keep an eye on them, as overripe corn is quite inedible. Carefully twist the cob off the stem when ready – which is likely to be in August.

Cook the cobs as quickly as possible after harvest, as the sweetness soon turns to starch. The 'supersweet' and 'tendersweet' varieties now available do store for longer in the fridge but, still, the fresher the better. Remove the husks first. Popcorn is made from dried cobs. There are some varieties specifically bred for popcorn, but these are not recommended for Scotland. Corn can be successfully frozen whole or as kernels removed from the cob, after blanching.

COMMON PROBLEMS

The main problem with Scottish-grown corn is that it simply does not ripen fast enough – so all the more reason to grow it under protection. The sun weakens quickly after September so you need the corn to be more or less ready by then. And it can be knocked over by wind – yet another reason to grow it under cover. George Anderson told us that at the Caley allotments in Edinburgh, rats climbed up the stems and ate the cobs.

SWEETCORN VARIETIES

For outdoors, and probably for indoors too in Scotland, go for early maturing, supersweet varieties.

'**Candy Mountain**' F1 Very sweet, early maturing.
'**Earlibird**' F1 ♀ An early maturing supersweet and said to have more cold tolerance than most.
'**Minipop**' A succulent, small cob grown very successfully in a tunnel at Dunrobin in Sutherland.
'**Minor**' Dwarf plants up to five feet tall producing mini-cobs ideal for stir-fries.
'**Northern Extra Sweet**' F1 ♀ The name suggests it should do well and it is a reliable performer.
'**Ovation**' F1 ♀ Supersweet, mid season, good reports from Jo Hunt on the Black Isle. He tried eight varieties and this was the best.
'**Prelude**' ♀ A supersweet variety with huge cobs, early to mid season.
'**Snobaby**' Low growing with delicious white mini-cobs.
'**Sundance**' F1 ♀ Early maturing. Good at *Beechgrove Garden* and at trials at Harlow Carr, Yorkshire.
'**Supersweet**' Early maturing with large cobs.
'**Swift**' F1 ♀ Very early, said to be extra tender and very sweet.

Sweet Potato (*Ipomoea batatas*) H2 E3

Nothing to do with potatoes, these are actually members of the bindweed (*Convolvulus*) family. They are produced from root cuttings or 'slips' and need to be grown indoors in a greenhouse or tunnel in high soil and air temperatures – higher than most other crops, so you may have to grow them on their own. The best-known variety is '**Beauregard**'. The Beechgrove Garden has tried various protected cropping methods, with the tunnel house the most successful. Ian Thorne grows them commercially on the Black Isle.

CULINARY HERBS, EDIBLE FLOWERS
AND FURTHER INFORMATION

Scots have used herbs for food and medicine for hundreds of years. Many medieval monasteries had herb gardens and Scots have long gathered wild herbs such as celandine, yarrow, mint, self-heal, henbane and many others for the treatment of illnesses. The Royal Botanic Garden Edinburgh was originally founded in 1670 as a physic garden to produce medicinal herbs.

I must confess a particular fondness for the growing of herbs. Not only did my mother and step-father, who likes to think he is a descendant of the great sixteenth-century herbalist William Turner, start a culinary herb business in the Carse of Gowrie, now Scotherbs, with their friends Bob and Sylvia Wilson, my family, the Beatons, were reputed to have been the hereditary doctors to the Lords of the Isles and there is a monument to them at the site of their herb garden on the road to Iona on Mull.

Herbs, annual and perennial, are often planted in a great burst of culinary aspiration and then left to grow on un-harvested, so do consider which herbs you would most like to try growing – that is, what you will honestly use. Next, choose a site for your herbs as close as possible to the kitchen, then at least lethargy won't stop you harvesting them. Even if you don't use them for cooking, many herbs add a blousy attractiveness to your garden and many are an excellent food source for bees.

Many herbs are easy to grow and we have seen them thriving in all parts of Scotland, even on an old airstrip on Benbecula. They are rarely troubled by pests and diseases, and they really do need relatively little looking after. If you want more information than can be provided here, any book by Jekka McVicar can be recommended and, to buy the rarer ones, try Poyntzfield Herb Nursery on the Black Isle (www.poyntzfieldherbs.co.uk).

Beyond the traditional herb bed, consider inter-planting herbs with flowers or vegetables. Chives and pot marigolds make good companion plants, for example. In the herbaceous border, herbs such as bronze fennel and angelica can add their own particular strengths in structure, colour and aroma.

And, if you have no garden at all and only space for window boxes or small containers, then herbs are ideal – contained, beautiful and useful. But do remember to add some soil-based compost and a little grit to your multi-purpose compost. Most herbs grow well under protection too and, for tender ones like basil, indoors is much better than out. Container growing is also a solution to gardens with heavy soil and it means that you can bring your herbs indoors or under some protection over winter. Herbs unhappy in containers are angelica, borage, caraway and sweet cicely.

All herbs can be grown from seed but, as you probably only want one or two of most of them, buying small plants might be a better option. In any case, some herbs, such as parsley, are erratic germinators, so buying plants is a good investment. Annual herbs tend to be sown *in situ* as they often react badly to transplanting. You may want to succession plant to get several crops throughout the season.

Garden centre chains and DIY sheds will try to sell you herb plants flown in from Spain in March and April. These are totally inappropriate for Scotland, with growth too far advanced to plant out at that time. Don't touch them unless you can keep them going indoors. Most of the independent garden centres know better and won't make this mistake, we'd like to think. Wait to plant out until the second half of April for milder and coastal gardens and well into May and beyond for colder gardens. Gradually harden off herbs before planting out. Many perennial herbs are quite easy to propagate from cuttings, division or layering.

Some commonly used herbs have both a medicinal and a culinary profile. This book deals only with herbs for the kitchen. Note that one or two common culinary herbs can be harmful if used excessively – for example, parsley is potentially damaging to the liver and pennyroyal is not recommended during pregnancy.

SITE, SOIL, SOWING AND PLANTING

For herb seed germination, a little bottom heat will work wonders if you can provide it. The majority of herbs enjoy a light, gritty, free-draining soil. Herbs less fussy and more amenable to heavier soils include caraway, chives, horseradish, lemon balm, lovage, mint, salad burnet and sorrel.

Almost all herbs like a good deal of sun. The exceptions, that can be grown in semi-shade, are angelica, chervil, horseradish, lovage, mint, parsley, salad burnet, sorrel and sweet cicely.

As ever, keep your plants weeded. Once established, most are quite drought tolerant. You'll get a much longer cropping season if you can protect herbs from frost in autumn. Remember to pay attention to feeding and watering container-grown herbs and protect their roots from frost. Bay and rosemary have particularly frost-sensitive roots and are often killed in containers in cold winters.

HARVESTING, STORAGE AND SEEDS

To store leaves, freeze them, chopped, in ice-cube trays to which a little water has been added, packing the resultant cubes in freezer bags. Or just freeze them as they are. Don't mix different herbs in the one bag. They will last for up to six months, with flavour and colour diminishing considerably after this and defrosted they are really only fit for adding to sauces and stews. You could also try storing herbs by making flavoured oils and vinegars with some. Try tarragon or rosemary.

To gather the seeds to use in the kitchen, wait until you can see the seeds loosening or falling from the flower heads. Cut the heads and place upside-down in paper bags. Label and leave in a warm place to dry. Shake the seeds into the bag and then remove any debris and transfer to an airtight jar. Keep in a dark place, such as your kitchen cupboard. To store them for future sowing, keep them dry and cool. The fridge is ideal if you have space. You can freeze them.

COMMON PROBLEMS

Long, cold, wet winters are the most common cause of herb failure in Scotland, especially if the herbs are in a heavy soil. For much of Scotland, keeping herbs going for more than a year or two is quite an achievement. Having said that, they are relatively cheap to buy and quick to grow, so regular replanting may not be too much of an issue. For perennials, you can always arrange an insurance policy – take cuttings in late summer and overwinter them in a cold frame. The majority of herbs are unlikely to be troubled by pests and diseases. As a general rule, if you see something untoward, remove the leaves or stem affected and burn. Lift and destroy the entire plant if the whole thing is affected.

We have divided the herbs into two groups – the short-lived annuals and biennials are in the first section followed by the perennials, which live longer.

CHAPTER 1

Annual and Biennial Herbs

Angelica (*Angelica archangelica*) *H5 E2*

A large, architectural plant which grows well in Scotland, its young stems can be candied and the leaves and stalks can be cooked with tart fruit to reduce the need for sugar. Only plant it if you have lots of space – it may reach up to 2m in height. Angelica likes a rich soil in a slightly shaded spot. Sow seed *in situ* in autumn or plant out in spring from autumn-sown modules, but do this before the taproot develops. Keep well watered in dry weather. Angelica is a biennial, so once the plant flowers and seeds it will die. Remove seed heads before seeds drop to prevent self-seeding.

Basil (*Ocimum basilicum*) *H1C-2 E3*

There is nothing like home-made pesto and that is reason enough to try growing your own basil. Indeed, many things are beautifully partnered by it, including garlic and tomatoes. Generally it must be grown under glass or inside on a sunny windowsill, although you may get away with growing some outside during the warmest summer months if you have a very sunny, sheltered corner in the garden and the night temperatures do not fall too low. It may well develop a stronger flavour if it withstands the rigours of the garden. It is probably best grown in a pot or trough. You can direct sow into these and this should give you a plentiful supply all summer if harvested carefully – nick off the large leaves and replacements will soon shoot from the same area of stem. Succession sowing will also help you to keep cropping. Remove any developing flower heads to encourage further bushing. In addition to sweet basil you might want to try the small-leaved Greek basil or the beautiful purple variety. And my herb-expert stepfather tells me that the large-leafed Neapolitan variety is well worth tracking down.

Alternatively, sow in seed trays indoors in April. Put in a sunny and warm place until the seed germinates. When large enough to handle, transplant to a trough or pot at a spacing of around 7cm. Be careful with watering – water in the morning to avoid damping off and consequent seedling collapse. It should grow to around 30cm or more in height.

Although you want a warm and sunny place for your basil, shade it from the hottest midday rays. The flavour is best fresh, needless to say, and it is barely worth eating dried. To store the basil, try preserving the flavour as a herb oil, as a flavoured butter or frozen in an ice cube tray. You could simply pop the leaves in a plastic box and put them in the freezer. Rip the leaves – you don't cut basil leaves – and only add them at the end of cooking hot dishes otherwise you will lose most of the flavour.

Annual herbs: basil, angelica, dill and parsley.

COMMON PROBLEMS

This herb is so sensitive to cold winds and cool nights that Scotland outdoors is often too much for it to bear. We therefore recommend it is grown under cover – probably inside. A cloche might do. It can suffer a bit from **moulds** and **rot**, and the leaves begin to turn brown or the entire stem collapses. Remove the leaves, or the entire stem, as soon as you see this happening and destroy them.

Borage (*Borago officinalis*) H4–5 E1

A delightful and bee-friendly herb that I let self-seed freely among the vegetables, its reputation as a bringer of happiness is certainly deserved even if only because of its beauty.

The delicate blue flowers are easily picked by pinching the middle point. Put fresh into salads or freeze one to each ice cube and pop into your Pimms or rum and coke. The young leaves, hairy though they are, can be picked and cut into a green salad or used in pea and bean soups. They have a slight cucumber flavour.

Borage quite likes poor soil, as long as it is light and well drained. Sow the seeds *in situ* in drills once the earth has warmed and after the danger of frost has passed. Thin them to at least 45cm, as they are rangy plants of up to 75cm high.

Caraway (*Carum carvi*) H4 E2

Commonly used, especially in Eastern European cookery, to flavour cakes, breads and rich meats, caraway seeds are also reputed to aid digestion – and to prevent lovers going off piste. The young feathery leaves can be used in salads. This biennial, producing flower heads and seeds in the second year, is pretty forgiving of most soils and situations. Seed is best sown in summer *in situ* – this is another herb that hates to be transplanted. Thin seedlings to 20cm. Rotate this herb to protect against **carrot root fly** and use a fine mesh to avoid them too. Will reach up to 60cm in height. Not for containers.

Chervil (*Anthriscus cerefolium*) H4 E2

Chervil, with its delicate aniseed flavour, can be used as a tea to help stimulate digestion and lower blood pressure. Like a number of herbs, it can also be added to a green salad and adds a nuance to many foods, including fish, eggs, carrots and tomatoes – especially if it is added to a dish just before serving.

A biennial, it will reach 40cm tall. It is fairly hardy. Succession-sow *in situ* from spring, in a hearty soil in light shade. Thin to 23cm. Remove flower heads as they appear, although you may want to allow some to mature for seed next year.

It's best in spring and autumn – pick the leaves as you need them. Regular picking encourages growth.

Coriander (*Coriandrum sativum*) H2–3 E2

An annual grown for both leaf and seed, coriander leaves are essential for curry and couscous salads. Succession-sow *in situ* from spring in short, shallow drills for a constant supply. It likes a well-fed soil and can be container grown, outside or in a tunnel or greenhouse. It is not happy started in modules, as it dislikes being transplanted. It will grow up to 60cm tall. The flower heads are also edible. Snip the stems when you need them. Use the ice-cube method to store or just stuff stems into a bag and freeze.

Dill (*Anethum graveolens*) H4 E2

An annual herb used in Scotland at least as long ago as the Roman period. Named from the Old Norse word *dilla* 'to lull' – it is reputed to have a soothing affect when taken medicinally and is still found as a constituent of gripe water for babies. Fabulous with fish, used to make gravadlax, great with broad beans, makes lovely dill and potato scones and the seeds are essential in pickled cucumbers. Dill is easy to grow with fortnightly succession plantings across the growing season – and beyond that indoors in containers.

Dill does not like to be transplanted. Sow *in situ* from spring until summer 0.5cm deep in short drills and thin to 20cm. It can grow to 1m but is best harvested at 15-20cm. If you are not gathering seed, remove developing flower heads. Harvest the feathery leaves as you need them. Gather the seed as noted above. The leaves can be frozen in containers but will then have to be used cooked.

Parsley (*Petroselinum crispum*) H4–5 E2

Probably another Roman introduction and an absolutely essential herb because of its nutritional value and culinary versatility – the best to grow for flavour is the flat-leafed French variety. And, like coriander, much flavour lies in the stems, so do not discard them. In some countries it is used in enormous quantities as a major ingredient – think of the bulgur wheat salad, tabbouleh.

Although a biennial, parsley is, in Scotland, best treated as an annual and brought on every year. Parsley is a hungry plant and likes a rich soil and a slightly shady position, growing well between other plants. If starting from seeds, sow them in early spring in trays under protection, covering the seeds lightly in vermiculite. Germination can be tricky, so soak the seed overnight before sowing and keep the soil warm and moist until it happens. Sow *in situ* in late spring and again in late summer for a winter crop if your conditions allow, in a drill 0.5cm deep. Seedlings, plugs or potted seedlings are best thinned/planted at a spacing of about 25cm. **Curled parsley**, which Ken abhors, is slightly hardier and is likely to crop longer before flowering than **French parsley**. Plants grow to 20cm high for curly and 30cm for French. **Root Parsley** has the added bonus of small white carrot-like roots, with a mild sweet taste. Ken grew it and found the leaf flavour quite intense.

Protect against **carrot root fly** and feed occasionally. Remove flower heads as they appear, unless you hope to save seed. If you wish to overwinter – even just to gather seed – you should cut the plants back a little in early autumn then cloche or offer some other sort of protection. Picking encourages further growth, so harvest as you need it, as it does not store well in the fridge. You could try making parsley butter, which should store for a week or more in the fridge and much longer in the freezer.

Take a pot or two of parsley indoors over winter for the kitchen.

Summer Savory (*Satureja hortensis*) *H4 E2*

This very old culinary herb is said to diminish the wind that results from eating too many beans, hence the name 'bean herb'. Traditionally paired with broad beans and lentil soup, it also goes well with egg-based dishes and adds depth to the taste of a green salad. It is thought to be sweeter and more interesting than the perennial winter savory.

It is happy in poor soil. Sow seeds in trays in early spring under protection. Plant out when the earth has warmed, spacing at 15cm. The plants will grow to 15cm and more. Harvest before flowering. Cut back after flowering for a second flush of leaves. To store, you could try the ice-cube tray method.

CHAPTER 2

Perennial Herbs

In theory, perennial herbs will grow indefinitely and can be harvested each year. In practice, in Scotland, most of them are a little on the tender side and their Mediterranean origins make them prone to winter freezes and fungal disease in our long, wet and cold winters. For that reason, grow these for as long as they remain healthy but don't be dismayed if you have to replace them from time to time. Recent hard winters have been particularly harsh on herbs.

Bay (*Laurus nobilis*) H2–3 E2

This is the 'laurel' with which winners were crowned in ancient times, the 'noble berry tree' or *Baccae lauri*, from which the French qualification the baccalaureate derives its name. Bay, or sweet bay, an evergreen shrub, is a very widely used herb, most commonly in savoury dishes but it can also be used to flavour milk puddings. It is relatively easy to grow but is not fully frost hardy in the coldest winters. Potted bays are particularly vulnerable to having their roots killed. Digging the pot into the ground or bubble wrapping it should help, or move the pot right next to the house to protect from wind and rain and to benefit from the radiated heat. In the ground, once established in the right spot, you could have a very long-lasting and beautiful tree in your garden. In the brutal winters of 2010 and 2011, many people lost their potted bays to frost, but Ken's 1.2m

bay tree in the ground at Glendoick survived with only a little dieback. You can buy bays as small potted plants in garden centres and nurture them to a great size or you can blow the budget and go for a fully grown one. The most expensive are pruned into lollipops, spirals and pyramids. Do not re-pot bays too often, as they do quite like to be pot bound. As long as it remains in a container, feed the plant regularly or add slow release fertiliser granules or use nettle or comfrey 'tea'. Give it a fresh top dressing of compost and clip to shape in spring. As an ever-green, you can harvest fresh leaves year round. To store leaves, pick them and dry them at room temperature before putting them in a jar.

COMMON PROBLEMS

Frost and **wind** are probably the worst problems, especially when the tree is young and/or in a container, so protect it if you can. **Scale insects** may infest and the result will be visible on the underside of leaves like little suckers. Jekka McVicar recommends rubbing them with cotton buds dipped in alcohol. If you have better things to do with your booze, then try a moist rag or an insecticide, but you probably won't want to eat the leaves for a while afterwards.

Bay with its beautiful but scentless flowers.

Fennel, both the bronze and green varieties.

Bergamot (*Monarda fistulosa*) H4–5 E2

Wild bergamot is a very pretty plant indeed. With the common name of American bee balm, you'll see and hear why it gets this name as soon as it flowers. You'll notice the leaf fragrance reminds you of Earl Grey though, in fact, it is the plant *Citrus bergamia* which is used to flavour the tea. The petals of bergamot flowers can be added to salads, as can the chopped leaves.

Bergamot likes a rich and moisture-retentive soil and a sunny position and grows to 90cm high. You can lift and split it every three years or so, thereby increasing your plant stock. Pick the leaves and flowers as you need them and use in salads or fruit salads but don't bother trying to store it. Try to obtain mildew-resistant forms, mostly named after Native American tribes.

Chamomile (*Chamaemelum nobile*) H4 E2

Roman chamomile makes the tea beloved of many insomniacs. In spring, as the seeds are really tiny, sow in trays under protection. Or you could use cuttings or divide your existing stock. Plant out to a spacing of 20–25cm. Once established, chamomile will creep around quite happily, so cut it back if it becomes too enthusiastic. Lift, divide and replant every three years or so. It will grow to around 20–30cm tall when in flower and it is happy in a container. Chamomile does not like wet soil but nor does it like to be too dry in summer. Water as necessary. Dead head to encourage further growth. Harvest the flowers when they are just fully open and at the start of the day. Wash well and then lay them on a piece of muslin on a rack. Put them in a warm place to dry, then store in an airtight jar. Steep two teaspoonfuls of dried flowers or one tablespoon of fresh in a cup of boiling water. Strain and add honey to taste. Not to be confused with the non-flowering *Chamaemelum nobile* 'Treneague', lawn chamomile.

Chives (*Allium schoenoprasum*) H5 E1

Great for attracting bees, one of the easiest and toughest herbs, great for adding to salads, scrambled eggs and vinaigrettes, chives are a member of the onion family. Both flowers and stems are edible and flowers look great sprinkled on a potato salad. Garlic chives (*Allium tuberosum*) are also worth growing, although they are less hardy and you may want to overwinter them indoors. Their beautiful, white star-like flowers can be eaten too.

Chives are not fussy but prefer a rich and moisture-retentive soil in sun or partial shade. They are also happy in containers. I plant them at the ends of quite a few of my vegetable beds as companions and because I use them a great deal in the kitchen. You can grow from seed, buy small plants or split up a large clump. Sow seed in spring, thinning to about 20cm. Plants will grow to around 25cm tall. Cut off the flowers as they pass their best and you may get a second flush. Indeed, the plants get a bit scruffy come midsummer, so cut down the whole lot and wait for the fresh growth. Harvest the leaves by cutting at the base of the plant. Chives will keep in the fridge for a few days but are not really suitable for storing and, in any case, you can probably keep some going year round if you divide one of your clumps and grow it indoors in a container over winter. Chives may suffer from **rust** – browning of the leaves. Remove and destroy affected parts.

Fennel (*Foeniculum vulgare*) *H5 E1*

Often confused with dill and Florence fennel, as they look similar, this is a tall handsome perennial in green and bronze forms – the filigree leaves make a striking foliage plant for the back of a border. The bronze form (*Foeniculum vulgare* 'Purpureum' *H4*) is less hardy than the green. Fennel can reach 1–1.5m and has a strong aniseed flavour to its seeds and a mild flavour to its leaves. The seeds can be used in breads, soups and in Indian-style dishes. The leaves can be chopped into salad or used to flavour cooked dishes. Chopped and dried foliage is good for repelling dog fleas apparently. Buy a small plant or two, or you can grow it from seed sown in spring early under protection or outdoors in late spring after the threat of frost has passed. Cut back in autumn to within 7cm of the ground and it will

reappear in spring, when it would enjoy a mulch of well-rotted manure. If not supported by surrounding planting, it may need staking. Remove flower heads unless saving seed or you may end up with a fennel forest. It is best to replace every few years, although self-sown seedlings will generally provide replacements.

Horseradish (*Armoracia rusticana*) *H5 E1*

Its Latin name sounding like a jolly operetta, horseradish is said to stimulate the digestive system – it will certainly stimulate the tear ducts when you peel and grate it to make your horseradish sauce. It is wonderful with beef, smoked mackerel and in a beetroot salad, mixed with mayonnaise. The young leaves can be used in salads.

Unless you want a garden full of horseradish, plant this in a large pot, in a moisture-retentive compost – and place the pot on a paving slab too, to prevent the roots escaping and beginning the colonisation process. Buy as a small potted plant or beg a piece of root from a friend. Unlike most herbs, it will grow in partial shade. Expect it to grow to 60cm tall. Dig up, split and replant every three years or so. Take the roots as you need them and use them fresh, as the flavour is quickly lost. If you wish, preserve the prepared root in vinegar.

Hyssop (*Hyssopus officinalis*) *H2–3 E2*

Hyssop has a strong, distinctive taste – somewhere between mint and sage. Used sparingly, it works well with fatty dishes, as it aids digestion. It is also good paired, in the form of a syrup, with fruits such as plums, apricots or peaches. Although not fully hardy, it is worth growing, as it makes really attractive semi-evergreen little bushes of blue, pink or white flowers in late summer (the blue is most common), which can be used to decorate salads. It makes a very good alternative to a lavender border and the bees love it. It will grow happily in a container.

Sow seeds in early spring, in a seed tray under protection. Prick out and transplant into modules or small pots and harden off once they are large enough to plant out. Reaching 50cm or so, plant at a spacing of 30cm as low hedge and 40–50cm in the border or herb garden. Pinch out the growing tip in the first year to encourage bushiness. Each spring, cut the plants hard back and give a compost top dressing. Snip stems and strip leaves as you need them. As it is evergreen, there is no need to store. Replace plants every four or five years.

Lavender (*Lavandula angustifolia*) H3 E2

With its long-lasting flower spikes, this is a must for the bee-friendly garden. A slightly tender evergreen, it has a number of uses in the kitchen, with the leaves and flowers used in biscuits, vinegars or ice creams, for example. Pick the flowering stems just before they are fully out, dry and tie into little bundles with ribbon and give to friends to hang in their bedrooms to scent the space and help keep away bedbugs. If you want the individual flowers for ice cream or biscuits, put stems in paper bags in a warm dry place. Once dry, carefully strip the flowers from the stem. Store in a dry, dark place in an airtight container.

It is easy to root from cuttings in late summer in gritty compost or buy small or large plants from a garden centre in spring. Plant lavender at 30cm spacing for a hedge effect – '**Hidcote**' and '**Munstead**' varieties are probably the best for Scotland. Lavender hates heavy, wet soil and grows well in containers, even tolerating drying out for short periods. Dead head to prolong flowering and prune to keep in shape but don't cut too much into old wood. It

A lavender hedge at Culross Palace, in Fife – a stunning colour contrast between plant and building.

Variegated lemon balm (left) is best used raw in fruit salads, whereas golden marjoram is usually cooked in Italian-style dishes.

suffers in cold, wet winters and often looks ragged and half dead after five years or so and is best replaced.

Lemon Balm (*Melissa officinalis*) H4 E1

Also known as sweet balm, lemon balm has long been used to treat anxiety disorders. It is now, interestingly, being tested as an anti-agitation herb for people with Alzheimer's. Best eaten raw, the chopped leaves make an interesting addition to a fresh fruit or green salad. They can also be used for a refreshing tea sweetened with honey.

Reaching up to 60cm in height and suitable for a container, lemon balm will grow in most soils in most aspects. Start with a shop-bought plant or a piece of a plant divided in the spring. It has a tendency to spread, so try to keep it in check by removing roving and adventitious rooty bits. Remove the fairly insignificant flower heads to encourage good, bushy growth. Around midsummer, chop the whole plant back to 15cm and it will produce another flush of scented leaves before autumn. Lift and divide to propagate. It is not worth trying to store it.

Lemon Verbena (*Aloysia triphylla*) H2 E3

With a beautiful lemon scent, the leaves can be used sparingly, chopped in drinks, cakes and puddings, and it can be made into a herb tea reputed to aid digestion. A tender shrub that will grow in excess of 90cm, it is not hardy away from the coast. Plant outdoors, if you want to risk it, in well-drained soil in a sheltered site – a south-facing wall is ideal – and consider a cloche or grow in a pot to bring indoors. Water well in the growing season. Give it a bit of a prune in late summer to maintain its shape, removing flower heads as you go. Pick the leaves fresh or dry and store for kitchen use. They can also be used in potpourri. It's prone to **whitefly**.

Lovage (*Levisticum officinalis*) H5 E2

Commonly called 'love parsley' because of its reputation as a passion-inducing potion, this is another architectural specimen for the back of the border. It has a flavour similar to that of celery and its young leaves, picked before flowers appear, can be used in small amounts in salads and stews. Its stems used to be cooked as a celery replacement. The smaller Scots lovage (*Ligusticum scoticum*) ✉ is found in coastal areas amongst rocks and was prized by our forebears, who ate it raw or cooked it with fish.

Lovage likes a rich and moisture-retentive soil in sun or partial shade. Start with shop-bought specimens. Plant at least 60cm apart. It will, in three years, reach a height of around 1.8m. It's happy in a container but it will clearly need to be in a large one. Keep well watered in dry spells. Remove the flower heads as they appear unless you are saving seed, as it can spread all over the garden. The plant will die back in autumn. Cut the stems to ground level. Mulch with well-rotted manure or compost in spring. Not a plant that stores.

Mint (*Mentha*) H5 E1

Mint has a long and interesting history. Pliny recommended that students wear wreaths of mint to keep the mind active – worth a try, though people may point and laugh. Scotland has its native species including *Mentha aquatica*, the water mint, which was used in the kitchen but has also been recommended as a cure for athlete's foot amongst other things. And mint was also used to keep flies away from the larder and mice away from the grain stacks. I wonder if it would keep them away from my seed peas? On a more contemporary note, mint is being used along with reeds in natural effluent cleansing activities. There is a large range of mints available for the gardener and, by extension, the cook. If you are to have only one in the garden, look for spearmint (*Mentha spicata*) or apple mint (*Mentha suaveolens*). Bowles mint (*Mentha x villosa* var. *alopecuroides*) is also well flavoured and has good disease resistance. But you could try ginger mint (*Mentha x gracilis*) or pennyroyal (*Mentha pulegium*), which is a strong-flavoured mint traditionally used in Britain as one of the flavourings in black pudding (and to keep body lice and fleas at bay in the Middle Ages). My favourite, when my mother

Spearmint in a pot to contain the roots (left) and rosemary in a container (right) which can be moved under protection in winter.

and stepfather ran their herb farm, was the wonderfully named red raripila (*Mentha x smithiana*).

Some are hardier than others but all are relatively easy to grow. Use it in all the usual ways – with lamb, in refreshing salads and yoghurt dips, on new potatoes and peas. Try a few leaves of mint in a pot of boiling water on a hot summer's day – with the addition of a few grains of sugar, the most delicious and refreshing tea.

PLANTING, ROUTINE CARE, HARVESTING AND STORING

Beware of planting mint in the open ground, as it can take over the garden. Plant it in a large pot with the base cut out, plunged into the soil or, as they have done at Heligan in Cornwall, sink some slabs into the ground to stop the roots spreading sideways. Mint is not really fussy about soil type but use a rich and moisture-retentive mix for your pots. Start with a plant from the garden centre or a piece of root from a friend. Make sure it is good and flavourful stock. Plant this in the pot and keep well watered until it is established. Mint is always best trimmed to stop it flowering, as the flavour of leaves is best before the flowers appear. Chop it back in mid season and it will come away again. Ideally, you should lift mint every year or two, splitting and/or re-potting it in spring. For a winter supply, dig up and split one of your plants, popping a few of the roots into a pot. Take it indoors to grow on. To store, freeze leaves in ice-cube trays or make mint sauce. Mint may suffer from **rust** – browning of the leaves. Remove and destroy affected parts.

Oregano (*Origanum vulgare*) ✉ and Pot Marjoram (*Origanum x onites*) H4–5 E1

Taking its name from the Greek *ore gamos*, meaning 'joy of the mountain', it is impossible not to be wooed by the poetry inherent in this herb. From the cultivation and cooking points of view, these two are so similar that they are included here together. They are thought of in this country very much as Italian herbs and they find their way into many tomato-based dishes. Oregano, in Italy, is one of very few herbs which is regarded as worth eating dried and you will see huge bunches of the stuff hung up to dry outside houses in the countryside. Poyntzfield Herb Nursery on the Black Isle offers '**Tomintoul**' oregano, a hardy variety from the Grampians.

Buy as small potted herbs, as you don't need more than one, or they are easy to propagate by taking a rooted section off the side of a clump. They will grow to 30cm high and spread gradually to 50cm or more, and they do well in a container. These were one of the few herbs to sail through the harsh 2010–11 winter at Glendoick. To dry them, harvest the stems before the flowers open and hang upside down in bunches in a warm place. Once dried, store in an airtight jar in a cupboard.

Rosemary (*Rosmarinus officinalis*) H2–3 E2

An evergreen, shrubby flowering plant, attractive to bees and said to grow well if there is a strong woman in the house, rosemary is a pungent herb that needs to be used sparingly. It is especially well matched with lamb or pork and with courgettes as part of a herby, mustardy vinaigrette. The Greeks wore rosemary garlands when sitting exams, as they thought it improved memory and concentration. The common variety is the hardiest, although there are some very attractive alternatives. '**Mrs Jessop's Upright**' is a good bet for Scotland.

As rosemary is slightly tender and the 2010–11 winter certainly did for most of the Scottish ones, you may want to keep it in a pot so that it can be put beside a south-facing wall or brought under protection over winter. It is a very resilient seaside plant but keep it safe from cold winds. You are probably best to start with a shop-bought plant, as you are likely to only want one or two. Space at least 1m apart. It will grow to 90cm high and more and dislikes boggy, heavy or very acid soil.

Clip it lightly in spring and again after flowering to keep it bushy and prevent it from becoming woody at the base. Use the pretty blue flowers as well as the spindly, sticky and aromatic leaves. It can be dried and it stores well as flavoured oil. Easy to propagate from cuttings, it will tend to need replaced every five years or so in colder areas.

Sage (*Salvia officinalis*) *H3 E2*

This shrubby herb is beautiful, pungent and a key ingredient of stuffing. Its strong flavour counteracts pleasantly the richness of meats such as duck or pork. It matches very well the earthiness of squash in a delicious soup. It is also good in tomato dishes and raw – in small measure – in salads. Quite easy to grow in well-drained soil and suitable for a container, wet Scottish winters can cause it to die back (grey mould) and it is easy to lose all or parts of it. A cloche to keep foliage dry can help it survive. At Glendoick we find we are doing well to keep it going for three years without starting again. Start with a shop-bought plant, which you can expect to grow to 50 × 30cm or so. Trim the bush lightly after it flowers in summer.

As an evergreen, you can take the leaves as you need them, although they do taste best in midsummer before they flower. To store, either dry them in a warm place on cake cooling racks covered with muslin then keep in containers in a cupboard or chop and freeze using the ice-cube method.

Purple sage '**Purpurescens**' is more compact and less hardy and has a slightly milder flavour than the common green, while the variegated form is less hardy than both. Tricolour sage is more ornamental than edible.

Sage-lined paths at Culross Palace, Fife. Dipping sage leaves in hot water just before cooking improves their flavour.

Salad Burnet (*Poterium sanguisorba*) *H4 E1*

This is an attractive evergreen with branches of tiny leaves which give a slight cucumber flavour to salad, yoghurt or mayonnaise – particularly when bruised.

Salad burnet is not too fussy about site or soil. Sow seed *in situ* in spring and thin to 30cm. Or start with a shop-bought plant. It will grow to a height of 30cm or so. It self-seeds like mad if you let it so one plant will inevitably lead to more if you wish. Otherwise, remove the flowers as they appear. It can be container grown. Cut it back in autumn and give it a top dressing of compost in spring. It can be lifted and divided to produce more plants. Not for storing.

Sorrel (*Rumex acetosa*) H5 E1

Broad-leaved sorrel – or sourocks, in Scots – is an easy-to-cultivate herb which is productive from March each year, even in the severe climate at 300m of Chisholme, near Hawick. It grows to about 60cm. The smaller and milder-flavoured buckler-leaved variety (*Rumex scutatus*) is so easy it will sow itself in every available space in the herb garden. It sits at about 23cm tall. Used in soups and with fish, sorrel is delicious both raw and cooked. Include it in omelettes, salads, sauces and mayonnaise, allowing the release of its lovely lemony tang.

Sorrel likes a well-fed, moisture-retentive soil and sun or light shade. It is easily grown from seed or root division and, for the best harvest, should be replaced every three years. Sow where it is to crop from late April and thin to 30cm apart. Buckler-leaved sorrel would be the best to grow in a container.

Feed and mulch in spring and keep well watered as, if the plants dry out, the leaves end up tasting so bitter as to render them inedible. Simply pick the leaves from the base of the broad-leafed variety when you feel they are large enough. Smaller and younger leaves are milder – the older ones can make you wince when you bite into them. The leaves of buckler-leaf sorrel are uniformly small and can just be harvested in handfuls. Remove the flower heads, especially in the case of the buckler-leaved variety with its tendency to self-seed. Not really for storing – unless you freeze sorrel soup.

Sweet Cicely (*Myrrhis odorata*) H4–5 E1

Sweet cicely is a beautiful plant that can become invasive. The entire thing smells and tastes of aniseed and the seeds in particular were popular with children of old, who collected them and ate them as sweeties. The seeds, harvested when green, can be eaten as they are or added to salads or fruit salads, and leaves can be chopped and added to a salad. As with elderflower flower heads and angelica stems, this is a 'sugar-saver' plant. Its chopped leaves and stems will take the acid sting from tart fruits like gooseberries and rhubarb when stewed alongside them (discard after cooking).

Select a rich and moisture-retentive soil and light shade for this plant. It is another that will go towards the back of the border, as it will eventually reach in excess of 45cm tall so not really suitable for containers. As you will only need one or two plants, start with shop-bought specimens. If you are trying seed, sow it *in situ* as soon as the seed ripens – that is in autumn. Space plants at 60cm. Cut back in the autumn and top dress with compost in spring. Remove the flower heads assiduously when they appear unless you want the seeds to eat or to sow. Harvest the leaves, stems and seeds as you need them.

Tarragon (French) (*Artemisia dracunculus*) H2–3 E3

This is a perennial herb but not a hardy one and you will do well to keep it going through the winter in many parts of Scotland. It is, however, well worth the effort, as its strong flavour is central to a number

French tarragon at Islay House Community Garden. Divide plants every couple of years to maintain their flavour and vigour – if you can keep them going outdoors.

Two of the many different varieties of thyme, showing flowers and variegated foliage.

of dishes, including those with a chicken or fish base. Tarragon vinegar is easy to make and a store cupboard necessity. Do not make the mistake of buying the weaker flavoured Russian tarragon. It is French tarragon you need.

Tarragon needs a sunny, sheltered site. French tarragon does not come true from seed, so you need to buy plants or use divisions from an existing clump. It can be container grown – and, indeed, you may find this the best way to keep the stuff going. Protect in winter with a mulch of straw or frost-grade fleece. Don't let its roots get waterlogged. It should start to come to life as early as February under protection. If you can keep it going, divide the underground runners or take cuttings and replant every two or three years. Snip the stems as you need them and strip off the leaves, remove flowers to maintain vigour and cut back in June for lovely fresh shoots. Like basil, the flavour is easily destroyed by heat so add it at the last minute to your dishes. Freeze, chopped, in a tub, use the ice-cube method or try tarragon vinegar.

Thyme (*Thymus*) H5 E1

A must-have intensely aromatic herb, delicious with onions roasted in butter or with tomatoes and garlic and lots more. There is a great range of thymes to choose from. It is probably best to start with the 'ordinary' garden thyme (*Thymus vulgaris*) as the basis of your collection and then branch out to things like lemon thyme (*Thymus x citriodorus*) or broad-leaved thyme (*Thymus pulegioides*). The smaller thyme varieties, for example wild mountain thyme (*Thymus polytrichus* ssp. *britannicus*) ✉, make great plants to pop into the spaces between flagstones and they smell lovely when walked over.

Choose a well-drained and sunny spot or container with a gritty, not too acid soil for preference. Keep cropping it to keep it compact and productive. Lift and divide every three years or so in spring to maintain vigour. The creeping varieties can be left to creep.

As an evergreen, it can be harvested year round so there is no need to store. Snip branches and use whole in stews and soups, removing the stalks before serving. For other dishes, strip the leaves and discard the stalks before adding.

Winter Savory (*Satureja Montana*) H3 E2

Winter savory is useful as it is a year-round, more-or-less evergreen plant and so, unlike summer savory, is always available to the cook – although it doesn't taste as good. Start with a shop-bought specimen. Growing to about 30cm tall, it is likely to become leggy so should be replaced every two years or so. Lightly cut back in spring and top dress with compost. It can be grown in a container but ensure it is kept adequately watered and regularly fed with your comfrey or nettle 'tea' or with a proprietary brand of plant food. Propagate by cuttings.

CHAPTER 3

Edible Flowers

It is possible to eat the flowers of many garden plants and herbs but do your homework before you start experimenting lest you make yourself ill – for example, tomato, potato and many other flowers are toxic. The petals of most edible flowers make a beautiful addition to a mixed salad – and quite a groovy-looking omelette or stunning fruit jelly. Flowers can also be used to flavour and colour oils and vinegars as well as for tisanes. And don't forget that companion planting with some flowers may distract predators. To taste flowers at their best, pick them just as you need them and remove all the bits of stem and other potentially chewy bits to ensure only the flower goes into your mouth. Give them a shake too, as many a flower has a resident insect which you may not want to crunch as part of your salad.

You could start by trying the following, some of which have already been covered in the fruit and vegetable sections:

Bergamot (*Monarda fistulosa*) – sprinkle the petals over a salad, savoury or fruit.

Borage (*Borago officinalis*) – individually preserved in ice cubes they look great in summer drinks and even better in midwinter ones!

Chives (*Allium schoenoprasum*) – great in scrambled eggs, as a garnish for lots of dishes, in soured cream for baked potatoes or as a dip and in egg sandwiches. A useful companion in the vegetable garden and also believed to inhibit rose black spot (*see* p. 275).

Cornflower (*Centaurea cyanus*) – pretty much just for salads this one, including tabbouleh.

Daylily (*Hemerocallis* spp.) – cook Jenny Leggatt suggests this as part of a stuffed sole, as well as a decoration on salad.

Elderflower (*Sambucus nigra*) – cook with gooseberries to remove their sharpness, use to make cordial or try deep frying in a light batter, as does Nigel Slater (*see* p. 116).

Evening primrose (*Oenothera biennis*) – add to a mixed salad.

Hyssop (*Hyssopus officinalis*) – another for a salad. Also a good companion near cabbages to redirect cabbage whites.

Nasturtium (*Tropaeolum majus*) – 'Indian cress', a lovely peppery addition to salads, along with the chopped leaves, which are rich in vitamin C. Shake the flowers well, as they tend to have earwigs in them. A useful weed-suppressing spreader for under fruit or beans.

Pinks (*Dianthus* spp.) – into the salad with this. The more you pick, the more they flower.

Pot marigold (*Calendula officinalis*) – the petals look lovely in sponge cakes and scones and behave a bit like saffron when cooked with rice. A good companion near asparagus and tomatoes amongst other things.

Primrose (*Primula vulgaris*) – add the flowers to

Edible flowers: nasturtium, borage, viola and bergamot.

salads, if you can bear to pick them from your garden. But don't pick them in the wild, of course.

Sage (*Salvia officinalis*) – for salads and other foody decorative purposes and good on soups.

Viola (*Viola odorata* and *V. tricolor*) – the heartsease pansy is a delightful and possibly romantic addition to a salad. Try crystallising them, too, to decorate your cupcakes.

Eating 'Weeds'

You may wish to experiment with eating what we now regard as weeds. **Ground elder** (*Aegopodium podagraria*) can be added to a green salad or cooked as spinach, and **chickweed** (*Stellaria media*) is good in egg sandwiches. **Wild garlic** (*Allium ursinum*), commonly called ramsons, grows prolifically in woodland settings and the leaves and flowers are worth using in salads, soups and to make a pesto. **Fat hen** (*Chenopodium album*) used to be commonly used as a spinach-style vegetable. The closely-related **Good King Henry** (wild spinach) (*Chenopodium bonus-henricus*) (*see* p. 200) can also be eaten in place of spinach, and its young shoots, peeled and cooked, apparently taste a little of asparagus. Kellie Castle walled garden grows it in the vegetable patch. **Nettles** (*Urtica dioica*), picked very young and in an area clearly free of car fumes and herbicide sprays, can be eaten as soup or as a spinach-style vegetable. **Dandelion leaves** (*Taraxacum officinale*), again picked young, are good in a mixed green salad (common in Greece) or they can be boiled like spinach or added to soup.

CHAPTER 4

Further Information

The National Vegetable Society

Scotland retains a strong tradition of growing fruit and vegetables for showing and competition as can be witnessed in late summer at the Ayr and Dundee flower shows and Gardening Scotland, for instance. The National Vegetable Society (NVS – www.nvsuk.org.uk) encourages, supports and judges vegetable growing. Founded in London in 1960 with the aim of improving the growing of vegetables through innovative practice, the Scottish branch was founded in 1974. In addition to offering advice to those new to this activity, they also train and examine horticultural judges and offer lecturers.

Having started as a society comprising almost exclusively men (although a Miss L. E. Plumpton had the honour of membership number one) and with a focus on show vegetables, there has, over the past few years, been a move to encourage a wider membership and to include information on growing to eat. Exhibitor Sherie Plumb is currently experiencing considerable success as a woman breaking into this traditionally male domain. The quarterly magazine *Simply Vegetables* is included in the annual membership for which a modest fee is charged.

Show vegetables, at times the butt of unkind remarks, are in fact entirely edible. NVS members do like to grow them large but, they would suggest,

Medwyn Williams' stand at Dundee Flower and Food Festival 2010 is a very fine example of the art and craft of the show grower.

Medwyn Williams, winner of many RHS Chelsea Flower Show gold medals, with Caroline at Dundee Flower and Food Festival 2010.

they are growing in conditions and with feeding regimes from which all gardeners can learn. The days of secret recipes and dastardly undermining of fellow competitors are gone too – if they ever existed – and NVS members are keen to share their knowledge with others.

Where to see Fruit and Vegetables in Scottish Gardens

Many Scottish gardens have good fruit and vegetable displays. For fruit, notable places to visit include the Garden of Scottish Fruit at **Fyvie Castle** in Aberdeenshire. **Castle Fraser** nearby has some of the best espaliered fruit you'll see anywhere, while **Anton's Hill** walled garden near Coldstream has an amazing collection of cordon apples. For both fruit and vegetables, **Culross Palace** on the Forth has a recreated seventeenth-century garden with outdoor grapes and figs. We are big fans of **Kellie Castle's** charming organically run walled garden in Fife and **Culzean Castle** walled garden in Ayrshire has lots of

vegetables, fine fruit on the walls and a spectacular greenhouse range with vines and peaches. Hard to beat is the amazing, productive walled garden at **Mertoun** in the Borders, full of fruit, vegetables and cutting flowers – one of the last full-blown production gardens attached to a big house. We love **Inverewe's** curved walled garden which follows the line of the beach. **Geilston** near Dumbarton has extensive vegetables and fruit. Many **allotments** have annual open days and this is a chance to see what grows well locally and how to grow it. We always come away with produce to try and seedlings to plant.

Fruit, Vegetable and Growing Equipment Suppliers

Agroforestry Research Trust, ART, 46 Hunters Moon, Dartington, Totnes, TQ9 6JT, UK – www.agroforestry.co.uk

Blackmoor Fruit, Near Liss, Hampshire, GU33 6BS – www.blackmoor.co.uk

Fyvie Garden of Scottish Fruits, in Aberdeenshire.

Mertoun near St Boswells, one of the oldest Borders gardens, is a fine example of a classic working kitchen garden where an impressive array of fruit and vegetables is cultivated.

Geilston in Dunbartonshire has an extensive vegetable and fruit garden as well as an orchard.

Brogdale National Tree Fruit Collection, Faversham Kent ME13 8XZ – www.brogdale.org

Chris Bowers & Sons, Wimbotsham, Norfolk PE4 3QB – www.chrisbowers.co.uk

Harrod Horticultural, Pinbush Road, Lowestoft, Suffolk NR33 7NL – www.harrodhorticultural.com

James McIntyre & Sons, Moyness Nurseries, Coupar Angus Rd, Blairgowrie, PH10 6UT – www.jamesmcintyre.co.uk

John Hancox, The Children's Orchard, 75 Clouston St, Glasgow G20 8W – www.scottishfruittrees.com

Keepers Nursery – www.keepers-nursery.co.uk

Plants with Purpose, Middlebank Cottage, Smiths Brae, Bankfoot, Perthshire, PH1 4AH – www.plantsandapples.co.uk

Poyntzfield Herb Nursery, Black Isle, by Dingwall, IV7 8LX – www.poyntzfieldherbs.co.uk

Riverford Organic Vegetables Limited, Buckfastleigh, Devon TQ11 0JU – www.riverford.co.uk

Wondermesh, Redford Farm, Garvock, Laurencekirk, AB30 1HS – www.wondermesh.co.uk

Mail Order Seeds

Alan Romans, 72, North St, Kettlebridge, Fife, KY15 7QJ – www.alanromans.com.

Dobies, Long Road, Paignton, Devon, TQ4 7SX – www.dobies.co.uk

Garden Organic, Coventry, Warwickshire, CV8 3LG – www.gardenorganic.org.uk

Kings Seeds, Monks Farm, Kelvedon, Colchester, Essex, CO5 9PG – www.kingsseeds.com

Kokopelli, Oasis, 131 Impasse des Palmiers, 30100 Alès, France – www.kokopelli.asso.fr

Medwyn Williams, Anglesey, Wales Llanor, Old School Lane, Llanfair P.G., Anglesey, LL61 5RZ – www.medwynsofanglesey.co.uk

Real Seeds, PO Box 18, Newport near Fishguard, Pembrokeshire SA65 0AA – www.realseed.co.uk

Rebekah's Veg – www.rebekahsveg.org.uk (Internet and shows only)

Sarah Raven, 2 Woodstock court, Blenheim Road, Marlborough SN8 4AN – www.sarahraven.com

Scottish Seed Exchange Network, East Kilbride – www.ekdevtrust.com

Tamar Organics, Carta Martha Farm, Rezare, Lauceston, Cornwall PL15 9NX – www.tamarorganics.co.uk

Thomas Etty, Seedsman's Cottage, Puddlebridge, Horton, Ilminster, Somerset, TA19 9RL – www.thomasetty.co.uk

Tuckers Seeds, Brewery Meadow, Stonepark, Ashburton, Newton Abbot, Devon TQ13 7DG – www.tuckers-seeds.com

Contacts and Organisations

Aberdeen Biodynamic Land Trust – www.biodynamic.org.uk.

Binn Soil Nutrients Ltd, Binn Farm, Glenfarg – www.binnsoilnutrients.com

Fife Diet Office, 6–7, Old Station House, Forth Place, Burntisland, Fife KY3 9DR – www.fifediet.co.uk

Gardening Leave, Gardens Unit, SAC Auchincruive, Ayrshire KA6 5HW – www.gardeningleave.org

Greenspace Scotland, 12 Alpha Centre, Stirling University Innovation Park, Stirling FK9 4NF – www.greenspacescotland.org.uk

Landshare – www.landshare.net

Macaulay Institute (James Hutton Institute), Craigiebuckler, Aberdeen AB15 8QH – www.macaulaysoils.com

Nourish Scotland – www.nourishscotland.org.uk

Permaculture Scotland (launched February 2011) – www.permaculture.co.uk

Royal Horticultural Society (best website for pest and disease information) – www.rhs.org.uk

Scottish Allotments and Gardens Society (SAGS) – www.sags.org.uk

Soil Association (all things organic – includes a very useful section on community supported agriculture (CSA)) – www.soilassociation.org

Transition Scotland, 8/2 Marlborough Street, Edinburgh EH15 2BG – www.transitionscotland.org

Trellis, 40 St John Street, Perth PH1 5SP – www.trellisscotland.org.uk

And Finally …

For updates on this book, supplier details and useful fruit and vegetable information, visit www. glendoick. com and follow links to *Fruit and Vegetables for Scotland.*

Acknowledgements

KEN

This book could not have been written without the help of many Scottish growers, farmers, gardeners and policymakers from almost every corner of the country.

The fruit section was completed with input, advice and invaluable proof-reading by John Butterworth, Willie Duncan, Nick Dunn (Frank Matthews) and Alec West.

Thanks to Colin Stirling (Hortics), Professor Mike Lean (Glasgow University), Steve Mercer (*Gardening Which?*), Catherine Erskine, Elliot Forsyth and Ruth McHuchon (Cambo), Christopher Dingwall, Mark Armour (Kellie), Mark Jeffery (Culross), David McIntyre, John Stoa (*Dundee Courier*), Toby and Kate Anstruther (Balkaskie), Ann Steele, Melissa Simpson, Robert Grant (NTS), Jo Hunt, Pete Ritchie (Nourish), Alan Grant, John Ferguson, Jennifer Cook (Seer Rockdust), Peter and Melanie Thomson (fruit farmers, Blairgowrie), Susan Russell, (Culzean), Graham Bell (permaculture), Rex Brennon and Gavin Ramsay (James Hutton Institute/SCRI), Alan Smith (Strathdon), Damon Powell and Sarah Earney (Castle Fraser), Eileen Heavens (Inverleith Allotments), Carole Inglis, Christine Campbell, Ian Brown, Dede MacGillivray, Deidre Peppe, Roger Whiddon, Claire MacDonald (Skye & Food Van) Paul Brooker and Rosie Gibson, Tom Mabbott for giving us a set of RCHC journals, Alan Romans, John Marshall and Ian Barbour for invaluable potato information and proof-reading, Medwyn Williams, Lynn Wotherspoon, Paul Gill, David and Jane Shields, Stewart Smith (vines), Tom Sharples (Suttons Seeds), Ronald Gilchrist (vermiculture), Catriona Graham, Dave Allen (*Glasgow Herald*), Patricia Stephen and Liz Paterson, (Phantassie Farm and Earthy Foods), David Catt (Borders Organic Gardeners), Richard Owen (Chisholme, Hawick), Fiona J. Houston, Frances Brown, Mike Small, Matthew Love (Scottish Seed Exchange), Pam Whittle, Maureen Meldrum, George Anderson, Jim McColl, Carole Baxter (*Beechgrove Garden*), Chris Scratchard, Rora Paglieri, Barrie Andrian (Scottish Crannog Centre), Alison Schofield (Tweed Valley Organics), Elspeth Bruce (Scone Palace), John Cook, Moira Stevenson (The Caley), Sue Tindell, Mary Cannon, Patrick Kelsey, Catriona Murray and Neil Cameron (Jura), Mary Kennedy and Ursula Fearn (questionnaires), Nick Hoskins (Broughton House), Will Soos (Dundonell), Mrs James Duff (Hatton Castle), Jamie MacKenzie and Rosa Steppanova (Shetland), Patricia Cox (Glendoick), Vicki Fergusson and Fiona Thackery (Trellis). The SNP Scottish Government have been very supportive of food growing and helping with aspects of this book – Rosanna Cunningham MSP, Jared Stewart, Jon Rathjen, John Swinney MSP, Richard Lockhead MSP. I'd like to thank my cousin Peter Milne and my perfect co-author Caroline Beaton who kept me on my toes. I'd like to thank my wife Jane for agenting this book, proof-reading and letting me take over her borders for vegetable experiments and for tolerating being a fruit and vegetable widow for many a long evening.

CAROLINE

My vegetable-related contribution to the book could not have been completed without valuable help from many people – not least, those I met during my island-hopping 'veg on the edge' tour in the early autumn of 2010. Grateful thanks to them all. Feri Bartai, Alan Crowe, Sarah McBurnie (Shetland); Les Bates (Torridon); Denise Bridge, Laura Donkers (Uist); Clive Chaddock, Eric Hutchison, Kathy Pickles (Orkney); Chris Conniff, Elizabeth Harrison (Poolewe); Ian Crisp (Dunrobin Castle); David and Jane Eastwood, Emma Elliott, Kirsty Macdonald,

Rowena and Stuart Oakley, Barry Shelby, Cris Stubbington (Lewis); Vicki Ferguson, Fiona Thackery (Trellis); Alison Graham (Achiltibuie); Sue MacDonald, David Newman (Benbecula); Tammy McKinlay, Bill and Sheena Thomson (Perth); Peigi MacLean (Barra); Sandy Pattullo (Eassie); Olga Ridley (Castle of Mey); Graham and Maureen Thom (Blackness); Jim Williams (National Vegetable Society Scotland); and special thanks to Peter for getting me started and keeping me going, to my mother and stepfather for inspiration and sound advice and, of course, to Ken for asking me to give him a hand.

Thanks to all at Birlinn for seeing this project from idea to publication: Hugh Andrew, Andrew Simmons, Mark Blackadder, Helen Black, Patricia Marshall, Chris Brown, Jim Hutcheson, Tom Johnstone, Kenny Redpath and Jan Rutherford.

Bibliography

Books

Albala, K., *Beans, A History* (Berg, 2007)

Anderson, J. (ed.), *The New Practical Gardener and Modern Horticulturist* (William Mackenzie, c. 1875)

Ayres, A. (ed.), *The Gardening from Which? Guide to Gardening Without Chemicals* (Which? Books, 1990)

Baker, H., *The Fruit Garden Displayed* (Cassell, 1986)

Bannerman, J., *The Beatons: A Medical Kindred in the Classical Gaelic Tradition* (John Donald, 1998)

Brickell, C. (ed.), *Encyclopedia of Gardening* (Dorling Kindersley, 1992)

Burns, J., *Gardening in Orkney and Shetland* (The Shetland Times Limited, 1976)

Butterworth, J., *Apples of Scotland: A Practical Guide to Choosing and Growing Our Favourite Fruit* (Langford Press, n.d.)

Campbell, S., *A History of Kitchen Gardening* (Frances Lincoln, 2005)

Caplan, B. (ed.), *The Complete Manual of Organic Gardening* (Headline Book Publishing plc, 1992)

Cox, E. H. M., *A History of Gardening in Scotland* (Chatto & Windus, 1935)

Cox, K., *Scotland for Gardeners* (Birlinn, 2009)

Cox, K., and Curtis Machin, R., *Garden Plants for Scotland* (Frances Lincoln, 2008)

Crawford, M., *Directory of Apple Cultivars* (Agroforestry Research Trust, 2001)

Crawford M., *Directory of Pear Cultivars* (Agroforestry Research Trust, 1996)

Crawford, M., *Fruit Resistant to Pests and Diseases* (Agroforestry Research Trust, 1997)

Darton, M., *A Potted History of Fruit* (Ivy, 2011)

Darwin, T., *The Scots Herbal: The Plant Lore of Scotland* (Birlinn, 2008)

Davidson, A., *The Oxford Companion to Food* (Oxford University Press, 1999)

De Witt, D., and Bosland, P., *The Complete Chilli Pepper Book* (Timber Press, 2009)

Dowding, C., *Organic Gardening the Natural No-Dig Way* (Green Books, 2010)

Ellis, A., *Kitchen Garden Cook Book* (Stanley Paul & Co. Ltd, 1972)

Fedor, J., *Grow Your Own Organic Fruit and Vegetables* (Frances Lincoln, 2011)

Fenton, A., *Scottish Life and Society: The Food of the Scots: A Compendium of Scottish Ethnology, Volume 5* (Scottish Life & Society) (Birlinn, 2008)

Fern, K., *Plants for a Future* (Permanent Publications, 1997)

Flowerdew, B., *Bob Flowerdew's Organic Bible* (Kyle Cathie Limited, 1998)

Ford, S., *50 Ways to Kill a Slug* (Hamlyn, 2003)

Fowler, A., *The Edible Garden* (BBC Books, 2010)

Gilchrest, J., *Old and New Fruit Varieties for the Clyde Valley* (self-published, 2008)

Gilchrist, R., Grand, A., and Jess, M., *Grow Food Nature's Way* (Greenway Consulting, 2011)

Gillman, J., *The Truth about Organic Gardening* (Timber Press Inc., 2008)

Gross, P., *Superfruits* (McGraw Hill, 2010)

Guillet, D., *The Seeds of Kokopelli* (Association Kokopelli, n.d.)

Hawthorne, L. (ed.), *The Northern Pomona* (Pomona Publications, 2007)

Hessayon, Dr D. G., *The Fruit Expert* (Transworld, Expert Books, 1999)

Hessayon, Dr D. G., *The Vegetable and Herb Expert* (Transworld, Expert Books, 2002)

Hobhouse, P., *The Story of Gardening* (Dorling Kindersley, 2002)

Hogg, R., *The Fruit Manual* (London, 1860, 1883)

Kent-West Kent Federation of Women's Institutes, *The Country Housewife's Handbook* (5th Edition) (Kent-West Kent Federation of Women's Institutes, 1968)

Larkcom, J., *Grow Your Own Vegetables* (Frances Lincoln Limited, 2002)

Laws, B., *Spade, Skirret and Parsnip: The Curious History of Vegetables* (Sutton Publishing, 2004)

Leggatt, J., *Cooking with Flowers* (Century Hutchinson Ltd, 1987)

Louden, J., *An Encyclopedia of Gardening* (n.p., London, 1822, 1835)

Lyle, S., *Ultimate Fruit and Nuts* (Frances Lincoln, 2006)
McVicar, J., *New Book of Herbs* (Dorling Kindersley, 2002)
Millican, W., and Bridgewater, S. *Flora Celtica* (Birlinn, 2004)
Mollison, B., *Permaculture One, Two* (Tagari Press, 1990, 1979)
Morgan, J., *The Book of Apples* (Ebury, 1993)
Muck, Lady, *Magic Muck: The Complete Guide to Compost* (Pavilion Books, 1994)
Neil, P., *The Fruit, Flower and Kitchen Garden* (n.p., 1849)
Pavord, A., *The New Kitchen Garden* (Dorling Kindersley, 1999)
Pollan, M., *The Omnivore's Dilemma* (Bloomsbury, 2007)
Pollock, M. (ed.), *Vegetable and Fruit Gardening* (Dorling Kindersley, 2002, 2008)
Reader, J., *The Untold History of the Potato* (Vintage, 2009)
Reader's Digest Association Limited, *Food from Your Garden* (Reader's Digest Association Limited, 1977)
Reid, J., *The Scots Gard'ner* (n.p., 1683)
Reynolds, R., *On Guerrilla Gardening* (Bloomsbury, 2008)
Roach, F., *The Cultivated Fruits of Britain* (Wiley Blackwell, 1985)
Roberts, J., *Cabbages and Kings: The Origins of Fruit and Vegetables* (HarperCollins, 2001)
Robertson, F., *Early Scottish Gardeners and Their Plants* (Tuckwell, 2000)
Romans, A., *The Potato Book* (Frances Lincoln, 2005)
Sanders, R., *The Apple Book* (Frances Lincoln, 2010)
Shepherd, A., *The Organic Garden* (Collins, 2007)
Slater, N., *Tender, Volume 1 (Vegetables)* (Forth Estate, 2009)
Slater, N., *Tender, Volume 2 (Fruit)* (Forth Estate, 2010)
Stocks, C., *Forgotten Fruits* (Windmill, 2009)
Stuart, T., *Waste: Uncovering the Global Food Scandal* (Penguin, 2009)
Szmidt, R., and Ferguson, J., *Co-utilisation of Rockdust, Mineral Fines and Compost* (SEPA, 2004)
Titchmarsh, A., *Growing Fruit* (How to Garden) (BBC Books, 2010)
Titchmarsh, A., *Pests and Problems* (How to Garden) (BBC Books, 2011)

Titchmarsh, A., *The Kitchen Gardener* (BBC Books, 2008)
Walker, Dr A., *Garden of Herbs Traditional Uses of Herbs in Scotland* (Argyll Publishing, 2003)

Government Publications & Reports

Finding Scotland's Allotments (SAGS, 2007)
Food and Drink in Scotland 2010 (Scottish Government)
Food Justice: The Report of the Food and Fairness Enquiry (Food Ethics Council, 2010)
Healthy Eating in Schools: A Guide to Implementing the Nutritional Requirements for Food and Drink in Schools (Scotland) Regulations (Scottish Government, 2008)
Recipe for Success: Scotland's National Food and Drink Policy (Scottish Government, 2009)
Report for Grow-Your-Own Working Group (Scottish Government, 2011)
Review of the Climate Challenge Fund (Brook, Lyndhurst and Ecometrica, Scottish Government, 2011)

Periodicals

'Fair Miles: Recharting the Food Miles Map' (Oxfam, 2010)
'Herbicide tolerance and GM crops' (Greenpeace, 2011)
Kovach, J. et al., 'A method to measure the environmental impact of pesticides' in *New York's Food and Life Sciences Bulletin* (1992)
Oszmianski, J., and Wojdylo, A., 'Aronia melanocarpa phenolics and their antioxidant activity' in *European Food Resource Technology* (2005, 221, pp. 809–13)
Mabbott, T. W., 'The Scottish Potato' in *The Caledonian Gardener* (1998)
Maclean, D., 'Potatoes Yesterday and Today' in *Royal Caledonian Horticultural Society Journal* (1982)
Storrie, D. I., 'Apples and Pears in Scotland' in *The Fruit Year Book* (1949, pp. 28–35)

Index

Note: Page numbers in **bold** refer to illustrations